THE PROJECTIFICATION OF THE PUBLIC SECTOR

In recent decades, we have witnessed an increasing use of projects and similar temporary modes of organising in the public sector of nations in Europe and around the world. While for some this is a welcome development which unlocks entrepreneurial zeal and renders public services more flexible and accountable, others argue that this seeks to depoliticise policy initiatives, rendering them increasingly technocratic, and that the project organisations formed in this process offer fragmented and unsustainable short-term solutions to long-term problems.

This volume sets out to address public sector projectification by drawing together research from a range of academic fields to develop a critical and theoretically-informed understanding of the causes, nature, and consequences of the projectification of the public sector. This book includes 13 chapters and is organised into three parts. The first part centres on the politics of projectification, specifically the role of projects in de-politicisation, often accomplished by rendering the political "technical". The chapters in the second part all relate to the reframing of the relationship between the centre and periphery, or between policy making and implementation, and the role of temporality in reshaping this relation. The third and final part brings a focus upon the tools, techniques, and agents through which public sector projectification is assembled, constructed, and performed.

Damian Hodgson is Professor of Organisational Analysis at Alliance Manchester Business School and Co-Director of the Institute for Health Policy and Organisation, University of Manchester, UK.

Mats Fred is a post-doctoral researcher at the Department of Global Political Studies, Malmö University, Sweden.

Simon Bailey is a researcher at the University of Kent, UK. His interests are in the sociological study of medicine, organisation, learning, and policy.

Patrik Hall is Professor of Political Science at the Department of Global Political Studies, Malmö University, Sweden.

ROUTLEDGE CRITICAL STUDIES IN PUBLIC MANAGEMENT

Edited by Stephen Osborne

The study and practice of public management has undergone profound changes across the world. Over the last quarter century, we have seen

- increasing criticism of public administration as the over-arching framework for the provision of public services,
- the rise (and critical appraisal) of the 'New Public Management' as an emergent paradigm for the provision of public services,
- the transformation of the 'public sector' into the cross-sectoral provision of public services, and
- the growth of the governance of inter-organizational relationships as an essential element in the provision of public services

In reality these trends have not so much replaced each other as elided or co-existed together – the public policy process has not gone away as a legitimate topic of study, intra-organizational management continues to be essential to the efficient provision of public services, whist the governance of inter-organizational and inter-sectoral relationships is now essential to the effective provision of these services.

Further, whilst the study of public management has been enriched by contribution of a range of insights from the 'mainstream' management literature it has also contributed to this literature in such areas as networks and inter-organizational collaboration, innovation and stakeholder theory.

This series is dedicated to presenting and critiquing this important body of theory and empirical study. It will publish books that both explore and evaluate the emergent and developing nature of public administration, management and governance (in theory and practice) and examine the relationship with and contribution to the over-arching disciplines of management and organizational sociology.

Books in the series will be of interest to academics and researchers in this field, students undertaking advanced studies of it as part of their undergraduate or postgraduate degree and reflective policy makers and practitioners.

Crossing Boundaries in Public Policy and Management
Tackling the Critical Challenges
Edited by Luke Craven, Helen Dickinson and Gemma Carey

The Projectification of the Public Sector
Edited by Damian Hodgson, Mats Fred, Simon Bailey, and Patrik Hall

THE PROJECTIFICATION OF THE PUBLIC SECTOR

Edited by Damian Hodgson, Mats Fred, Simon Bailey, and Patrik Hall

NEW YORK AND LONDON

First published 2019
by Routledge
52 Vanderbilt Avenue, New York, NY 10017

and by Routledge
2 Park Square, Milton Park, Abingdon, Oxon OX14 4RN

Routledge is an imprint of the Taylor & Francis Group, an informa business

Library of Congress Cataloging-in-Publication Data
Names: Hodgson, Damian E., editor. | Fred, Mats, editor.
Title: The projectification of the public sector / edited by Damian Hodgson, Mats Fred, Simon Bailey, and Patrik Hall.
Description: New York : Routledge, 2019. |
Series: Routledge critical studies in public management | Includes index.
Identifiers: LCCN 2018053859| ISBN 9781138298545 (hardback) |
ISBN 9780367183332 (pbk.) | ISBN 9781315098586 (ebook)
Subjects: LCSH: Project management. | Public administration–Case studies.
Classification: LCC HD69.P75 P7633 2019 | DDC 352.3/65--dc23
LC record available at https://lccn.loc.gov/2018053859

ISBN: 978-1-138-29854-5 (hbk)
ISBN: 978-0-367-18333-2 (pbk)
ISBN: 978-1-315-09858-6 (ebk)

Typeset in Bembo
by Taylor & Francis Books

For Kay, Jude, and Madeleine – Damian
For Lina, Sture, and Billy-Bo – Mats
For Sarah, Charlotte, and Vivien – Simon
In memory of Olle Hall – Patrik

CONTENTS

ILLUSTRATIONS

Figures

Tables

Box

PREFACE AND ACKNOWLEDGEMENTS

This book is the result of researchers from all over the world working together towards a better understanding of the challenges to the public sector posed by processes of projectification. Our ambition has been to cover both different geographical and empirical fields as well as a diversity of theoretical perspectives on projectification.

The first steps towards the creation of this book was taken in Malmö, Sweden, in 2016 when critical management scholars and public administration researchers from Finland, Poland, Sweden and the UK gathered to critically reflect upon what we all saw as a neglected but important area of study – namely public sector projectification. The symposium in Malmö generated a conversation between different research traditions and backgrounds, contrasting theoretical perspectives with a wide range of empirical examples, and we were keen to broaden the debate further. Therefore we organised a panel in Budapest at the 2017 International Research Society for Public Management (IRSPM) conference. The result of that panel was a wider network of researchers, both empirically and theoretically, now including scholars from across Europe, Australia, New Zealand, and North America. The panel was also a starting point for a whole range of activities including calls for papers, reading sessions, revisions, and re-revisions, copyright agreements, and of course copious e-mails and meetings that underpin the actual text you now have in front of you!

Although we – Damian Hodgson, Mats Fred, Simon Bailey, Patrik Hall – are responsible for pulling this network of researchers together and assembling this volume, we owe many people our deepest gratitude for helping us reach this point. First, we would like to acknowledge the contributing authors to this book for their hard work and patience – without you the result would have been a less exciting book. We also would like to thank our partners and families, two of which have grown in number during the gestation period of the book. We would also like to acknowledge the support and encouragement of our editorial team at Taylor & Francis, including David Varley for kick-starting the "project" and Brianna Ascher and Mary del Plato for carrying it through to delivery. Also Kristin Trichler at Alliance Manchester Business School for her careful and patient work in preparing the final text.

INTRODUCTION

Damian Hodgson, Mats Fred, Simon Bailey, and Patrik Hall

In recent decades, we have witnessed an increasing use of projects and similar temporary modes of organising in the public sector of nations in Europe and around the world. There is now a widespread reliance on projects across many parts of the public sector, both to deliver routine services or else to reform/transform services in the form of pilots, programmes, task forces, and similar organisational arrangements. This gradual shift towards non-permanent structures in public organisations has been argued to be "one of the most important – although still very much neglected – administrative changes of the past decades" (Sjöblom, 2009, p. 165). This change is heavily influenced by perceptions of best practice within the private sector centred on maximising flexibility and innovation without sacrificing control. Temporary, task-focused organisational arrangements in the form of projects have been mainstream within large companies for several decades (Morris, 1997; Whittington et al., 1999) and there is a vast management-oriented literature regarding how to effectively organise and manage projects in the private sector.

However, little has been written regarding how this organisational practice has spread to the public sector with very limited critical attention directed towards this process of public sector projectification. This perhaps reflects the widespread association of project management with the hard disciplines of engineering and technology, and with technical rather than political matters. Indeed, to quote Sjöblom (2009), it seems "project management has trickled down from these sectors to public administration gradually and rather silently" (p. 166).

This volume sets out to address public sector projectification by drawing together research from a range of academic fields, from organisation theory to social policy, from regional studies and political science to innovation research. Our aim is to develop a critical and theoretically informed understanding of the causes, nature and consequences of the projectification of the public sector.

First, however, we will introduce the phenomenon of public sector projectification, critically assessing the nature and consequences of this phenomenon to make clear the importance of studying this development in detail. We describe in this introduction the specific context of the public sector in relation to processes of projectification, the relation between projectification and politics in state-owned and state-managed sectors, and consider the embedded tensions between permanent organisations and temporary organising. We then introduce the three sections of the volume and their chapters, unpacking how these chapters develop and advance our understanding of these critical issues.

Projectification and Its Discontents

The growing reliance on projects and project management techniques to structure activity has been identified since the 1990s, defined as a process of "projectification" (Midler, 1995; Packendorff & Lindgren, 2014). Initially, the term "projectification" was coined to describe organisational restructuring within a firm to place projects as key units by which production could be organised, drawing on Christophe Midler's seminal work within Renault. This "narrow" definition of projectification (Packendorff & Lindgren, 2014) – also referred to as "organisational projectification" (Maylor et al., 2006) – has generated an extensive literature in the field of project management studying such structural changes in organisations, frequently focused on identifying the advantages and disadvantages of this change (for instance, Hobday, 2000; Arvidsson, 2009) or providing practical guides to facilitate projectification. Broadly, this work tends to celebrate the potential inherent within project organising, and thus project management, to enable other positive developments within organisations (Frame, 1994; Gemünden, 2013) such as increasing flexibility, innovation, customer focus, and efficiency – when implemented effectively.

In a parallel debate, however, a number of writers have extended this concept, arguing that this "narrow" projectification is accompanied by a "broad" projectification (Packendorff & Lindgren, 2014) referring to the more fundamental discursive spread of projects and related phenomena as they become embedded, naturalised, and institutionalised across organisations, societies, and in everyday lived experience. Over time, the narrow and broad definitions of projectification come to reinforce one another, as practical organisational arrangements meet a greater degree of acceptance in a broader and broader array of socio-cultural settings. This work draws its inspiration from a sociological rather than a managerial framing and reflects societal shifts towards greater fragmentation and discontinuity (Bauman, 2012; Sennett, 1998) as well as expectations of greater individual flexibility and entrepreneurial zeal (Boltanski & Chiapello, 2005). At its broadest, this shift has been described as the "projectification of society" (Lundin & Söderholm, 1998) or even the "projectification of everything" (Jensen et al., 2016).

Without even going so far, it is difficult to dispute the growing prevalence of projects in contemporary societies, with increasing numbers of employees being redefined as project leads or project managers, and a creeping adoption of the language and forms of projects and project management outside of their traditional heartlands of engineering and technology into the media, healthcare, research, and performing arts (Packendorff & Lindgren, 2014). Given the range of definitions from narrow to broad, it is perhaps unsurprising to find that establishing the degree of projectification in a society is far from simple. The various attempts to measure projectification bear this out, ranging from efforts to count bibliographic references to projects (Boutinet, 1996); to research which traces the membership of professional associations of project managers (Hodgson & Muzio, 2011); to studies which count the number of projects undertaken in particular countries (Schoper et al., 2018), or to surveys of the growing employment of project managers in the public sector (Löfgren & Poulsen, 2013). Each of these studies shows an increase in our reliance on projects and a parallel increasing influence of bodies which govern the development of project managers and the bodies of knowledge which inform their practice (Hodgson & Muzio, 2011).

Whether this is a cause for celebration or concern is a question which is still very much in play. There are many cheerleaders for the cause of projects, including a large number of actors engaged in promoting and delivering project management training at universities or private companies around the globe (Clegg & Courpasson, 2004) and, of course, the different professional associations for project management which exist across the world (such as the Project Management Institute, with 500,000 members worldwide[1], and the International Project Management Association, connecting national associations in over 60 countries[2]), issuing, among other things, certificates to project managers all over the globe. There is also a large number of best practice journals bearing evidence of project management as an evolving academic field. In addition, the ISO (International Organization for Standardization) has developed a specific standard for project management (ISO21500, effectuated in 2012), heavily influenced by the International Project Management Association.

However, there is also a strong tradition of work which has developed a broader critique of the process of projectification, exemplified by work associated with the Making Projects Critical movement (Hodgson & Cicmil, 2006; Lindgren & Packendorff, 2006). From this perspective, pragmatic questions about "how to make projects more successful" are "bracketed" in favour of more fundamental debates inspired by Critical Management Studies (Alvesson & Willmott, 1992; Fournier & Grey, 2000). In particular, this movement was inspired by a concern at the tendency of project management to reduce social activity of all kinds to instrumental and rationalised action, and in doing so efface the political, social, and ethical dimensions of activity structured as projects (Hodgson & Cicmil, 2006; Lindgren et al., 2014). Over two decades of work, the Making Projects Critical movement developed a critique articulated around three core concerns, defined as follows:

> give voice to issues of morality, equality and ethics in project-based work, organising and management and create a dialogue with those more traditional functionalist concerns of project's effectiveness and efficiency; challenge the apparent inevitability of projects by drawing attention instead to political and power relations underpinning any "status quo"; and open up possibilities for fairer, more affirmative and caring forms of organising and management.
>
> *(Hodgson & Cicmil, 2016, p. 745)*

From this critical perspective, it is argued that rather than simply celebrating and seeking to better implement projectification, there is instead a pressing need to look critically at this phenomenon. For many, this entails challenging what is seen as the growing colonisation of all quarters of life by project-related principles, rules, techniques, and procedures, seeing this as the formation of a new "iron cage" of project rationality. Alongside this critical challenge, it is equally important to examine the changing social and political conditions from which projectification has developed into a legitimate set of forms and techniques for government, in order to develop a critique which is grounded in the complexity of contemporary processes of national, and increasingly supra-national, governance and policy making.

Projectification in the Public Sector

As tax revenues have reduced and demands on public services increased in many developed countries, many governments are seeking to move beyond the search for marginal economies within their public sector, to instead transform the manner in which the sector operates.

Project-based arrangements such as projects, policy pilots, or task forces seem to offer attractive and relatively cheap ways to "test out" or roll out new ways of working, to encourage bottom-up innovation from within those organisations who deliver services and even to generate a mode of entrepreneurship, or "intrapreneurship" (Kanter, 1989) from a sector frequently accused of bureaucracy and defensive complacency. Even outside explicit projects in the public sector, Sahlin-Andersson and Söderholm (2002, p. 15) argue that many routine and continuous work processes in the public sector are increasingly organised in temporary forms and indeed, "many processes are presented and understood as projects" (cf. Abrahamsson & Agevall, 2010; Sjöblom & Godenhjelm, 2009).

In Europe in particular, there is little doubt that the European Union has been an influential vehicle for driving projectification since the beginning of the 1990s (Büttner & Leopold, 2016; Freeman, 2018) with more than 60% of the entire EU budget now managed through different project funding systems regarding research, social, and regional development, etc. (Mukhtar-Landgren & Fred, 2018). Globally, similar processes can be observed through the workings of the World Bank and similar global institutions (Ika & Hodgson, 2014; Neu & Ocampo, 2007). These influences alone, however, do not fully account for the uptake of project organising at a national level across continents in recent decades. In some countries, this process of projectification is driven by the privatisation or pseudo-privatisation of public services, with the state offering fixed-term contracts for competitive tender to leverage market competition and maximise quality or value for money. In this way, many services and organisations that have traditionally been characterised by permanence are now described and understood as projects – defined by assignments (rather than goals), by time (rather than survival), by teams (rather than working organisations), and by transition (rather than continuous development) (Fred, 2015). Launching projects may also be rewarding to politicians, at least in the short term, since time-limited project activities make the bureaucracy an instrument for strategic purposes and signals more clearly than before that the bureaucracy actively delivers a political agenda (Fred & Hall, 2017).

Projectification has emerged in close inter-relation with broader discourses of managerialism in public services, often collectively described as "new public management" (NPM). NPM is a broad and contested term covering a substantial and often poorly defined range of activities and processes. However, it is commonly associated with the political discourse of neo-liberalism, which emphasises decreased state involvement in, and funding for, public services in favour of market-based forms of administration. In so doing, NPM emphasises competitive relationships between public organisations, and encourages a more decentralised approach, which allows organisations flexibility to manage their own income and investments. NPM therefore seeks to describe the changing nature of public managerial activities, forms, and processes that accompany this decentralised and competitive public sector. In terms of organisation, NPM reforms called for something beyond bureaucracy, with ideals of flat hierarchies, teamwork, networking, flexibility, and customer-orientation – ideals captured in the concept of post-bureaucratic organisations (Donnellon & Heckscher, 1994; Iedema, 2003).The rise of projects and project management has been welcomed by many as an organisational form which enables both flexibility and control, and as a practical apparatus for the production and documentation of measurable outputs. What is novel in the turn towards projectification of the public sector is the manner in which the technical apparatus of projects and project management can come to stand in for the more conflicted and contestable aspects of politics and political decision making, such as ideologies, party politics, and electoral cycles. If projects can provide a rational language with which to describe, monitor, and rank the value-laden work of politics, then they represent an alluring, and potentially de-politicising, mode of political organisation.

Projects as the Re-allocation of Responsibility

One of the fundamental challenges of policy making is that it must have a vision for the future, and must find the means for constructing that future in concrete terms. Project forms are often perceived to be more "agile" than what are conventionally understood to be more centralised and bureaucratic forms of organisation (Styhre, 2007). This makes the logic of projectification politically attractive (Fred, 2018), as it involves delegation of responsibilities for implementation of policy further down the hierarchy. Delegating implementation means deferring the necessarily complex and uncertain task of describing policy in terms of concrete matters prior to those matters being tried out in context. Considered in light of the increasing internationalisation of public administration, for example through super-states such as the European Union (EU), projects are thus enrolled into managing the "ungovernable" on limited resources.

Taking the EU as an example, the funds and infrastructure do not exist to govern the micro-details of member activities; neither would this be politically palatable. The use of projects within the EU structural and investment funds is a way to obtain visible impacts on a local level which the EU do not have any other means to control in detail. Projectification operating through the allocation and administration of EU funding therefore offers the central European administration the opportunity to guide member states towards broad aims while devolving to more local levels the task of finding "what works" for them. Similar dynamics can be seen in the operation of other supra-national organisations (such as the World Bank) and also in the relation between national governmental policy and regional/local implementation within sovereign countries around the world. In this way, governments and meta-governments can be seen to be "taking action" in relation to "wicked" problems in a manner which is both regulative and non-prescriptive. This constitutes a form of "government at a distance" (c.f. Foucault et al., 1991).

Projects are thus a means for government to delegate responsibility for policy outcomes, sharing responsibilities between central and local levels (not least through the method of co-financing), while still remaining in control in terms of programme development, funding, and evaluation. This can be seen at the institutional, organisational, and individual level; that is to say, the introduction of project forms requires system level governance that is flexible to the requirements of particular projects, and offers a degree of autonomy to those responsible for project management. Meanwhile, using project management techniques from the private sector makes this type of political action appear as "modern" and "rational". This mode of government may be seen as a deliberate attempt to de-politicise implementation, but the logic behind delegation is still a deeply political one.

Projects and Temporality: From Routine to Continuous Renewal?

Connecting projects to the ongoing governance of public administration also highlights the critical question of temporality. There is, inevitably, a temporal challenge inherent to projectification reflecting the dynamic tensions that emerge between permanent organisational arrangements and "time-limited" project operations. The public sector is traditionally associated with routine, hierarchy, and stability, whereas projects connote in principle a conflicting logic of discontinuity, flexibility, and innovation. The temporality of the routine oriented, or permanent, organisation is cyclical – phenomena are repeated, recurring time and time again (Burrell 1992) – whereas the project follows a linear, teleological temporality, progressing from a starting-point to termination (Ibert, 2004, p. 1530). These different conceptions have an impact on the organisations in several aspects. The future in projects is framed in terms of strategies and goals in which the present is viewed as a passing phase from the past to the future, while "ordinary" activities are characterised by repetition and routine where more or less the same activities are repeated every day.

How these distinct temporalities can be reconciled is a key concern of much of the research literature into projects as temporary organisational structures, processes and forms. Combining routine and time-based organisational arrangements implies a degree of hybridity (Annell & Wilson, 2002; Clegg & Courpasson, 2004) and typologies of such hybrids typically posit four broad types: permanent, routine-based organisation; coexisting routine/project-based organisations; project-based organisations; and organisations that are projects (Annell & Wilson, 2002). The shift implied by the projectification of the public sector is a move by permanent and routine-based organisations towards increasing "temporariness" (Annell & Wilson, 2002), affecting not only the way specific projects are run but also how "ordinary" public service activities are organised and executed. The increasing hybridity that results demands situated attention to the boundaries of the routine and non-routine and the increasingly dynamic interaction between them (Clegg & Courpasson, 2004). Projects are conventionally conceived as something apart from "the everyday", yet their increasing use makes this distinction of the ordinary from the project more and more problematic, as projects themselves become the norm.

One example of this process taking place in contemporary public services is the increasing use of pilots and other experimental temporary organisational forms in order to test out policies, ostensibly in the interests of building a rational case for the ongoing redesign and spread of policy ideas (Ettelt et al., 2014). As noted above, project rationalities offer an appealing means through which to manage the inherent uncertainty associated with policy making, and on the face of it, pilots and other similar forms offer genuine opportunities for a broadened engagement with policy making by policy recipients. Nevertheless, policy making by piloting might have a number of other effects, in part due to the relations of temporality inherent to project forms. Pilots thus can be seen to delegate power to localities insofar as they authorise local experimentation, but project rationalities also lend this experimentation a regulative "buffer", helping to ensure that such pilot projects remain accountable to policy makers. Temporality therefore offers one mechanism through which policy can be "recentred", as experimentalism gives way to the need to demonstrate outcomes, and political-normative questions about potential policies become obscured by technical questions of what can be achieved in limited time (Bailey et al., 2017).

However, questions remain concerning the introduction of new temporal logics in the public sector and whether this might also imply the construction of a new bureaucracy of plans, strategies, project managers and coordinators, steering groups, and evaluative committees whose core purpose is applying for, planning, executing, and accounting for projects. For instance, the ISO21500 standard presents instructions on how to implement excessive bureaucracy rather than effective project management. The reconciliation of the different temporalities of permanent and project organisations may very well lead to the routinisation of projects – that "bureaucracy eats projects" rather than the other way around. Less dramatically put, it seems accurate to state that projectification is a new stage in the successful history of bureaucracy rather than its replacement (Styhre, 2007).

The relation between "cyclical" and "linear" organisation is also central for the construction of organisational knowledge. In traditional conceptions of such knowledge, the public sector organisation is a "container" for various professional "knowledges". As many commentators have demonstrated, the NPM movement seems to challenge these various knowledges through a more general organisational knowledge in terms of organisational construction, financial steering, and control and audit (cf. Power, 1997). As Chaib (2018, p. 213) indicates, even "counter challenges" to NPM (such as "collaborative innovation" [see Sørensen & Torfing, 2011]) seem to be obsessed with organisational form rather than content. Project management is yet another form of organisational knowledge, a form of micro-management in organisational terms, but one where the planning, execution, and termination cycle may challenge the accumulation of knowledge in another way. What happens to the accumulation of knowledge when knowledge itself becomes a time-limited project?

Implementing Projectification

In line with the "broad" definition of projectification, attention needs to focus not only on the structural changes which define projectification in the public sector, but also the transformation in the roles and orientation of those individuals involved in public services in line with a "project rationality" – one which is distinct from a traditional public sector ethos. At the same time, this shift is supported by discursive changes in the language employed in the public sector (Rombach & Zapata, 2010), and in places by the introduction of novel techniques, instruments, and methodologies to govern and structure the organisation of activity in this sector. Such techniques are typically imported from the methodologies employed in traditionally "projectified" sectors such as construction and engineering; they frequently rely upon a system of arms-length, contractualised relations between project sponsor or commissioner and project delivery organisation, with competitive tendering and contract performance management, and are accompanied by standardised governance tools such as dashboard, stage-gates, and traffic-light systems. There is therefore a need to attend to the changing forms of agency which accompany projectification, as well as the corresponding forms of regulation that are afforded by the projectification of politics and policy making.

The proliferation of project forms and consequent increase in the numbers of individuals employed in project settings is most clearly evident in the creation of posts to manage and administer project funding, to evaluate project performance and delivery, and, of course, the multiplication of designated project managers or leads whose employment is often directly related to the duration of the project and its fixed-term funding. In accordance with the issue of bureaucratisation highlighted above, Styhre (2006) describes the bureaucratisation of the project manager role within the construction industry, and calls for a discussion of the dangers of excessive administrative work which follows from the introduction of specific project models. However, within the public sector, such calls seem to go unheeded.

Apart from the issue of bureaucratisation, the broad implementation of project "managers" in both private and public organisations also complicates power relations as these individuals often work across the boundaries of subunits. In his study of Swedish chief executives of state agencies, Hall (2015) found that the introduction of (boundary-crossing) projects in their agencies was mainly an ambition – from their part – to "reshuffle" and "make something happen" in their ordinary units. As Courpasson (2006) and Courpasson and Clegg (2006) argue, with examples from the private sector, the appointments of project managers aid the "circulation of elites" in organisations, at least from the view of top managers. However, the actual power and authority of this "quasi-manager" position is frequently problematic in practice, with contested claims to professionalism (Hodgson & Muzio, 2011) and multiple sources of positional pressure (Lindgren et al., 2014; Paton & Hodgson, 2016). If there is indeed a "projectocracy" in this setting, it is more likely to be found in the project sponsors, evaluators, and the proliferating expert project consultant positions which accompany the process of projectification.

A less visible but equally important aspect of projectification in the public sector is the status of those on the frontlines of public administration or public service delivery who are increasingly enrolled in project working, including professionals such as social workers, doctors, and teachers. In structural terms, this may simply change the conditions of work for such public servants, with a greater focus on short-term deliverables and perhaps shorter-term employment contracts. Such changes are often more than structural, however; this enrolment frequently seeks to embed a kind of project management "ideology" in an organisation and in these actors themselves, seeking to reform them not as drones but as active and passionate converts and missionaries to the cause of project management. Doing this involves a movement from simply providing instruction on project management methods to a more sophisticated cultural process, encouraging and promoting project management as a value in itself in order to generate an entrepreneurial project mentality, or perhaps a disciplined conformity with project management governance mechanisms. Hence the introduction of standard project management reporting tools (Räisänen & Linde,

2004) is facilitated by embedding among staff an understanding of why these are appropriate, important, and valuable alongside a technical understanding of how to collect and provide information in this format. Whether this presents a liberating and empowering new identity in public bureaucracies, or generates greater precarity and work intensification as public servants are converted to a new "projectariat", is an empirical question, and one which is explored in several of the chapters in this volume.

Of course, such a process faces challenges; this shift may entail a fundamental rethinking of what it is to provide a public service, and this is particularly the case where an embedded public sector or professional ethos perceives this as an alien, instrumental, or managerialist logic of project management. For some, this may be seen as a revolutionary and liberating new framing, or an opportunity to deliver changes which cannot be achieved in traditional public sector settings (cf. Styhre, 2007). How this plays out in different contexts, and the processes of compliance or resistance which result from efforts to embed project ideology in a public sector setting, merits careful attention if we are to understand how projectification unfolds in practice.

Overview of the Collection

Projectification in the public sector is a fairly new field of study and perhaps unsurprisingly, as with broader discussions of projectification, it remains contested in various ways. While, for some, projectification is a welcome development which unlocks entrepreneurial zeal and renders public services more flexible and accountable, others argue that it seeks to de-politicise policy initiatives, rendering them increasingly technocratic and therefore less accountable to democratic processes (Burnham, 2014). For some, the whole notion of public sector projectification appears paradoxical given the long-term policy challenges in health, employment, infrastructure, social services, and environmental issues both nationally and regionally (cf. Kerratt, 2012), offering what appear short-term fixes to long-term problems (Abrahamsson & Agevall, 2010). Others emphasise how this process serves to de-politicise interventions by prioritising managerialism over elected politicians and democratic accountability (Burnham, 2014, 2001; Hodgson & Cicmil, 2006). A further stream of research questions the purpose of such projects (cf. Ettelt, Mays, & Allen, 2015) – whether it is truly to learn from experiments, to test implementation, to gain public support/defuse public resistance, or to transform a (contentious) political act into a technical one (Bailey et al., 2017) There is therefore a pressing need for critical and theoretically-informed analyses of the causes, nature, and consequences of this mode of projectification.

Following the format of this introduction, the volume is organised into three parts, with a focus upon: Part I, projects, politics, and de-politicisation; Part II, de-centring, re-centring, and temporality in projects; and Part III, new instruments, techniques, and agents of projectification.

The first section centres on the politics of projectification, specifically the role of projects in de-politicisation, often accomplished by rendering the political "technical". Stefanie Ettelt and Nicholas Mays (Chapter 1) introduce this section by examining policy pilots in the health and social care system in the UK, arguing that pilots represent a novel form of politics in emphasising "how" rather than "why" questions. Rendering the political technical in their argument is accomplished by situating pilots in broader discourses of evidence-based policy, in turn linked to neutral scientism. Although Ettelt and Mays consider the de-politicising effect this may have, they adopt a pragmatic stance, arguing that pilots represent one way in which policy makers attempt to reduce complexity and uncertainty around specific policy problems. Recognising that piloting might represent de-politicisation, Ettelt and Mays also expose the shortcomings of the assumptions of evidence-based policy underlying piloting, arguing that in practice pilots might not fulfil the policy makers' ideals of definite answers and reduced conflict over policy aims.

In contrast to Ettelt and Mays' focus upon a specific form of project, Patrik Hall (Chapter 2) broadens the debate, exploring the history of Swedish innovation policy in order to draw attention to the inter-relationships between what he calls the political logic and the project logic. He argues that the role of politics as both driver and vehicle of projectification has been underestimated, precisely because of what he identifies as the role of projectification in the accomplishment of government at a distance. Through a historical policy study of the central and regional innovation systems in Sweden, Hall shows how projectification results in fragmentation at both the organisational and system level, but on the other hand, this fragmentation also represents key political tensions, the necessity of political reaction to the unforeseen as well as the apparent will to delegate substantial issues "downwards" in the policy system.

Tania Murray Li (Chapter 3) extends the discussion of de-politicisation through an analysis of the rural development policy in Indonesia, which is administered through what she refers to as the project system. Li's argument is that projects have replaced policy as conventionally understood, in guiding practices of rural development. Through two empirical studies, Li illustrates how the project system gives a diverse and disparate set of actors access to decisions about which problems might be amenable to intervention and what kind of solutions might be found. What results is a system reliant on the co-emergence of policy problems and solutions. Like Hall, one of Li's concerns is that not only is this a technical and highly selective system, but also a fragmented one.

Josef Chaib (Chapter 4) zooms out to focus upon innovation discourse in the Swedish public sector, arguing that projectification offers a "third way" of political organisation that appears different to either "outdated" bureaucracy or much-criticised new public management reforms. He argues that projects are seen by policy makers as attractive vehicles for innovation in appearing to make possible the articulation of specific and achievable goals on a limited scale. In this way the rise of innovation discourse in the public sector has given rise to a preference for project forms of organisation, and projectification in turn has bolstered the discourse of innovation. Recognising the appeal of this approach to public administration, Chaib is nevertheless concerned that rather than merely being a convenient vehicle for the organisation of politics, projects could in this way render politics invisible.

Concluding this first section, Karl Löfgren and Barbara Allen (Chapter 5) examine official documentation associated with the New Zealand government's major projects programme. Through a discursive analysis, they illustrate the managerial rationalities at work in political project reporting. Here, reductive narratives are mobilised through which governments can maintain an optimistic and productive appearance of tending to substantive problems, while simultaneously being seen to hold themselves to account. Nevertheless, Löfgren and Allen argue, this cannot simply be seen as some kind of technical and managerial void, but rather is embedded in a deeper political context. Official reporting therefore accomplishes a detachment of politics (and politicians) from the practical realities of projects, enabling the restriction of discussions about success and failure to a binary of "deliver–not deliver".

The chapters in the second section all relate to the reframing of the relationship between the centre and periphery, or between policy making and implementation, and the role of temporality in reshaping this relation. Christian Jensen, Staffan Johansson and Mikael Löfström (Chapter 6) open this section with a conceptual chapter focusing upon the relationship between permanent human service organisations and temporary project organisations in the broad context of policy innovation within the EU. They identify problems between the temporary and the permanent that project managers and public administrators must come to terms with if they are to understand the active role temporality plays in the outcome of policy change processes. They pay particular attention to the attempt to absorb project work into the "ongoing work" of the organisation, using the institutional logics framework to illustrate competing and supportive institutional contexts.

Simon Bailey, Damian Hodgson, and Kath Checkland (Chapter 7) return to the specific but critical case of policy pilots, examining this same dynamic between the "normal" organisation and the "exceptional" project, drawing on research within the English health service. They argue that policy piloting requires a suspension of the ordinary rules in order to enable innovation, with both practical and political consequences. In the immediate term of the pilot, the creation of conditions that are out of the ordinary means that the pilot itself is not necessarily a good test for how things might work in the long run. At the same time, the proliferation of temporary policy projects, each bringing its own suspension of the rules, threatens the integrity of the "ordinary bureaucracy" within which the project is embedded. Echoing some of those concerns raised in the first section, Bailey et al. conclude with a discussion of what the exceptional nature of piloting might represent for core political values such as deliberation and accountability.

Concluding this second section, Sebastian Godenhjelm, Christian Jensen and Stefan Sjöblom (Chapter 8) offer a wider perspective on the sources, meanings and implications of projects as tools to manage an increasingly complex public sector. Foreshadowing the third and final section, they argue that individuals become embedded in a rationale whereby politics must become embedded into projects in order to reduce complexity and maintain a focus on outcomes. However, this creates problems, particularly in the capacity of government institutions to operate within collaborative structures and to coordinate policy development. Godenhjelm et al. then seek to conceptualise the broader institutional conditions necessary for governing public administration as a project-based enterprise, with a focus upon the inter-relations between embeddedness, autonomy, and the intersection of the permanent and temporary.

The final section brings a focus upon the tools, techniques, and agents through which public sector projectification is assembled, constructed, and performed. Sebastian Büttner (Chapter 9) opens this section, adding to the cluster of chapters here presented which focus upon the EU as a significant contemporary vehicle of projectification. Büttner argues that as such a vehicle, the EU has contributed to the development of a distinct sphere of professional practice, associated with the shift towards project-based forms of policy implementation. Büttner associates this move towards projectified policy with the establishment of a "professional core" of project experts of different forms, which together constitute the "project world" of the EU. In the context of a super-structural state which often lacks effective authority over its members, Büttner argues that these "carriers" of projectification play an important role in translating highly bureaucratic and technical EU funding processes. Although this accomplishes the local participation upon which the EU relies, Büttner argues that it results in mass standardisation of policy goals and the means to both achieve and evaluate these, as well as driving forward a particular specialisation of EU policy implementation.

Mats Fred and Dalia Mukhtar-Landgren (Chapter 10) follow directly on from Büttner's broad overview to bring a micro focus on the roles and techniques through which the mediation of EU policy is accomplished at the local level of municipal government in Sweden. Situating their analysis within an understanding of projectification as a transformation of local government towards project management-inspired language, techniques, and tools, Fred and Mukhtar-Landgren bring a focus on the "how" and the "who" of this transformation at a regional and local level. Their analysis illustrates the work of individual change agents in different forms of translation work: changing, adjusting, matching, facilitating, and informing. This builds a picture of EU project funding as an instrument or tool of government and an emerging EU funding project market. This chapter concludes with a discussion of this emergent field, where the local discretion opened up by EU funding structures is increasingly captured by an emergent "project class" of policy implementation experts.

In the last of these three EU-focused chapters, Beata Jałocha and Małgorzata Ćwikła (Chapter 11) examine the process of projectification through the cultural regeneration of the City of Kraków, Poland. Setting their analysis in the context of the post-communist era in Poland, Jałocha and Ćwikła focus particularly on the process through which Kraków became European City of Culture as the catalyst to a project-based form of cultural production and management. This created a space for a number of new agents of projectification, who the authors illustrate as grappling with a set of unresolvable tensions between aesthetic and commercial values. Jałocha and Ćwikła convey a vivid sense of cultural agents as both active and entrepreneurial *and* constrained and precarious. As these agents appear to view the idea of "deprojectification" as an abstract utopia, the question the authors pose in conclusion is how the work of cultural projectification might be carried on in a manner which does not completely obscure the aesthetic values of art.

Sara Shaw, Gemma Hughes, and Trish Greenhalgh (Chapter 12) move the analysis onto a focus on the process of becoming an agent of projectification, through an examination of the kind of work that gets done in order for individuals to complete the PRojects IN Controlled Environments (PRINCE2^{TM}) training. The authors bring a novel methodological approach, drawing upon an autoethnographic case study in which Shaw undertook this training and studied the process as she was being asked to internalise it. This gives rise to an examination of the manner in which project management is constructed, the discourses and categories it brings into play, and the consequences of this for considerations of how to manage public sector health care in practice. The authors examine the values and practices of PRINCE2^{TM}, underscored by principles of linearity, "tidiness", efficiency, and cost-effectiveness, which work together to promote and sustain the idea of a "market" and a set of principles to "manage" it. This holds the potential to translate concerns over sickness or care into a language of "value" creation, reflecting the "de-politicisation" arguments in the first section; in so doing, this creates the potential for moral blindness in the transformation of healthcare as project logics dominate.

In the final chapter of this collection, Ewan Mackenzie and Edward Barratt (Chapter 13) show how efforts to promote project management at a British local authority rely on the work of freelance consultants. As such, they bring a sustained focus to a phenomenon raised in previous chapters by Büttner and Fred and Mukhtar-Landgren, mobilising a governmentality framework in order to examine the constrained but active shaping of the practices and identities of consultants. Mackenzie and Barratt show how consultants are afforded an active advocacy of their own distinctive understandings and ways of enacting project expertise, while also showing how certain forms of tactical "resistance" are defined by the key targets of their expertise; local government workers, who are sometimes able to "disidentify" with the consultants and their project logic. Behind such public rebuffing of consultancy and project management, the authors conclude in sobering style, showing that workers in this turbulent and insecure context often actively drew upon this discourse as a defensive resource for demonstrating individual and departmental achievements and protecting their employment.

In sum, projectification represents a novel and challenging set of organisational practices which challenge how we think and do public organisation and administration. Our concern in this collection is to raise awareness of the many different means through which this occurs, and to critically examine the diverse consequences of these activities, for actors from the local to the super-state level across a variety of international contexts, as well as for our understanding of the core values at the heart of public service. If this volume manages to raise an interest among researchers and students in the diverse forms in which the large-scale introduction of project management forms may affect the public sector – be it in terms of power and influence, democracy, or new forms of agency – then it has fulfilled its ambition.

Notes

1 www.pmi.org/annual-report-2017/at-a-glance Accessed 26/9/2018.
2 www.ipma.world/about-us/membership-associations/ Accessed 26/9/2018.

References

Abrahamsson, A., & Agevall, L. (2010). Immigrants caught in the crossfire of projectification of the Swedish public sector: Short-term solutions to long-term problems. *Diversity in Health and Care*, 7(9), 201–209.

Alvesson, M., & Willmott, H. (1992). *Critical management studies*. London, England: Sage.

Annell, B., & Wilson, T. (2002). Organizing in two modes: On the merging of the temporary and the permanent. In K. Sahlin-Andersson & A. Söderholm (Eds.), *Beyond project management: New perspectives on the temporary–permanent dilemma* (pp. 170–186). Liber, Sweden: Copenhagen Business School Press.

Arvidsson, N. (2009). Exploring tensions in projectified matrix organisations. *Scandinavian Journal of Management*, 25(1), 97–107.

Bailey, S., Checkland, K., Hodgson, D., McBride, A., Elvey, R., Parkin, S., Rothwell, K., & Pierides, D. (2017). The policy work of piloting: Mobilising and managing conflict and ambiguity in the English NHS. *Social Science and Medicine*, 179, 210–217.

Bakker, R. M., DeFillippi, R. J., Schwab, A., & Sydow, J. (2016). Temporary organizing: Promises, processes, problems. *Organization Studies*, 37(12), 1703–1719.

Bauman, Z. (2012) *Liquid Modernity*. Cambridge, UK: Polity Press.

Boltanski, L., & Chiapello, E. (2005). *The new spirit of capitalism* (G. Elliott, Trans.). New York, NY: Verso.

Boutinet, J.-P. (1993). *Anthropologie du Projet*. Paris, France: Presses Universitaires de France.

Bredin, K., & Soderlund, J. (2006). Perspectives on human resource management: An explorative study of the consequences of projectification in four firms. *International Journal of Human Resources Development and Management*, 6(1), 92–113.

Burnham, P. (2001). New Labour and the politics of depoliticization. *The British Journal of Politics & International Relations*, 3(2): 127–149.

Burnham, P. (2014). Depoliticisation: Economic crisis and political management. *Policy & Politics*, 42(2), 189–206.

Burrell, G. (1992). Back to the future: Time and organization. In M. Reed & M. Hughes (Eds.), *Rethinking organization: New directions in organization theory and analysis* (pp. 165–183). London, England: Sage.

Büttner, S. M., & Leopold, L. M. (2016). A "new spirit" of public policy? The project world of EU funding. *European Journal of Cultural and Political Sociology*, 3(1), 41–71.

Chaib, J. (2018). *Evidence, expertise and "other" knowledge: Governing welfare collaboration*. Lund, Sweden: Lund University (Doctoral Diss.).

Clegg, S. R., & Courpasson, D. (2004). Political hybrids: Tocquevillean views on project organizations. *Journal of Management Studies*, 41(4), 525–547.

Courpasson, D. (2006). *Soft constraint: Liberal organizations and domination*. Malmö, Sweden: Liber and Copenhagen Business School Press.

Courpasson, D., & Clegg, S. R. (2006). Dissolving the iron cages? Tocqueville, Michels, bureaucracy and the perpetuation of elite power. *Organization*, 13(3): 319–343.

Donnellon, A., & Heckscher, C. C. (1994). *The post-bureaucratic organization: New perspectives on organizational change*. Thousand Oaks, CA: Sage.

Ekstedt, E., Lundin, R. A., Söderholm, A., & Wirdenius, H. (1999) *Neo-industrial organizing: Action, knowledge formation and renewal in a project-intensive economy*. London, England: Routledge.

Ettelt, S., Mays, N., & Allen, P. (2015). The multiple purposes of policy piloting and their consequences: Three examples from national health and social care policy in England. *Journal of Social Policy*, 44(2), 1–19.

Foucault, M., Burchell, G., Gordon, C., & Miller, P. P. D. (1991). *The Foucault Effect: Studies in governmentality: with two lectures by and an interview with Michel Foucault*. Chicago: University of Chicago Press.

Fournier, V., & Grey, C. (2000). At the critical moment: Conditions and prospects for critical management studies. *Human Relations*, 53(1), 7–32.

Frame, J. D. (1994). *The new project management: Tools for an age of rapid change, corporate reengineering, and other business realities*. San Francisco, CA: Jossey-Bass.

Fred, M. (2015). Projectification of Swedish municipalities: A case of porous organizations. *Scandinavian Journal of Public Administration*, 19(2): 49–68.

Fred, M. (2018). *Projectification, the Trojan horse of local government*. Lund, Sweden: Statsvetenskapliga institutionen.

Fred, M., & Hall, P. (2017). A projectified public administration: How projects in Swedish local governments become instruments for political and managerial concerns. *Statsvetenskaplig tidskrift*, 1, 185–205.

Freeman, R. (2018). Europe in translation: Governance, integration and the project form. In T. Berger & A. Esguerra (Eds.), *World politics in translation: Power, relationality and difference in global cooperation* (pp. 135–153). London: Routledge.

Gemünden, H. G. (2013). Projectification of society. *Project Management Journal*, 44(3), 2–4.

Grabher, G. (2001). Locating economic action: Projects, networks, localities, institutions. *Environment and Planning A*, 33(8), 1329–1331.

Hall, P. (2015). *Makten över förvaltningen: Förändringar i politikens styrning av svensk förvaltning*. Stockholm, Sweden: Liber.

Hobday, M. (2000). The project-based organisation: An ideal form for managing complex products and systems? *Research Policy*, 29, 871–893.

Hodgson, D. E. (2002). Disciplining the professional: The case of project management. *Journal of Management Studies*, 39(6), 803–821.

Hodgson, D. E., & Cicmil, S. (2006). *Making projects critical*. Basingstoke, England: Palgrave Macmillan.

Hodgson, D. E., & Cicmil, S. (2016). Making projects critical 15 years on: A retrospective reflection (2001–2016). *International Journal of Managing Projects in Business*, 9(4), 744–751.

Hodgson, D. E., & Muzio, D. (2011). Prospects for professionalism in project management. In P. Morris, J. Pinto, & J. Soderlund (Eds.), *The Oxford handbook on project management* (pp. 107–130). Oxford, England: Oxford University Press.

Hood, C. (1991). A public management for all seasons? *Public Administration*, 69, 3–19.

Ibert, O. (2004). Projects and firms as discordant complements: Organisational learning in the Munich software ecology. *Research Policy*, 33(10), 1529–1546.

Iedema, R. (2003). *Discourses of post-bureaucratic organization*. Philadelphia, PA: John Benjamins.

Ika, L. A., & Hodgson, D. (2014). Learning from international development projects: Blending critical project studies and critical development studies. *International Journal of Project Management*, 32(7), 1182–1196.

Jensen, A., Thuesen, C., & Geraldi, J. (2016). The projectification of everything: Projects as a human condition. *Project Management Journal*, 47(3), 21–34.

Kanter, R. M. (1989). *When giants learn to dance: Mastering the challanges of strategy, management and careers in the 1990s*. London, England: Simon & Schuster.

Kerratt, S. (2012). The need to shift rural community development from projects towards resilience: International implications of findings in Scotland. In S. Sjöblom, K. Andersson, T. Marsden, & S. Skerratt (Eds.), *Sustainability and short-term policies: Improving governance in spatial policy interventions* (pp. 127–152). Farnham, England: Ashgate.

Lindgren, M., & Packendorff, J. (2006). What's new in new forms of organizing? On the construction of gender in project-based work. *Journal of Management Studies*, 43(4), 841–866.

Lindgren, M., Packendorff, J., & Sergi, V. (2014). Thrilled by the discourse, suffering through the experience: Emotions in project-based work. *Human Relations*, 67(11), 1383–1412.

Löfgren, K. & Poulsen, B. (2013). Project management in the Danish central government. *Scandinavian Journal of Public Administration*, 17(2): 61–78.

Lundin, R. A. (1995). Editorial: Temporary organizations and project management. *Scandinavian Journal of Management*, 11(4), 31–318.

Lundin, R. A., & Midler, C. (1998). Evolution of project as empirical trend and theoretical focus. In R. A. Lundin & C. Midler (Eds.), *Projects as arenas for renewal and learning processes* (pp. 1–9). Boston, MA: Springer US.

Lundin, R. A., & Söderholm, A. (1998). Conceptualizing a projectified society discussion of an eco-institutional approach to a theory on temporary organisations. In R. A. Lundin & C. Midler (Eds.), *Projects as arenas for renewal and learning processes* (pp. 13–23). Boston, MA: Springer US.

Maylor, H., Brady, T., Cooke-Davies, T., & Hodgson, D. (2006). From projectification to programmification. *International Journal of Project Management*, 24(8), 663–674.

Midler, C. (1995). "Projectification" of the firm: The Renault case. *Scandinavian Journal of Management*, 11(4), 363–375.

Morris, P. W. G. (1997). *The management of projects*. London, England: Thomas Telford.

Mukhtar-Landgren, D., & Fred, M. (2018). Re-compartmentalizing local policies? The translation and mediation of European structural funds in Sweden. *Critical Policy Studies*, 1–19. doi:10.1080/19460171.2018.1479282

Neu, D., & Ocampo, E. (2007). Doing missionary work: The World Bank and the diffusion of financial practices. *Critical Perspectives on Accounting*, 18(3), 363–389.

Packendorff, J., & Lindgren, M. (2014). Projectification and its consequences: Narrow and broad conceptualisations. *South African Journal of Economic and Management Sciences*, 17(1), 7–21.

Paton, S., & Hodgson, D. (2016). Project managers on the edge: Liminality and identity in the management of technical work. *New Technology, Work and Employment*, 31(1), 26–40.

Peters, T. (1992). *Liberation management: Necessary disorganization for the nanosecond nineties*. London, England: Macmillan.

Power, M. (1997). *The audit society: Rituals of verification*. Oxford, England: Oxford University Press.

Räisänen, C., & Linde, A. (2004). Technologizing discourse to standardize projects in multi-project organizations: Hegemony by consensus? *Organization*, 11(1), 101–121.

Rombach, B., & Zapata, P. (Eds.) (2010). *The rise of management-speak*. Stockholm, Sweden: Santérus.

Sahlin-Andersson, K., & Söderholm, A. (2002). *Beyond project management: New perspectives on the temporary–permanent dilemma*. Copenhagen: Liber.

Schoper, Y.-G., Wald, A., Ingason, H. T., & Fridgeirsson, T. V. (2018). Projectification in Western economies: A comparative study of Germany, Norway and Iceland. *International Journal of Project Management*, 36(1), 71–82.

Sennett, R. (1998). *The corrosion of character: The personal consequences of work in the new capitalism*. New York, NY: WW Norton & Co.

Sjöblom, S. (2009). Administrative short-termism: A non-issue in environmental and regional governance. *Journal of Environmental Policy and Planning*, 11(3): 165–168.

Sjöblom, S., & Godenhjelm, S. (2009). Project proliferation and governance implications for environmental management. *Journal of Environmental Policy and Planning*, 11(3), 169–185.

Sørensen, E., & Torfing, J. (2011). Enhancing collaborative innovation in the public sector. *Administration and Society*, 43(8), 842–868.

Styhre, A. (2006). The bureaucratization of the public sector manager function: The case of the construction industry. *International Journal of Project Management*, 24(3), 271–276.

Styhre, A. (2007). *The innovative bureaucracy: Bureaucracy in an age of fluidity*. Routledge Studies in Innovation, Organization and Technology. London, England: Routledge.

Whittington, R., Pettigrew, A., Peck, S., Fenton, E., & Conyon, M. (1999). Change and complementarities in the new competitive landscape: A European panel study, 1992–1996. *Organization Science*, 10(5), 583–600.

1

POLICY PILOTS AS PUBLIC SECTOR PROJECTS

The Projectification of Policy and Research

Stefanie Ettelt and Nicholas Mays

LONDON SCHOOL OF HYGIENE AND TROPICAL MEDICINE

Policy pilots are an intellectual cornerstone of evidence-based policy (EBP) as they hold out the promise, at least ostensibly, that policy will be rigorously tested before being rolled out more widely. Pilots are thus usually accompanied by evaluations designed to establish whether the policy change being tried out has the potential to generate the intended effects and is worth the investment. In England, national policy pilots have been promoted as an important instrument for central government, in particular, to better inform policy formulation and to manage the risks arising from new policy. While much attention has been given to the role of evaluation in generating the evidence from pilots (Cameron et al., 2011; Craig et al., 2008; HM Treasury, 2011), policy pilots have yet to be analysed as a specific type of policy project.

There is now a substantial literature analysing, and critiquing, the role of projects and project management in the public sector. Projects have become the dominant mode of organising activity in the corporate world and, in countries such as England, are widely used in the public sector. By now, some sectors are entirely organised through projects, notably international development. The European Union exercises a large swathe of its policy influence through project funding, either in regional development or through funding of the arts and sciences (see Fred and Mukhtar-Landgren, Chapter 10, and Jalocha and Ćwikła, Chapter 11, this volume). Nowadays, scientific research is almost exclusively organised through competitively acquired funding in the form of project grants and commissioned research. In innovation policy of all kinds, projects are ubiquitous, with policy-making itself also becoming increasingly "projectified" (see Hall, Chapter 2, this volume).

Policy pilots share many of the characteristics of projects discussed in the project and project management literature. Like other public sector projects, pilots promise to accelerate change (Jensen et al., 2013), and to combine "controllability and adventure" (Sahlin-Andersson and Soderholm, 2002), qualities that are highly desirable in policy-making. They offer the prospect of enabling policy-makers to control the risks of new policy while also creating a space for policy experimentation. They also operate within a set time frame, usually compatible with electoral cycles, occupy a particular space as a "temporary organisation" (Lundin and Soderholm, 1995) within a permanent (host) organisation, and are normally funded through distinct budgets rather than mainstream funding. Thus, there are boundaries drawn between the pilot as a project and the routine work of the host organisation, aimed at focusing energy on achieving project goals by prioritising specific activities aimed at facilitating a desired change from usual practice. Policy pilots also seem to share some of the problems attributed to projects and projectification, including concerns about short-termism, the difficulty of sustaining change beyond the duration of the pilot, and the potential for de-politicisation (Parsons, 2002).

This chapter aims to contribute to the literature on projects and projectification by considering the role of policy pilots in policy-making as a form of public sector project. Our observations are derived from our research on policy piloting and our experience as evaluators of policy pilots in health and social (long-term) care in England (Ettelt et al., 2015a; Ettelt et al., 2015b). The first part examines the conceptual overlap of projects and pilots, and identifies the project characteristics of policy piloting, drawing on the literature on project and project management. In doing so, we draw attention to the dual structure of pilot programmes since they typically comprise one or more implementation projects (i.e. pilots implemented in pilot "sites") and a linked research project (i.e. the evaluation of these pilots).

In the second part of this chapter, we make three observations based on our research on policy piloting in health and social care in England that resonate with the literature on projects and projectification. These are: (1) the relevance of the centre–periphery relationship as the governance context in which policy piloting takes place; (2) the importance given to evaluation and generating evidence; and (3) the difficulty of sustaining achievements and "scaling up" efforts after the end of the pilots that explains their limited contribution to policy change. We conclude by reflecting on the political implications of policy piloting in health and social care in England, arguing that piloting is politically convenient as it shifts the responsibility for potential failure to local actors while reflecting positively on the aspirations of central government.

Policy Pilots as Projects

Policy piloting is a type of policy project. Pilots have a deadline, budgets, a project management team, and a declared goal of promoting policy change. In instrumental terms, they are a change management tool that policy-makers can use when, or before, introducing policy change more widely. In English policy-making, pilots typically come in clusters, as pilot programmes, which then consist of a number of projects that are embedded and layered in a pilot programme, and are given a distinctive name such as "demonstrators", "pioneers" or "trailblazers". We here distinguish three layers within a national policy pilot programme: a national policy project that is the pilot programme; pilot projects through which the policy is implemented (and tested) locally; and a research project that aims to find out whether the policy "works" by evaluating the local policy pilots (occasionally, this includes evaluating the effectiveness of national level management of the programme). In this model, drawing on Jensen and colleagues (Chapter 6, this volume), policy piloting often combines characteristics of the "change project", intended to change existing organisational practices, with those of the "experimental project", aimed at testing new activities to be added to an existing practice.

In England, central government initiates and funds policy pilots with the stated aim to test policy before it is rolled out more widely.[1] Such programmes typically consist of several local pilots, but the number of sites per programme varies widely. These are implemented, for example, by local authorities, local organisations within the National Health Service (NHS) or other organisations in the public, private or voluntary sector, often in combination (e.g. local authorities working with NHS Clinical Commissioning Groups and care homes that are owned by private businesses or voluntary organisations). National policy-makers, in this case usually officials at the Department of Health and Social Care or one of its arm's-length agencies such as Public Health England or NHS England, also commission an evaluation, typically involving a research team, often, but not exclusively, based in academia.

Lundin and Söderholm (1995) distinguish "task", "time", "teams" and "transition" as central dimensions of projects and we will use these attributes to further disentangle the organisation of health and social care policy pilots. The *task* of pilot sites is to implement the policy that is being piloted, meaning that their task is to operationalise policy and put ideas set out in policy papers into organisational practice. In this sense, implementation in pilot sites can be seen as a "single project as unit of analysis" that is "understood as a manageable and researchable item whose intrinsic mechanisms were to be uncovered in pursuit of project success" (Packendorff, 1995; Packendorff & Lindgren, 2014). Project success, however, is typically not clearly specified ex ante and pilot sites can vary hugely in how they interpret national policy aims and what they aim to achieve. Instead, it is often the task of the evaluators to define clearly the outcomes sought and the related indicators that help specify and measure these outcomes, and it is their responsibility then to establish whether these outcomes can be attributed to the policy that is being piloted.

The task of implementing policy in pilot sites is usually presented as orderly and straight-forward, but inevitably turns out to be as messy and complex as implementation in any other policy "swamp" (Argyris & Schön, 1978). Pilot implementation includes a large number of decisions, trial and error, and eliminating alternatives. It also involves "unlearning" previous ways of working and typically relies on actors within the host organisation and its wider network of public and private sector organisations to come together and agree on a course of action, especially in those pilots that aim for "integration" between sectors. Policy implementation is complicated by the fact that it is sometimes not clear what is to be implemented. A broad policy idea may appear plausible in a Green Paper in which a government consults on its plans for future policy, but remains aspirational if there is no clear idea of how it can be operationalised in practice.

The research project is also broken down into a number of sub-projects, usually an outcome evaluation, process evaluation and an economic evaluation, to establish whether the policy can produce certain outcomes, how these are produced, and whether it constitutes value for money. The task therefore is to complete the evaluation and produce findings within given timeframes and budgets. Compared to the task of implementing the pilots, the research project is significantly more structured ex ante with a predefined sequence of tasks (e.g. research ethics and governance approvals, development of tools, data collection, data analysis, etc.) set out in a proposal or protocol. There is space for adjustments, but this depends on the research design with some designs being more flexible than others (e.g. randomised controlled trials rely on a stricter protocol and a more narrow definition of the nature of the policy as an "intervention" than, say, case study research).

It is interesting to consider what constitutes the "task" from the perspective of national policy-makers who initiate pilots and commission their evaluations. Their task usually includes clarifying policy objectives, selecting pilot sites, and developing implementation guidelines. However, as our research has shown, objectives of pilots are rarely stable and are likely to change over time, especially in an environment in which policy-makers change frequently, with ministers being replaced and civil servants reorganised or made redundant to reduce the government's administrative headcount (Ettelt et al., 2015a). After the end of a pilot programme, the tenets of evidence-based policy assert that policy-makers "make use" of the findings from the evaluations and deliberate on their implications for the roll-out of the policy. In some cases, evaluation findings are instrumental in informing policy decisions. Yet, in other cases, priorities for policies have shifted during the life of the programme. If findings are less favourable than expected, policy-makers may be inclined to drop the policy, postpone its wider implementation, or try to find solutions to overcome problems identified by the research. Alternatively, they could "cherry pick" findings to make them sound more positive in pursuit of wider policy goals (e.g. in the case of the evaluation of the Whole Systems Demonstrators[2], which were testing the use of assistive technologies for people with long-term conditions, the government highlighted the positive findings in order to justify further technological investment) (Ettelt et al., 2015b).

Time is of obvious relevance to policy pilots, which are time-limited by definition. Since it is the declared purpose of policy pilots to inform policy decisions, the programme needs to be organised in a way to allow for the evaluation to report when the findings are needed. Thus, pilot programmes often depend on political schedules (e.g. legislative cycles) to determine their endpoint. The problem is that this can leave too little time to implement the pilots, let alone to evaluate them, especially if the pilots need to produce a sufficient number of observable outcomes. There is an increasing recognition by policy-makers that more time needs to be allocated to allow pilot programmes to be set up. However, it is often hard to predict how much time is sufficient for pilot sites to operationalise the policy and when a programme is mature enough for its evaluation to capture the policy's true potential (Ogilvie et al., 2011). It is sometimes claimed that policy pilots would have produced better outcomes if they had been allowed more time and that this explains why very similar pilot programmes are frequently mounted in swift succession (Bardsley et al., 2013). Yet while it seems obvious that programmes should be allowed to "bed in", this is often not realistic within the time constraints that come with national policy-making. Lurking behind this empirical problem is an unresolved question as to how much time is enough to be able to judge whether a programme has generated sufficient evidence to determine whether the policy is worth persisting with or should be discontinued.

The pilot projects and their research projects are typically executed by separate *teams*. Staff implementing the pilots may be recruited from the permanent workforce of the organisation or employed on temporary contracts, with pilot managers often having other responsibilities within the host organisation. The project literature emphasises that the project team simultaneously anchors the project in the structure of the host organisation and separates it from its routine operations (Lundin & Soderholm, 1995; Jensen et al., 2013; Godenhjelm et al., 2015). This resonates with pilot projects that typically rely on project managers to collaborate extensively with other members of the organisation and with other organisations, while at the same time keeping the team focused on implementing change. In addition, many contemporary pilot programmes in England aim to improve the collaboration between different organisations (e.g. to promote "integration" of health and social care). In such programmes, pilot teams can sit between existing organisations, making it more difficult to maintain links with the existing structures and secure their support. Typically, such pilots do not sit within a legal entity, nor do they form their own one, which means they are not allowed to hold their own budget, which arguably exposes them even more to tensions between, or simply lack of interest from, their participant organisations.

The research project is also organised around a team, typically brought together for the purpose of the evaluation and based on individual competencies. Temporary contracts are the norm for the majority of research staff with the exception of senior researchers, who tend to work on other projects alongside contributing to a particular evaluation. There are different schools of thought with regards to the separation of implementers and evaluators (more about this below), yet evaluators are typically expected to be independent from policy-makers, for example, by limiting the ability of policy-makers to influence, or prevent, the publication of findings, although this varies across different policy fields with health being the most wedded to independent evaluation.

The stated purpose of national policy piloting is to promote policy change and thus facilitate *transition*. While this is in line with other types of public sector projects (Jensen et al., 2013), policy piloting, at least in theory, aspires to a different route to transition: policy change based on evidence produced from evaluation. The assumption is that findings from evaluation will be used by policy-makers to inform future policy decisions, so that these decisions are taken on a more informed basis, which then leads to decreased opposition and increased support for the policy change. However, this instrumental logic is problematic. Findings appear to be most palatable when they confirm a decision, rather than challenge it. They are also not always conclusive enough to support a specific decision. Frequently, more research is needed, for example, because the pilot sites have taken longer than expected to implement the intervention and more time is needed to measure patient/client outcomes in comparison with some sort of "control" group. In most cases, it is difficult to generalise beyond the remit of the programme and questions arise about the transferability of findings to other prospective areas.

More familiar from a project perspective is the idea that pilots are used to "pump prime" change nationally by initiating projects locally from which other places can then learn. This intention is reflected in programmes in which pilot sites are selected based on their experience with, and success in, implementing existing policy. However, this approach generates concerns about a potential lack of sustainability of local change and the difficulty of "rolling out" the programme to less "expert" sites, especially if pilot sites have been selected primarily to be able to "show off" their achievements (Ettelt et al., 2015a). There can also be substantial confusion about the mechanism of change that policy pilots are expected to promote, which in turn can have an impact on the options and opportunities for evaluation. For example, if pilot sites are selected because of their experience, it will be difficult to organise a trial that measures the likely costs and benefits when sites start implementing "from scratch" (Hendy et al., 2012).

To summarise, policy pilots share many of the characteristics of other types of public sector projects, but there are also some qualifications. The task of implementing policy pilots is often less clear in operational terms than it appears in policy documents. Pilots also sit within a political environment that both enables and compromises the tasks of implementation and evaluation. As pilots are a temporary organisation, there is usually a firm deadline to work towards, but deadlines are typically politically determined, not based on a realistic estimate of the time it is likely to take to implement the policy change and have it "bed down" sufficiently to allow for meaningful evaluation of its long-term consequences. The different teams involved emphasise the separation of implementation, evaluation and policy-making, and also highlight that policy piloting is a multiple team effort that requires substantial coordination. Finally, while facilitating change is the obvious purpose of policy piloting, there can be confusion as to how transition is to be brought about and the role of evaluation in facilitating policy change.

Three Observations from Policy Piloting in Health and Social Care in England

In the next section, we make three observations based on the findings from our research on nationally initiated policy pilots in health and social care in England that resonate with debates in the projectification literature. These are: (1) the observation that national policy piloting is embedded in, and relies on, the specific centre–periphery relationships prevalent in health and social care governance in England; (2) the importance of generating evidence from evaluation in policy piloting as its proclaimed mechanism of change; and (3) the difficulty of sustaining achievements in policy implementation and rolling them out following the end of a pilot programme.

Piloting Cuts Across the Centre–Periphery Relationship

National policy piloting relies on local actors to implement national policy and therefore spans the centre and periphery involved in policy-making. In England, central government initiates national policy pilots by inviting local actors to participate in a pilot programme, sometimes, but not always, associated with the promise of additional funding. Local statutory actors who volunteer to participate in the programme then implement the pilots in their locality, often in collaboration with other organisations in the voluntary or private sector (e.g. care homes) or across policy sectors (e.g. NHS organisations working with elected local authorities). In addition, there are all sorts of local and regional initiatives that may be pilot programmes, but are not usually piloting national policy (Bailey et al., 2017). The centre also commissions any national evaluation. At times, this is complemented by a requirement to invest in additional local evaluation. Central government also tends to support networking activities between pilot sites to foster the exchange of local experience, knowledge and inspiration. These activities are typically run separately from the evaluation process. Before the financial crisis of 2007–08, there would often be a substantial support infrastructure at the centre for some pilot programmes, but this has been massively reduced in recent years, in part, in response to financial pressures, but also reflecting a new vision for a more restrained, scaled-down role for central government in policy innovation.

Policy piloting – as practised in health and social care policy in England – reflects an understanding of an existing mode of governance and its established centre–periphery relationships. The received wisdom is that central government is responsible for policy formulation but has limited ability to engage in, or even control, implementation. There are many ways in which central influence filters through the system, but responsibility for implementation is largely delegated to local actors (Flinders, 2002; Exworthy & Frosini, 2008; Pratchett, 2004). Local actors, in turn, including local government, do not participate in national policy formulation. They may be consulted or "listened to" and their staff may or may not support implementation in their role as "street-level bureaucrats" (Lipsky, 1980), but they do not have a formal role in decision-making (Ling, 2002). There are of course differences between the two policy sectors: central government is more or less directly responsible for the NHS which is overseen by its administrative agency, NHS England; social care, in contrast, is organised entirely by elected local governments. Local government, however, is dependent on a centrally allocated social care grant and operates within a centrally set policy and regulatory framework. Yet local authorities have a larger degree of separation from the centre than, say, organisations of the NHS. They raise some of their own funds locally from business rates and household taxes and thus do not depend entirely on national resource allocation. Their leaders are primarily accountable to local voters rather than central government, even though local councillors also have to account for their use of central government funds. Despite this, the centre acts as the initiator of policy piloting, while leaving "implementation" to local actors. In recent years, there has been renewed interest in the idea of "localism" and the devolution of responsibilities from the centre to the periphery (mostly to the large metropolitan centres through a series of "devolution deals") (Lowndes & Pratchett, 2012; Cox, 2010), but on the whole central government in England still conceives of itself as the main driver of policy innovation.

In practice, policy ideas launched by the centre are often broad and still require a substantial amount of thought, work and effort to operationalise. The pilot is thus a mechanism to delegate the task of operationalisation to local actors who deal with the hard graft of working through the problems that implementation throws up. For example, as a policy idea, the integration of health and social care seems to make eminent sense as it promises both a better service for patients and a possibility of reducing costs in the face of increasing demands from an ageing population. Yet integration has so far been largely elusive (although it has been tried in multiple ways and many places) and consequently central government has initiated a series of locally implemented pilot programmes to test different approaches, establish the evidence and diffuse the knowledge of how better integration can be achieved. System integration remains out of reach, but the effort is ongoing and the idea of integration, despite its many setbacks, is still very much alive. An alternative policy approach would have been to bring the health and social care systems under one legislative umbrella, develop a unified funding approach and systematically organise a (more) integrated approach to system governance and service delivery. Yet this would require national politicians and their policy advisers to resolve a series of awkward policy dilemmas made more difficult by tightly constrained public finances. So far, this approach has been seen as "too difficult" to be contemplated. In contrast, initiating a series of local pilots allows for an incremental approach to promoting change by devolving the responsibility for progress to local actors.

It also shifts the risk of policy failure from the centre to the periphery, while leaving the existing governance infrastructure intact. From a central government perspective, there are at least three types of risk related to policy "failure". First, there is the practical risk of a policy failing either because its implications were insufficiently thought through or because other stakeholders, on whom implementation relies, withhold their support. The project management literature emphasises the risks of time overrun and budget overspend of projects, especially in the public sector (Jensen et al., 2013). By initiating a pilot programme, government is able to control these risks as the programme is given a fixed budget and timeline within which pilot implementers have to operate. There have been occasions in which the length of a programme has been extended, typically to give the evaluation more time to measure outcomes, but these extensions have been limited in scope. Perhaps more importantly, if the government decides after the end of a programme that it no longer wishes to roll out the policy it is able to abandon it (although there is still the risk of some reputational damage).

Second, there is the reputational risk for government of being seen as complacent. By initiating a pilot programme, and commissioning its evaluation, the government gives the policy some prominence, devotes (limited) resources to it and makes a commitment to engage with the knowledge produced from the process. Initiating pilots signals that the government intends to address a problem and that it is willing to embark on a new approach. In this respect, national policy piloting is no different from other public projects that cater for a demand for change by signalling innovation and entrepreneurship (Sahlin-Andersson & Soderholm, 2002) and a "crystallisation of intent" (Pellegrinelli, 2011, p. 236). However, government often seems most comfortable about its pilot programmes at the stage when they are announced, suggesting that there is symbolic value in initiating pilots and commissioning their evaluation, as opposed to having to deal with their results (Ettelt et al., 2015a).

The third risk that central government will aim to avoid is the risk of opposition to the policy growing, and of losing control over the policy discourse. Opposition to a policy is more likely to be manageable when the policy is contained within a pilot programme, which is ostensibly only meant to "test" the policy on a limited scale. This gives less room for critics to oppose the policy. The management of this third type of risk through piloting contributes to concerns about the de-politicisation of policy-making. By focusing attention on local implementation and testing, piloting creates a distance between the politics of policy-making and the government that is testing its implementation. In a similar fashion, it is much more likely that policy pilots are evaluated locally than evaluation being applied to projects that government embarks on within its own ranks (e.g. projects undertaken by the Cabinet Office). It also focuses on questions of policy-effectiveness and cost-effectiveness, while other issues, such as distributional fairness (e.g. in respect to finding alternative ways of collecting and distributing funding for social care, which has been discussed as a matter of urgency for many years) can easily be side-lined. Thus, while piloting is a mechanism for testing policy, it is also a tool to contain criticism and control the discourse, by which the centre maintains its power over policy-making, while simultaneously delegating the practical problem solving to local actors.

The Importance Given to Evaluation and the Production of Evidence

Many projects involve monitoring and evaluation, but in policy piloting generating evidence from evaluation is usually a key purpose of the exercise, at least ostensibly and at the outset, which sets it apart from other types of policy projects (Cabinet Office, 2003; Sanderson, 2002). The idea is that by evaluating a pilot programme, insights can be gained that can inform national policy-making and create the "evidence" in support of a policy. The hope is that the evidence generated from the pilots is sufficiently conclusive to support a decision and the typical assumption is that it will demonstrate that the new policy "works", i.e. it will produce the effects desired.

However, in practice, the evaluation process often does not work like this. Frequently, the findings from the evaluation are equivocal. Evaluators often find it difficult to measure outcomes to an extent that they are conclusive, with some recent pilot programmes simply unable to attract the number of study participants required to measure outcomes validly in the time available. In such cases, evaluation is likely to produce a good understanding of the difficulties of implementing the pilots, but it is much harder to establish whether the mechanism underpinning the policy can generate the desired outcomes and how these outcomes may differ in a wide range of different contexts.

However, from an implementation perspective, there is also the question as to whether the evaluation is targeted at the right audience. Should the evaluation be aimed at informing mainly local policy implementers rather than central government decision-makers? There are a number of approaches to evaluation that do exactly this, such as action-research that aims to involve implementers strongly in the research to foster learning while the pilots are being developed; but these are rarely requested when evaluations of national policy pilots in health and social care are commissioned. This also raises the question as to whether findings from evaluation should be made available more quickly (as in "real-time" evaluation), rather than at the end of the programme as is customary and more feasible for rigorous outcome evaluation. In practice, evaluators are often encouraged to report early and often, yet it is entirely possible that early findings differ from, even contradict, later conclusions that take account of all the data collected during a programme. Though each of these propositions sounds desirable, they tend to conflict with the idea of outcome evaluation that is both scientifically robust and independent, since this requires that the influence of implementers (and policy-makers) is kept to a minimum.

There can also be tension between the purpose of the pilots and the purpose of the evaluation, suggesting conflicting ideas about the mechanisms through which policy change influences changes in local practice. Should pilots be organised to enable evaluation to be as robust as possible? If so, local variation between interventions should presumably be kept to a minimum. Or should the pilots be more flexible and allow more variation to encourage local innovation, in which case the chances of robust outcome evaluation would be reduced dramatically? Having substantial variation between different pilots within a programme means that effects of the policy cannot be pooled across pilot sites (as they all implement something different), hence limiting the "evaluability" of the programme (Ogilvie et al., 2011). Presumably, such decisions, if taken consciously, hinge on different ideas about the mechanisms of policy change. From an evidence-based policy perspective, it is assumed that policy change should be determined by the best available evidence; robust evaluation is therefore vital. Yet policy piloting also allows for a more bottom-up type of policy change that invites local actors to experiment less formally and develop their own solutions to policy problems. This mechanism of policy change tends to be favoured by local organisations, perhaps especially local authorities; yet it can conflict with ideas of evidence use in policy that favour robust evaluation and a more prescriptive approach to policy piloting.

The Difficulty of Sustaining Achievements in Policy Implementation

To allow project managers in pilot sites to develop new ways of working, the temporary organisation that is the pilot requires a degree of separation from the permanent (host) organisation. At the same time, project managers typically rely on the host organisation, its resources, structures and networks, for support and to achieve the effects they are expected to produce.

Yet by separating the pilots from their host organisations, the pilots face the same challenge that many other projects face: how can the achievements of the pilot be "mainstreamed" into the normal ways of working of the host organisation? For example, if the pilots set out to test the impacts of providing frail individuals with telecare devices to improve their care at home (as attempted in the Whole System Demonstrators), how are local authorities expected to continue offering these devices and provide the new service alongside existing services after the funding for the pilots has expired? This problem is not trivial, as few policy pilot programmes appear to have been sustained beyond the end of the programme (though this may be an artefact of the fact that this phenomenon is difficult to research). Those interventions that have continued after the formal end of a pilot programme have often been scaled down. Given current funding constraints, at least in England, it is difficult to imagine how this could be different, unless the intervention piloted clearly shows it can save money. Arguably, this is neither unexpected, nor necessarily undesirable. It is not unexpected, given that much research has demonstrated that it takes a long time to embed almost any type of change into routine practice; and it may not be undesirable, if we concede that piloting should be undertaken without fixed expectations as to its results, similar to the concept of equipoise that justifies randomised clinical trials (Petticrew et al., 2013).

There is an added challenge for policy piloting, arising from the aspiration associated with evidence-based policy: how can the achievements of the pilots be "scaled" and rolled out nationally? If the intention is that after a successful experience (however defined) the policy is to be implemented in other areas beyond those that participated in the pilot programme, how can the learning from the pilots inform these efforts? Evidence-based policy stipulates that the evaluation will generate the generalisable knowledge that will help others to follow suit. However, evaluation, especially of the national, outcome-focused variety, is often not well placed to provide the level of detailed, contextual knowledge that implementers are likely to require if they are to extend the innovation to other places. In addition, those studies with strongest claims to internal validity (e.g. research designs that test causality such as randomised controlled trials) tend to have particularly limited external validity, that is, they cannot easily be generalised or their findings applied to other places, and researchers may hesitate to provide the kind of prescriptive steer desired by project managers and policy-makers.

One aspect of this problem is the relationship between the pilot and the host organisation and its wider network. In the language of piloting and evaluation, this is how the "intervention" relates to the "context" or, more precisely, how the variables associated with the context influence the intervention/policy and thus the outcomes observed. One way of examining this relationship is to require pilot sites to standardise the intervention as much as possible. However, this requires prior definition of the intervention and agreement among the parties that this definition is the correct one to pilot, which is not always the case, particularly not with genuinely innovative pilots. Standardising the implementation may help the robust measurement of outcomes, taking account of contextual variables, but it does so by precluding the option of exploring alternative approaches to operationalising the policy and by reducing the options for adaptation that may make the experience of participating in the programme more meaningful to local sites.

This problem is amplified where pilots set out to make a significant change to existing practices and systems. There can be a significant contrast between the scale of the ambition and the ability of pilot programmes to achieve it, almost irrespective of how the evaluation is conducted. Programmes such as the Whole System Demonstrators ostensibly set out to show how the "whole" local health care and social care systems could become involved in the integration of services by introducing patient-operated supportive technologies (telehealth and telecare). This did not materialise during the pilot programme because too few people could be identified who had both a health care and a social care need that could be appropriately met via a technical intervention, so there was little opportunity to integrate care in this way. With hindsight, it seems curious that policy-makers should believe that telehealth and telecare could be expected to transform entire local health and care systems or at least to make a noticeable difference to any of them. If this was ambitious, this was matched by the high expectations placed on the evaluation in that it was meant to provide definitive proof of the superiority of such technology compared with usual care. Not surprisingly, this did not materialise either.

Final Reflection: Policy Piloting in the Shadow of "Politics"

In this chapter, we have argued that policy pilots have much in common with other types of public sector projects, but that there are also some differences insofar as policy piloting in our experience tends to put special emphasis on national evaluation and a proclaimed commitment to test whether pilots produce desired outcomes. By drawing on our research on policy piloting in health and social care in England, we have shown that national policy piloting is ostensibly embedded in a particular version of public sector governance, in which central government formulates policy and initiates national programmes while local actors solve problems of implementation. Policy piloting is therefore directly exposed to the "politics" of central government policy-making, its contestation, vagaries and uncertainties, and its desire to control the risks associated with policy change, which can be practical (avoiding policy failure) as well as reputational (by delegating risk) and political (by defusing opposition).

We have also highlighted the role of evaluation in policy piloting and its importance as a mechanism of policy change, which is in line with the central tenets of evidence-based policy. However, this approach means that the stakes for evaluation are high in policy piloting and much depends on the "evaluability" of the pilots as they are implemented locally (Ogilvie et al., 2011; Ettelt & Mays, 2015). Hence, policy-makers are faced with a dilemma: should pilots be organised to allow for robust evaluation and therefore risk stifling flexibility and local innovation; or should they be organised to encourage local variation, yet at the price of reducing the possibility of evaluation to assess whether the policy "works" in a more generalizable sense? A further, related observation focuses on the difficulty facing policy pilots in maintaining their achievements and transferring their experience to other localities that have not participated in the programme, but are expected to learn from the pilots, especially through their evaluation. The long-term effects of policy pilots in health and social care on local change have yet to be investigated in any depth. There is much less research on long-term developments in local governments than on the short-term implementation of evidence-based practice (May et al., 2007).

Examining policy piloting through the lens of the project and projectification literature leads us to the question as to why policy-makers embark on pilot programmes. Based on the analysis presented above, we conclude that piloting allows policy-makers to influence the policy process in at least three ways: first, policy piloting shifts attention away from the question of the desirability of a new policy to the practical problems of implementation. The pilot evaluation will tend to focus on "how" the policy is interpreted and translated into practical change rather than "why" it is being suggested in the first place. Second, it allows policy-makers to delegate the responsibility for success and failure of pilots and policy to local actors, and away from the centre. This is particularly tempting when the risk of failure is high, since it is difficult, both conceptually and practically, to distinguish whether "failure" (in itself a socially constructed phenomenon) was the result of a conceptually flawed policy or because local actors did not implement it correctly (policy failure versus implementation failure). Third, piloting helps to mobilise claims to objectivity derived from independent, outcome-focused evaluation, which strengthens the authority of policy-makers by lending scientific authority to policy decisions (Bijker et al., 2009; Weingart, 1999). In conjunction, these strategies can partly, and perhaps only temporarily, de-politicise the policy process, an observation made by critical commentators on the claims of evidence-based policy-making, as well as on projectification in the public sector more widely (Parsons, 2002; Cicmil & Hodgson, 2006).

This is striking, given the obvious mismatch between the scale of the ambition loaded onto programmes aimed at whole system change, system transformation or integration between public policy sectors and the deliberately limited investment of political capital and resource associated with most pilots. Whether this suggests the survival of pragmatism in English policy-making (the optimist's view) or an attempt to obfuscate politics by devising a smoke-screen behind which to hide a lack of willingness to address complex social problems (the cynic's view) remains a matter of debate (including between the authors of this chapter). However, the ambiguity associated with these two readings may explain why policy piloting, although initially a New Labour initiative in the UK, has remained popular with successive (Conservative) governments, including those devoted to the "small state" and austerity governance. Projectification helps policy-makers to manage a whole set of complex relationships, uncertainties and expectations that they would otherwise have to deal with much more explicitly and laboriously.

Notes

1 We refer to England instead of the United Kingdom (UK), as responsibility for health and social care policy is devolved to the four countries that form the UK: England, Northern Ireland, Scotland and Wales.

2 The "Whole System Demonstrators" were a government-funded pilot programme conducted between 2008 and 2011 that tested the use of assistive technologies such as pendant alarms for older people at risk of falling (referred to as telecare) or diabetes management devices (referred to as telehealth) used in people's homes. The name of the programme was aspirational, indicating the intention to use these technologies to help integrate services at the boundary between the health and social care systems. While the evaluation of the individual technologies showed moderate positive effects, the programme did not achieve its overarching aim of integrating systems of care.

References

Argyris, C. & Schön, D. A. (1978). *Organizational learning*. Reading, MA: Addison Wesley.

Bailey, S., Checkland, K., Hodgson, D., McBride, A., Elvey, R., Parkin, S., Rothwell, K., & Pierides, D. (2017). The policy work of piloting: Mobilising and managing conflict and ambiguity in the English NHS. *Social Science & Medicine*. Retrieved from http://dx.doi.org/10.1016/j.socscimed.2017.02.002

Bardsley, M., Steventon, A., Smith, J., & Dixon, J. (2013). *Evaluating integrated and community-based care: How do we know what works?*London: Nuffield Trust.

Bijker, W. E., Bal, R., & Hendricks, R. (2009). *The paradox of scientific authority: The role of scientific advice in democracies*. Cambridge, MA: MIT Press.

Cabinet Office (2003). *Trying it out: The role of "pilots" in policy-making: Report of a review of government pilots*. London, England: Cabinet Office Strategy Unit.

Cameron, A., Salisbury, C., Lart, R., Steward, K., Peckham, S., Calnan, M., Purdy, S., & Thorp, H. (2011). Policymakers' perceptions on the use of evidence from evaluations. *Evidence & Policy: A journal of research, debate and practice*, 7, 429–447.

Cicmil, S., & Hodgson, D. (2006). Making projects critical: Introduction. *Making projects critical* (pp. 1–25). Basingstoke: Palgrave.

Cox, E. (2010). *Five foundations of real localism*. Newcastle Upon Tyne, England: Institute for Public Policy Research/IPPR North.

Craig, P., Dieppe, P., Macintyre, S., Michie, S., Nazareth, I., & Petticrew, M. (2008). *Developing and evaluating complex interventions: The new Medical Research Council guidance. British Medical Journal*, 337, a1655.

Ettelt, S., & Mays, N. (2015). *Advice on commissioning external academic evaluations of policy pilots in health and social care: A discussion paper*. London, England: Policy Innovation Research Unit.

Ettelt, S., Mays, N., & Allen, P. (2015a). The multiple purposes of policy piloting and their consequences: Three examples from national health and social care policy in England. *Journal of Social Policy*, 44, 319–337.

Ettelt, S., Mays, N., & Allen, P. (2015b). Policy experiments: Investigating effectiveness or confirming direction? *Evaluation*, 21, 292–307.

Exworthy, M., & Frosini, F. (2008). Room for manoeuvre? Explaining local autonomy in the English National Health Service. *Health Policy*, 86, 204–212.

Flinders, M. (2002). Governance in Whitehall. *Public Administration*, 80, 51–75.

Godenhjelm, S., Lundin, R. A., & Sjöblom, S. (2015). Projectification in the public sector: The case of the European Union. *International Journal of Managing Projects in Business*, 8, 324–348.

Hendy, J., Chrysanthaki, T., Barlow, J., Knapp, M., Rogers, A., Sanders, C., Bower, P., Bowen, R., Fitzpatrick, R., & Bardsley, M. (2012). An organisational analysis of the implementation of telecare and telehealth: The whole systems demonstrator. *BMC Health Services Research*, 12, 403.

HM Treasury (2011). *The magenta book: Guidance for evaluation*. London, England: HM Treasury.

Jensen, C., Johnsson, S., & Löfström, M. (2013). The project organization as a policy tool in implementing welfare reforms in the public sector. *International Journal of Health Planning and Management*, 28, 122–137.

Ling, T. (2002). Delivering joined-up government in the UK: Dimensions, issues and problems. *Public Administration*, 80, 615–642.

Lipsky, M. (1980). *Street-level bureaucracy: Dilemmas of the individual in public services*. New York, NY: Russell Sage Foundation.

Lowndes, V., & Pratchett, L. (2012). Local governance under the coalition government: Austerity, localism and the "Big Society". *Local Government Studies*, 38, 21–40.

Lundin, R. A., & Söderholm, A. (1995). A theory of the temporary organization. *Scandinavian Journal of Management*, 11, 437–455.

May, C., Finch, T., Mair, F., Ballini, L., & Al, E. (2007). Understanding the implementation of complex interventions in health care: The normalization process model. *BMC Health Services Research*, 7.

Ogilvie, D., Cummins, S., Petticrew, M., White, M., Jones, A., & Wheeler, K. (2011). Assessing the evaluability of complex public health interventions: Five questions for researchers, funders, and policymakers. *Milbank Quarterly*, 89, 206–225.

Packendorff, J. (1995). Inquiring into the temporary organization: New directions for project management research. *Scandinavian Journal of Management*, 11, 319–333.

Packendorff, J., & Lindgren, M. (2014). Projectification and its consequences: Narrow and broad conceptualisations. *South African Journal of Economic and Management Sciences*, 17, 7–21.

Parsons, W. (2002). From muddling through to muddling up-evidence based policy making and the modernisation of British government. *Public Policy and Administration*, 17, 43–60.

Pellegrinelli, S. (2011). What's in a name: Project or programme? *International Journal of Project Management*, 29, 232–240.

Petticrew, M., McKee, M., Lock, K., Green, J., & Phillips, G. (2013). In search of social equipoise. *British Medical Journal*, 347, 18–20.

Pratchett, L. (2004). Local autonomy, local democracy and the "New Localism". *Political Studies*, 52, 358–375.

Sahlin-Andersson, K., & Soderholm, A. (2002). *Beyond project management: New perspectives on the temporary–permanent dilemma*. Copenhagen, Denmark: Liber.

Sanderson, I. (2002). Evaluation, policy learning and evidence-based policy making. *Public Administration*, 80, 1–22.

Weingart, P. (1999). Scientific expertise and political accountability: Paradoxes of sciences in politics. *Science and Public Policy*, 26, 151–161.

2

WHY IS INNOVATION POLICY PROJECTIFIED?

Political Causes in the Case of Sweden

Patrik Hall

MALMÖ UNIVERSITY

In this chapter, it is argued that the projectification of innovation policy – the organisation and implementation of a policy field where the project form dominates – is the product of political processes, despite the consensual and seemingly "apolitical" character of the contemporary innovation discourse. A political science perspective may contribute with significant insights into the general issue of what is driving projectification in the contemporary public sphere. In the Swedish case considered in this chapter, innovation policy has relied on government-funded innovation projects for at least 100 years, which gives the opportunity to draw a general picture of the most important traits of projectification in policy contexts. Furthermore, contemporary innovation policy is related to typical coordination problems within politics, such as multi-level governance and inter-organisational relations (not least between the public and the private sphere), where the project form tends to become a dominant outlet as several chapters in this volume show (see Büttner, Chapter 9, this volume).

The fundamental feature of innovation policy is that it is inter-organisational, developing in the boundary between public and private, between politics, bureaucracy, industry, and academia, sometimes referred to as the triple helix model of innovation (Etzkowitz & Leydesdorff, 2000). Inter-organisational relations are looser and more unpredictable than intra-organisational, without established methods of resolving conflicts, although several actors within such relations – specifically "meta-governors" such as national governments or the European Union (EU) – frequently try to establish rules and predictability. However, as long as there are uncertainties regarding the jurisdiction of such rules, a possible scenario is continuous negotiations regarding commitments and spheres of authority, a form of inter-organisational diplomacy. Many organisational arenas serve as sites for such diplomacy within innovation policy, where intriguing issues such as who is going to pay development costs for innovations, how to share risks, and how to handle potential company secrets are continuously negotiated but never entirely solved. In such an organisational system, ideas and beliefs (of innovation) seem to serve as the rationale behind coordination (Valaskivi, 2012), in line with the "ideational turn" in policy studies (Béland & Cox, 2011). However, the project form is a way of delegating the complexity of "innovations" and "innovation systems" to actors who carry out projects in the form of inter-organisational collaborations, predominantly within technological research but increasingly also within human services.

The configuration of "politics" in such a system of relations, characterised by consensual ideas and collaborative forms, is of course alien to conceptions of politics as antagonism or (visible) conflicts (Mouffe, 2005; Hay, 2007). The concepts and ideas within innovation policy are of academic origin and often become bureaucratic mainstream within the EU, states, and regions. It may even reasonably be claimed that innovation policy is not only contrary to conceptions of politics as antagonistic, but sometimes also contrary to conceptions of the market as based on competition, since industries within specific sectors or within specific regions are often expected to be able to cooperate without problems (Hall & Löfgren, 2017).

However, if politics instead is conceptualised as ambitions to organise authority (*Herrschaft*), innovation policy is definitely politicised. Innovation policy maintains ideas about how society ought to be organised, based on academic theories, ongoing negotiations regarding responsibilities and allocation of resources, representations in the form of public agencies with great importance for actors who want support, and delegations of responsibilities to other political authorities such as regions. The most important outflow of these ideas, representations, and delegations is the funding of innovations. By qualifying funding according to the lines of ideas of triple helix, clusters or regional innovation systems, political ideas (or politicised academic ideas, see Lovering, 1999) are institutionalised into a system of government. Researchers who describe the phenomenon of "de-politicisation" point to the delegation of politics to non-political bodies ("arena-shifting", Burnham 2001; Flinders & Buller 2006), such as funding agencies regarding innovation systems, in support of their argument. By contrast, Fenwick et al. (2012) view modern governance structures, such as partnerships, as an extension of bureaucratic and political control. Bell and Hindmoor (2009) also argue that states are enhancing their capacity to govern by developing closer ties with non-government actors. Arena-shifting moves issues to new arenas, but cannot be seen as the same thing as de-politicisation. Institutionalised rules regarding the support of innovation systems are rather a case of far-reaching governmental, and thus political, control. Furthermore, these rules may be circumvented politically when new situations must be acted upon, as we shall see examples of in the following.

This study of Swedish innovation policy will illustrate how and why innovation policy relies on a logic of projectification, as well as show that, rather than de-politicising policy, it re-politicises policy at various levels. The aim of this chapter is to describe the political origins of projectification within Swedish innovation policy in a historical perspective. The reason for this exposé is that it is important to understand the key political logics, which still are at play in a process where projects are increasingly used as legitimation, means, and end. This chapter will claim that projects: (1) legitimise and represent specific political constellations; (2) are used to react politically to perceived industrial crises, and (3) become ends in themselves in an effort to responsibilise other actors for innovative development.

The Projectification of Innovation Policy

The inter-related concepts of "innovation" and "innovation systems" have dominated efforts to rejuvenate globalised capitalism since the 1990s. According to the Organisation for Economic Co-operation and Development (OECD), more and better innovations have become the default policy solution to many fiscal and industrial policy problems. From the outside, innovation policy is a cross-sectorial policy which bridges several policy domains and which requires a whole-of-government approach capable of coordinating different layers of government and stakeholders (OECD, 2010). In particular, the interplay and interdependence between public, private, and third sectors are conceived as prerequisites for generating "innovation" and subsequently further economic development in Europe (European Commission 2011). While the definitions of innovation abound with several different meanings and alignments, innovation is mainly defined as "new creations of economic and/or societal significance, mainly carried out by firms (public or private)" (Edquist, 2011, p. 5), whereas the modern concept of innovation systems (invented by Bengt-Åke Lundvall in 1985) refers to the interactions between actors that are necessary for producing innovations.

At present, the existing body of innovation policy research is dominated by best-practice perspectives in which the researchers are pursuing actual cases with the capacity of being replicated in other realms. Policy prescriptions take the form of simplified rationalist models where the (rational) master decision-maker is conceived as an actor with the ability to choose from a tool box of policy instruments (Flanagan et al., 2011). In addition, traditional motivations of innovation policy mainly regard politics as a form of action, which is only motivated in situations of "market failures". Flanagan et al. (2011, p. 705) call this dominant approach "prescriptive innovation policy studies". Equally, current national (and European) policies are clearly intertwined with the academic knowledge production, as models, theories, and concepts of the policy are progenies of theoretical academic output. Regardless of buzz words such as "smart specialisation", innovation policy, as well as regional development policy in the EU, seem to produce broadly isomorphic outcomes in terms of discourse and practice

(Lagendijk & Varró, 2013). In terms of policy instruments, short-term and co-financed development programs and projects are almost invariably chosen.

Büttner and Leopold (2016; see also Büttner, Chapter 9, this volume) describe the EU project world as an "enormous standardisation" in terms of goals, models for implementation, and evaluative practices. There is a reason for this standardised projectification: the possibility of governing at a distance through delegating implementation to other actors. However, projectification differs from ordinary implementation within public administration – projects actively perform a political, strategic, and operational agenda. Through projectification, public actors as well as partner actors in knowledge institutions, firms, and non-governmental organisations (NGOs), make themselves instruments for strategic purposes; in the case of innovation policy, in order to realise "innovation systems" throughout Europe. At the core of projectification thus lies the phenomenon of "responsibilisation" (Rose, 1999). The projects are responsibilised for the government of innovation, but are also held to account and rendered auditable by the centrally-organised funding systems (ibid., pp. 154–155). Gross investments are thus made in innovations, but in a centrally-stipulated form. As stated above, the technologies of the project may seem de-politicised, but on the other hand, this centrally-stipulated form allows for more governmental control over forms of innovation than ever before. However, the interesting thing with innovation policy is that it has a history of projectification, which goes much further back (at least in Sweden) than the EU funding schemes.

Method and Structure

Swedish innovation policy has a more than century-long history. This history is quite well researched (Sundin, 1981; Weinberger, 1997; Björck, 2004; Eklund, 2007; Persson, 2008). This chapter is based on these secondary sources regarding the history of Swedish innovation policy, as well as my own interviews and studies of documents and discourse of Swedish innovation policy. The funding patterns of Sweden's Innovation Agency (Vinnova, *Verket för innovationssystem*) has also been documented through their "project bank" on their web page.

- Nine interviews were conducted, with: two senior analysts and the deputy CE of Vinnova,
- three former officials at the Ministry of Enterprise,
- one project leader at the Royal Academy of Engineering Sciences, and
- two officials in charge of innovation at Region Skåne.

The interviews were semi-structured and aimed at getting a description of contemporary innovation policy – its ideas, structures, and forms of organising. These interviews are generally more interesting than official reports regarding innovation policy since the actors have much experience and generously shared this wide experience from the policy milieu, whereas most of the reports only reproduce ideas. Specifically, the interviews on a national level were mainly quite frank and outspoken since these officials believe strongly in innovation systems; it seems that this political outspokenness among officials in the innovation sector is a general pattern (interview with former official at the Ministry of Enterprise). This pattern also implies discontentment and frustration since Swedish politics does not seem to function according to the ideas of innovation systems.

From out of these various descriptions of Swedish innovation policy, I have compiled a story of how the politics of innovation has become projectified. First, I trace historical patterns of projectification. Second, modern forms of industrial support through research programs is exemplified. In the third section, I first describe the projectification of innovation policy itself, and then proceed to understand how delegation is a consequence of national failures to collaborate beyond the level of ideas. Fourth, I describe the regional turn within innovation policy and how this amplifies projectification as a consequence. In the final section of this chapter I propose three decidedly political factors behind the projectification of Swedish innovation policy.

The Development of Swedish Innovation Policy

As in many other Western countries, efforts to stimulate industrial development and technological research has been seen as crucial in Sweden during the entire 20th century, regardless of whether these efforts have been labelled technological research policy, industrial policy, or innovation policy. A formative moment was the establishment of the Royal Academy of Engineering Sciences (*Ingenjörsvetenskapsakademin*) in 1919, the first academy of its type in the world (www.caets.org)[1], which has remained a co-financed meeting arena for the state, industry, and leading representatives of the engineering profession (Sundin, 1981). This is an arena of the inter-organisational, diplomatic kind referred to in the introduction. A central issue has been responsibility for advanced technological research, where the boundaries between political and industrial responsibilities often have been unclear. Furthermore, within industry, there has been a tension between the will to cooperate internally (and with the government) in order to enjoy the fruits of co-financed research, and the opposing interest of keeping one's "innovations" secret in order to outflank competitors. There has also been a continuous tension within government between those more business-friendly ministries with a "user-oriented" inclination towards research and those ministries that view academic research as a collective good for the whole of society.

A temporary settlement of these tensions regarding responsibilities saw the construction of a governmental agency, the Technological Research Council, in 1942, with a mission of sponsoring industrially-relevant technological research projects. This decision was formative for the entire area of research funding in

Sweden which ever since has been strongly driven by state agencies under the government. Originally, the Royal Academy of Engineering Sciences was proposed to take this role, but it was decided that the issue was better handled by a more "neutral" state agency. This may be seen as the second formative moment within Swedish innovation policy where the government took the overall responsibility for promoting advanced industrial development with the role of mediating relations between universities, schools of technology, research institutes, and industry, primarily by funding collaborative projects (Weinberger, 1997). Furthermore, it equated technological development with research policy, a fact increasingly lamented by many commentators who want innovation policy to concern every sector of society (Borrás & Edquist, 2013; interview with deputy CE of Vinnova).

From the outset, this agency saw as its mission to sponsor projects with a strong product orientation. Weinberger (1997) has conducted two case studies of projects (from the 1950s and 1960s) where he finds the predominance of a kind of technological enthusiasm in which the "product" (for instance a hand prosthesis called "Sven") served as a boundary object (Star & Griesemer, 1989) between a large number of actors, but where ideas about potential markets and demand were lacking. According to the OECD, such fallacies were common in large-scale technological projects globally in the 1960s (OECD 2016, p.178). The number of actors involved in innovation increased and the leading role of government was challenged by private initiatives such as Wallenberg's development company Incentive (1963). Political interest in innovation issues grew as witnessed in OECDs new policies regarding a state-led industrial development (OECD, 1963). The growing number of actors and the focus upon single products and projects thus brought forward further calls for collaboration (Weinberger, 1997). In 1968, a larger and more inclusive government agency was created, the Council for Technological Development (followed by the Agency for Industrial and Technological Development in 1991 and Sweden's current innovation agency – Vinnova – in 2001). The organisational efforts in the area may thus be seen as representing inter-organisational relations at a particular moment in time ("frozen politics").

Support for technological research increased but was still dominated by single projects and products. However, in the late 1970s, the Council for Technological Development developed a more systematic thinking on innovations, following criticism that the central innovation bureaucracy was inflexible and that demand for products could not be planned (Agdur, 1974; interview with former senior analyst at the Council). The Council implemented "framework programs" (SOU, 1977, p. 64) where the focus was not upon developing products but on fostering relations between research and industry where collaboration was financed mainly according to the organisational qualities of fund recipients, the potential of their network. According to Weinberger (1997, pp. 449, 468–469), the framework programs may be seen as "venues", meeting arenas, where the different interested parties were "coerced" to negotiate compromises and form networks. This is probably the most important formative moment regarding the ideational content of innovation policy since focus shifted from the technological development of products in singular projects to the organisation of a *system of inter-organisational relations* between actors. In this system, the very establishment of "the project" forms the central area of governance; a system demanded by governmental actors as a prerequisite for receiving funds. As Weinberger finds in the Swedish case (also claimed by the deputy CE of Vinnova in interview), the evolving practice from the early 1980s of supporting organisational design rather than product development preceded more elaborated ideas of "innovation systems". According to Weinberger, the realisation that innovation is an organisational process replaced the technological determinism of earlier decades, and constituted a more attractive foundation for political interventionism:

> If research and development are social processes, then the future is also a social construction as are the images of the future. The future becomes an issue of negotiation where what matters is to form a common view regarding what may be done and ought to be done when it comes to supporting technological research and development.
>
> *(Weinberger, 1997, p. 440, my translation)*

The ideational content of innovation policy has thus been strengthened; for instance, the newly appointed CE of Vinnova in 2001 saw as his primary mission to promote the "idea" of innovation systems (Eklund, 2007). Since then, the potential conflicts of interests between actors described in the introduction of this section have been neglected in government innovation policy (as in the innovation policy of the EU and the OECD), regardless of the actual terminology (such as "material consortia", "clusters", or "regional innovation systems"). Lagendijk and Varró (2013) point to how the idea of "innovation systems" within the EU serves as an organisational script which has to be performed by regions, firms, and researchers in order to be funded. Potential conflicts are delegated to the collaborating actors themselves. The most important organisational development in the Swedish system thereafter has been the entrance of a new actor, the region, the site where actual innovations are to be performed, as well as a political endorsement of a much broader concept of innovations than just technological research projects. Today, among other things, "service innovation", "social innovations", and "public sector innovations" (see also Chaib, Chapter 4, this volume) are also included in the innovation concept, and implemented through projects. Collaborative projects thus politically *represent* and *legitimate* the inter-organisational character of innovation policy within wider areas than before.

Reactive Politics – Projectification as a Consequence of Industrial Support

The difference between investments in innovations and industrial support is seldom obvious, although these two types of interventions are judged entirely different nowadays. Unsurprisingly, since the dawn of innovation policy, the industry has been interested in government support for expensive investments in research, which may or may not be of use for particular companies. Uncertainties regarding the usability of research thus calls for government responsibility. Furthermore, industrial support for specific companies was not regarded as particularly strange until the formation of the strict European competition regime during the 1980s (Andersson et al., 2017). This regime was on its way in Sweden as well during the 1960s, although briefly paused during the economic crises in the 1970s, simultaneously motivating a more active government policy to compensate for so-called "market failures". In this light, innovation policy, as well as modern regional development policy, are outcomes of a new competition regime, whereas earlier economic policies often actively tried to construct industrial cartels (Lundqvist, 2003; Andersson et al., 2017).

New liberal ideas gained hegemony in the political arena, but this followed a very concrete and growing concern from Right to Left regarding the appropriateness of supporting sectors – such as shipbuilding and textiles – which seemed to be doomed to succumb to global competition. Since Sweden entered the EU in 1995, the only form of industrial support allowed is for R&D and innovation (European Commission, 2014; SFS, 2015, p. 208). This means that projectification becomes a default consequence of remaining forms of industrial support.

> In terms of large investments government funding is limited to research. The reason for this is of course the competition laws. However, it rests on a long-lasting tradition. Sponsoring research is easier to govern and control than for instance monitoring legal requirements for innovative public procurements … which may not adhere to the current competition legislation. So what came out of our industry talks in the form of concrete measures were research programs, the industry programs, channelled through Vinnova.
>
> *(Interview with former official at the Ministry of Enterprise)*

The case referred to by this interviewee is the "industry billion" 2005–2006, a consequence of the first governmental innovation strategy in 2004. The resources were channelled through Vinnova and represents a clear example upon how research and innovation funding becomes politicised in times of structural crises. Late in this process, the old Swedish automotive company, SAAB, faced an acute crisis which was countered by a vehicle industry program developed by the centre-Right government, a part of which was more political funding of innovation channelled through Vinnova. Hence an additional almost one billion Swedish crowns was directed to "innovation projects" in the vehicle industry, mainly to SAAB and VOLVO. Indeed, almost 30 per cent of the overall innovation funding from Vinnova in 2006 was directed to SAAB and VOLVO. Even today, VOLVO is the leading receiver of Vinnova projects on the company side (Vinnova project database). The tendency to counter structural crises through investment in "innovation" research has continued within life sciences in recent years:

> The Government was worried politically over what was happening, maybe especially so regarding the vehicle industry, but also in other industries. To them it was not really an ambition of research progress, it was more that these industries should stay in Sweden, even when they were foreign-owned. … Recently, we have seen the same thing within life science, some programs are like putting in the yeast after the dough. … It's about old-fashioned industrial policy, it is a structural crisis which we do not meet proactively but by reacting in order not for the worst thing to happen, but then the worst thing happens anyway.
>
> *(Senior analyst at Vinnova)*

Thus innovation policy in terms of financial support is clearly an heir of earlier industrial policy. In the critical verdict above it is portrayed as a form of *reactive* politics. Projectification becomes by default *the means* for carrying out such politicised interventions, due to the formal prohibition of industrial support.

National Political Mobilisation and Representation Through Projects

> Innovation policy can't be compared to traditional policy domains. We are here talking about the objective to create coordination, dialogue, mutual views and co-action between different domains.
>
> *(Interview with project manager at the Ministry of Enterprise for the National Innovation Strategy, 2012)*

Since the early 2000s, the "high politics" of Swedish innovation has taken a peculiar form of mobilising different actors to rally themselves around the concept of a national innovation system through campaign meetings, projects, and strategies. Two governmental strategies – Innovative Sweden (2004) and The National Innovation Strategy (Ministry of Enterprise, 2012) – and three successive strategies from the Royal Academy of Engineering Sciences have been produced. This projectified form of mustering support for innovation policy is related to its inter-organisational character, as hinted at in the quotation above. However, the successive projects are also forms of lobbying towards the government (in the case of the Academy's projects) as well as efforts on the part of the Ministry of Enterprise to gain influence within the government over the overall economic policies of Sweden.

The responsible official for the first governmental strategy (in 2004) describes the background of the strategy as an effort to mobilise support for the concept of "innovation systems" in the wake of setting up Vinnova, and strongly inspired by the OECD work on innovation systems (interview). She describes the project as driven by engaged officials in the Ministry of Enterprise:

> We ran some high-level seminars in 2001 and 2002 with the aspiration of producing an innovation policy strategy. We invited the cream of the industry and others, and allowed them to share their views and needs regarding the innovation policy.
>
> *(Interview with former project manager at the Ministry of Enterprise)*

However, the results of the strategy were mainly to be taken care of regionally:

> Many of the measures, which will implement the strategy, are to be taken under the regional growth programs that will be implemented nationally 2004–2007. The programs are implemented in partnerships between public and private actors and should contribute to the implementation of the strategy "Innovative Sweden".
>
> *(Ds, 2004:36, p. 43, my translation)*

On the governmental level, "partnerships" did not function that smoothly. It was intended to be a governmental strategy, but actually, "Innovative Sweden" was only a strategy for the ministries of education and enterprise (the Prime Minister even switched the respective ministers in order to make collaboration between these mutually hostile ministries smoother; something which according to former officials meant that the ministers also "switched brains over a day"). The Ministry of Finance left the project at an early stage; according to the project leader because finding the strategy both too foggy and too sensitive in terms of financial policies (interview with former project leader). With hindsight, the former project leader views the impact of the strategy as primarily visionary.

What happened between the two national innovation strategies was that the Academy of Engineering Sciences took the lead in a kind of lobbying (we wanted to create a "sense of urgency" in the political sphere, according to the project leader) against the mainly tax-cutting centre-Right government (2006–2014). The stated argument was that the government did not take innovation seriously; specifically the project leader pointed to a round table group called the Globalisation Committee, the work of which was not "taken care of" by the government (interview with project leader for "Innovation for growth"):

> When IVA [The Royal Academy of Engineering Sciences] together with practically all relevant agencies and organisations start the project "Innovation for growth", somebody will probably ask if there is still one more

> investigation under way. A gigantic work as the Globalisation Committee, with a voluminous report after several years. The answer is no. Now action counts. … "Innovation for growth" is an action-oriented project. Which will involve politicians, decision-makers, organisational representatives, entrepreneurs, and all the good forces. All who want to help Sweden become a dynamic and innovative nation are welcome!
>
> *(Håkan Gergils/The innovation blog of the Royal Academy of Engineering Sciences, 24 September 2009)*

As stated in the blog post, there were many influential people involved. The chairman was Sweden's leading industrialist, Marcus Wallenberg, and one of the sub groups was led by the CE of VINNOVA who actually then came to lobby her own government.

This project and its two successor projects "Innovative power for Sweden" and "Attractiveness for growth: boundless innovation for increased affluence" were also characterised by mobilisation in the form of seminars and conferences, as the Academy itself states in their first final report "Innovation Plan for Sweden" (IVA, 2011): "The process has been characterised by dialogue and activities. Within the national dialogue we have conducted meetings with parliamentary and youth politicians, politicians and officials in the Government Office, young innovators and representatives for the industry" (p. 3). The project leader for the IVA projects explains:

> These projects summit people from the whole range of the political life of Sweden, organised interests, industry and academics. You bring both your personality and your competence to the table. Moreover, these meetings transcend ideological differences, at least partly, and then you really get the best out of all individuals. It has been fantastic!
>
> *(Interview)*

If the IVA-projects thus mainly were characterised by talk about what others ought to do, they still served as an important agenda-setter for national politics. Not least because the incoming Prime Minister, Stefan Löfven, was involved in them and promised to set up a standing innovation committee with himself as chair if he became elected. However, earlier than that, the centre-Right Minister of Enterprise decided to develop a new governmental strategy for innovation. Once again, it was set up in project form and characterised by inter-organisational dialogues. History more or less repeated itself from the 2004 strategy: the outcome in financial terms were research programs and regional projects, but these were simultaneous with severe restrictions to the government's ability to cooperate internally. Specifically, the ministers of the Ministry of Enterprise and Education, respectively, were party leaders of two of the small coalition parties, while the Moderate Party dominated the Ministry of Finance. In the end, the "governmental strategy" turned out to be

"Annie's strategy" (Annie Lööf was Minister of Enterprise and party leader of the Centre Party):

> During the whole innovation strategy process I worked for this to be a process including many ministries, many ministers, and many policy areas. When the government decided that this should be solely Annie's process, I realised that I do not want to continue doing this, because I do not believe in this. I believe in coordination, it is required in order to get legitimacy, strength, trustworthiness, you need several ministers' involvement. Since the government saw it differently, I felt that I could not stay as a project leader.
>
> *(Project leader for the National Innovation Strategy 2012, Ministry of Enterprise)*

Because of these internal problems, it becomes a necessity to delegate responsibilities for innovation. Even if (activist) bureaucrats drive the national projects, there is also a strong interest among all political parties to *represent* the innovation ideology as such, not least in order to maintain good relations with the industrial interests within IVA. However, specifically when many parties are involved in government with different ministerial responsibilities, coordinated, national action of the form that the innovation ideology seems to demand is impossible. National representatives are able to collaborate on the ideational level – in successive expressions of belief in the innovation system, but not when it comes to actual interventions. The consequence of this is projectification on the regional level as shown below.

Delegating and Responsibilising Other Actors

What is the reason for these successive campaigns whose main output has been the production of rhetoric and internal collaboration problems? The answer would also explain projectification, since the more long-term effects of the government strategies are research and regional development projects.

First, the Swedish government is a negotiation machinery where the importance of reaching consensus stems from the Swedish Constitution stipulating that all government decisions are to be taken collectively.

> This is the classical corporatist challenge. The Industry has been enticed into participation under the premises that this was going to become a co-decided and integrative process ... But the Ministry of Finance feels no obligation to herald the original commitments. The internal affairs of [Swedish] Cabinet Government are based on a logic of inter-departmental negotiation, and this logic takes precedence over all agreements with external partners.
>
> *(Former project leader for the National Innovation Strategy 2012, the Ministry of Enterprise)*

This system makes individual ministers comparatively weak, and mostly incentivised to profile themselves. The result is delegation of innovation policy as well as funding in the form of projects to regions and research actors, since such investments produce the only visible short-term results during the term of office (interview with retired analyst at Vinnova). The internal, collaborative problems within the government are reproduced on the agency level, with many competing national authorities:

> Sweden has a "veneer" system of governance, with a relatively thin, lightly staffed layer of ministries overseeing a thick layer of well-staffed agencies. This means that while ministries can ask agencies to coordinate activities requiring concerted action across agencies, the ministries themselves have little scope to play a significant role in these coordinating activities. These are not new issues. Indeed, some have persisted at least since the time of the Malm Commission (1942).
>
> *(OECD, 2016, p. 179. The Malm Commission resulted in the setting up of the Technological Research Council and is referred to as the formative moment in equating innovation policy with research.)*

Second, the significantly broadened innovation concept raises sensitive issues not only within the government but also between the more traditional industrial branches and newer competitors, specifically in the service sector. The former project leader of the National Innovation Strategy 2012 relates to the concerns of the industry when the Minister of Enterprise and Centre party leader wanted to include the service industry and smaller entrepreneurs in discussions regarding innovation:

> Actually, she had a point because innovation policy had become an issue for big industry and big capital, it was the clique around the Academy of Engineering Sciences really, and they kidnapped it and excluded the whole service sector. I saw it clearly when I developed the governmental strategy for service innovation in 2010, I received a lot of criticism: "we don't need any strategy for service innovation, we need an innovation strategy, are we going to wash each other's shirts and get rich?" Really, the classical argument against the service economy, showing that they did not understand anything, if I speak frankly. Of course, it was incredibly threatening.
>
> *(Former project leader for the National Innovation Strategy, the Ministry of Enterprise)*

Whereas innovation support is still overwhelmingly directed to traditional industrial branches and technological universities, social and service innovations are also funded, making the "innovation system" a quite fragmented area of project support where sensitive issues about how the different branches are related to each other are delegated to regional and local actors.

Third, and a more overall answer to why delegation in the form of projectification is the politically chosen form of innovation policy, are the broader developments within OECD and specifically EU innovation policy, which points to the regions as the centres of growth and innovation (Lagendijk & Varró, 2013). The reasons seem to be the same as at the national, Swedish level: what it is possible to accomplish at a central level are very general, consensual policy declarations and policy instruments, suggesting that lower levels have to take care of more concrete, collaborative problems and produce short-term results with political implications.

However, fourth, these negative and reactive effects are countered by a type of positive responsibilising of other actors. When Vinnova was established in 2001, its CE, Per Eriksson, came from a position as vice chancellor at the regional university college in Blekinge. Eriksson was trying to apply both the cluster and the triple helix concepts emphasising regional collaboration as the centre of innovation.

> Some sort of an innovation system thinking for Blekinge. He brought it back to Vinnova. So, one of our first programs, around 2003, was for stimulating all regions in Sweden to focus on how they should innovate themselves into the future, a program called Vinnväxt ("winning growth"). We made a competition where the regions had to partake, create their triple helix on paper, because there was a concrete connection to Leydesdorff och Etzkowitz. Triple helix is not complicated on paper, three partners contemplating a joint task and trying to mobilise commitment around it. So Vinnväxt was an effort to get the same commitment as Per Eriksson thought that they managed to do in Blekinge, without any program. From a Vinnova perspective, a good form of regional policy is a regional policy where you try to reach some sort of a competitive strength, maybe world class in one area, and innovate themselves out.
>
> *(Interview with deputy CE of Vinnova)*

The main method of supporting innovation became programs such as the one mentioned in the quotation, consisting of applications for funding which strongly resembled research applications and the formerly mentioned material consortia, but with an explicit regional focus. Since 2004, Vinnova has also supported research centres on innovation systems in different universities, which also carry out research targeted at regions. At about the same time, the EU picked up the idea of regional innovation systems and has ever since tried to support this more development-focused conception of regions.

Even if all regions have their own, or at least conceive of themselves as having their own, unique positions, they formulate similar strategies. Apart from having the same consultants, it is the funding systems that forms this similarity. The funding of regional innovation systems in Sweden is almost exclusively of EU and national origin. The role of the structural funds as well as the national programs – often inspired by the structural funds – in shaping isomorphic processes within European innovation policy is surprisingly seldom discussed in the scholarly literature.

> There's a lot of EU subsidies. The structural funds have become all the more important for innovation policy. In the period 2014–2020 innovative purposes will be decisive for who gets funding. This is not to say that the projects will be better. Many projects maybe will be protective, to keep what you have. Or grand visions of becoming the leading biotechnical region in Sweden, or even the world.
>
> *(Senior analyst at Vinnova)*

This dependence on funding automatically means projectification. Indeed, the EU structural funds are referred to as the most consequential driver of projectification in the Swedish public sector (Godenhjelm et al., 2015). This probably goes for the EU at large: "Most EU policies in almost all areas of EU policy-making are implemented, in one way or another, via project funding" (Büttner & Leopold, 2016, p. 62); at least half of the total EU budget is devoted to direct project funding (ibid., p. 49). Through the instrument of co-financing, regional actors are also enrolled financially to the EU agenda. The importance of EU funding shapes a standardisation regarding problems and solutions, but by default also an environment characterised by applying for new projects and implementing and auditing existing and old ones.

The degree of projectification within regional innovation policy goes very far. The effect of this development is a lack of unitary government and, as a consequence, fragmentation (Godenhjelm et al., 2015). The Skåne newspaper *Sydsvenskan* has written about the "innovation galaxy" in Skåne: a regional innovation system consisting of over 100 private, public, and semi-public actors, mainly funded through EU and national funds. This fragmentation is in itself dependent upon the demand on funded actors to comply with the organising principles of project management (see Fred and Mukhtar-Landgren, Chapter 10, this volume). Lavén (2008) has made a case study over time (between 2003 and 2008) of one such satellite in the innovation galaxy: an initiative regarding microwave technology (Microwave Road, MWR, described successively as a network, an innovation system, a cluster, and an association) in Västra Götaland (Lavén, 2008, p. 17). From the beginning, the initiative concerned raising funds for the development of microwave technology products. It consisted of a handful of researchers from two industrial research institutes and the companies Ericsson and SAAB Ericsson Space. What triggered their interest in joining forces, besides their keen interest in microwave technology, was the launching of Vinnova's first regional program, *Vinnväxt*. Their application for funding was turned down, however: "The growth potential is not presented concretely in the application. Strategic idea and vision are undeveloped. The triple helix leadership is weak with regards to politics/society" (from Vinnova Rejection Decision).

As Lavén states (p. 141), this shows how the collaborative project model of innovation has become canonical – if you do not follow the script, funding is impossible. In this case, the "weak triple helix leadership" implied that the researchers had to search for project collaboration with the public sector. The microwave initiative learnt its lesson and assembled a larger group with participation from the public sector, renamed itself a "cluster", and managed to obtain funding from another program with co-financing from Region Västra Götaland. Lavén shows that much of the actual activities concern organisational development rather than technological development, that is, the establishment of a collaborative management structure and the inclusion of public sector actors in order to perform the collaborative script and satisfy the donors.

However, this did not satisfy the driving spirits of the initiative, since their primary interest was to start technological projects in order to develop new microwave products, to go from "words to action" and to doing things "for real" (very common sayings within MWR according to Lavén who observed their meetings) and thus adhere to the practical ideals of the engineering tradition (ibid., p. 145). But since most funding was directed at new organisational initiatives and meetings, the group became absorbed by "incessant attempts at raising funds … first you have to have money, then you can start working" (ibid., pp. 168–169).

Lavén followed two projects regarding "doing things for real": a collaborative venture called "the automotive group" and an internal project called "the ceramics project". The idea of the automotive group was to link telecom and automotive technology in Västra Götaland through microwave technology and to shape a new market opportunity for microwave companies. This endeavour was a complete failure since representatives of the automotive industry (to whom the new products were supposed to be sold) did not even show up at the meetings, which instead were devoted to theoretical discussions about what type of microwave applications could hypothetically be of interest to the automotive industry. Lavén interprets this failure not only as neglect on the part of automotive companies, but as a real problem in merging different organisational cultures and interests in different industries into a collaborative structure. The ceramics project turned out to be successful, however; according to Lavén, "the only technology development project to be undertaken in MWR to date" (ibid., p. 218). Lavén's explanation for this is that ceramics is a technology which those companies involved saw as "neutral ground", it did not contain the sensitive issue of business secrets. Furthermore, ceramic substrates were a form of boundary object, a technology which could move across the borders of the different companies. However, the project was mainly funded by Region Västra Götaland, and when the involved companies were to have financed the collaborative project on ceramics on their own, interest seemed to wane.

What Lavén shows is how the system of government in innovation policy creates a logic of projectification. This logic is not entirely dependent on the EU system of government since the funding programs in this case are funded and managed by national authorities, and are ultimately a political responsibility, but the EU system serves as an important role model. The system *responsibilises* actors to do other things – forming horizontal collaborations – than merely devote themselves to technological products. They also, and as it seems even predominantly, have to organise and perform a system of relations that follows the script of how an innovation policy ought to be organised. This means that the professional experts of technology (in Lavén's case microwave technology) are outflanked by the responsibilising technologies of accountability demanded by the funding system: instead of working with research, they have to sit in meetings, form strategies, and perform cross-sectorial collaboration. Thus projectification is not only a means for reaching other ends; it becomes a *goal in itself*, since it performs what are ultimately the political ideas and relations which are the basis for innovation policy.

Concluding Discussion: Projectification as Political Representation, Reaction, and Responsibilisation

The role of politics is underestimated in studies of projectification. Politicians seldom have a direct role in the sponsoring, launching, and government of individual projects – as for instance Li (Chapter 3), Chaib (Chapter 4), and Löfgren and Allen (Chapter 5) argue in this volume, there is an "invisibilisation" of politics in both the discourses of innovation and projectification. However, as shown in this chapter, innovation policy in Sweden is politicised, and has become increasingly more so during latter decades. Without political decisions (or non-decisions), the formation of particular funding systems, and sometimes very detailed and concrete political instructions for specific funding programs in light of perceived industrial crises, the projectified innovation systems of modern Sweden would not exist. In the following, I will point to three mechanisms through which projectification becomes a consequence of politicisation: projectification represents tensions between different sectors and legitimates innovation policy; projectification is a reaction to perceived industrial crises; projectification responsibilises other actors for political purposes.

First, projectification *represents* tensions between the political system and the industrial sector. Here we find a strong path dependency in Swedish innovation policy. The formative moment for this was the creation of the Technological Research Council in 1942 which became a project funding agency (and a role model for future Swedish research funding in other sectors) for industrially relevant research, a role that has remained with its successors. This stability is a consequence of tensions regarding investments in and responsibilities for innovations. Technological investments represent a political "neutral ground", both for industrial interests with a general scepticism about political interventions, as well as for political interests with an imperative of reaching a consensus (see Björck, 2004, p. 465). These legitimating tendencies have amplified: the market ideology and the competition regime partly disguise the political basis for technological development and, whereas there used to be some political conflicts regarding national development, regional innovation policies proceed with remarkable, and often quasi-scientific consensus. What seems like a system of de-politicised governance is actually a system of governance within government based on the political consensus that technological investments must be made in order for Sweden to remain competitive.

Projectification can thus be seen as the effect of long-term traits in the history of Swedish innovation policy. Innovation policy has been related to research and product development during its entire history. R&D is most commonly organised in projects. Furthermore, the policy area was from the beginning inter-organisational in character, situated as it is in the meeting arena of government, industry, and universities, and thus facing complex and often sensitive issues such as who is to be responsible for large-scale investments and how companies, with an incentive to maximise profits by keeping "innovations" secret, are to collaborate among themselves and with universities. Traditionally, as well as in contemporary innovation policy, co-financed projects are a way to handle such sensitivities by enrolling actors from the different sectors in "triple helix" collaborations.

Second, projectification is a politicised *reaction* to economic crises as well as the recurrent failure to collaborate on the national, governmental level. From the 1970s onwards, successive structural crises within Swedish industry have been countered by political programs with projects as their main organisational form as a way of swiftly responding. Many recipients of funding have been satisfied with the projectified system and the politicians may (and do) actively intervene regarding the content and purpose of different funding programs. Simultaneously, the development from funding products to funding organisational efforts constructs government-dependent networks of actors who become co-opted by projectification. Innovation projects are a means to politicise economic actors (as shown in the microwave case) and to outflank the competition regime.

Projectification in the form of delegating collaboration is also a reaction to political failures to collaborate at the national level. The tensions between different government ministries are old and hard to ease. Furthermore, the constitutional feature of collective government decisions, as well as the modern trait of multi-party minority governments, serve to solidify the tensions on the central level. Instead, in the last two decades, the politics of innovation on the national level has been projectified as well, consisting in campaigns for mobilising the industrial elite and leading academics in expressions of belief in the national innovation system, but with few practical consequences other than new, politically-designed research programs to be channelled through the innovation agency. This does not mean that these mobilising projects are unimportant. Expressions of joint beliefs in the innovation systems and recurrent projects and meetings where actors continuously re-negotiate and re-constitute their relations to each other are important in order to keep the innovation system high up on the national agenda, as well as on the European agenda. The visionary level is a level of expressions of belief producing ideational consensus on a discursive level (the forging role of ideas has in recent years been emphasised by many writers, cf. Peters et al., 2005; Hay, 2011; Daigneault, 2014). This level serves as the diplomatic means for linking a large number of actors from different sectors. However, the consequence of this ideational consensus is the delegation of the responsibility for concrete innovations to other actors.

The comparatively small Government Office in Sweden uses delegation in order to avoid overload, keep a distance, and, through organisational measures, get other actors (agencies or actors outside the governmental sphere or both) to solve or at least handle the problems themselves (Jacobsson et al., 2015). This chapter has shown that innovation policy broadly functions along these lines, but it is not a form of government that ought to be equated with "de-politicisation". To the contrary, actors are co-opted and/or enrolled into the political system by the third factor of projectification emphasised here: *responsibilising actors*. Through projectification, public administration, as well as the other involved actors (in the innovation system typically firms and universities), make themselves visible instruments for strategic purposes and signal in a more transparent manner than for ordinary activities that they actively perform a political agenda according to collaborative scripts such as triple helix and regional innovation systems. In this system, projects and project leaders are "responsibilised" with the carrying out of innovation policies decided at other levels. The organisation of "the project" thus becomes a goal in itself as the collaborative model is established in not only the organisation but also the performance of innovation policy. As witnessed in the case of the microwave cluster, money buys loyalty to the system and enrols important actors into the governmental sector. Political scientists point to delegation as the survival factor of the Swedish system of government. OECD refers to this in very critical terms as a "veneer system of governance" (see above). This means that the division between a visionary level of belief and the short-term form of action will remain the key feature of Swedish innovation unless the central level of government is fundamentally reformed. This, if anything, demonstrates the inherently political nature of projectification.

Note

1 Caets. International Council of Academies of Engineering and Technological Sciences, Inc. Retrieved from www.caets.org.

References

Agdur, B. (1974). Utan möjlighet att arbeta på de större problemen. *Dagens Nyheter*, 26 April 1974.

Andersson, C., Erlandsson, M., & Sundström, G. (2017). *Marknadsstaten: Om vad den svenska staten gör med marknaderna – och marknaderna med staten*. Stockholm: Liber.

Béland, D., & Cox, R. H. (Eds.) (2011). *Ideas and politics in social science research*. Oxford, England: Oxford University Press.

Bell, S., & Hindmoor, A. (2009). *Rethinking governance: The centrality of the state in modern society*. Cambridge, England: Cambridge University Press.

Björck, H. (2004). *Staten, Chalmers och vetenskapen: Forskningspolitisk formering och sociala ingenjörer under Sveriges politiska industrialisering 1890–1945*. Nora, Sweden: Bokförlaget Nya Doxa.

Borrás, S., & Edquist, C. (2013). The choice of innovation policy instruments. *Technological Forecasting & Social Change*, 80(8), 1513–1522.

Burnham, P. (2001). New Labour and the politics of depoliticisation. *The British Journal of Politics & International Relations*, 3(2), 127–149.

Büttner, S., & Leopold, L. M. (2016). A "new spirit" of public policy? The project world of EU funding. *European Journal of Cultural and Political Sociology*, 3(1): 41–71.

Daigneault, P.M. (2014). Reassessing the concept of policy paradigm: Aligning ontology and methodology in policy studies. *Journal of European Public Policy*, 21(3), 453–469.

Ds 2004:36, Innovativa Sverige. Swedish Government Report, Stockholm.

Edquist, C. (2011). Innovation policy design: Identification of systemic problems. Paper no. 2011/06. Lund, Sweden: Lund University.

Eklund, M. (2007). *Adoption of the innovation system concept in Sweden*. Uppsala, Sweden: Uppsala University.

Etzkowitz, H. & Leydesdorff, L. (2000). The dynamics of innovation: From national systems and "Mode 2" to a triple helix of university–industry–government relations. *Research Policy*, 29(2), 109–123.

European Commission (2011). State of the innovation union. Brussels, Belgium: DG for Research and Innovation.

European Commission (2014). European Commission Regulation 651/2014 of 17 June 2014. Brussels, Belgium.

Fenwick, J., Miller, K. J., & McTavish, D. (2012). Co-governance or meta-bureaucracy? Perspectives of local governance "partnership" in England and Scotland. *Policy & Politics*, 40(3), 405–422.

Flanagan, K., Uyarra, E., & Laranja, M. (2011). Reconceptualising the "policy mix" for innovation. *Research Policy*, 4(5): 702–713.

Flinders, M., & Buller, J. (2006). Depoliticisation: Principles, tactics and tools. *British Politics*, 1(3), 293–318.

Godenhjelm, S., Lundin, R. A., & Sjöblom, S. (2015). Projectification in the public sector: The case of the European Union. *International Journal of Managing Projects in Business*, 8(2), 324–348.

Hall, P., & Löfgren, K. (2017). Innovation policy as performativity: The case of Sweden. *International Journal of Public Administration*, 40(4), 305–316.

Hay, C. (2007). *Why we hate politics*. Cambridge, MA: Polity.

Hay, C. (2011). Ideas and the construction of interests. In D. Béland & R. H. Cox (Eds.), *Ideas and politics in social science research* (pp. 65–82). Oxford, England: Oxford University Press.

IVA (The Royal Academy of Engineering Sciences) (2011). *Innovationsplan Sverige – underlag till en svensk innovationsstrategi*. Stockholm.

Jacobsson, B., Pierre, J., & Sundström, G. (2015). *Governing the embedded State: The organizational dimension of governance*. Oxford, England: Oxford University Press.

Lagendijk, A., & Varró, K. (2013). European innovation policies from RIS to smart specialization: A policy assemblage perspective. In E. G. Caravannis & G. M. Korres (Eds.), *The innovation union in Europe: A socio-economic perspective on EU integration* (pp. 99–120). Cheltenham, England: Edward Elgar.

Lavén, F. (2008). *Organizing innovation: How policies are translated into practice*. Gothenburg, Sweden: BAS Publishing.

Lovering, J. (1999). Theory led by policy: The inadequacies of the "New Regionalism" (illustrated from the case of Wales). *International Journal of Urban and Regional Research*, 23(2), 379–395.

Lundqvist, T. (2003). *Konkurrensvisionens framväxt: Konkurrenspolitik, intressen och politisk kultur*. Stockholm: Institutet för framtidsstudier.

Ministry of Enterprise (2012). *Den nationella innovationsstrategin*.

Mouffe, C. (2005). *On the political*. London, England: Routledge.

OECD (1963). *Science, economic growth and government policy*. Paris.

OECD (2010). *OECD innovation strategy: Getting a head start on tomorrow*. Paris.

OECD (2016). *OECD reviews of innovation policy: Sweden 2016*. Paris.

Persson, B. (2008). *The development of a new Swedish innovation policy: A Historical institutional approach*. Lund, Sweden: Lund University.

Peters, B. G., Pierre, J., & King, D. S. (2005). The politics of path dependency: Political conflict in historical institutionalism. *The Journal of Politics*, 67(4), 1275–1300.

Rose, N. (1999). *Powers of freedom: Reframing political thought*. Cambridge, England: Cambridge University Press.

SFS (2015) *Förordning om statligt stöd till forskning och utveckling samt innovation*. Stockholm.

SOU (1977) *STU:s stöd till teknisk forskning och innovation. Betänkande av STU-kommittén (Official Government Report)*. Stockholm.

Star, S. L., & Griesemer, J. R. (1989). Institutional ecology, "translations" and boundary objects: Amateurs and professionals in Berkeley's museum of vertebrate zoology 1907–1939. *Social Studies of Science*, 19(3), 387–420.

Sundin, B. (1981). *Ingenjörsvetenskapens tidevarv*. Stockholm: Almqvist & Wiksell.

Valaskivi, K. (2012). Dimensions of innovationism. In P. Nynäs, M. Lassander, & T. Utriainen (Eds.), *Post-secular society*. London, England: Transaction.

Weinberger, H. (1997). *Nätverksentreprenören: En historia om teknisk forskning och industriellt utvecklingsarbete från den Malmska utredningen till Styrelsen för teknisk utveckling*. Stockholm: Kungliga Tekniska Högskolan.

3

PROBLEMATISING THE PROJECT SYSTEM

Rural Development in Indonesia[1]

Tania Murray Li

UNIVERSITY OF TORONTO

In Indonesia as elsewhere in the global south, the arena of rural development is dominated by the project system. This system provides a relatively consistent way of thinking about, and acting on, rural development problems. It is a system around which different sets of actors converge, for different reasons, without anyone deliberately putting it into place. It defines the plausible space of action, precluding alternatives which seem unworkable, or just off the map. A rough equivalent would be the school system as a mode of education. We could think more broadly about what education is, and what the role of schools is, but most of the time we do not. Instead, we worry over the quality of schools, the curriculum, teacher training, etc. Similarly, the project system shapes the field of rural development. My question is, why?

Following Foucault, to pose a "why" question means to identify an apparatus we have come to take for granted, and problematize it: to stand back from it and make it strange, so we can turn it into an object of critical inquiry (Garland, 2014). Critique here does not mean evaluation (is the project system good or bad, could it be better) but, more fundamentally – why projects at all? (Cicmil & Hodgson, 2006) Is it not odd that the attempt to improve the lives of rural people should be organized in terms of projects: time-bound interventions, with a fixed goal and budget, framed within a technical matrix in which problem "a" plus intervention "b" is expected to produce "c", a beneficial result? How did we get to this?

Scholars who have examined the projectification of public management highlight the problems that projects are supposed to solve: more efficient targeting of funds and quality control (did we get what we paid for?) (Büttner & Leopold, 2016); the release of creativity from stultifying bureaucracy (Chaib, Chapter 4, this volume); accelerated decision making and problem solving (Öjehag-Pettersson,

2017); the management of risk through pilots to test the effects of policies on a limited scale (Ettelt and Mays, Chapter 1, and Bailey, Hodgson, and Checkland, Chapter 7, this volume). Since the list of reasons scholars give for the prevalence of projects in different arena is a long one, I argue that it is useful to view the project system not as a unitary formation cut from whole cloth, but as an assemblage of elements of diverse provenance: a set of rationales, authoritative knowledge, inscription devices, and modes of perception and evaluation that congeal contingently (and provisionally) in forms which are not identical, but have enough family resemblance to merit critical inquiry into how they hold together, and what they do (Li, 2007a).

The project system I examine here is specific to rural development in the global south. I began to examine it in *The Will to Improve* (Li, 2007b), where I used the analytic of governmentality to trace centuries of "improving" intervention from the colonial period to the present, as different parties diagnosed problems with Indonesian society, and came up with prescriptions to fix it. I showed how core political-economic questions concerned with the distribution of the means of rural livelihood (land, jobs, wages) were sidelined, and the problem of rural poverty reposed in technical terms (e.g. as a deficit of training, or credit, or high-yielding seeds). It was the project system that made it possible to imagine reducing rural poverty without addressing the processes through which poverty was systematically produced.

In this chapter I want to historicize my analysis of the project system, exploring why it has become so compelling in Indonesia at the present conjuncture. After a brief theoretical orientation, I proceed to make the project-dominated present strange by comparing it with previous eras in which rural development was addressed as a political question, a matter of contestation and debate. Next, I consider enrolment: why the project system so effectively enrolls different actors, such as government officials, politicians, transnational donors, non-governmental organizations (NGOs), scientists, and villagers, whose interests are quite distinct, and sometimes opposed. Then I draw from my research on a massive community development project devised by the World Bank, to examine more closely how projects work, how they enroll people, and the planned and unplanned outcomes that result. The conclusion summarizes my account of why it is projects, and not policy or politics, that currently dominate in the field of rural development.

Governing Through the Project System

To govern, in the sense elaborated by Foucault, is to direct conduct, optimize processes, and devise interventions to secure the "welfare of the population, the improvement of its condition, the increase of its wealth, longevity, health, etc." (Foucault, 1991, p. 100). In the global south, colonial authorities took responsibility for governing under a dual mandate which involved improving native welfare alongside the pursuit of profit. In contemporary post-colonies in Africa and Asia, governing to enhance the welfare of populations merges with the endeavour glossed with the label "development" (Li, 2007b; Ludden, 1992; Moore, 2000). Defined in these broadly Foucauldian terms, governing involves diverse actors, both inside and outside the state apparatus, national and foreign, who attempt to intervene in relations between "men and things," to orient social, economic, and ecological processes in an "improving" direction (Foucault, 1991, p. 93).

Specific projects of improvement require two key practices. One is diagnosis – the identification of deficiencies that need to be rectified. The second is "rendering technical," my shorthand for representing

> the domain to be governed as an intelligible field with specifiable limits and particular characteristics … defining boundaries, rendering that within them visible, assembling information about that which is included and devising techniques to mobilize the forces and entities thus revealed.
>
> *(Rose, 1999, p. 33)*[2]

Rendering technical simultaneously involves rendering non-political, closing down contestation, struggle, and democratic debate in favour of expert calculation, even though such closure tends to be provisional and incomplete (Li, 2007b, pp. 7–12).

The practices of diagnosis and rendering technical are not separate. As James Ferguson (1994) explained in his landmark study of rural development projects in Lesotho, the bounding and characterization of an "intelligible field" appropriate for a transnational intervention anticipates the kinds of intervention that development experts can supply. The identification of a problem is intimately linked to the availability of a solution, with projects taking pride of place. Problem and solution co-emerge within a governmental assemblage in which certain sorts of diagnoses, prescriptions, and techniques are available to the expert who is properly trained. This is a crucial insight, because it disrupts the assumed sequence in which a problem is identified, then a policy is devised to respond to it, and interventions follow. In the policy-centred sequence, projects are just one form of intervention among others that might be used to meet policy objectives (others might include changes in law, prices, or institutions). But when the anticipated intervention takes the form of a project, the entire sequence may be reversed: first comes the potential project, then the definition of a problem in terms that render it solvable by the project at hand. Put this way it is easy to see why policy is not the guiding principle of rural development interventions.

The most important function of policy in the orbit of projects is legitimation: sustaining a coherent account of project activities and authorizing them, often *post hoc* (Mosse, 2004). Legitimation may be light and late because, as Richard Freeman observes, projects are "secluded enterprises" in which negotiation and decision making can be conducted away from public forums (Freeman, 2009). Seclusion from debate is a core element that renders the project system attractive for diverse sets of actors drawn into it. Seclusion is also a key limitation of projects as a vehicle for improving the welfare of rural populations, because it evades critical scrutiny of a project's premises and prescriptions, and an assessment of whether it could – even if perfectly delivered – actually meet the policy objectives of rural development.

Politics, Historicized

While all governing requires diagnosis and rendering technical, the extent to which these practices are expected to yield project-style interventions, and are secluded from political debate, varies over time and space. Some examples from different periods in Indonesia's history will illustrate. One era of heightened political debate occurred in the late colonial period, when Dutch parliamentarians and colonial officials took different positions on the principles to apply when governing relations between land and population in the Netherland East Indies (Li, 2010). The problem had technical elements, but the protagonists in the debate (all of them Dutch) were quite aware that vastly different visions of the future of the Indies and its population were at stake. The protagonists concurred that the Indies should produce both profits for corporations and welfare for the Native population, but what was the proper balance between these two objectives, and how could they be accomplished?

The colonial-era discussion was focused on law, which officials understood as a key instrument for shaping social and economic processes, and governing conduct. Should there be one land law for everyone, enabling (and obliging) Native farmers to compete in a land market, thereby spurring productivity and rural development? Or should Natives be protected from land markets, their authentic traditions of oriental communalism and spiritual attachment to the land restored (and enforced), leaving the business of profit making to westerners better suited for it? The debate was inconclusive, and – remarkably – no specific projects followed from it. There was no cadastral survey or land titling program, nor was there an effort to map Native communities and their territories. The Indies government granted land concessions to private corporations, but the legal basis of the government's claim to control and dispose of land was not clarified, and it remains disputed today.

Fast forward to the land arena in 2014, and political debate about the proper way to govern relations between land and population is being deflected into a technical project to amalgamate dozens of conflicting maps prepared by different government agencies and by self-defined indigenous communities onto one map.[3] Somehow, proponents seem to imagine, an upgrade in the technical infrastructure of land information will quell the heated political struggle that pits villagers against corporations and their state sponsors, and pits government agencies promoting plantations or mining against agencies with environmental mandates (Peluso, Afiff, & Rachman, 2008). The "one map project" is funded by transnational donors, especially those concerned to promote the climate-change related project to "Reduce Emissions from Deforestation and Degradation" (REDD+). The global politics of the REDD+ project have hardly been debated. Why is it reasonable for nations in the global south to be asked to limit forest clearance so that industrial economies can continue to pollute? A necessary, national debate over how to balance different goals (e.g. corporate profits versus farmer control, local incomes versus global conservation) has not taken place. Instead, technical projects to map forest boundaries and link forests to particular actors who can be made responsible for conserving them have taken centre stage. The money attached to the REDD+ project is substantial: Norway committed a billion dollars to Indonesia in return for demonstrated reductions in emissions from deforestation, and a host of technical sub-projects (mapping, measuring, community preparedness, capacity building, pilots, and demonstrations) are underway.[4]

Another period of intense political debate occurred in Indonesia between the declaration of independence in 1949, and the 1965 massacre of half a million people, many with communist and union affiliations, when the military led by General Suharto (and backed by the CIA) took power. This period is described in Indonesian official history as excessively political, because mobilized groups affiliated with different parties (nationalist, Islamic, and communist) advanced contending visions of how best to secure the welfare of the population. A populist land reform law was passed in 1960, but not implemented. To push the matter forward, farmer groups affiliated with the communist party took "unilateral actions" to occupy land which the law had granted to them, antagonizing landowners who joined with the military in exacting bloody revenge. General Suharto's New Order government made the evacuation of politics from all arenas of public life its explicit goal: from parliament right down to rural villages, democratic debate was foreclosed in favour of a focus on development, conceived as a technical enterprise (Li, 2007b, pp. 51–59). A massive and rather successful project comprising improved infrastructure and miracle rice seeds, backed by subsidized credit channelled through authoritarian village elites, undermined both the need and the capacity for rural mobilization around land reform: the green revolution effectively forestalled the red one (Hart, Turton, & White, 1989).

Historicizing the project system makes it strange, enabling critical scrutiny of the social forces that work to politicize development in one period, and to render it technical and apparently non-political in another. Projects do not always dominate, but when they do, they have remarkable powers of enrolment.

Enrolment in Indonesia's Contemporary Project System

In contemporary Indonesia, technical projects to improve rural livelihoods are scattered and largely ineffective at achieving their stated goals, yet they persist. As in the New Order, projects continue to serve as vehicles for channelling funds to favoured members of the rural elite, and to discipline villagers who are told to wait patiently for state largesse to come their way. Hence villages are awash with small projects sponsored by dozens of different national and transnational agencies that distribute free goats, sewing machines, water systems, and micro-credit schemes. Villagers do not expect these projects to bring about rural development, but they accept the inputs offered because something is better than nothing (Li, 1999; Schiller, 1990). The main effect of these projects is to diminish the role of policy and limit (but not quite eliminate) political debate.

Indonesia has many political parties, but they do not campaign on distinct policy platforms, nor do they advance such platforms once in power (Aspinall & Van Klinken, 2011; Hadiz, 2007). Elections are won by individuals who can mobilize networks and gain financial support from different sectors of society (the military, big business, and regional and religious groups, each with their own factions). Indonesians call this "money politics," and it includes buying votes. Members of parliament expect to be paid for passing legislation and approving budgets. Standing committees are classified as wet or dry, according to their potential to generate illicit income streams (Dick & Mulholland, 2011, p. 80). Managerial level civil servants are paid wages that are only 10–50% of private sector equivalents, and expect to make up the shortfall through allowances, license fees, kickbacks, and various forms of rent (McLeod, 2011, p. 45). Hence positions in the bureaucracy are purchased by the applicants, the price reflecting the estimated return on investment (e.g. the expected revenue from a position as a forest guard, or school principal, or police chief) (Dick & Mulholland, 2011, pp. 72–73; McLeod, 2011, p. 58).

Viewed from a revenue perspective, successful implementation of Indonesia's official policy to Reduce Emissions from Deforestation and Development (REDD +) would turn a very wet ministry (forestry) into a dry one. Many observers and participants enrolled in REDD+ activities are aware that implementation will not happen, because REDD+ policy offers no durable replacement for the disrupted revenue streams of forestry officials and their associates. The main function of the REDD+ policy is to legitimate the flow of REDD+ project funds, which are sufficient to keep bureaucrats on side until the funding ends, when they will again need to search for supplementary income.[5]

Scholars who have studied Indonesia's "neo-patrimonial" system of government stress that it is not unique to Indonesia, nor to the global south. It should not be interpreted in cultural, still less orientalist, terms (Baker & Milne, 2015; Barker & Van Klinken, 2009; Van Klinken & Barker, 2009). Election related spending goes on almost everywhere, as do practices that embed social relations in state functions and vice versa (Mbembe, 2001). It is the role of the project I want to stress. Projects are the flexible element of state budgets that make funds flow. These can be transnational projects that run, perforce, through the Indonesian state-system, or domestic projects funded by national revenue or loans. Rather than waiting passively for projects to come their way, government officials and politicians seeking to establish a revenue stream must define an arena of intervention and make a project of it, hence the coining of a new verb, *di-proyekkan* (to projectify) (Aspinall, 2013; Dick & Mulholland, 2011, p. 72).

After a project is over, no one expects to see a lasting result of the kind anticipated in the technical matrix that served to legitimate it. A successful project is one that generates a flow of revenue, and more projects. In relation to the state apparatus, using project funds to provide honoraria, travel allowances, bonuses, and kickbacks is not an aberrant practice that undermines the operation of the bureaucratic system: currently, it is the system, a "public secret" that everyone knows (McLeod, 2011; Van Klinken & Barker, 2009).[6] The estimated level of "leakage" from state financed projects is 30% per annum (Dick & Mulholland, 2011, p. 60). President Joko Widodo, elected in 2014 on the promise to stamp out corruption in the public sector, won widespread popular support, although Indonesians recognize that the "rogue elements" investigators expose are small tips of vast icebergs that are deeply entrenched, and in which tens of millions of ordinary Indonesians who receive routine though not-quite-legal payments have a direct stake.

Indonesia's NGOs are similarly enrolled in the project system, because donor funds for projects are their main source of revenue to maintain their organizations and pay salaries. Critics use this rather obvious fact to level the accusation that NGOs instrumentalize poverty to generate funds. The purpose of the critique is usually to delegitimize NGOs, especially those that attempt to maintain an activist political agenda alongside their funding-driven project work. Indonesian NGOs are certainly not unique in straddling this awkward project/politics divide (Hulme & Edwards, 1997). Yet like state officials, they cannot maintain themselves, nor have an effect in the world, without the funds and legitimation that projects supply.

Transnational Governing, Historicized

Rural development projects are compelling to Indonesian officials and NGOs, and pragmatically accepted by village beneficiaries as the best they can hope for under the current system. They are also compelling to transnational development agencies that converge on the project system for quite different reasons. Transnational development agencies intervene in the global south in order to enhance the welfare of the population, to conserve biodiversity, to promote democracy, ensure accountability, and bring about sundry other improvements. Seen in this light, they share in the burden of governing, as Foucault defines it. Yet there is core tension in transnational attempts to govern populations situated (overwhelmingly) in the global south: their interventions lack a democratic mandate. What gives transnational agencies the authority to intervene in the affairs of a sovereign nation? For colonial authorities, the absence of a democratic mandate was not a problem: they ruled more or less benevolently, but always absolutely. Their right to rule was not subject to a vote (Mbembe, 2001). Today's transnational governors and development agencies are on much thinner ground. They must operate with, through, or around national regimes with their own sets of practices, which are sometimes corrupt and often authoritarian. They must foreground expertise, for if not for superior knowledge or technology, why are transnational agencies intervening at all? Tactical diplomacy (not causing offence to the national "host" or "partner") and the emphasis on technique combine to make many arena crucial to the well-being of rural populations – access to land, fair wages, the right to organize, for example – off limits for transnational development intervention.

Transnational agencies cannot engage in political debate or support social groups (e.g. workers, farmers) involved in political struggle; nor can they dictate policy, although they may attempt to engage in "policy dialogue" to persuade recalcitrant governments to do the right thing. Hence they divide development problems into project-sized pieces, and hope that the big prize will follow: scaling up, improved policies, and a transformation of delinquent social, political, and economic relations. Intervening on society at the scale of the project is also conducive to showing the results necessary to sustain the flow of funds (Mosse, 2004, 2005). Tellingly, donor agencies seldom demand a quantified result that would relate directly to the policy goal: rural poverty reduced by *x* percent. Instead, they require project proposals to use a standard, technical matrix such as the "logical framework analysis" to justify how a given set of inputs is plausibly related to the expected results.[7]

Host governments are less threatened by delimited, time-bound, technical projects, and officials positively embrace them not only for the financial benefits that flow from them, but for professional reasons as well. Collaborating with foreign experts to render rural development problems technical and devise projects to solve them affirms professional credentials, and separates development officials from the deficient rural subjects whose conduct needs to be improved (Pigg, 1992). This is one important way in which the project system is installed and naturalized. The process of planning and implementing projects both expresses and creates a divide between experts and targets of expertise. It shapes social hierarchies in ways that are deep and enduring, even though entrenching hierarchy is not part of the plan.

Although it now seems quite natural, it is only recently that the project system has become entrenched as the modus operandi of transnational development agencies. Henry Bernstein (2006) makes the compelling argument that transnational development practice mutated between the period of national development planning (1950–1980) and the present age of neoliberalism in which market processes are supposed to dominate. In the era of development planning, he argues, transnational development experts contributed to political debate about how best to improve the welfare of populations. They compared the pros and cons of the various development paths that were being attempted in different corners of the global south: socialist paths, capitalist paths, nationalist paths based on import substitution, and so on. They drew on their studies to provide and defend policy advice to national governments in the global south that were actively engaged in their own processes of development planning, and sometimes also in political debate (Bernstein, 2006, p. 53).

Since the 1980s, neoliberal orthodoxy suggests that governments should not try to plan or manage national development, but trust in markets to deliver growth and welfare for all. Yet ironically, as Bernstein argues, it is in the era of neoliberalism that transnational development agencies and some national governments are, in fact, doing more. To paraphrase Bernstein (2006), they are doing more and more about less and less (pp. 54–56). Since there appears to be no alternative to capitalist modes of growth as the engine of economic development and poverty reduction, there is no more need for big-picture, policy debate. It turns out, however, that there is still a lot of work to do, managing a host of new issues of concern: environmental protection, gender equity, good governance, public participation, human rights, and care of vulnerable populations, to name just a few. Each of these concerns opens up new arena for technical interventions of a piece-meal, project kind.

In Indonesia, the proliferation of issues of concern from the mid-1980s onward made it possible to bring the transnational development apparatus into alignment – awkwardly, contingently – with national bureaucrats and politicians, with NGOs, and with rural villagers seeking to improve their situation. Their interests and practices converged around the project system. In the next section, I draw on my Indonesian research to explore how this convergence worked out in practice. I also highlight the unsettled remainder that continues to trouble the technical matrix, keeping open the possibility that political contestation around the processes producing rural poverty may still erupt.

Transforming Society from Below

The intervention I will examine here is a massive, US$1.2 billion project that was designed by the social development team at the World Bank in Jakarta around 1996, expanded exponentially, and came to an end in 2016 when it was merged into the government's rural development system under a new Village Law. The World Bank project's goals were good governance, peoples' empowerment, and poverty reduction. The project designers took these goals as self-evident, and did not attempt to stimulate political debate about the need for social or bureaucratic reform, or the priority that should be accorded them. Several transnational development agencies had undertaken "good governance" projects since the fall of Suharto, with meagre results. An attempt by the Bank team to engage officials in a dialogue about policy reform in this field would have alienated the "host" government upon which the World Bank, like all other transnational agencies, depends for its license to operate in the territory of a sovereign nation. Besides, policy dialogue is difficult to "projectify", and it does not move money on a significant scale – a matter of concern for Bank loan officers as well as Indonesian "hosts". Instead, the Bank's social development team planned a "community driven development" project with extremely ambitious goals: it would transform the conduct of tens of millions of rural villagers, and empower them to transform the conduct of government officials through exerting pressure from below (Guggenheim, 2004; Li, 2007b).

In the eyes of its Bank designers, Community Driven Development was an intensely political empowerment project that masqueraded in mundane, technical garb in order to fly under the radar of members of the oligarchy who benefited from the status quo. The Bank team crafted its project interventions with the deliberate intention of disrupting the unaccountable, inefficient, neo-patrimonial regime that had become entrenched under Suharto's New Order rule. Spurred by enthusiasm for the popular capacities embedded in social capital, it planned to enhance that capital and direct it, freeing Indonesian villagers to pursue development on their own terms. To understand how social capital worked, the Bank team sponsored detailed ethnographic studies of Indonesian village life. The team's commitment to careful research set their approach apart from the clumsy, top down development projects for which the Bank is often criticized. But the Bank team's ethnographies were of a particular kind. To pave the way for Bank involvement, they had to yield a diagnosis/prescription couplet in which a Bank-funded project could plausibly play a role. Indeed, the Bank team had already begun to plan its project while the studies were being undertaken, so diagnosis and prescription proceeded in tandem. The problem the Bank-sponsored ethnographies identified was the poor quality of village level infrastructure planning. The studies confirmed that corruption, lack of transparency, and lack of participation had resulted in a chronic misconnect between the infrastructure villagers wanted, and the infrastructure the top down government machinery gave them. Hence the technical focus for the Bank project was to reform the process of village level infrastructure planning.

The project had two levels of explicit operation. One was the multi-billion dollar project, Community Driven Development, which aimed to empower villagers and transform Indonesian society by training tens of thousands of villagers to design and deliver village infrastructure projects. At this level, building infrastructure was not the purpose of the project, but the vehicle through which villagers and, eventually, government officials would be schooled in the forms of participation, accountability and pro-poor sensitivity the Bank experts had devised for them. The second level was the funding of village infrastructure and other small scale projects planned by villagers. The content of the village level projects hardly distinguished them from scores of similar rural development projects run by different agencies, but they had a twist: villagers would drive the planning process (hence "community driven") and government officials would be excluded from any share in the project funds that normally flow towards them – funds they should not have.

The Bank's project design team argued that deficiencies in village planning and entrenched corruption were not cultural attributes of the Indonesian people, but the result of delinquent habits formed in the Suharto era. To transform these habits, strict rules were needed to govern village-level project planning and manage the disbursement of funds. The resulting rule book was a thick one, in which every element had an educative purpose. The team's idea was that villagers who were initially obliged to follow rules as a condition of accessing project funds would learn to value the new practices, and then adopt them as their own. For example, villagers had to engage in a competitive process to access the funds, with the idea that the best "pro-poor" projects would win. Villagers who failed in one round would think harder and more creatively about how they could address poverty in the next round. When a village project had been approved, the budget had to be posted on the wall of the village meeting hall so everyone could see how much money had been allocated and check on implementation.

The Bank team commissioned studies to examine the culture of corruption, and devised techniques to change villagers' views on which kinds of conduct they should accept as normal, and which they should reject. Inspired by institutional economics, the team attempted to understand the existing incentive structure and change it: they would increase the risk of getting caught for corrupt behaviour and decrease the potential rewards to the point where corrupt behaviour would no longer be rational. Concretely, project staff who were found guilty of corruption were fired, and village committees that misappropriated project funds were barred from further funding, together with the entire sub-district of which they were a part. Entire provinces were coded red or green according to the risk of corruption based on project performance to date. It was a system of carrots and sticks with clear "rules of the game" in which right conduct was rewarded, and misconduct punished (Friedman, 2014, pp. 9–11). The level of detail at which the Bank team studied and dissected village life, and devised techniques to intervene in the problematic processes thus revealed was quite extraordinary. It was through attention to minutiae that the team proposed to empower villagers to demand better projects from their own government.

After my description of the Bank project went to press (Li, 2007b, chapter 7), the project expanded exponentially and an increasing share of the budget was met from Indonesian government and loan funds. Some other donors also contributed. Yet the original project structure hardly changed. In 1998, the Bank project had been approved by top officials in the planning ministry and it was supported by a succession of presidents, but its underlying premises were not subject to a parliamentary debate. There was no discussion about whether improving villagers' capacity to plan local infrastructure projects was the most urgent task of the day, and worth the hefty cost to the national treasury. Nor was there a debate about the project's unusual delivery mechanism: a complete bypass of the government rural development planning system. The Bank team insisted from the outset that government officials could not be trusted to deliver the project, and its Indonesian partners at the top levels of government agreed to have the project administered separately from, but parallel to, the government system. This meant hiring private sector management firms and thousands of project facilitators, 11,000 of them by 2009 (Friedman, 2014, p. 8). Officials from the department of Home Affairs had oversight and coordination roles, but no license to "meddle" in project activities (Friedman, 2014, p. 12; Guggenheim, Wiranto, Prasta, & Wong, 2004, p. 2). The by-pass model, which was integral to the project's transformation agenda, was one of several crucial limitations.

Project Limits

Beginning in 2011, the government and the Bank sought ways to integrate the project's massive parallel bureaucracy into the standard rural development project planning system, but the structural impasse to integration was severe: government officials had little incentive to work on a project that made a virtue of deliberately excluding them from their customary project-derived revenue streams. Since plenty of funds for micro-projects flow into Indonesian villages from multiple ministries, village-level officials had no particular incentive to become involved in the Bank-designed process, with its lengthy participatory process and onerous rules. Villagers reached the same conclusion: they were willing to abide by the Bank rules to access the project funds, but they did not alter their conduct in the way the Bank's social development team had anticipated – by demanding the same standards of participation, transparency, or accountability from regular projects, or from the officials who deliver them. A Bank-sponsored evaluation attributed the problem to elite dominance in village affairs and lack of commitment by government officials (Friedman, 2014, p. 17). Since these were precisely the problems the project was designed to solve, it seems the ambition to empower villagers to transform Indonesian society was not achieved.[8]

In 2011, Indonesian critics of the World Bank project were raising another problem (Gapri & Tifa, 2011). The original World Bank Community Driven Development project was focused on empowerment, but it drew further post hoc legitimacy from its contribution to poverty reduction, mainly in the form of days of paid work on village infrastructure projects. At a cabinet meeting in 2005 at which then President Yudhoyono was presented with summaries of different poverty alleviation programs currently operating in Indonesia, ranked by their effectiveness, the Bank's Community Driven Development project came out on top. The result was a decision by the President to make a greatly expanded, successor project Program Nasional Pemberdayaan Mandiri (PNPM) the mainstay of Indonesia's poverty reduction program, which was being stepped up to meet the UN's global Millennium Development Goals. The number of villages reached by PNPM expanded from 33,000 in 2007 to around 61,000 in 2011. The village infrastructure projects carried out in that period comprised upgrades or new construction of 69,000 kilometres of roads, 6,500 irrigation systems, 30,000 schools, and 11,000 health facilities, at a cost of US$4.4 billion, including facilitator wages (Friedman, 2014, p. 14). But it was unclear whether or how PNPM, which retained the Community Driven Development project's intensive focus on improved processes for village level infrastructure planning, made a dent in poverty (McCarthy et al., 2017).

Despite the project's emphasis on transparency, and the demand that villagers meticulously account for every rupiah they spent, neither the Bank's project designers nor the Indonesian parliament set any specific poverty-reduction goal. The director of poverty reduction at the state planning agency Bappenas admitted that he could not measure the project's contribution to poverty reduction, although he was confident the project was playing a role (Friedman, 2014, p. 15). An evaluation based on comparison with "non treatment" villages concluded that poor households served by the project had increased their consumption expenditure by 9% more than control households, which amounted to US$4 per month. But the evaluation did not demonstrate a causal connection nor the durability of this result beyond the three-year project span (Friedman, 2014, p. 16; Voss, 2012, p. 16). Something is better than nothing, as villagers would confirm, but for a billion dollar poverty reduction project this was a meagre result.

Marginal performance on poverty reduction could hardly be otherwise: since the project did not identify the processes producing rural poverty, it had no realistic means to address them (Gapri & Tifa, 2011; Li, 2007b). Project managers attributed the limited gains to the exclusion of marginalized social groups such as street children, widows, and sex-workers from project benefits, and devised a sub-project called "Caring for the Invisible" to provide micro-credit and training schemes for these groups (Friedman, 2014, p. 22). In keeping with the trend among donor agencies to do "more and more about less and less," assiduous attention to the needs of specific marginal groups left the causes of poverty among tens of millions of rural Indonesians (no land, few jobs, low wages) out of the project's diagnosis–prescription chain.

The end of this remarkable project came in 2016, with another surprising twist. A new president with a populist orientation rushed through a new Village Law (2014) that absorbs and expands on one part of the World Bank's project system, while transforming it in crucial ways. The Law gives large, standard, annual block grants to every village to spend on village infrastructure and other projects of their choosing (up to ten times the amount villages previously received). But the Law and its attendant regulations lack the provisions for competition, participation, transparency, and accountability that were central to the Bank's educative version of block funding. There is no more system of carrots and sticks to direct conduct, prevent elite capture, and ensure the poor get a share. All villages will get the same grant, with little or no scrutiny of how they use it. The Bank's supra-project – the one that monitored, evaluated, tutored, and piloted – has gone.[9] So too has the Bank's parallel project system – the "state of exception" (Bailey et al., Chapter 7, this volume) that, posing as a pilot, bypassed government officials and left them out of their accustomed revenue streams. The Village Law states repeatedly that village development is to be conducted in a spirit of collective harmony and mutual assistance – and leaves it there (Berenschot & Vel, 2017; White, 2017; Zakaria & Vel, 2017). The Law is a travesty of the project system as a regime for the tight management of funds around technically-defined objectives. It is, however, a rather full realization of a project system Indonesian style, one that meets the objective of securing clients, votes, and the networks of collusion that are the modus operandi for the actually-existing state.

To the regret of Indonesia's politically oriented NGOs (Gapri & Tifa, 2011), Indonesia has not translated increased space for democratic debate post-Suharto into serious discussion about rising poverty and inequality, the processes that produce these trends, or the kinds of policies that would be needed to change them. In the period 1990–2011, Indonesia had the second biggest increase in income inequality of any Asian country (after China), with steeper growth after the end of the dictatorship in 1998 (ADB, 2012, p. 47); it had the second lowest per capita spending on health in all of Asia (just ahead of Myanmar), and its social protection expenditure as a percent of GDP was also very low, far behind India and China (ADB, 2012, pp. 77, 79). Although money spent on Indonesia's social programs is growing, in 2017 it was still less than half that of other lower middle-income countries as a percentage of GDP, and the depth and reach of the programs continues to be limited (World Bank, 2017, p. 21). Social programs have proven to be effective means of reducing rural poverty in countries such as Brazil and Mexico (Ferguson, 2015). In Indonesia, in contrast, social programs come second to the project system, which – despite the severe limits on what it can accomplish – continues to enrol a range of different actors in assemblages that morph and realign.

Conclusion

Rural development in Indonesia is dominated by the project system. For quite different reasons, Indonesian villagers, government officials, NGOs, and transnational development agencies have converged on the project – a time-limited, funded, technically-defined and limited intervention – as the solution to rural development problems. For government officials and the staff of NGOs, projects provide flows of funds, and confirm their professional standing and expertise. For transnational development agencies, projects enable interventions into the affairs of sovereign nations to be framed in technical terms, avoid diplomatic upset, and evade political questions they cannot resolve. For villagers, projects bring concrete benefits – a village road, a sack of free fertilizer – although they do not reverse processes of impoverishment or redistribute the key resources upon which rural livelihoods are based. Particular projects sometimes collapse under the weight of their contradictions, but mostly they just reach the end of their limited life, and discretely fizzle out.

Although projects have proliferated and the project system has become entrenched in Indonesia as the principle way of thinking about and conducting rural development, my brief historical review confirmed that this was not always the case: there were periods when political struggle and debate over the proper way to organize rural economic and social relations took centre stage. For transnational development agencies too, the current dominance of the project system must be historicized. It is the age of neoliberalism that has brought us to the curious position identified by Henry Bernstein in which transnational development interventions have become more and more about less and less. Contemporary development experts, driven by demands for accountability in spending development funds, devise ever more restricted, technical interventions like giving children vitamins or de-worming pills, and measure the outcome in terms of indicators like school attendance.[10] They do not engage in debate over different possible futures, since the market can be counted on to direct human affairs efficiently and there is no alternative to it, or so we are told.

The Bank's Community Driven Development project was hugely ambitious: it aimed to transform delinquent social and political relations and replace them with improved, more democratic and accountable ones. But the technical matrix guiding the project overestimated the extent to which involvement in new planning processes could reform conduct in an enduring way. Poverty reduction was introduced by the Bank project designers as a light and late *post hoc* legitimation, but was taken up by Indonesia's President as the project's main purpose, increasing the gap between what was promised, and what could actually be achieved through the project mechanism. Under the Village Law, the funds that flow to villages to devise and implement their own projects have increased enormously, and – for better or worse – villagers and government officials have been freed from the constraints of the Bank's version of improvement. In Indonesia's villages today it is projects, projects everywhere, as there is money to spend, and (a version of) the project system is ever more fully entrenched.

As Ferguson (1994) pointed out, projects that fail to do one thing may nevertheless succeed at doing something else. Their form may be generic, but their outcomes depend upon the constellation of powers shaping the historical conjuncture into which they are inserted. In the Lesotho livestock project Ferguson examined, the unplanned outcome was an expansion of the state apparatus, an "infestation of petty bureaucrats wielding petty powers" (Ferguson, 1994, p. 273). In contemporary rural Thailand, projects serve to consolidate communities and productively engage government officials in village networks and political schemes (Walker, 2012). In northern India, democratic politics disrupt the orderly pursuit of development in project mode (Witsoe, 2013). In the Indonesian case I described, a World Bank-designed project was expected to do a lot of work – to transform society from the bottom up. It failed to do this, but it succeeded in generating more projects, and also in generating dissent and debate among critics who prised open political questions the project's technical matrix sought to contain.

Project outcomes present rich fields for empirical analysis that expand far beyond the parameters usually considered in an evaluation report, or social impact assessment (Vanclay & Esteves, 2012). In Indonesia and perhaps elsewhere, projects are more significant than policy in shaping how lives are lived. They shape and align the conduct of diverse actors and intervene in social and economic processes. Some of their effects are planned, but the most significant and enduring one is so obvious we hardly notice it: directing us to think about rural development in terms of projects, when we could think about it quite differently.

Notes

1 This chapter is derived from a paper previously published in 2016 in the journal *Critical Policy Studies, 10*(1), pp. 79–94, by Tania Murray Li "Governing rural Indonesia: Convergence on the project system" © Institute of Local Government Studies, University of Birmingham, reprinted by permission of Taylor & Francis Ltd, www.tandfonline.com on behalf of Institute of Local Government Studies, University of Birmingham.
2 I adapt the term "rendering technical" from Rose, who glosses it as making something – his example is bonds of solidarity – "amenable to technique"(Rose, 1999:79). On problematization, see (Dean, 1999; Rose, 1999). See also Timothy Mitchell's discussion of enframing as a practice that produces an apparently exterior object world susceptible to management (Mitchell, 1988, 2002).
3 www.downtoearth-indonesia.org/story/indonesia-s-one-map-policy
4 (Angelsen, 2010, 2009; Indonesian REDD+ Task Force, 2012); www.downtoearth-indonesia.org/story/redd-indonesia-update
5 See (Indonesian REDD+ Task Force, 2012); www.forestcarbonportal.com/content/rimba-raya-debacle-casts-pall-over-indonesian-redd
6 Graft, skimming and side-line enterprises were also pervasive among Dutch officials serving the Netherlands East Indies Company in colonial times. The Company devised procedures to limit these practices, but did not attempt to stamp them out, as without supplements Company pay was too low to attract competent staff (Adams, 1996).
7 www.gdrc.org/ngo/logical-fa.pdf
8 Early evaluations of the empowerment benefits were more positive. In 2002 Bank officers and some Indonesian government officials touted the project as a model of effectiveness and best practice that should be replicated in other countries (Edstrom, 2002; Friedman, 2014, p. 15; Guggenheim et al., 2004, p. 4).
9 Bank project staff were given the task of managing the hasty transition from their project system to the one prescribed under the Village Law. They prepared a document outlining the significant risks and challenges of the path the government had taken, while continuing to proffer recommendations on how to reinstate project-style management over what is now supposed to be a fully integrated part of "normal" government functioning (TN2PK, 2015).
10 http://aidwatchers.com/2009/07/development-experiments-ethical-feasible-useful/; http://blogs.worldbank.org/africacan/can-randomized-control-trials-reduce-poverty

References

Adams, J. (1996). Principals and agents, colonialists and company men: The decay of colonial control in the Dutch East Indies. *American Sociological Review*, 61(1), 12–28.

ADB (2012). *Asian development outlook 2012: Confronting rising inequality in Asia*. Manila, Philippines: Asian Development Bank.

Angelsen, A. (Ed.) (2009). *Realising Redd+: National strategies and policy options*. Bogor, Indonesia: CIFOR.

Angelsen, A. (2010). The 3 Redd 'I's. *Journal of Forest Economics*, 16(4).

Aspinall, E. (2013). A nation in fragments. *Critical Asian Studies*, 45(1), 27–54.

Aspinall, E., & van Klinken, G. (Eds.) (2011). *The state and illegality in Indonesia*. Leiden, Netherlands: KITLV.

Baker, J., & Milne, S. (2015). Dirty money states: Illicit economies and the state in Southeast Asia. *Critical Asian Studies*, 47(2), 151–176. doi:10.1080/14672715.2015.1041273

Barker, J., & Van Klinken, G. (2009). Reflections on the state in Indonesia. In G. Van Klinken & J. Barker (Eds.), *State of authority: The state in society in Indonesia* (pp. 17–46). Ithaca, NY: Cornell Southeast Asia Program Publications.

Berenschot, W., & Vel, J. (2017). New law, new villages? *Inside Indonesia*, 128 (April–June).

Bernstein, H. (2006). Studying development/development studies. *African Studies*, 65(1), 45–62.

Büttner, S. M., & Leopold, L. M. (2016). A "new spirit" of public policy? The project world of EU funding. *European Journal of Cultural and Political Sociology*, 3(1), 41–71. doi:10.1080/23254823.2016.1183503

Cicmil, S., & Hodgson, D. (2006). Making projects critical: Introduction. In D. Hodgson & S. Cicmil (Eds.), *Making projects critical* (pp. 1–25). London, England: Palgrave.

Dean, M. (1999). *Governmentality: Power and rule in modern society*. London, England: Sage.

Dick, H., & Mulholland, J. (2011). The state as marketplace: Slush funds and intra-elite rivalry. In E. Aspinall & G. Van Klinken (Eds.), *The state and illegality in Indonesia* (pp. 65–88). Leiden, Netherlands: KITLV Press.

Edstrom, J. (2002). Indonesia's Kecamatan developmentproject. Is it replicable? Design considerations in community driven development. World Bank Social Development Paper No. 39. Washington, DC: World Bank.

Ferguson, J. (1994). *The anti-politics machine: "Development," depoliticization, and bureaucratic power in Lesotho*. Minneapolis, MN: University of Minnesota Press.

Ferguson, J. (2015). *Give a man a fish*. Durham, NC: Duke University Press.

Foucault, M. (1991). Governmentality. In G. Burchell, C. Gordon, & P. Miller (Eds.), *The Foucault effect: Studies in governmentality* (pp. 87–104). Chicago, IL: University of Chicago Press.

Freeman, R. (2009). Articulation, assemblage, alignment: The project in/of EU governance. Unpublished paper. Retrieved www.richardfreeman.info/articulation-assemblage-alignment-the-project-inof-eu-governance-2/, accessed 12 December 2018.

Friedman, J. (2014). *Expanding and diversifying Indonesia's program for community empowerment 2007–2012*. Washington, DC: World Bank.

Gapri & Tifa (2011). *Laporan audit sosial program nasional pemberdayaan masyarakat mandiri kasus: PNPM perkotaan dan perdesaan*. Jakarta, Indonesia: Gerakan Anti Pemiskinan Rakyat Indonesia (GAPRI) and Yayasan TIFA.

Garland, D. (2014). What is a "history of the present"? On Foucault's genealogies and their critical preconditions. *Punishment & Society*, 16(4), 365–384.

Guggenheim, S. (2004). *Crises and contradictions: Understanding the origins of a community development project in Indonesia*. Jakarta, Indonesia: World Bank.

Guggenheim, S., Wiranto, T., Prasta, Y., & Wong, S. (2004). *Indonesia's Kecamatan development program: A large-scale use of community driven development to reduce poverty*. Jakarta, Indonesia: World Bank.

Hadiz, V. R. (2007). The localization of power in Southeast Asia. *Democratization*, 14(5), 873–892.

Hart, G., Turton, A., & White, B. (Eds.) (1989). *Agrarian transformations: Local processes and the state in Southeast Asia*. Berkeley, CA: University of California Press.

Hulme, D., & Edwards, M. (1997). NGOs, states and donors: An overview. In D. Hulme & M. Edwards (Eds.), *NGOs, states and donors: Too close for comfort?* (pp. 3–22). New York, NY: St. Martin's Press/ Save the Children.

Indonesian REDD+ Task Force (2012). *REDD+ national strategy*. Jakarta, Indonesia: Indonesian REDD+ Task Force.

Li, T. M. (1999). Compromising power: Development, culture and rule in Indonesia. *Cultural Anthropology*, 14(3), 1–28.

Li, T. M. (2007a). Practices of assemblage and community forest management. *Economy and Society*, 36(2), 264–294.

Li, T. M. (2007b). *The will to improve: Governmentality, development, and the practice of politics*. Durham, NC: Duke University Press.

Li, T. M. (2010). Indigeneity, capitalism, and the management of dispossession. *Current Anthropology*, 51(3), 385–414.

Ludden, D. (1992). India's development regime. In N. B. Dirks (Ed.), *Colonialism and Culture* (pp. 247–288). Ann Arbor, MI: University of Michigan Press.

Mbembe, A. (2001). *On the postcolony*. Berkeley, CA: University of California Press.

McCarthy, J. F., Steenbergen, D. J., Warren, C., Acciaioli, G., Baker, G., Lucas, A., & Rambe, V. (2017). Community driven development and structural disadvantage: Interrogating the social turn in development programming in Indonesia. *The Journal of Development Studies*, 53(12), 1988–2004. doi:10.1080/00220388.2016.1262024

McLeod, R. H. (2011). Institutionalized public sector corruption: A legacy of the Suharto franchise. In E. Aspinall & G. Van Klinken (Eds.), *The state and illegality in Indonesia* (pp. 45–64). Leiden, Netherlands: KITLV Press.

Mitchell, T. (1988). *Colonizing Egypt*. Berkeley, CA: University of California Press.

Mitchell, T. (2002). *Rule of experts: Egypt, technopolitics, modernity*. Berkeley, CA: University of California Press.

Moore, D. S. (2000). The crucible of cultural politics: Reworking "development" in Zimbabwe's Eastern Highlands. *American Ethnologist*, 26(3), 654–689.

Mosse, D. (2004). Is good policy unimplementable? Reflections on the ethnography of aid policy and practice. *Development and Change*, 35(4), 639–671.

Mosse, D. (2005). *Cultivating development: An ethnography of aid policy and practice*. London, England: Pluto Press.

Öjehag-Pettersson, A. (2017). Working for change: Projectified politics and gender equality. *NORA – Nordic Journal of Feminist and Gender Research*, 25(3), 163–178. doi:10.1080/08038740.2017.1370011

Peluso, N. L., Afiff, S., & Rachman, N. F. (2008). Claiming the grounds for reform: Agrarian and environmental movements in Indonesia. *Journal of Agrarian Change*, 8(2), 377–408.

Pigg, S. L. (1992). Inventing social categories through place: Social representations and development in Nepal. *Comparative Studies in Society and History*, 34(3), 491–513.

Rose, N. (1999). *Powers of freedom: Reframing political thought*. Cambridge, England: Cambridge University Press.

Schiller, J. (1990). State formation and rural transformation: Adapting to the "new order" in Jepara. In A. Budiman (Ed.), *State and civil society in Indonesia* (pp. 395–420). Victoria, Australia: Monash University.

TN2PK (2015). *Integrating community-driven development principles into policy: From PNPM Mandiri to the Village Law*. Jakarta, Indonesia: National Team for the Acceleration of Poverty Reduction, Secretariat of the Vice President, Republic of Indonesia.

Van Klinken, G., & Barker, J. (2009). Introduction: The state in society in Indonesia. In G. Van Klinken & J. Barker (Eds.), *State of authority: The state in society in Indonesia* (pp. 1–16). Ithaca, NY: Cornell Southeast Asia Program Publications.

Vanclay, F., & Esteves, A. M. (Eds.). (2012). *New directions in social impact assessment: Conceptual and methodological assumptions*. Cheltenham, England: Edward Elgar.

Voss, J. (2012). *PNPM rural impact evaluation*. Retrieved from http://psflibrary.org/catalog/repository/PNPM%20Rural%20Impact%20Evaluation%20April%202012_English_20130627.pdf, accessed 12 December 2018.

Walker, A. (2012). *Thailand's political peasants: Power in the modern rural economy*. Wisconsin: University of Wisconsin Press.

White, B. (2017). The myth of the harmonious village. *Inside Indonesia*, 128 (April–June).

Witsoe, J. (2013). *Democracy against development*. Chicago, IL: Chicago University Press.

World Bank (2017). *Towards a comprehensive, integrated, and effective social assistance system in Indonesia*. Jakarta, Indonesia: World Bank.

Zakaria, Y., & Vel, J. (2017). New law, old bureaucracy. *Inside Indonesia*, 128 (April–June).

4

PUBLIC SECTOR INNOVATION PROJECTS

Beyond Bureaucracy and Market?

Josef Chaib

MALMÖ UNIVERSITY

Across the public sector, organisations are increasingly carrying out their services in the form of temporary projects. Projects allow different actors and stakeholders to collaborate around specific challenges or target groups; outside the everyday silos and with external funding, new ideas can be developed and implemented on a limited scale (e.g. Bailey et al., 2017; Godenhjelm et al., 2015). Although research has widely acknowledged the proliferation of public sector projects – as indicated by the concept of "projectification" – there is still a need for more critical debate about projectification, and especially its role in politics and the public sector.

In this chapter, I describe projectification in relation to discourses on public sector innovation. Utilising Carol Bacchi's (2012, 2015) problematising approach, I focus on how certain problems about the public sector are represented within discourses on public sector innovation and how projects provide organisational solutions to these problems. Following this approach, I ask, firstly, *what are the problems that public sector innovation is supposed to solve?* and, secondly, *how could projects be part of the solution?*

Projects, I argue, are seen as appropriate for undertaking innovations on a limited scale, and they are often the preferred organisational form to receive external funding. More importantly, however, insofar as innovation discourses entail a critique against bureaucracy, hierarchy and traditional politico-administrative relations, projects appear to offer an alternative to this in that they are not seen as bureaucratic. Projectification thus feeds on a broader anti-bureaucratic sentiment, which endows them with a certain attractiveness in contemporary public administration. As opposed to the public sector reforms of recent decades, however, contemporary reforms are not inspired by market relations and competition to the same extent. Instead, innovation is seen as located beyond both bureaucracy and market, and projects fit well into this rationality as they are seen as enabling collaboration – as opposed to competition – as well as realising an inherent potential and creativity of the public sector.

While the concept of innovation has primarily been associated with the industrial realm (see for example Hall, Chapter 2, this volume; Hall & Löfgren 2017; Lavén 2008), the concept has broadened to also include social policy (Fougère et al., 2017) and administrative reforms. In this chapter, "public sector innovation" refers to innovation that targets the public sector, primarily seeking to improve organisation and/or work practices.

In the first section after this introduction, I present the methodological approach of this study, focusing on the problematising approach and the methods employed in the empirical study. In section two, I describe the discourse and rationality of innovation, zeroing in on how public sector problems are represented within the innovation discourse, and in section three, I describe the project rationality and the organisational solutions that projects offer. In section four, the Swedish discourse on public sector innovation is described through three separate but related empirical cases. These cases show how the rhetoric and rationality of innovation drives projectification, and how this takes places on national as well as local levels of government. The cases thus capture *how* certain rhetoric and practices connect projects to the innovation discourse. In the fifth section, I provide my theoretical reflections on these cases and the relation between innovation and projectification, and in a sixth and final section I summarise the main findings and arguments of this chapter.

The Problematising Approach

The problematising approach departs from a poststructuralist perspective, where processes of power and discourse are set centre stage. By making specific problems – such as the alleged inefficiency of the public sector – seem natural, or taken for granted, solutions can be launched as rational responses as opposed to being explicitly political or ideological. Following this, the solutions – such as projects as a way of organising innovation – are "rendered technical" and thus contribute to an invisibilisation of politics (see Li, Chapter 3, and Bailey et al., Chapter 7, this volume).

According to Bacchi (2015, p. 7), the problematising approach "rests on the simple idea that what we propose to do about something indicates what we think needs to change and, hence, what we think is problematic." Rather than accepting the assumptions and claims explicitly presented in policies, the problematising approach focuses on "the implicit representations of 'the problem' (problem representations) they purport to address" (Bacchi, 2015, p. 7; see also Triantafillou, 2012).

Following Bacchi (2015, p. 3), discourse signifies "broad, socially produced forms of knowledge" – in which issues are construed as problems or not, and thereby made subject to political action or not (see also Townley, 2008). Discourses thus enable certain practices, while making others unfeasible. Additionally, discourses constitute actors – such as individuals or organisations – rather than being something that actors can use at their discretion, or deliberately choose to adhere to or not. In other words, policies, reforms and changes should not be attributed to particular political interests or preferences; they emanate from the innovation discourse, and are thereby more profound social and political constructs. An important contribution of the problematising approach is therefore its ability to make politics visible (Bacchi, 2015).

Although the overall ambition of this chapter is to illustrate how discourses of innovation drive projectification, I will not describe this strictly in terms of cause and effect. That kind of inference is not possible to ascertain, following the problematising approach. Instead, I describe the rational foundation of public sector innovation and of projects, and how these coincide in discourses of innovation as expressed in the Swedish public sector. My overall method is thus to juxtapose the concepts of innovation and projectification, to illustrate how projects as organisation connect to the problem representations of innovation.

In poststructuralist analyses of politics and public administration, the role of knowledge is important. The establishment of facts and dominating narratives is part of governing practices – they are not tools of government that actors choose to use or not (Townley, 1993; Triantafillou, 2012). In accordance with this, the theoretic accounts of public sector innovation, described in the next section, is not just a research overview; it is an introduction to the problem representations of the public sector, which underpins the discourses on innovation, as I describe later. By problematising not only the discourses on innovation as they appear within the Swedish public sector, but also their appearance in academic writing, I am able to show the contingency of the represented problems. By problematising the scholarly debate on innovation and public sector reform, I emphasise that discourses and their problem representations are attributable to historical circumstances and scientific argument (see Bacchi, 2012). Likewise, projectification and the project rationality – described in section three – provides the foundation for why projects are seen as conducive for public sector innovation.

The three cases, described in section four, show how discourses on innovation appear on different levels within the public sector in Sweden. The *Innovation Council* represents a particular government-appointed initiative to promote public sector innovation, whose investigations, descriptions and proposals were presented in a report within the series of national public commissions (SOU 2013:40). Secondly, I describe the role of *Vinnova*, the national agency of innovation systems, by highlighting their so-called strategic areas and funding programmes for public sector innovation. Thirdly, I focus on how the innovation discourse is articulated locally, by a describing a municipal organisation, called *DEAL*, devoted to innovation and methods development within child welfare, by initiating and supporting local collaboration projects. This case – studied ethnographically, through observations, interviews and documentation, as part of a broader research project on public sector collaboration – shows projectification in a local context, but clearly resonating with the broader innovation discourse.

The selection of the cases stems from my ethnographic study of DEAL. In following the projects and practices of DEAL, government reports, government funding programmes and associated public organisations and agencies were referenced – sometimes explicitly, at other times mentioned only in passing. The three cases are thus related in that they have appeared within the practices of DEAL, but they have not been orchestrated as part of an overarching government initiative or programme; the appearance at local level of the Innovation Council and Vinnova is rather a testament to the innovation discourse's multi-level character. In other words, the comparative purpose of these cases is to demonstrate the different ways in which the innovation discourse is expressed, and also to show how the innovation discourse travels between national and local levels.

Combined, this study employs different methods, inspired by ethnographers of politics and organisation (cf. Schatz, 2009; Ybema et al., 2009), where the Innovation Council and Vinnova have been approached through document studies, and the case of DEAL is based upon extensive field observations (approximately 40 visits during 18 months), informal interviews (15) and studies of protocols and reports (totalling some 40 documents). For the purpose of this study, I have analysed protocols, reports, transcriptions and field notes with regards to the problematising approach, focusing on problem representations in relation to innovation, and how they are addressed organisationally.

The Innovation Rationality: Problem Representations

In recent decades, the public sector of many Western European countries has undergone significant political and organisational change. Many efforts of change and modernisation have targeted an allegedly archaic public sector, accused of being unfit to address the challenges that face contemporary society (see for example Byrkjeflot & du Gay, 2012). As a remedy, organisational and managerial reforms have promised to deliver a modern, flexible and efficient public administration. Inspired by private sector management, New Public Management (NPM) implied a greater focus on results. By calculating cost and benefits at organisational level – or on the level of individual cost units, such as a school or hospital clinic – the idea was to make the public sector more efficient and to rid it from unnecessary administration and superstructures (cf. Triantafillou, 2012).

NPM-reforms, however, have brought disappointment and criticism. On the one hand, they have been criticised for not delivering what they had promised; rather than producing efficient and expedient organisations, the reforms entailed new procedures of control and administration, creating a "management bureaucracy" (Hall, 2012; cf. Forssell et al., 2013). On the other hand, the reforms have been criticised, not for failing to deliver what they had promised, but because of the promises' underlying ideas and assumptions. Critics have challenged the representation of the public sector as something archaic which is in desperate need of change (e.g. Bevir, 2013; Byrkjeflot & du Gay, 2012; Triantafillou,

2012). Among the many critics, at least three strands could be identified in the scholarly debate, all touching upon public sector organisation and its alleged shortcomings.

In a first category, scholars have advocated a return to the principles of bureaucracy. Lamenting the anti-bureaucratic rhetoric, Byrkjeflot and du Gay (2012, p. 101) say that

> traditional bureaucratic forms of public administration are represented as out of step with the demands of the present and future, and their continued presence within the machinery of government is regarded as testimony to the rigidity and inefficiency of that machinery and its need for its complete overhaul

but argue that this critique is inequitable and simplistic. Hierarchy is necessary to secure political and democratic rule, and the traditional organisation still harbours indispensable values and skills (e.g. Byrkjeflot & du Gay, 2012; Diefenbach & Todnem By, 2012).

Others have envisioned more interactive processes of government and organisation, emphasising trust, collaboration and innovation – offering a third way, beyond hierarchical bureaucracies and fragmented market solutions (e.g. Axelsson & Axelsson, 2006; Meyers, 1993; O'Toole, 2015; Powell, 1990; Rhodes, 2007; Sørensen & Torfing, 2011; Torfing et al., 2012). As a response to the critique against markets and NPM, but without resorting to the principles of bureaucracy, "collaborative innovation" has been launched as a third way of public sector reform (Sørensen & Torfing, 2011; see also Axelsson & Axelsson, 2006).

From a third viewpoint, however, advocates of collaborative innovation and network governance have been accused of hanging on to the same functionalist problem-solving agenda as the one driven by NPM-reforms (Bevir, 2013). Instead, it has been argued that contemporary forms of organising and governing public administration – by empowering organisations and employees, and encouraging bottom-up initiatives – are based on the same modernist assumptions of progression and continuous improvement as the NPM-driven performance apparatus – no matter how different and contradictory they seem (e.g. Bevir, 2013; Deetz, 2003; Townley, 2008; Triantafillou, 2012). Rather than criticising particular policies and organisational and managerial reforms, they focus on the assumptions, problems and knowledge that underlie such reforms (e.g. Bejerot & Hasselbladh, 2011; Triantafillou, 2012). It is in this third strand that I situate myself and this analysis.

Much simplified, one could say that the praise of bureaucracy does not seem to have struck a chord with politicians and other decision-makers in contemporary public sector, while the calls for collaboration, networks and innovation indeed have. Consequently, the representation of the public sector as anachronistic and overly rigid has gained ground along with the discourses on innovation.

The Many Problems of Bureaucracy

In the discourse of collaborative innovation, the problem with the public sector is its fragmentation and competition, driven by NPM, as well as the traditional bureaucratic silos and the mind-set of politicians and professionals. While traditional hierarchical public administration may encourage innovation to some extent – and so may the quasi-market organisation often associated with NPM – network-based forms of collaboration are seen as necessary to obtain more profound change (Axelsson & Axelsson, 2006; Bommert, 2009; Sørensen & Torfing, 2011).

> The bureaucratic silos and narrow-minded professionals associated with public hierarchies and the failure of competitive markets to find favourable ways of sharing the costs, risks and benefits of innovation tend to stifle innovation, but these problems can be overcome by the formation of networks that facilitate collaboration across organisational and institutional boundaries.
>
> *(Sørensen & Torfing, 2011, p. 845)*

The need for innovation supposedly stems from several demands, or challenges, that the public sector has not been able to meet. First of all, the public sector has not been able to deliver results, or take proper action, in the face of newly emerging issues – such as the climate – and in relation to so-called "wicked" issues, which have proven difficult to solve (see also Bailey et al., Chapter 7, this volume, on policy pilots in a "state of exception" and Harrison & Wood, 1999, on "manipulated emergence"). In relation to this, there are also rising expectations from the public and from private business, demanding public services with better quality, availability and effectiveness. This, in turn, also demands of the public sector to become more cost-efficient in organising and providing services (Bommert, 2009; Sørensen & Torfing, 2011).

The overall problem represented is that of bureaucracy, which encompasses organisational deficiencies as well as cultural. Sørensen and Torfing (2011, p. 848) describe that "it is often asserted that the strong adherence to legal and bureaucratic rules and the lack of competition and economic incentives in terms of patents and bonus payments tend to stifle public sector innovation." In addition, "[n]ext to these organisational barriers to innovation in the public sector there are cultural restrictions," Bommert (2009, p. 21) explains. The culture of politicians and managers' propensity for risk aversion is emphasised, but also the inability to tap into the innovation resources within their own organisation, and those of potential collaborating partners (Bommert, 2009; Sørensen & Torfing, 2011).

Taken together, the many deficiencies of the public sector – such as the failure to take political action, the absence of an entrepreneurial culture, and limitations of a hierarchical and rule-bound organisation – can be summarised as "the bureaucratic nature of government" (Bommert, 2009, p. 22). But as mentioned, this critique is not framed in political-ideological terms. Instead, innovation is needed because of exogenous political factors, and because there is virtually no alternative but to become more innovative (Bommert, 2009; Bailey et al., Chapter 7, this volume; Harrison & Wood, 1999; see also Fougère's et al., 2017 "critical reading of EU social innovation policy discourse").

The kind of collaborative innovation proposed represents a way beyond hierarchy and market. As an alternative to "the visible hand" of management and hierarchy, and the "invisible hand" of market relations, Axelsson and Axelsson (2006, p. 79) propose organising public services in networks – meaning "a more or less voluntary co-operation or collaboration between organizations." More specifically, Sørensen and Torfing (2011) emphasise the need for collaborative public sector innovation, but without signing on to "the neo-liberal critique" which they consider "highly exaggerated." The problem with the public sector, they say, is not that innovation has not taken place, "but rather that most public innovations are episodic and driven by accidental events that do not leave public organizations with a lasting capacity to innovate" (Sørensen & Torfing, 2011, pp. 846–847).

The Project Rationality: Organisational Solutions

The connection between discourses on public sector innovation and the emergence of projects is not easily discernible in terms of cause and effect. Projectification can be seen quantitatively – as an increasing number of projects – but also qualitatively – as proliferation or adaptation to a *project rationality*. By focusing projects qualitatively, projects appear rational – as a natural solution – to perceived organisational problems. As described by Fred (2018, pp. 43–44), the project rationality (what he calls "project logic") "encompasses two almost contradictory features: one innovative, flexible feature expressed as a break with traditional, bureaucratic ideals and practices, and the other supporting control, standard operating procedures and hierarchical structures" (see also Hodgson, 2004). The first of these features is notably non-bureaucratic, reflecting the critique against bureaucracy described earlier. In addition, projects are typically temporary and to some extent organisationally isolated – as opposed to the permanent or cyclical features of ordinary government procedures. Therefore, projects can harbour processes and practices that the ordinary bureaucracy cannot (Fred, 2018; Hodgson, 2004).

More specifically, projects provide organisational solutions to the public sector problems represented in the discourses on innovation in three important aspects.

Projects Enable Swift Action and External Funding

The increase in projects is attributable to push and pull factors working together. As described by Li (Chapter 2, this volume), contemporary initiatives of rural development in Indonesia are almost exclusively carried out as projects, which means that different actors who wish to partake in initiatives of rural or regional development, for example, must adhere to the project rationality. But also in Europe, similar instruments of government are among the main drivers of projectification, where "the most obvious external push factor is perhaps the Cohesion policy of the European Union (EU) and especially the implementation of the Structural Fund policies" (Godenhjelm et al., 2015, p. 331). In order to receive funding from the EU, applicants must present their proposals in the form of projects; and, trying to secure funding for longer periods of time, projects tend to replace each other and occasionally develop into a parallel organisation (see Forssell et al., 2013). But the way EU organises and funds initiatives – on national as well as regional and local level – has been mimicked also on local level, as local and regional governments have developed similar funds of their own, using similar project applications (Fred, 2018). One rationale behind these funds and project organisations is that the launching of projects implies swift action – a signal of something being done. In this respect, the project rationality resonates with a political rationality, where politicians – either on local, national or EU-level – undertake a symbolic action, conveying that they are handling various problems and situations.

Policy pilots are a particular kind of projects that fill this function. Through policy pilots, politicians can introduce new polices, but on a limited scale, and while leaving it up to civil servants – or the projects themselves – to settle on the details and specifics on each project. Politicians can thus present themselves as decisive, by initiating policy, but without being accused of too much governing top-down (Ettelt & Mays, Chapter 1, this volume). In the United Kingdom (UK), for example, over the course of three decades, the governing of the National Health Service (NHS) "changed away from the production of a blueprint of what was to be implemented and towards the promulgation of a 'bright idea' which local actors were given incentives to develop in accordance with government philosophy" (Harrison & Wood, 1999, p. 765; see also Bailey et al., Chapter 7, this volume). Following this development, the government launched further initiatives to "liberate" the NHS – making it easier for professionals to develop ideas bottom-up, without the involvement of politicians and bureaucrats.

It is worth noting here, that the distancing from a political and/or bureaucratic discourse is not predicated on a simple turn to the market – for example by advocating privatisation or business-like management. In the case of the NHS, the role of medical professionals, and their proximity to the patients, was brought forward, as well as collaboration among professionals and public sector organisations, as opposed to increased competition. Similar tendencies have been described in the public sector at large, where public organisations as well as individuals and families are "responsibilised" to govern themselves, but only in accordance with what is expected of them (Rose, 2004; see also Hall, Chapter 2, this volume).

Projects provide a middle-way between political control and distance. By allocating funds and launching projects – either as policy pilots or more "traditional" projects – political bodies and other public organisations strike an important balance between flexibility – for example by showing resolve and quickly taking action – and control (see Hodgson, 2004). In addition, projects can make initiatives and policies visible in a way that ordinary politics and public administration cannot. As described by Mackenzie and Barrett (Chapter 13, this volume), the introduction of a project management rationality into that of local authority results in conflicts and attempts of resistance – on behalf of the local authority employees – but the project also provides an outlet for employees to act upon. Public employees could thus make use of the projects in order to learn new skills (project management) and make themselves more attractive on the labour market.

Projects can Organise Creativity

Although projects may speak a language of politics – by offering swift action – there is also a significant demand from below, where managers and employees within the public sector want to work with projects (see Fred, 2018, and Mackenzie and Barrett, Chapter 13, this volume, on freelance project managers). And while the importance of external funding should not be underestimated – the public sector often operates on a tight budget – projects have an appeal that goes beyond the merely material. Projects become a way to handle – or, more precisely, to *organise* – a will to improve within the public sector (Li, Chapter 2, this volume).

In his study of a Swedish municipality, Fred (2018) shows how projects stimulate a "sense of excitement" on both an individual and an organisational level. Whereas individual civil servants consider projects to be more attractive than their ordinary job – and allow for them to do something else, develop their own ideas, or perhaps work closer to top management and politicians – the organisation as a whole benefits from projects as a free zone for experimentation.

There is a tension in the public sector, between change and continuity, and between temporary and permanent organisation, where projects are easily seen as representing the former (change/temporary). But in practice, projects offer a way to handle, or bridge, this tension by allowing for change and manoeuvrability to co-exist with the continuous and bureaucratic environment (Forssell, Fred, & Hall, 2013; Hodgson, 2004). Again, policy pilots can serve as an example, in that they so clearly speak to the professionals' contribution (the "bright idea", see quote above), and steer away from a hierarchy (blueprint) where politicians and managers give instructions top-down (Ettelt & Mays, Chapter 1, and Bailey et al., Chapter 7, this volume; Harrison & Wood, 1999). Like other public sector projects, pilots promise to accelerate change (Jensen et al., 2013) and to combine "controllability and adventure" (Sahlin-Andersson & Söderholm, 2002) – qualities that are highly desirable in policy-making (Ettelt & Mays, Chapter 1, this volume).

Projects Break with Bureaucracy

The explicitly organisational features of projects are an important part of their character and attractiveness. But in order to understand how problems are represented, and how they are construed as natural and taken-for-granted issues that must be addressed, it is equally important to acknowledge the more discursive features of projects, and how projects are conceived within public administration. In this regard, projects are ostensibly non-bureaucratic. In a public administration context, they appear as "the other" of the ordinary organisation, which is instead seen as highly bureaucratic and rigid (Hodgson, 2004; Jensen et al., Chapter 6, this volume; see also Triantafillou, 2012). Public sector projectification can thus be positioned within in a post-bureaucratic discourse, where the push away from a perceived "bureaucratic rationality" is perhaps as important as the pull towards a "project rationality" (Fred, 2018; Hodgson, 2004).

Anti-bureaucratic sentiment, as I described earlier, was imperative in previous decades' promotion of market-inspired reforms and business-like management. But this does not mean that all initiatives to steer away from an allegedly bureaucratic public sector are by definition inspired by the market, or NPM. On the contrary, projects are often seen as a way to handle the problems that marketisation and NPM have caused – such as the fragmentation of the public sector into isolated cost units, and an inability to venture into new initiatives. The conceptualisation of projects as something essentially different than "traditional" public sector work is important in order to understand why projects continue to spread, despite repeated critique of isolation and short-sightedness. Projects are more than their formal-organisation character, and projectification is something else than merely "lots of projects" (e.g. Fred, 2018; Godenhjelm et al., 2015).

Summing up, I have argued that organisational arrangements for carrying out policy should not be approached as if they were instruments chosen at the discretion of policy makers or other actors. Instead, organisational, managerial and political reforms should be seen as discursive; they emerge as responses to problems and assumptions that are often taken for granted. In other words, the drivers for projectification should be searched within the broader problematisations – the underlying rationality – that informs those actors. If the EU, national and local governments require public organisations and employees to organise projects, it is because projects are seen as the adequate solution to a perceived problem.

I have suggested here that the rationality of public sector innovation distances itself from both bureaucracy and market, and that it – because of this – is linked to projectification. But exploring how this linkage plays out in practice – studying the *how* of government (Rose & Miller, 2008; Townley, 2008) – requires a closer look at the innovation discourse and how it is enacted in a multi-level political and administrative setting. In the next section, I pursue the question of how problem representations are expressed on national and local level – rhetorically as well as in practices – and how projects are seen as the organisational solution to these problems. Through what rhetoric and practices are projects proposed as an organisational third way, beyond bureaucracy and market?

Discourses on Public Sector Innovation in Sweden

In this section, I describe discourses on public sector innovation in Sweden, as it is articulated on national and local level. In all of the three cases, introduced in section two above, innovation is promoted and coupled with projects. The relation between innovation and projects is not explicitly causal, but the cases all juxtapose innovation and projects in a way that illustrates how discourses on innovation drive projectification. In the section after this one, I provide my theoretical reflections on these cases and the relation between innovation and projectification.

The Innovation Council: Presenting Public Sector Innovation

In 2013, the National Council for Innovation and Quality in the Public Sector (henceforth: the Innovation Council, or the Council) – a commission appointed by the Swedish government – delivered their final report (SOU, 2013, p. 40). The main message of the report was that the public sector needs improvement, and that this can be achieved by applying new perspectives to how public services are organised and provided. The Council states: "it is our firm belief that public administration could do a great deal more than is currently the case – at the same cost or lower" (p. 19). But the report is not presented as a critique; it is rather a praise of the public sector, emphasising that it is capable of great things if only creativity is set free: "It is our impression that the municipalities, county councils and government agencies are bubbling with ideas and a desire for change" (p. 19).

The Council had been tasked to investigate the prospects of public sector improvement, and to promote such improvement. The government instructions were rather general, describing how the previous industrial society has been replaced by a society of service production and management, and that in this context, the public sector needs reform. The instructions to the Council focused on the efficiency and quality of public services, and identified innovation as the guiding principle to achieve this. "The task of the Council is to support and stimulate innovation and change in public services that can result in considerable improvement for citizens and business, as well as making existing processes more efficient" (p. 229, *my translation*).

In accordance with this, the Innovation Council describes how the public sector must become more customer oriented, more efficient as to how services and processes are organised and carried out, and – not the least – more audacious. Managers and employees must be allowed "controlled risk-taking" in order to develop and test ideas on a limited scale. To move the public sector in this direction, the Council presents general as well as specific proposals. The more specific ideas concern coordinating organisations and efforts to allow for ideas to be developed and tested, while the more general notes concern organisational culture and politics that do not interfere too much.

> One success factor in innovative organisations is that every employee is seen as a potential innovator and implementer of change. This approach should also be integrated into the public sector to a greater extent. Public sector

> employees have a great deal of knowledge and a wealth of ideas that, if there were clearer support, could be used and better channelled than is currently the case. … The National Council for Innovation and Quality in the Public Sector considers that new working methods for the development of ideas, combined with idea management systems, can help to unleash employees' innovative capacity, steer ideas to where they are needed, clarify the process for improvement suggestions and feedback, and bring together people working on similar problem-solving issues in various parts of public administration.
>
> *(p. 24)*

The Innovation Council points to certain immaterial factors – such as fostering a culture and relations that promote innovation and change – and some more tangible factors – for example how to organise the development and implementation of ideas and methods, and how to encourage a collaboration between different actors. In this latter regard, the innovation discourse has clear implications on public sector organisation, and not the least the proliferation of projects as a way of organising for creativity and change.

The Council argues that the public sector needs to be more customer oriented, as opposed to being self-centred; and it must be more focused on collaborating for the greater whole, as opposed to doing things in isolated cost units. The public sector must therefore encourage collaboration between agencies, administrations, and professions. And it must allow for projects to be launched on a limited scale, where ideas can be developed and tested – through so-called "pilots". Development and testing in a real-life environment provides important knowledge on what consequences a change actually brings about, the Council says. Since every employee should be seen as a potential innovator and implementer of change, their ideas and capability need supporting structures in order to be put into practice.

The envisioned structures include concrete measures, such as digital platforms, but they also point to a way of more generally organising for innovation. In this respect, however, the Council expresses a certain hesitance. They warn against an overemphasis on projects, and point out that many ideas take time to implement and integrate into the permanent organisation. A sustainable and long-term promotion of innovation should therefore be a priority, the Council argues. Despite this caution – against what is best understood as projectification – the project as organisational form is present throughout the Innovation Council's report. Although not explicitly promoted as the sole preferred organisation, it is implied in their reasoning on innovation, and this is most likely why the words of caution are necessary. As I turn to the case of Vinnova, the agency responsible of innovation systems, the promotion of innovation through projects is further illustrated.

The Innovation Agency Vinnova: Promoting Innovation Projects

The agency of Vinnova promotes innovation in various areas, primarily by funding programmes and by stimulating collaborations. One of their so-called strategic areas is "Innovation Capacity in the Public Sector," where Vinnova "supports the development of an innovation-oriented public sector by stimulating and enabling investment in research and innovation activities which clearly address the public sector's capacity to promote innovation" (Vinnova (2017a) webpages on public sector innovation). The agency offers funding for innovation projects carried out within the public sector, and they provide information and publications where local authorities are encouraged to initiate their own programmes for innovation projects, such as social investment funds and social impact bonds (see for example Fred, 2018).

The strategic area of public sector innovation has been identified in a national strategy for innovation, Vinnova describes, but they also say that it is an internationally established area, and that organisations such as the EU, OECD and the UN work actively with the issues. "The background for Vinnova's activities within the area is that an innovation-oriented public sector can promote innovation capacity in society as well as a more efficient use of resources within the own organisation" (Vinnova, 2017b, called: FRÖN 2016, p. 10).

For the public sector, there are different funding opportunities. Funding can be obtained, for example, for "innovation centres and test beds within healthcare," and, more generally, for "the planning, development and implementation of public sector innovation projects." The former is described as an opportunity "to commercialise ideas into innovations within the health service" – where Vinnova seeks to support local and regional authorities (who has a shared responsibility for Swedish health services). Similar to the Innovation Council, Vinnova describes that there is a great interest and potential within the public sector, but "systems/milieus need to be developed which can advance concrete ideas from those working in the health service." The repeatedly emphasised inherent potential of the public sector is also reflected in the name of the programme – where *innovation capacity* (Swedish: "*innovationskraft*") in Swedish also implies a force, or power, that resides inside the public sector.

Vinnova offers several funding opportunities for both public and private organisations devoted to public sector innovation, and these opportunities employ projects as their default organisation. The programme that funds planning, development and implementation of innovation projects – called FRÖN (English: "Seeds") – aims to unleash an already existing potential within the public sector. Apart from this, however, Vinnova invites public organisations to describe their plans and needs, so that these can be considered for future funding programmes – and in this respect, pilot projects are given extra attention.

> But we would really like to finance *pilots* in that or those directions we consider to support going forward. It is not yet clear exactly how this will be

> designed, but the pilots are likely to be within a few themes and financed mainly during autumn 2017. The investment in public services will continue in the same scale as before.
>
> Although *FRÖN Continuation* [a specific call] is not available for others than previously financed projects, we are interested in your needs/wishes regarding initiatives. Please contact us with a brief proposal of the project/s that you would like to implement. We can then use this as input in our discussions during spring. You are of course also welcome to provide us more general input.
>
> *(Vinnova, 2017b, webpage on FRÖN Continuation, my translation, bold in original)*

As shown here, Vinnova reaches out to public actors who are potential applicants and organisers of projects, to include their ideas and proposals in future programmes. In Sweden, agencies such as Vinnova enjoy a considerable autonomy from political bodies – in this case, the Ministry of Enterprise and Innovation – and by identifying needs and demands, the agency can affect the direction and design of future initiatives. In other words, the agency programmes not only affect how innovation is organised and implemented throughout the public sector; they also encourage innovation to be organised and implemented from below (see also Vinnova, 2014, letter of appropriation).

One public sector organisation which follows this imperative of bottom-up innovation, and which displays the ambition and devotion stipulated by both Vinnova and the Innovation Council, is described next. The organisation, here referred to as DEAL, has received funding from Vinnova for their innovation projects, but they have also established an organisation of their own to initiate and support various collaboration projects that aim to develop and test new methods within welfare services.

DEAL: Local Collaboration Projects for Innovation

DEAL was established in 2005, with the purpose of supporting a specific collaboration project between the municipal departments of education and social services in a Swedish city. DEAL was formed as an organisation to help administer the project, and to benefit from its positive results. Over the course of ten years, the organisation of DEAL took shape to organise different collaboration projects between the departments of education and social services – projects that involved different professional groups within the departments, such as social case workers, teachers and school counsellors. A key element in the projects was to develop methods or new knowledge of some kind. These projects should not be entirely administrative or routine; they were expected to involve an innovative component of some sort – a new method for screening and assessing children, a new procedure to make casework more efficient and time-saving or a new technical device to motivate young people to better health and sleep.

DEAL was subsequently broadened, to include the equivalent municipal departments in a neighbouring city, and at a later stage it was also significantly reorganised. It went from being an organisation of ten to twenty employees, to being a very small office of only one manager and a few administrative employees. The idea with the reorganisation was for the bulk of the work to be carried out within the different projects that DEAL initiated and/or supported – and the projects should be staffed by employees from the permanent organisations, thereby establishing a closer tie between the departments and the different projects. The modus operandi of DEAL was for the small office – where the manager is the centrepiece – to initiate projects, or to identify project ideas within the departments that could be put into practice.

The knowledge production and methods development, which was imperative in all projects, had different sources. In several projects, researchers participated as consultants, participants or evaluators. Evidence-based practices were also frequent, especially in the screening and assessment of children. But in interviews and conversations with me – in relation to me attending meetings and conferences – the manager of DEAL often emphasised the role of the professionals in the projects. She explained that she and the few co-workers at the office of DEAL should work with methods development, but they should not be the ones who develop. Their role is merely about coordination, administration and project management, while the developers are the ones who work within the participating administrations. By this, she presented the public sector employees as a key resource in the innovative practices. According to the manager, they are the ones who can say what works and not, and what needs to be changed in order to work better. She was clear in her description of the project participants doing the greater part, if not all, of the knowledge production, while her office mainly administrates and compiles that knowledge.

DEAL's role to stimulate and promote innovation projects includes administrative work, argumentation, and convincing the right people of what needs to be done in order to put ideas into practice, as well as securing funding for certain project ideas – including applying for funds from Vinnova. In relation to the innovation credo described by Vinnova and the Innovation Council, DEAL serves as a case in point – focusing on how to unleash the creativity and devotion of welfare employees, and put their capabilities into projects, through organisational and systematic support structures. The manager, much like the Innovation Council, praises the inherent creativity and contribution within the ordinary organisations, while at the same time incorporating this into projects. To a greater extent than Vinnova, however – and more than the Innovation Council – DEAL shows how the innovation discourse is realised in organisational practice, namely through temporary collaboration projects.

In particular, DEAL demonstrates explicitly what is envisioned and encouraged by the Innovation Council and Vinnova, namely that individual welfare professionals take part in the public sector innovation. Addressing the question of *how* the anti-bureaucratic rationality, underpinning the innovation discourse, is enacted in the public sector – and how projects are part of this rationality – these cases all point to the collaborative ethos of innovation projects, supposedly located beyond market and bureaucracy. The Innovation Council is explicit in its denouncing of NPM-reforms and market-inspired competition; Vinnova encourages the collaborative and bottom-up perspective of local authorities in developing their future funding programmes; while DEAL emphasises the contribution of local and individual welfare professionals in staffing and carrying out innovation projects. In these regards, the Swedish discourse on public sector innovation – and its project organisation – show similarities with as well as differences from other cases of projectification described in this volume.

The Innovation Discourse as Driver for Projectification

By adopting a problematising approach, this study has focused on the problem representations that underlie discourses on public sector innovation, and how these representations contribute to the projectification of the public sector. Following Bacchi (2015), the purpose has not been to argue for or against projectification, but to study the drivers and implications of said representations. Apart from the methodological benefits of such an approach – in the sense that underlying assumptions and problem representations are focused – it is especially useful in studying projectification, as this concept and phenomenon is often dressed in technical or functionalist terms (e.g. Li, Chapter 2, this volume).

Accordingly, in section three above, I described how projects enable politicians and managers to *take swift action* and *secure external funding*; how they can *organise creativity*; and how they imply a *break with traditional bureaucracy*. In the Swedish discourse on public sector innovation, as described in the previous section, these are all sought-after organisational features.

The issue of politicians *taking swift action* is perhaps the least explicit in the cases described, although local politicians who oversee the organisation of DEAL – and whom I have met repeatedly – affirm that DEAL is important to address politically significant issues, regarding children and youth, and that it allows them to take important action. On a national level, the very appointment of an Innovation Council also testaments to a political resolve, and an ambition to handle an alleged inertia of the public sector. The issue of *external funding* is closely related to politicians' need of addressing acute problems, or handling things in a non-traditional manner. Funds from the EU or from national agencies such as Vinnova allow projects to run outside of the permanent organisation, which means that externally funded innovation projects do not have to interfere with the ordinary budget cycle and fiscal year.

Overall, the role of politicians is equivocal within the innovation discourse. On the one hand, politics and politicians are construed as a threat to innovation and creativity. They are associated with the traditional public administration, where creativity and new ideas are frowned upon, and there is no room for mistakes.

This needs to change, the story goes, as politicians need to distance themselves from the organisation to unleash the potential of managers and individual employees. On the other hand, the innovation discourse – as articulated by the Council – promotes "controlled risk-taking," and in this regard it is not necessarily the managers and agency directors who take action; also politicians may use projects as an outlet for their needs and interests. As described by Vinnova, politicians have a need to test ideas on limited scale; launching initiatives which may become highly successful, but without the risk of them drawing criticism (see Bailey et al., Chapter 7, this volume, on the "multi purposes" of pilots).

However, a more prominent feature of projects is their perceived aptitude to *unleash and organise creativity*. As shown in the case of DEAL, the temporary character of projects sometimes fit into a more permanent superstructure – a permanent organisation devoted to initiate, lead or support projects (see Jensen et al., Chapter 6, this volume). By doing this, the host organisations – agencies or local governments – seek to combine the adventurous and risk-taking element of innovation, with the controllable project organisation. On a national level, this follows the view on innovation promoted by Vinnova, whose focus is on innovation *systems* as a way of reducing the ad hoc manner in which innovation is allegedly carried out – as argued by Sørensen and Torfing (2011) for example – by providing an innovation infrastructure (see Hall, Chapter 2, this volume, for a discussion on Vinnova and innovation systems).

Projects' perceived appropriateness in organising creativity is closely linked to its anti-bureaucratic character. The Innovation Council argues that the current interest in public sector innovation is "an expression of frustration with politics and societal institutions not being able to sufficiently govern society"; but, they continue, "also for a belief in people's inherent ability to see new solutions and realise these" (p. 47, *my translation*). The anti-bureaucratic rhetoric is thus very different from that of earlier decades, where the market and private business were seen as leading the way.

Lastly, the innovation discourse signals a sought-after *break with bureaucracy* which effectively separates the interests and contributions of public sector employees, on the one hand, and from their organisation, on the other; and this is where projects come in. Projects, as described above, may stimulate "a sense of excitement" on individual as well as organisational level, which allows employees and managers to remain in the public sector but untethered from the bureaucracy (see for example Triantafillou, 2012). Hence, projects speak to the alleged cultural deficiencies of the public sector, which by innovation advocates is seen as detrimental to a much-needed entrepreneurial spirit.

However, this break with bureaucracy also construes politics and politicians in a particular way. Rather than discarding politics – by arguing that politicians' power should be reduced for the benefit of experts, professionals or the market, for example – politics is acknowledged, but as something potentially problematic and which must be ascribed a clearer and more predictable role. Politics is thus not made entirely invisible, but it is severely "reined in" and subjugated to a rationality of innovation and improvement. In the empirical examples provided here, however, this is mostly seen implicitly (I elaborate on this issue elsewhere, see Chaib, 2018).

Another implication of the break with bureaucracy is that it risks throwing the baby out with the bath water. As described by Byrkjeflot and du Gay (2012), for example, bureaucracy does not only provide important mechanisms for decision-making and accountability; the bureaucracy also contains a set of skills, established practices and institutional memory which is often necessary for the organisation and which is only missed once it is gone.

Conclusion

To summarise, according to the innovation discourse, the public sector is rigid, self-absorbed and burdened by traditional politico-administrative relations, and projects offer a non-traditional organisation that may unleash the administration's inherent creativity and potential. Projects speak to a rather vague, albeit widespread, anti-bureaucratic sentiment, without necessarily resorting to the much criticised path of market solutions and NPM. Public sector innovation projects are thus clearly located beyond the dualism of hierarchy versus markets – just as prescribed by researchers who advocate collaborative innovation and similar forms of governing. Innovation in general, and especially innovation that draws upon collaboration between different agencies and professions, is seen as counteracting the fragmentation that NPM has brought. Consequently, innovation, collaboration and projectification are fuelled by an anti-NPM rhetoric, besides its more obvious anti-bureaucratic rhetoric.

But this third way is still based on the premise that public sector organisations must pursue effectiveness, continuous improvement, and that the employees' creativity and contribution cannot be unleashed within the ordinary, allegedly bureaucratic, organisation. In addition, there is a view that the public sector must rid itself of traditional politico-administrative relations, where politicians take a step back and/or encourage the audacity of managers and employees to experiment and take risks. Although this latter issue has not been fully addressed in this chapter, it actualises the issue of the public sector's legitimacy and what values, ethos and purpose the public sector is set to serve. In accordance with this, some important areas for future investigation would be the way politics is construed within the innovation discourse; the adaptation of politics to the project rationality; and the incorporation and compartmentalisation of politics into project-oriented organisations.

References

Axelsson, R. & Axelsson, S. B. (2006). Integration and collaboration in public health: A conceptual framework. *International Journal of Health Planning and Management*, 21, 75–88.

Bacchi, C. (2012). Why study problematizations? Making politics visible. *Open Journal of Political Science*, 2(1), 1–8.

Bacchi, C. (2015). The turn to problematization: Political implications of contrasting interpretive and poststructural adaptations. *Open Journal of Political Science*, 5, 1–12.

Bailey, S., Checkland, K., Hodgson, D., McBride, A., Elvey, R., Parkin, S., Rothwell, K., & Pierides, D. (2017). The policy work of piloting: Mobilising and managing conflict and ambiguity in the English NHS. *Social Science & Medicine*, 179, 210–217.

Bejerot, E. & Hasselbladh, H. (2011). Professional autonomy and pastoral power: The transformation of quality registers in Swedish healthcare. *Public Administration*, 89(4), 1604–1621.

Bevir, M. (2013). *A theory of governance*. Berkeley, CA: University of California Press.

Bommert, B. (2009). Collaborative innovation in the public sector. *International Public Management Review*, 11(1), 15–34.

Byrkjeflot, H. & du Gay, P. (2012). Bureaucracy: An idea whose time has come (again)? In T. Diefenbach & R. Todnem By (Eds.), *Reinventing hierarchy and bureaucracy: From the bureau to network organization*. Research in the Sociology of Organization, Vol. 35, 85–109.

Chaib, J. (2018). *Evidence, expertise and "other" knowledge: Governing welfare collaboration*. Lund, Sweden: Lund University Department of Political Science.

Deetz, S. (2003). Disciplinary power, conflict suppression and human resource management. In M. Alvesson & H. Willmott (Eds.), *Studying management critically* (pp. 23–45). London, England: Sage.

Diefenbach, T. & Todnem By, R. (2012). Bureaucracy and hierarchy – what else!? In T. Diefenbach & R. Todnem By (Eds.), *Reinventing hierarchy and bureaucracy – from the bureau to network organizations*. Research in the Sociology of Organizations, Vol. 35, 1–27.

Forssell, R., Fred, M., & Hall, P. (2013). Projekt som det politiska samverkanskravets uppsamlingsplatser: en studie av Malmö stads projektverksamheter [*Projectification as a response to political demands for collaboration: A study of projects in the City of Malmö*]. *Scandinavian Journal of Public Administration*, 17(2), 37–60.

Fougère, M., Segercrantz, B., & Seeck, H. (2017). A critical reading of the European Union's social innovation policy discourse: (Re)legitimizing neoliberalism. *Organization*, 24(6), 819–843.

Fred, M. (2018). *Projectification: The Trojan horse of local government*. Lund, Sweden: Lund Political Studies.

Godenhjelm, S., Lundin, R. A., & Sjöblom, S. (2015). Projectification in the public sector: The case of the European Union. *International Journal of Managing Projects in Business*, 8(2), 324–348.

Hall, P. (2012). *Managementbyråkrati. Om organisationspolitisk makt i svensk offentlig förvaltning.* [*Management bureaucracy. On organisational power in Swedish public administration.*]Malmö, Sweden: Liber.

Hall, P. & Löfgren, K. (2017). Innovation policy as performativity: The case of Sweden. *International Journal of Public Administration*, 40(4), 305–316.

Harrison, S. & Wood, B. (1999). Designing health service organization in the UK, 1968 to 1998: From blueprint to bright idea and 'manipulated emergence. *Public Administration*, 77(4), 751–768.

Hodgson, D. E. (2004). Project work: The legacy of bureaucratic control in the post-bureaucratic organization. *Organization*, 11(1), 81–100.

Jensen, C., Johansson, S., & Löfström, M. (2013). The project organization as a policy tool in implementing welfare reforms in the public sector. *The International Journal of Health Planning and Management*, 28, 122–137.

Lavén, F. (2008). *Organizing innovation: How policies are translated into practice*. Göteborg, Sweden: BAS Publishing.

Löfström, F. (2010). Inter-organizational collaboration projects in the public sector: A balance between integration and demarcation. *International Journal of Health Planning and Management*, 25, 136–155.

Meyers, M. K. (1993). Organizational factors in the integration of services for children. *Social Service Review*, 67(4), 547–575.

O'Toole, L. J. (2015). Networks and networking: The public administrative agendas. *Public Administration Review*, 75(3), 361–371.

Peterson, O. (2013). Statens backspeglar skymmer sikten. [*The government's rear-view mirrors are blocking the view, review article*]. *Respons. Recensionstidskrift för samhällsvetenskap & humaniora* No.4/2013.

Powell, W. W. (1990). Neither market nor hierarchy: Network forms of organization. *Research in Organizational Behaviour*, 12, 295–336.

Rhodes, R. A. W. (2007). Understanding governance: Ten years on. *Organization Studies*, 28(08), 1243–1264.

Rose, N. (2004). *Powers of freedom: Reframing political thought*. Cambridge, England: Cambridge University Press.

Rose, N. & Miller, P. (2008). *Governing the present: Administering economic, social and personal life*. Cambridge, England: Polity Press.

Sahlin-Andersson, K. & Söderholm, A. (Eds.) (2002). *Beyond project management: New perspectives on the temporary–permanent dilemma*. Lund, Sweden: Liber/Abstrakt.

Schatz, E. (2009). Ethnographic immersion and the study of politics. In E. Schatz (Ed.), *Political ethnography: What immersion contributes to the study of power* (pp. 1–22). Chicago, IL: University of Chicago Press.

SOU (SOU 2013:40) (2013). *Att tänka nytt för att göra nytta – Om perspektivskiften i offentlig verksamhet. Slutbetänkande från Innovationsrådet.* [*New thinking for doing good – Shifting perspectives in public services. Final report from the Innovation Council. English summary available*]. Stockholm, Sweden: Fritzes.

Sørensen, E. & Torfing, J. (2011). Enhancing collaborative innovation in the public sector. *Administration & Society*, 43(8), 842–868.

Torfing, J., Peters, B. G., Pierre, J., & Sørensen, E. (2012). *Interactive governance: Advancing the paradigm*. Oxford, England: Oxford University Press.

Townley, B. (1993). Foucault, power/knowledge, and its relevance for human resource management. *The Academy of Management Review*, 18(3), 518–545.

Townley, B. (2008). *Reason's neglect: Rationality and organizing*. Oxford, England: Oxford University Press.

Triantafillou, P. (2012) *New forms of governing: A Foucauldian inspired analysis*. Basingstoke, England: Palgrave Macmillan.

Vinnova letter of appropriation (2014). The government's letter of appropriation to the agency of Vinnova for the fiscal year 2014. Retrieved from www.esv.se.

Vinnova (2017a). Webpage on public sector innovation. Retrieved from www.vinnova.se/innoff, April 2017 (summary in English available).

Vinnova (2017b). FRÖN fortsättning – För ökad innovation i offentligt finansierad verksamhet [*FRÖN Continuation – For increased innovation in public service. Call for applications*], https://www.vinnova.se/e/fron-for-okad-innovation-i-offentligt-2015-00082/fron-fortsattning/.

Ybema, S., Yanow, D., Wels, H., & Kamsteeg, F. (2009). Studying everyday organizational life. In S. Ybema, D. Yanow, H. Wels, & F. Kamsteeg (Eds), *Organizational ethnography: Studying the complexities of everyday life* (pp. 1–20). London, England: Sage.

5

IN AND OUT OF AMBER

The New Zealand Government Major Projects Performance Reporting

Karl Löfgren and Barbara Allen

VICTORIA UNIVERSITY OF WELLINGTON

How do we *perceive* the measuring of public sector project processes? Why is the perception of the reporting important? These questions allude to the fact that project management (PM) in the public sector is more than just technically organising policy implementation through discrete time frames, budget allocations, and quality requirements. By studying the project management in the public sector, and more precisely, the reporting of public sector projects, we are engaging a unique lens for understanding current processes of de-politicising (Christensen & Lægreid, 2006) and technicalising (or "rendering technical", Li, Chapter 3, this volume) modern bureaucracy in the next phase of New Public Management. Although the performance reporting of projects often is the only part of a project that is visible to decision-makers, media, the public, and indeed academic research, the literature on projectification in the public sector has by and large disregarded performance reporting. This chapter is an explorative attempt to discern what is conveyed in the New Zealand Government's "*Major Projects Performance Reporting*" (MPPR) – a high-level assessment of the government's most complex high-value investments. We will apply two aspects of the academic literature on reporting project management; first the discussion about what constitutes success in project management, and secondly, how to manage risks, or uncertainty, in projects. Our research questions are: *How is performance for public sector projects reported in terms of success, failure, risks and outcomes? To what extent does the nature of this reporting represent de-politicisation and technicalisation of the policy programmes?*

In terms of methodology, we will employ a policy discourse approach based on Maarten Hajer (2006) with the objective of analysing how outcomes, successes, failures, and risks are constructed in the reporting documents.

The chapter is structured as follows. In sections two and three, we present our theoretical framework, and the methodology employed. In the subsequent section four, we describe our unit of analysis the New Zealand Government Major Projects Performance Reports, and the New Zealand context. Section five contains our discursive analysis of the MPPR. Finally, in section six, we identify implications and questions for research and practice.

Theorising PM and Reporting

At a general level, project management is undertaken in similar ways in both the private and public sector, and are both informed by standard business management practices. However, there are noticeable differences arising from the nature of public work and the pursuit of public values through government investments (Baldry, 1998). Above all, public sector projects are subjected to political control, a patchwork of regulatory principles and conventions, and constitutional chains of political accountability. Despite the fact that project management practice does not seem to adhere to either classic bureaucratic or post-bureaucratic organisational models in principle, the strict applied standards and conventions, through professional project management, is fairly technocratic and de-politicised. Through introducing project management in the public sector, policy decisions seem to be transformed from a political ambition about what is achievable in terms of creating public values to an issue regarding what is technically possible to implement within some given time and budget frames (cf. Hodgson, 2004; Sjöblom et al., 2013; Löfgren & Poulsen, 2013; Fred, 2018; Ettfelt, & May, Chapter 1, and Hall, Chapter 2, this volume). Political and normative complexity becomes reduced to quantifiable measures and benchmarks, and hence more easily managed (more below).

The whole undertaking of appraising projects and their management, the chosen success criteria, and the factors affecting success (and failure) date back to the establishment of the project management methods in the 1950s. Already at a very early stage, the literature differentiates between *project success* (attaining the desired outcome) and *project management success* (achieving a purposeful method). For a considerable time, project management measures of success revolved around the "iron triangle" in which the projects were managed: (a) on time, (b) within the budget, and (c) to a quality/performance standard (cf. de Wit, 1988; Atkinson, 1999; Turner, 1999). In a review of the project management literature, Ika (2009) shows that the vast majority of articles in PM journals (from the 1960s and onwards) adhered to this iron triangle until the 1990s. More recently there have been shifts to emphasising benefits and value management and their role in project success (Fleming & Koppelman, 2016; Chih & Zwikael, 2015; Badewi, 2016).

In terms of the empirical focus in this paper, we may conclude that the academic literature normally juxtaposes public sector project management with the private sector equivalents. The mainstream PM literature has primarily been focussing on the private sector (engineering, IT, etc.) and has rarely attempted to envision different models for the public sector (although there is a growing focus on public sector, see Crawford et al., 2003; Crawford & Helm, 2009). That being said, there are many similarities between how we perceive project management as a process with different stages in the public policy literature (cf. Hogwood & Gunn, 1984; DeLeon, 1999). Actually, some of the thoughts in McConnell's heuristic framework on policy success (and more recently policy failure, McConnell, 2015) can without too much difficulty be converted to project management studies. His framework contains three dimensions: policy, programme, and politics (McConnell, 2010; see also Marsh & McConnell, 2010). These dimensions are by no means objective in a strict positivist sense, but neither completely a matter of (arbitrary) interpretations. Instead, McConnell suggests a definition able to accommodate what he calls a realistic definition:

> A policy is successful insofar as it achieves the goals that *proponents* set out to achieve. However, only those supportive of the original goals are liable to perceive, with satisfaction, an outcome of policy success. Opponents are likely to perceive failure, regardless of outcomes, because they did not support the original idea.
>
> *(McConnell, 2010, p. 39, our italics)*

Consequently, the subjective perception of a policy is the main determinant for success. The three following dimensions are vital for understanding different perceptions.

First, one may perceive success in light of whether the *process* was perceived successful or not. This includes factors such as preserving government policy goals and instruments, ensuring policy legitimacy (see Hall, Chapter 2, and Li, Chapter 3, this volume) and symbolising innovation. This resonates well with the project management literature's focus on project management success, and in particularly the pursuit of avoiding project failures. Second, success can be measured in the language of *programmes* including, among other things, meeting objectives, producing certain outcomes, and meeting internal policy domain criteria. This is the traditional quest for achieving desired outcomes which also is covered in the PM literature. Finally, success can be appraised on its *political* merits including the survival and reputation of decision-makers, the control of the agenda, and sustaining government policy values and ideology ("stand by your ground"). This final dimension has been one of the less evident elements of performance measurement in NPM. Henman (2016) notes that

> the centre is capable of governing by numbers aggregated and disaggregated at the centre to make visible the various parts of an organisation or network … reporting performance data, rather than the rules, becomes the *sine qua non* of managerialism, contractualism, marketization and the consequent mixed economy.
>
> *(p. 501)*

The de-politicised use of numbers in the public sector has a similar variant in the private sector, where company narrative and numbers are employed to indicate to the market and shareholders that a company remains viable or is on the rise (Froud et al., 2006). Indeed, the authors explain how (financial) numbers are socio-technically constructed in a variety of ways that enable different narratives to be empirically supported (ibid., p. 133). Both the public and private sector contexts present tensions between the role of performance reporting as politically visible (thereby accountable) or "democratic" and performance reporting as corporate internal strategy building and performative – getting the numbers to do what you want them to do. The "narrative" of performance reporting and the performativity of the numbers themselves is something we will return to.

Another important factor affecting our study on the reporting of public sector projects is "uncertainty", or "risks" (see "state of exception", Bailey et al., Chapter 7, this volume). Just like performance, the whole systematic planning approach to project management, including identifying, monitoring, and controlling risks, has been around since the advent of the project management theory and practice. Although focussing on so-called "megaprojects", some of the arguments mentioned by Flyvbjerg (2014) in a recent article can be retrieved and converted to characteristics relevant to the type of risks public sector projects we are discussing. Among others, these include plurality of actors, principal-agent problems, omitted longevity and stewardship, and poor channels of communication (ibid.).

Analytical Framework

Three aspects – project success, project risk/uncertainty, and outcomes – are going to be the focal points for our discursive analysis of the project management reporting. Through the concepts of *discourse, metaphor*, and *story line* (derived from Hajer, 2006) we will study how success and uncertainty are subjectively pronounced. The basic premise for discourse analysis is that the language we use in social interactions affect our perceptions of the world rather than just reflect the world. Paraphrasing Hajer and Versteeg (2005), the benefits of employing a discursive approach are manifold. First, by using this approach we become aware about the underlying rationality of the public-sector project management and performance. Second, they contribute to shape our views of the world, which in turn delimits what is possible to envision in practice. Third, the discourse is more than just a mutual understanding in a group of actors of problems and solutions (let alone a "discussion"). The discourses (or world-views) "discipline" us, and affect our behaviour (Foucault, 1991). Foucault inspired work that shows how performance measures affect the practice of public sector organisations by indicating relevant measures (benchmarks), criteria for good performance, and in so many other ways exercise "normalisation" of our practice as a subtle and implicit form of power ("governmentality") (cf. Triantafillou, 2007).

Although technical, the language of project management is telling us something about how the practitioners' world is constructed and reconstructed, and how meaning is given to their social practice. While discourse analysis "normally" adheres to spoken and written communication ("texts"), our unit of analysis (the MPPR reports) also entails visual forms of communication. We have here been inspired by Liu (2013) and his thoughts about interpretive strategies in multimodal texts (see below).

Discourse

In terms of our analysis, discourse is here defined as "an ensemble of ideas, concepts, and categories through which meaning is given to social and physical phenomena, and which is produced and reproduced through an identifiable set of practices" (Hajer, 2006, p. 67). Deeper understandings of rationality, structures, and positions embedded in the language emerge. These may be described both in terms of discourse structuration – how one specific discourse comes to dominate the conceptualisation of the world – and discourse institutionalisation – how the discourse solidifies itself through organisational practices (ibid., p. 70). Applying this to our specific study, we are asking the following questions: *Is the practice described in binary, or dualist terms (e.g. success/failure, safety/risks future)? What are the critical success factors? Also, which nouns and adjectives are used to describe the projects? Are they active or passive? Which roles are assigned to which actors? What is acceptable/legitimate (and not acceptable/illegitimate)?* With respect to the visual elements, we will pursue to understand what the graphical elements in our reports seek to symbolise as representations (based on Liu, 2013). This includes questions such as: *What are the constructing pieces of the graphic element? What are the dominant elements? What are the dominant colours? Do the graphical elements entail different font sizes that draw attention in particular ways?*

Metaphors

Most policy documents are full of various forms of figures of speech. A classic example is the "market" which metaphorically translates to "mechanism for exchange". While metaphors can be conceived as stylistic and functional devices to enhance interpersonal understanding, it also signifies what Hajer calls "emblematic issues". Moreover, they provide us with a unique vantage point for grasping the frames for a project. They are particularly important for understanding changes in practices, and why certain discursive practices become institutionalised. The questions we ask are: *what kind of metaphors are being used for describing the projects? Are they being employed regularly and consistently? Are the metaphors used for positive or negative entities and practices in projects?*

Storylines

Hajer uses the term storyline to a "condensed statement summarising complex narratives, used by people as 'short-hand' in discussions" (Hajer, 2006, p. 69).

Most policy speech comes in the shape of a narrative which portrays the blend of actual events, causality, definitions, and "culture" in a logic and rational fashion. In a public sector context, story-telling is an imperative part of the institutional memory of the organisation. It is often aligned with reforms and interventions, and certain significant individuals (such as for example Ministers/Chief Executives) are nominated as change agents.

Empirical Data

The attention in our article is on the "micro-discourse". By focussing on the actual reporting mechanism, we are provided with a unique vantage point for perceiving the institutionalisation of the broader public sector (macro-)discourse on project management. The analysis in this chapter is based on mainly two kinds of official documentary government sources. First, the actual performance reports, the so-called "Interim Major Projects Performance Reports". Since the first report in 2015 to the time of this chapter (2018), the Treasury has released a new report every six months (November and March). The chief element of these reports is the front-end list of those projects which are "likely to need support" in terms of delivery; these are allocated a front-end position with a full "dash-board" (see below). Although there have been some minor changes in the presentations, they have generally stayed the same in terms of design since the initial one. They are all written in a succinct and technical style avoiding any unnecessary comments and claims.

Second, we have studied the Question and Answers documents (Q&As) accompanying the interim reports. While the interim reports are presented in a mixed text and graphic design, the Q&As are media reports with predefined questions and subsequent answers. These, compared to the interim reports, are written in a more explanatory style, although much of the content is repeated. The Treasury has so far published five each of these reports since the beginning in 2015.

In addition to these two sources, we have also examined the original 2011 guidance document for monitoring major projects (SSC, 2011). This document was developed by the State Service Commission and was based on an older document from 2001: "Guidelines for managing and monitoring major IT projects".

In terms of our coding and analysis process, we pursued the following strategy. Following a reading, and re-reading of the sources with the aim of gaining familiarity, we started to code the material. We categorised the material according to underpinning assumptions, images, figures of speech, stylistic and rhetorical devices, and also narratives and storylines. We built up a database organising quotes and excerpts, with the aim of identifying the three overarching categories of discourse, metaphors and storylines, and subsequent sub-categories.

The Context: Major Project Performance Report

MPPR is now a common approach to dealing with the need to amass data across complex organisations, and publicly account for the investments being made by government. By and large, it follows the global idea of "managing for results", where New Zealand has been appointed one of the "benchmark countries" following its New Public Management reforms in the 1980 and 1990s (Moynihan, 2006). Australia, Canada, New Zealand, and the United Kingdom all have Major Projects offices at the central government level. However, they are all grappling with the methods in which to effectively communicate the complex linkages between policy – represented in this case in the form of Major Projects or investments – and the implementation, or actual expenditure, and demonstrating how this meets national objectives. From this perspective, it is noteworthy that the New Zealand practice has been strongly influenced by the experiences of the UK Office of Government Practice (OGC) and the Australian National Audit Office (ANAO), and the vast majority of the New Zealand departments are employing the same methodologies as the OGC (The Treasury, 2011, pp. 4, 33).

Like many other jurisdictions, New Zealand has had its own fair share of major project failures in the public sector. In particularly the failure of the "*Novopay*" system, a payroll system for all school staff in New Zealand, has been hanging like a cloud over public sector project management, and in particular large government IT-projects in New Zealand seem to be vulnerable to project failures with several examples making their way to the public (cf. Gauld & Goldfinch, 2006). The State Service Commission's overall 2011 guidance document (SSC, 2011) also shows that public sector project management in general has been affected by the government IT-project failures.

The MPPR in New Zealand is an overview of the government's largest and most complex investments which has existed since 2013. The July 2016 Report lays out fifty-five major projects being delivered across thirty-three agencies with a whole-of-life cost of $36b. The Report presents an "evaluation" of how "on-track" a project is as determined by whether it will deliver the planned benefits on time and within the budget. A Dashboard system presents data that has been collected three times per year from the sponsoring agency, Treasury, monitoring organisations, and the Corporate Centre (Treasury, State Service Commission, Department of the Prime Minister and Cabinet, and the "functional leaderships"[1]). The reporting is not based on a value judgement about how "good" or "bad" a project is. Instead, potential success or failure is indicated through a series of proxy indicators. This includes: (a) expected benefits, (b) costs, (c) schedule, (d) scope and quality, (e) governance and resourcing, (f) stakeholder engagement, (g) strategic alignment and business case development, (h) risk and issues, (i) market engagement and procurement, and (j) assurance (The Treasury, 2016c). As such, it follows a balanced scorecard logic (i.e. combining financial and non-financial perspectives) albeit not the original scorecard measures (Kaplan & Norton,

1992, 1996). The proxy indicators are similar to that of Ertürk et al. (2007) whereby managers promise value for shareholders, and then construct a narrative of purpose and achievement that covers their difficulty in generating appropriate financial numbers (p. 556).

Finally, the whole design of the MPPR resonates very well with the overall New Zealand government policy on public management in the 2010s which includes "clear expectations" and "no surprises" (cf. SSC, 2014).

Analysis

Discourse

From our perspective, we can conclude that the overarching discourse of the studied performance reports is one of *managerial and governance control.* The design of the reports, the reporting tools, the measures, etc., are all devised to generate easily accessible performance information linked to strategic goals, assurance of being on track in terms of time, and financial costs (and deviations from schedule and budget).

However, what is less observable is who is the "manager" or "recipient" of the information? Basically, the documentary sources are operating with three different recipients. First, the initial guidance report (2011) talks about the monitoring *Minister.* [The objective with the reports is] "to provide Ministers with ongoing second opinion assurance and risk, assessment advice on projects throughout their development (from concept stage until benefits realisation)" (The Treasury, 2011, p. 2). Although reiterated in subsequent reports, the focus seems to drift to the collective actor "*the Corporate Centre*" including the Treasury, the State Service Commission, the Department of Prime Minister and Cabinet, and the functional leaderships. Second, the *project owners* are portrayed as important receivers by being given advice and feedback on the major projects deliverables (and in particular on outlining business cases) and through being shared best practices from other departments and projects. Third, there are some elements (in the accompanying Q&As) that the reports aim to provide "the public with visibility over how the delivery of the Government's major projects is being managed" (also called "The New Zealand taxpayers"). It is probably not misplaced to suspect that the public in this context is synonymous with mass media since the presentations can be easily converted to "a good news story", as most of the reporting conveys "positive case stories". In that context, it is worth drawing the attention to a media article in 2016 that raised some "alarm bells" after the November 2016 report. This report indicated that five of government's biggest projects were running into major problems and were at risk of failure. The Finance Minister of the time, Steven Joyce, said in response, "These investments are instrumental for the provision of quality public services for our growing country, and it is important that they are delivered well. Transparent reporting is a key part of ensuring agencies lift their performance in investment management" (Radio New Zealand, 2016). This would indicate the "policy problem" is transparency, not the projects themselves, and that MPPR is the solution. As many of the major projects are deemed to be "risky investments", the need to find a way to be visible and accountable – or transparent – requires a vehicle such as the MPPR that can carry the narrative but bundle up the details into a manageable package.

Governance is otherwise a central part in the 2011 guidance report, in particularly project governance of *cross-sectoral* initiatives with two or more involved agencies. Governance is here defined as something more strategic than management, and refers in the document to roles, responsibilities and accountabilities of the different actors. These roles are dedicated specific definitions in the report, which will be elaborated below in the section on metaphors.

Another central element of the discourse is how *success and failure* is conceived and discussed in the reports. As mentioned above, success or "best practice" has been derived from the UK OGC and the Australian ANAO. The studied reports' balance scorecard approach (the "traffic lights") avoids binary categories (success/failure), but operates with projects with high and low *delivery confidence*. Rating a project amber/red, or red, is a signal that the project is slipping behind in one or more aspects, and that there is a risk for either delay of benefits realisation, or increased project costs. Important to notice here, is that "failure" is not considered to be a judgement of the project, or the idea, but whether the project is "on-track" to deliver benefits. There is an explicit expectation that projects at some point throughout the life-cycle are rated as red or amber/red. Finally, rather than identifying who should be held to account for the slip or delay, this amber/red rating is said to signal to the corporate centre that the project needs help to overcome the challenges and restore delivery confidence. While performance management in projects may be part of the solution in terms of dealing with complexity (the iron triangle), there are a huge number of other performance indicators including other values such as safety, satisfaction of stakeholders not immediately represented in the project, and other social and economic objectives.

There is also reason to discuss what is not expressed in the discourse. Overall, none of the documents define what constitutes a "major project". The closest to identifying a definition is that projects are made synonymous with major (and high-risk) government *investments*. As the purpose of MPPR is described in one of the many Q&A reports:

> To deliver on [robust and transparent stewardship of public funds], the Treasury oversees an *investment management system* that aims to:
>
> - optimise value from investments
> - increase efficiency and effectiveness of projects
> - enable investments to deliver benefits.
>
> *(The Treasury, 2016c, p. 1, our italics)*

This is an interesting drift in government language as while project management "normally" is a methodology for organising policy/strategy implementation according to temporal stages, the documents conceive "project" as hazardous investments. This is also reflected in the catalogue of included projects. These include rather diverse examples of government initiatives from the establishment of a new ministerial department (the Ministry for Vulnerable Children, Oranga Tamariki), replacement of the whole New Zealand tax system, modernisation of named navy vessels, various infrastructure programmes (e.g. roads), and modernisation of internal information systems. However, some clues are found in a section of the July 2016 report where the author(s) categorises the projects into three kinds (The Treasury, 2016b, p. 3): (a) "Keep the business running" – which involve investments that are directed at core services, such as schools rebuilding; (b) "Grow the business" – which are intended to improve and extend existing services, such as health screening programmes; and (c) "Transformational change", in fact the majority of Government projects where large-scale changes are required, such as e.g. the replacement of the tax system. The latter holds the biggest share of the three, and is also the one which is emphasised:

> It is expected that many major projects are innovative, as innovation typically involves significant business change, which can be complex and risky ... The MPPR indicates that almost two-thirds of major projects are delivering "transformational change". Transformational change is aligned with the idea that "investment can be a great opportunity for innovation".
>
> *(Ibid.)*

Nevertheless, on balance there is no good explanation in the documentary sources to why a government "activity" is put on this list of projects which needs to be monitored. Reviewing them, they contain everything from the implementation of traditional policy programmes and IT systems, to the establishment of new ministries and agencies. It is complicated to identify a leitmotif for why (and when) a government initiative becomes a "major project", let alone a project that is supposed to entail uncertainty.

Metaphors

On the whole, the language of the reports and the accompanying Q&A section is mechanical, terse, and non-colourful, such that unpacking the metaphors was a challenge. The number of details released from the various projects is mainly limited to descriptive details and comments from the agency itself and the "monitoring agent". However, in addition to the traditional PM "lingo" such as, for example, "value-for-money" and "project life-cycle", a few notable metaphors could be recognised.

First and foremost, the visual report mechanism of *the traffic lights*. In the MPPR, the traffic light system (Green, Amber/Green, Amber, Amber/Red,

Red) is called the *Monitoring Five-Point Delivery Confidence Scale* and the number of projects in each category are grouped and presented by quarter indicating issues of concern such as potential cost overrun. Traffic lights and indicative delivery confidence are then combined in a "dashboard summary" that shows change (i.e. from amber to red) by project along with identifying the Responsible Minister. The red or red/amber ratings are the significant ones, and have in the more recent reports become the only ones which are given some more detailed attention. The use of the wording "confidence scale" is evocative language and brings to mind the quantitative tool, the confidence "interval". The danger of this language is its power to encourage the reader to think that the scale represents a factual, scientifically, and mathematically-based certainty with the implication that assumptions will be made, and possibly policy made, on the basis of this reporting tool. Where the MPPRs are endeavouring to bring more certainty to the project management process, in fact, they are using a metaphor and particular language to make sometimes bold claims about the evidence.

Second, the *dashboard* in its most basic form is replicating the instrument panel of a modern car accommodating speedometers, odometers, warning indicators, and other devices and control functions. While there is an element of the traditional dashboard control gauges in the reports including coloured indicators, a design drawing the reader to focus on certain aspects (with other aspects are located in the periphery of the view), the dashboard is composed of short summaries in discrete text boxes. As a data-driven decision support system, a dashboard can provide significant detail to a decision-maker (Yigitbasioglu & Velcu, 2012), but at the MPPR level there is little detail from which to ascertain how and why a decision about a project might be made.

As metaphors, both traffic lights and dashboards envision a vehicle moving towards a destination. There may be interruptions, distances with reduced speed, and/or poor road conditions that will disrupt the journey. Still, it is predicted that the "vehicle" will reach its end-destination. The (formal) rationality of "dashboard-style" frames make no reference to the merit of any particular destination, and serve to de-politicise the project reviews. This feeds into the narrative that the projects are based on technical logic divorced from anything "political" or "normative".

Third, the chapter in the guidance on governance and management (SSC, 2011) presents a list of governance roles and responsibilities presenting some "shop terms" for both governance and management.

In addition to allocating responsibilities, these metaphors divulge a discourse in which managing uncertainty holds a central position. By including a broad group of actors, there will be enough safeguards to reduce uncertainty and increase the chances of attaining success. The language of the governance and management structures (the "shop terms") reflects a corporate project managerial world with little connection to political accountability. In fact, one may suspect that the whole structure is set up to deflect the political masters from the projects – a de-politicisation through technical means.

TABLE 5.1 Governance and management – actors and shop terms

"Governance"	
Actors	**"Shop term"**
Sponsoring group	"The investors"
Business change manager	"The change agent"
The sponsor/senior responsible owner	"The champion"
Project executive	"The decision maker"
Project board	"The voices of reason"
The portfolio/programme/project offices (P3O)	"The backstop"
"Management"	
Actors	**"Shop term"**
Programme/project director	"The strategist"
Project manager	"The planner and controller"
Project team	"The delivery specialists"
A reference/advisory group	"The quality team"

Storylines

The most evident feature of the documentary sources, in terms of the storyline, is perhaps the absence of any more complex storyline. What is presented is a rather mechanical and rational narrative of how investments/projects go through certain phases (through "pipelines"), sometimes falls of the wagon and needs support (goes amber/red), but eventually become successfully implemented and terminate, after which they disappear from the "books". These stories are cut for media use. For example, the concern over the "red" warning on the ANZAC Frigate Systems Upgrade made media reporting simple – a ready-made compilation of facts and figures mutable to a "bad news" clip. That being said, some elements of a storyline can be identified.

Perhaps most important, major projects are defined as critical social and economic "enablers". This imbues the notion that Major Projects make progress on social and economic objectives possible. However, there is nothing in the Reports that makes clear exactly what these objectives are or should be. The benefits of the projects are all considered to be paramount for the "New Zealand taxpayers", and the reports never question the value of them. In addition, there are two active parties involved; the lead agent as the implementing part, and then "the Government", sometimes represented by the collective actor "the corporate centre", sometimes by the individual actor, The Treasury. In addition, there are the passive subjects of "New Zealanders" or taxpayers, who being put in the front of the documents as the beneficiaries of the reporting, but in reality are excluded. This is really about the Government (and clearly at a few instances, the monitoring Minister) and the project owning agency.

Second, the interesting component in the reports' storyline is that the stories downplay the agency, and put the process at the centre. The driving force throughout the reports is the logic of project management, not the individual actors. Although the actors sometimes intervene, alter direction and/or give support, the process takes the centre stage in a programmed and technocratic manner. Anything that can reveal political and/or ideological issues are censored out of the reports. Value-conflicts, possible cross-agency disputes, and political salience are all influences reduced to a reduced matter of "confidence" in delivering the project mission in time, to the budget and to the prescribed quality standards. In this project management world of the reports there are no normative disputes, changes in external circumstances affecting the directions, or conflicts between various actors.

Concluding Remarks

The chief objective of this chapter has been to inductively study the New Zealand Government Major Project Performance Reporting (MPPR) on the backdrop of questions regarding risks and success/failure. We asked to what extent does the nature of this reporting represent de-politicisation and technicalisation of the policy programmes?

By employing a discursive approach, we have sought to identify some of the underlying rationality principles in the New Zealand government major project management reporting. Our research question on how performance for public sector projects is reported can be answered in various ways. While our empirical case is limited to New Zealand, there is reason to believe that some of the findings have some bearing in those Westminster jurisdictions that have inspired this reporting model (in particular the UK and Australia).

Overall, what we are witnessing in our study is how the policy implementation of a rather motley selection of large-scale New Zealand government initiatives are being subjected to a single and uniformed reporting system primarily addressing success and uncertainty in terms of delivering the anticipated outcomes. By and large, the reporting system reflects various governments in New Zealand's long-term adherence to managerial and de-politicising approaches in the public sector. Through the development of narrative and proxies for numbers, performance reporting provides a level of transparency and visibility solving the government's policy problem, but in a way that is simply reductive, performative, and of little use outside political reporting. So, despite the aspiration to use the MPPR mechanism to foster public sector innovation, the reporting system is far from radically innovative – quite the opposite. Apart from that, there are a few more lessons that can be learnt from this study.

First, it seems like one of the strong motives behind the MPPR is to shield the politicians from project "predicaments". Partly through raising red flags in time before a certain "project" comes out of hand, partly through proactively detach the "project" from the responsible (and accountable) elected politicians. The project is in the safe hands of a collective group of actors thereby securing shared ownerships of both risks and accountability. From this we may deduce that there are differences between projects in the private and the public sector with respect to success and failure. Political failure is an aspect private project management is immune from. However, throughout the different reports there is a tension between, on the one hand, a managerial and a private sector understanding of project management, and on the other hand, an array of politically sensitive government projects. One important finding in that respect is how the reports in their conceptualisations are making "projects" synonymous with "risky investments".

Second, project success is in the context of MPPR solely about delivery confidence. The classical iron triangle of time, cost, and quality is at centre of the attention, whereas reviewing the basis for the "project", let alone deviations from the schedule, is not part of the mechanism. In that sense, this reporting model is a rather crude audit mechanism for reporting progress. Without giving away to conspiracies, one could see this as an attempt to restrict the discussion about project management success and failure to a binary model of "deliver–not deliver" rather than raising more profound questions about alternative values, and the overarching trajectory of the project.

Third, and in relation to what has been said, the aesthetic and linguistic aspects are limited to a technocratic language with few and simple metaphors, and with a limited release of details from the different projects. Although one can perceive the MPPR as an attempt to enhance government transparency, it is an incomplete openness we are witnessing. Several aspects are omitted, and if one wishes to really learn about the progress of the projects, one has to go beyond these reports.

Finally, and for academic functions, this study has tried to illustrate how analysis of project reporting can shed light on the rationality behind public sector project management. Notwithstanding the limited scope of this study, we believe that there is a space for further development of both a theoretical and methodological nature. Public sector project management reporting does not operate in some technical and managerial void, but is embedded in a deeper political context beyond the PM iron triangle.

Note

1 Functional leadership was one of key pillars of the Government 2012 "Better Public Services change programme" where three central Chief Executives were given the role to drive performance across the state services in ICT (The Chief Government Information Officer), procurement (The Chief Executive of the Ministry of Business, Innovation and Employment) and property (The Chief Executive of the Ministry of Social Development) each respectively should wear an additional functional leader "hat" in order to achieve benefits for the whole of government.

References

Atkinson, R. (1999). Project management: Cost, time and quality, two best guesses and a phenomenon, it's time to accept other success criteria. *International Journal of Project Management*, 17(6), 337–342.

Badewi, A. (2016). The impact of project management (PM) and benefits management (BM) practices on project success: Towards developing a project benefits governance framework. *International Journal of Project Management*, 34(4), 761–778.

Baldry, D. (1998). The evaluation of risk management in public sector capital projects. *International Journal of Project Management*, 16(1), 35–41.

Chih, Y., & Zwikael, O. (2015). Project benefit management: A conceptual framework of target benefit formulation. *International Journal of Project Management*, 33(2), 353–362.

Christensen, T., & Lægreid, P. (2006). *Autonomy and regulation: Coping with agencies in the modern state*. Cheltenham, England: Edward Elgar.

Crawford, L., Costello, K., Pollack, J., & Bentley, L. (2003). Managing soft projects in the public sector. *International Journal of Project Management*, 21(6), 443–448.

Crawford, L., & Helm, J. (2009). Government and governance: The value of project management in the public sector. *Project Management Journal*, 40(1), 73–87.

DeLeon, P. (1999). The stages approach to the policy process: What has it done? Where is it going? In P. Sabatier (Ed.), *Theories of the policy process* (pp. 19–34). Boulder, CO: Westview Press.

de Wit, A. (1988). Measurement of project management success. *International Journal of Project Management*, 6(3), 164–170.

Ertürk, I., Froud, J., Johal, S., Leaver, A., & Williams, K. (2007). The democratization of finance? Promises, outcomes and conditions. *Review of International Political Economy*, 14(4), 553–575.

Fleming, Q. W., & Koppelman, J. M. (2016). *Earned value project management* (4th ed.). Newtown Square, PA: Project Management Institute Inc.

Flyvbjerg, B. (2014). What you should know about megaprojects and why: An overview. *Project Management Journal*, 45(2), 6–19.

Foucault, M. (1991). Governmentality. In G. Burchell, C. Gordon, & P. Miller (Eds.), *The Foucault effect: Studies in governmentality* (pp. 87–104). London, England: Harvester Wheatsheaf.

Fred, M. (2018). *Projectification: The Trojan horse of local government*. Sweden: Lund & Malmö University, Department of Political Science.

Froud, J., Johal, S., Leaver, A., & Williams, K. (2006). *Financialization and strategy: Narrative and numbers*. London, England: Routledge.

Gauld, R., & Goldfinch, S. (2006). *Dangerous enthusiasms: e-Government, computer failure and information system development*. Dunedin, New Zealand: Otago University Press.

Hajer, M. (2006). Doing discourse analysis: Coalitions, practices, meaning. In M. Brink & T. Metze (Eds.), *Words matter in policy and planning: Discourse theory and method in social sciences* (pp. 65–74). Utrecht, Netherlands: Netherlands Graduate School of Urban and Regional Research.

Hajer, M., & Versteeg, W. (2005). A decade of discourse analysis of environmental politics: Achievements, challenges, perspectives. *Journal of Environmental Policy & Planning*, 7(3), 175–184.

Henman, P. (2016). Performing the state: The socio-political dimensions of performance measurement in policy and public services. *Policy Studies*, 37(6), 499–507.

Hodgson, D. (2004). Project work: The legacy of bureaucratic control in the post-bureaucratic organization. *Organization*, 11(1), 81–100.

Hogwood, B. W., & Gunn, L. A. (1984). *Policy analysis for the real world*. Oxford, England: Oxford University Press.

Ika, L. A. (2009). Project success as a topic in project management journals. *Project Management Journal*, 40(4), 6–19.

Kaplan, R. S., & Norton, D. P. (1992). The balanced scorecard: Measures that drive performance. *Harvard Business Review*, 70(1), 71–79.

Kaplan, R. S., & Norton, D. P. (1996). *The balanced scorecard: Translating strategy into action*. Boston, MA: Harvard Business School Press.

Liu, J. (2013). Visual images interpretative strategies in multimodal texts. *Journal of Language Teaching and Research*, 4(6), 1259–1263.

Löfgren, K., & Poulsen, B. (2013). Project management in the Danish civil service. *Scandinavian Journal of Public Administration*, 17(2), 61–78.

Marsh, D., & McConnell, A. (2010). Towards a framework for establishing policy success. *Public Administration*, 88(2), 564–583.

McConnell, A. (2010). *Understanding policy success: Rethinking public policy*. Basingstoke, England: Palgrave Macmillan.

McConnell, A. (2015). What is policy failure? A primer to help navigate the maze. *Public Policy and Administration*, 30(3–4), 221–242.

Radio New Zealand (2016). Alarm raised for five of government's big projects [Online version]. Retrieved from www.radionz.co.nz/news/political/322734/alarm-raised-for-five-of-govt's-big-projects

Sjöblom, S., Löfgren, K., & Godenhjelm, S. (2013). Guest editorial: Projectified politics – the role of temporary organisations in the public sector. *Scandinavian Journal of Public Administration*, 17(2), 3–12.

State Service Commission (SSC) (August 2011). Guidance for monitoring major projects and programmes [Online version]. Retrieved from www.ssc.govt.nz/sites/all/files/monitoring-guidance_0.pdf

State Services Commission (SSC) (2014). Statutory crown entities. It takes three: Operating expectations framework [Online version]. Retrieved from www.ssc.govt.nz/sites/all/files/it-takes-three-operating-expectations-framework.pdf

The Treasury (2011). Guidance for monitoring major projects and programmes [Online version]. Retrieved from www.ssc.govt.nz/sites/all/files/monitoring-guidance_0.pdf

The Treasury (2015a). Proactive release process for major projects performance reports [Online version]. Retrieved from www.treasury.govt.nz/statesector/investmentmanagement/publications/majorprojects/pdfs/release-process-mppr.pdf

The Treasury (2015b). Major projects performance report, March to June 2015 [Online version]. Retrieved from www.treasury.govt.nz/statesector/investmentmanagement/publications/majorprojects/pdfs/mppr-jun15.pdf

The Treasury (2016a). Major projects performance report, July 2016 [Online version]. Retrieved from www.treasury.govt.nz/statesector/investmentmanagement/publications/majorprojects/pdfs/qanda-mppr-jul16.pdf

The Treasury (2016b). Interim major projects performance report, November 2016 [Online version]. Retrieved from www.treasury.govt.nz/statesector/investmentmanagement/publications/majorprojects/pdfs/int-mppr-nov16.pdf

The Treasury (2016c). Questions and answers on the major projects performance report, July 2016 [Online version]. Retrieved from www.treasury.govt.nz/statesector/investmentmanagement/publications/majorprojects/pdfs/qanda-mppr-jul16.pdf

The Treasury (2016d). Questions and answers on the major projects performance report, November 2016 [Online version]. Retrieved from www.treasury.govt.nz/statesector/investmentmanagement/publications/majorprojects/pdfs/qanda-mppr-nov16.pdf

The Treasury (2017a). Interim major projects performance report, April 2017 [Online version]. Retrieved from www.treasury.govt.nz/statesector/investmentmanagement/publications/majorprojects/pdfs/int-mppr-apr17.pdf

The Treasury (2017b). Q&A on the interim major projects performance report, April 2017 [Online version]. Retrieved from www.treasury.govt.nz/statesector/investmentmanagement/publications/majorprojects/pdfs/qanda-mppr-apr17.pdf

Triantafillou, P. (2007). Benchmarking in the public sector: A critical conceptual framework. *Public Administration*, 85(3), 829–846.

Turner, J. R. (1999). Editorial. Project management: A profession based on knowledge or faith. *International Journal of Project Management*, 17(6), 329–330.

Yigitbasioglu, O., & Velcu, O. (2012). A review of dashboards in performance management: Implications for design and research. *International Journal of Accounting Information Systems*, 13(1), 41–59.

6

PROJECT MANAGEMENT IN THE SHADOW OF PUBLIC HUMAN SERVICES[1]

Christian Jensen and Staffan Johansson

UNIVERSITY OF GOTHENBURG

Mikael Löfström

UNIVERSITY OF BORÅS

Many people associate public sector projects with large and spectacular construction projects – for example building roads, railways, subways, and airports – or they might think of more virtual investments such as telecommunications and Internet infrastructure. However, it has become common to use projects as a form of organisation when implementing new public policies and innovations in healthcare, social services, education systems, and other public human service organisations. The European Union (EU) is a key player in this development in Europe (Godenhjelm, Lundin, & Sjöblom, 2015). Most EU policies are implemented through project funding (Buttner & Leopold, 2016), including its structural funds that provide billions of euros for temporary projects within the public sector. One consequence is that public organisations in the member countries are forced to adapt and learn how to conduct project work to raise funds for their activities (Jalocha, 2012). These same trends can also be found at national, regional, and local levels in other countries (Marsden, Sjöblom, Andersson, & Skerratt, 2012). Project organisations are used to setting up new operations and changing existing ones. The observation that we live in a projectified society applies not only to issues related to infrastructure and events, but also to how we continuously develop public welfare activities (Jensen, Johansson, & Löfström, 2013, 2018). The project form seems to complying with an interest to introduce a short-term thinking among politicians (Fred & Hall, 2017).

The trend towards projectification in human service organisations has also led to widespread suspicion and fatigue among managers and professionals concerning the project as an organisational form due to perceptions that projects have limited long-term impact on operations outside projects themselves (Nytrø, Saksvik,

Mikkelsen, Bohle, & Quinlan, 2000). Projects are not only a form for organizing the implementation of policies. As Bailey et al. (Chapter 7, this volume) show in their analysis of policy pilots in the United Kingdom (UK) projects are also used as a powerful tool for giving authority to disseminate policies. Policy pilots seems to share characteristics of projects, but the difference seems to be that the projects have defined the focus on project results, while evaluating seems to be a key element for pilots and policymaking (Ettelt & Mays, Chapter 1, this volume).

The strong political, administrative, and organisational motives and drivers behind creating project organisations do not seem to guarantee a long-term sustainable impact on permanent operations in the human services (Jensen et al., 2013). We claim that there is an urgent need among policy makers, public managers, project managers, and public administration scholars to more fully understand the relationship between permanent human service organisations and temporary project organisations.

All parties first need to understand the importance of the different basic conditions of two organisational "mega-standards" (Røvik, 1998) and their relationships, and that the routines-based public bureaucracy and the time-based project organisation have different conceptions of time and space. Moreover, they need to understand the meaning and importance of institutional logics when trying to integrate experiences and practices from temporary organisations into permanent public bureaucracies. This need for understanding is pressing since human service organisations are highly institutionalised, which makes most kinds of change processes challenging. This relationship between permanent and temporary organisations is not only structural, but also involves identities, assumptions, values, traditions, and rules.

The purpose of this chapter is to identify problems and challenges that project managers and public administrators face when handling relationships between temporary project organisations and permanent public organisations, since these relationships influence the outcomes of change work and public policy implementation. Specifically, we will use empirical cases to illustrate aspects of the relationship between the project organisation and the permanent host organisation, which can help us understand how competing versus supporting institutional logics affect long-term change in permanent human service organisations.

In the next section of this chapter, we provide insights into temporary organisations, in particular the important interface between the project and organisational setting in which it operates. In the third section, we present some general characteristics of human service organisations, the context in which our empirical studies have been conducted. We link this to the theoretical discussion on institutional logics, which demonstrates how the projects could affect institutionalised settings. In the fourth section, we discuss the relationship between temporary projects and permanent organisations in terms of institutional logics based on empirical examples. In the fifth section, we offer central insights into the possibility of using projects to develop and introduce new or changed activities with long-term impacts. Finally, we draw conclusions on the possible contribution of our findings.

The Temporary Project Organisation in Relation to the Human Service Organisation

The primary reason to use projects in human service organisations is the need to develop and introduce something beyond the ordinary, something that cannot be done within the framework of current operations. Therefore, projects have become a common recurring organisational form when local authorities are tasked, for example, to implement a policy change or change operations. There are many indications that the concept of projects is associated with some kind of change, not least because they often focus on bringing about innovation, change, entrepreneurial action, and the possibility to explore new fields (Lundin et al., 2015; Sahlin-Andersson, 2002; Sundström & Zika-Viktorsson, 2009). This association between projects and change may also encounter challenges when the change is implemented in the permanent organisation or new activities are developed, maybe even creating a new organisation. The challenges for projects that will change existing operations is to distance themselves from prevailing thought and routines, develop new ones, and implement the change in the permanent organisation structures. The challenge for projects whose task is to create new operations is usually to try to distance themselves from current processes and structures in order to develop new solutions to specific problems. Sometimes the task also includes establishing a new organisation for the new operations, including its funding.

Projects in human service organisations are embedded in networks of relationships with other organisations – especially with those that own and/or have funded the projects (Grabher, 2002; Jensen, Johansson, & Löfström, 2006; Maurer, 2010; Sydow & Braun, 2017). Using project organisations to achieve change in permanent organisational structures may seem like a good idea because the project is considered accessible and manageable. However, it turns out that there are some difficulties when project results are to be implemented in the permanent organisation. These difficulties are based on the interaction between the project organisation and the permanent organisation. One aspect that clearly affects the relationship between the project and the permanent organisation is in what degree the project is separated from the permanent organisation (Coombs, 2015; Jensen et al., 2013, 2018). Another aspect that affects the relationship is the way in which the project's identity and the rationality of the operations differ from those of the permanent organisation (Johansson, Löfström, & Ohlsson, 2007; Jones & Lichtenstein, 2008).

Thus, the temporary project organisation and the permanent bureaucratic organisation are two different forms of organising activities. We use projects and bureaucracy as ideal types in a Weberian tradition and see ideal types like conceptual abstractions. They are mental constructs that shape our conceptions and actions. For example, schools and hospitals are stabilised through a formal organisation that is based on the notion that they are authorities, and therefore, procedures and processes for activities are designed as part of that perception. Projects, on the other hand, are used to create change in these organizations, based on the perception that projects are innovative and suitable tools for creating changes. It is useful to emphasise the difference between these two forms of organisations to show the conditions for developing a relationship between them (see Table 6.1).

The project organisation often has its source in the permanent organisation and is embedded in its activities, culture, structure, and processes. Consequently, the project organisation will operate in the shadow of the permanent organisation's activities, where the project is based on time and space, a more limited and subordinated entity. Nevertheless, projects can take a lot of space depending on whether the task is perceived as central to the regular operations or they can provide a necessary contribution to the permanent operations in a resource-intensive situation.

With regard to the ideal-type permanent organisation, the ordinary recurrent activities of most public organisations (or bureaucracies, according to Mintzberg, 1980) are essentially controlled by a routines-based rationality. The operations are production-oriented and coordinated through standardised work processes (machine bureaucracy) or standardised skills (professional bureaucracy). The environment is fairly predictable, and it is therefore possible to create a relatively uniform workload. The change process in this environment is often characterised by incremental change, and the most important restriction on public activities is the stipulated budget. In a permanent organisation, time is a continuum with no clearly defined beginning or end; time becomes linear, flowing, and independent of events (Dille & Söderlund, 2011; Jacobsson, Lundin, & Söderholm, 2015).

In contrast to bureaucracies, the ideal-type project organisation is initiated to solve a specific problem. In addition, projects are intended to contribute to change and renewal. Therefore, coordination is done by mutual adjustment where different professions, principals, and systems must adapt to each other

TABLE 6.1 Routine-based vs. time-based organisations

Routine-based organisation	*Time-based organisation*
Production-oriented	Task-oriented
Coordinated through the standardisation of work processes/skills	Coordinated through mutual adjustment
Predictable environment	Uncertain environment/future
Uniform workload	Uneven workloads
Incremental change	Radical change
The most important restriction: costs	The most important restriction: time
Time as a continuum	Time as a countdown

(Mintzberg, 1980). The project operates in an environment that is changing and is therefore uncertain. There is no fixed point to rely upon, only an unpredictable and unstable situation. Things happen suddenly and occasionally rather than continuously and constantly (Hietajärvi, Aaltonen, & Haapasalo, 2017; Kreiner, 1995; Olsson, 2006). Similarly, the workload is unpredictable. If it turns out that a new approach is successful, the result can bring about significant change. Therefore, change through projects is often radical because it is expected that the project will contribute innovative solutions. The most important restrictions for projects are their temporary status and what happens after completion. The notion of time as a countdown is an important prerequisite for project management. The project consumes time, and time divides the process into various parts (milestones) along the project life cycle (Lundin, Söderholm, & Wilson, 2001).

Although there is a point in making clear differences between projects and permanent organisations, the difference should not be exaggerated. On the one hand differences are not always clear, and it is therefore essential to problematise an overly one-sided description of projects as innovative, for example. There is empirical evidence that projects also tend to develop a bureaucratic form, not least by being characterised by the organisation it is part of (cf. Hodgson, 2004). On the other hand, the idea of bureaucracy as inflexible and restrictive when everything around constantly changes, is also a simplified and one-sided view of the formal organisation. In defence of the bureaucracy, du Gay and Lopdrup-Hjorth (2016) claim that bureaucracy has the ability to develop and handle change, but its purpose is not to be entrepreneurial and innovative or respond to experimental enthusiasm among politicians or officials. There is also reason to add that projects in human service organisations are not so project-like in their character, that is, they rarely resemble the descriptions in the project literature. There is not always a clear project organisation, and even if there is it is not always structural in its character. It seems that the temporary organisation is mainly used to create a framing or structure for the task (Jensen et al., 2013).

Human Service Organisations and the Concept of Institutional Logics

Human service organisations such as schools, hospitals, and social services agencies are often regarded as the core of the modern welfare state. These organisations are often regulated and funded by public sector agencies but are not always run and owned by these agencies, which sometimes is the case in the United States and some other countries.

The raison d'être of most human service organisations is often some combination of their three main functions: people processing, people sustaining, and people changing (Hasenfeld, 2010). Human service organisations are often also characterised on the one hand by the nature of the operational (moral) work, and on the other hand by the need to comply with norms and values of the surrounding society (Garrow & Hasenfeld, 2010). Moral work in highly institutionalised environments requires technologies that are socially approved and sanctioned. Hence, the ability of the organisation to select a service technology is constrained not just by the available repertoire of technologies (i.e., the technological environment) but mostly by the sanctioned practices (i.e., institutional logic) endorsed by key institutional actors, such as regulatory agencies, funding organisations, other human service organisations, academic and research organisations, and not least by concerned professionals and their associations (Garrow & Hasenfeld, 2010). The influence of these professions and associations on hospitals and other human service organisations has been given a lot of attention in classic neo-institutional theory, for example through the concept normative isomorphism (DiMaggio & Powell, 1983). In these respects, human service organisations may not have so much in common with some other public agencies responsible for basic public tasks such as physical infrastructure, public transport, water and sewage, and waste disposal.

Consequently, it could be difficult for management to achieve profound change in the basic institutional logics of such organisations, at least by using traditional management tools for planning and control. The concept of institutional logic can be defined as "socially constructed, historical patterns of material practices, assumptions, values, beliefs, and rules by which individuals produce and reproduce their material subsistence, organize time and space, and provide meaning to their social reality" (Thornton & Ocasio, 1999, p. 804). It is in the dynamics of symbols, culture, and structure, combined with how individuals and organisations reproduce meaning, that institutional logics exist. In that way organisations and their members constantly have to respond to many institutional logics (Besharov & Smith, 2014; Reay & Hinings, 2009; Thornton & Ocasio, 2008).

However, institutional logic can be conceived as fairly vague and has been used in many different ways in the literature on human service organisations. Some scholars used it for differentiating institutional logics at the macro level such as market logics versus civil society logics (Ramus, Vaccaro, & Brusoni, 2017), while others used it at the meso level to differentiate between healthcare logics versus social care logics (Fincham & Forbes, 2015). We join scholars who used the concept at the organisational micro level such as Currie and Spyridonidis (2016), who analysed and differentiated operational work – medical work logics versus nursing logics – within multi-professional units at hospitals. We agree with Garrow and Hasenfeld's (2010) claim that the institutional logics perspective is useful when analysing micro-processes in human service organisations that involve situated forms of organising. Thus, human service organisations embody multiple logics, and it is important to understand the relationship between different logics and how they interact and coexist. In a situation of multiple institutional logics, the question is whether it is possible to bring together disparate institutional logics to coexist (Reay & Hinings, 2009), or if they tend to compete (Arman, Liff, & Wikström, 2014), or maybe compete at the same time as they coexist (Greenwood, Raynard, Kodeih, Micelotta, & Lounsbury, 2011; Hill & Lynn, 2005).

Besharov and Smith (2014) theorised on different ways multiple logics manifest and their implications for organisations. Their theoretical framework categorises institutional logic into two dimensions – compatibility and centrality – and offers an analytical tool for studying how different institutional logics interact. Besharov and Smith (ibid.) define compatibility as the extent to which the instantiations of logics imply consistent and reinforcing organisational ideas and practices. In turn, centrality is defined as the degree to which multiple logics are each treated as equally valid and relevant to organisational functioning. Centrality is higher when multiple logics are instantiated in core organisational functioning and lower when a single logic guides core operations, while other logics manifest in peripheral activities not directly linked to organisational functioning (ibid., p. 369).

Besharov and Smith's (2014) first model incorporates multiple logics with low compatibility and high centrality, and has been denominated a "contested organization", where low compatibility implies that actors need to handle conflicting rationalities, values, principles, and goals, as well as different means to reach these goals. In addition, high centrality in the contested organisation implies that the institutional logics compete for dominance. As a result, the core of the organisation is continually disputed (Besharov & Smith, 2014, p. 371). Their example from a microfinance firm illustrates the conflict, wherein it was difficult to combine banking logic with social development logic with its roots in social work. In this case the conflict reached crisis proportions with significant employee turnover and forced resignation of the CEO (Besharov & Smith, 2014). Similar conflicts in a mental health organisation were observed by Arman et al. (2014), where professional logics were challenged by managerial logics.

The second model incorporates multiple logics with low compatibility and low centrality, and is denominated an "estranged organization" (Besharov & Smith, 2014, pp. 372–373). Similar to the contested organisation, low compatibility implies that the organisation is forced to handle conflicting rationalities, values, principles, and goals. In addition, the estranged organisation involves different strategies and practices for achieving these goals. However, different from the contested organisation, low centrality results in a situation where one logic exerts influence over organisational functioning (ibid.). Besharov and Smith's example is from a cultural organisation, where cultural logic was partly challenged by market logic, but the latter was subordinated and buffered from the former and was not causing a crisis in the same manner as in the first example of a "contested organization" (Besharov & Smith, 2014, pp. 372–373).

The third model involves high compatibility and high centrality, and is denominated an "aligned organization" (Besharov & Smith 2014, p. 373). High compatibility leads actors to draw on logics that offer consistent implications for organisational action, while high centrality pushes multiple logics to exert strong influence over organisational functioning. As a result, the core of the organisation is united, even as it reflects the goals, values, identities, and practices associated with multiple logics. Consequently, conflict in aligned organisations is likely to be minimal. Because these organisations have high centrality, multiple logics are represented among members and are reflected in the organisations' mission, strategy, identity, and core structures and practices. Besharov and Smith's example here is a childcare organisation where its core operations were infused by a state logic that emphasised formal rules and regulations, and also by professional social work logic. The two logics were different but relatively compatible with the goals and practices of the state logic, reinforcing those associated with the professional social work logic and resulting in only minimal conflict (Besharov & Smith, 2014, p. 373).

Besharov and Smith's (2014, pp. 373–374) fourth and last model combines high compatibility and low centrality. It is denominated a "dominant organization" as in aligned organisations, high compatibility leads actors to draw on logics that imply consistent goals for organisational action, and as in an "estranged organization", low centrality leads to core organisational features that reflect a single logic. Together, the combination of high compatibility and low centrality results in organisations where a prevailing logic is reinforced by one or more subsidiary logics. In the extreme, these organisations may seem as if they embody only a single logic, because other logics are consistent with the primary logic and have little influence on organisational functioning. Besharov and Smith's example of this is from the field of architecture, where a professional logic of aesthetic tradition was combined with a more functional architects' tradition dominated by a more commercial logic, but conflict between logics did not materialise internally in these organisations.

Thus, both the permanent human service and human service project organisations are arenas for various types of institutional logics. We claim that the concept of institutional logics is useful when analysing how these organisations interact and influence each other, and especially if and how more sustainable change is achieved in the permanent organisation.

Challenges when Temporary Project Organisations Interact with Permanent Public Human Service Organisations

In this section, we discuss factors that, when using temporary organisations or projects, explain why it can be difficult to change and develop public organisations and their activities in a long-term, sustainable manner. An answer to that question is in the relationship between projects such as temporary organisation and the hospital or school as permanent bureaucratic organisation. Another answer is in how different institutional logic relate to each other. From this point of view we identify two major challenges: whether the task of the project is about creating new operations or changing the current operations. For each challenge we give examples of two empirical projects: one that was perceived to be successful in having a long-term impact on surrounding permanent organisations, and another that ceased when the project ended and hence did not have as much of an impact. Defining a project as successful or unsuccessful is not done via a review, but rather through an assessment of whether the project had an impact on the surrounding permanent organisation or was itself transformed into a permanent organisation. We end this section with a brief comment on complexity – if the project involves more than one actor – for example a collaboration project between social services and the healthcare sector, wherein one needs to handle multiple rationalities, decision systems, identities, for instance, in order to add new operations or change current operations.

A Project Organisation is Used for Adding a New Activity to Current Operations

The combination of a single organisational relationship with the task of creating new activities leads to what we will call experimental projects. The primary responsibility of these projects is dealing with completely new challenges, and for this reason the projects require a temporary adhocratic organisation in order to develop and test new solutions. Thus, the project needs to question and challenge the existing organisational practices and its underlying operating principle. Finding the project to be successful is not enough to determine its overall success, as success is also defined by whether the project can develop and create an entirely new permanent operation or unit for dealing with the new activities. Therefore, success implies that the new operation must become indispensable and possible to fund. The condition for this success is that the new unit must be perceived to be consistent and will not threaten the organisation's identity and mission, and its overall goal and processes; it thereby becomes a permanent part of the administration with its own budget (Figure 6.1).

In a study of experimental projects within the Swedish welfare sector, challenges in the transition from bureaucratic permanent operations into projectified adhocracies, and then from adhocracies into new bureaucracies, have been described and analysed (Jensen et al., 2013). Some projects succeeded in establishing a new organisational unit, while others did not. One such successful project was in public health. Behind it were two nurses each with 20 years of experience working in community healthcare centres. They perceived that regular primary healthcare could not respond to the needs of a steadily growing group of patients with psychosocial

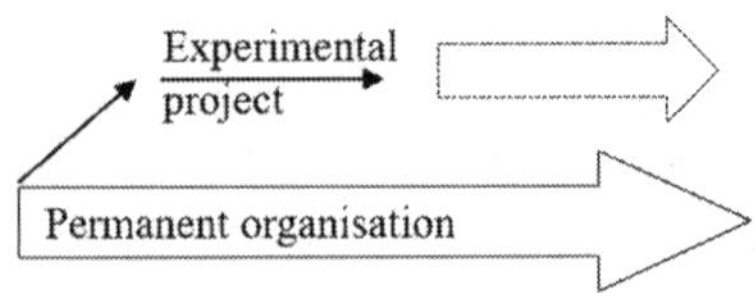

FIGURE 6.1 Experimental project; permanent organisation.

symptoms such as depression, stress, and sleep problems. They argued that simply prescribing pharmaceuticals helped very little. Therefore, their project idea was to empower patients: break their isolation, guide them to meet others in a similar situation, and have them start to learn from each other how to cope with their social situation. Focusing on prevention and involving the patient as a whole rather than offering only conventional care and cures based on symptoms and diagnoses was a completely new mission. Project managers made a conscious effort to promote the project to a range of stakeholders, especially within the social services in the municipality and to various patient associations – both of which represent organisations that traditionally have a wider view of the user than in the healthcare sector with its diagnostic focus. They managed to develop completely new working methods where affected and interested users were involved, and several of the project activities proved to be effective. Patients involved in the project also reported that they were better able to cope with their situations as a result of their involvement. Project managers' professional background and long experience were important, giving legitimacy to the activities and the project as a whole. But even reasons that have no basis in involved actors were of great importance for the successfulness. There was no competition and conflict between the two institutional logics of prevention and cure. They could coexist, mainly because the activities were separated from each other in both time and space. Because the different activities were kept separate, one logic could still dominate the activity while the other was perceived as peripheral. According to Besharov and Smith's model this situation can be called dominant. Thus, the experimental project succeeded both in developing a new logic of prevention (i.e., tested it and made it usable) and adapting it to an existing logic of cure. On the whole, the project came to be seen as a complement to the existing primary healthcare activities. The confidence of primary healthcare executives and other stakeholders in the project and its way of conducting complementary health work grew. As time passed, local actors viewed the project's activities as how preventive public health work should be carried out. In other parts of the municipality, similar projects started with similar wholehearted support and with similar positive results. Sometime later, the experimental project with all these activities was made permanent within the primary healthcare sector and was given its own budget for social security spending.

Another experimental project involving the introduction of newly arrived immigrants ended after project completion (Jensen et al., 2013), although the experiences of those concerned were generally positive and favourable. The project was financed within a national megaproject aiming to reduce exclusion in specific residential areas identified as socioeconomically disadvantaged (i.e., high unemployment, high welfare dependency, poor school performance, low participation in elections). The project owner was a city district administration that also coordinated other projects within the initiative in the district. The project manager and team consisted of immigrants living in the area who had been in Sweden for a number of years and who had practical experience with integration.

The project managed to build up a new operation that complemented the municipal social services. They also developed working methods that improved residents' living situations in many respects. The project was perceived as successful in the context of other similar projects within the megaproject, but was perceived as somewhat alien in the local governmental setting with more traditional public human services. The project management and team did not have a professional affiliation or a well-developed personal network within the city district administration. Lack of local legitimacy and newly developed approaches could therefore not affect the prevailing ones, and disagreements with the administration often became larger disputes. But aversion was due not only to different actors' lack of legitimacy, it was also about the notion of what public social service actually means. In Besharov and Smith's (2014) language, the newly developed logic was estranged from the traditional and uniform logic that permeated the social services. The project was told that such new services could belong to the civil society with a logic that allowed a greater degree of variation. As a result, the project team had great difficulty persuading the project owners and local politicians to continue the project with support from the regular budget. Consequently, it was just a successful project but with no long-term effects.

A Project Organisation is Used for Changing Current Operations

A change project has the task to make changes to structures or operational processes in an existing organisation. It is carried out in relation to, but temporarily separated from, the regular operations. The challenge is to create a distance and decouple the project from the prevailing thought, routines, and procedures, and to develop new working methods during the project and implement them in the permanent organisations (Jensen et al., 2018). This not only means that the change project challenges the prevailing institutional logic, but that the new institutional logic may need to coexist with an existing institutional logic (Reay & Hinings, 2009) (Figure 6.2).

The first example is a project about a social service agency that wanted to improve the quality of services for disabled adults (Johansson et al., 2007). Its purpose was to facilitate the relocation of disabled adults from poorly functioning

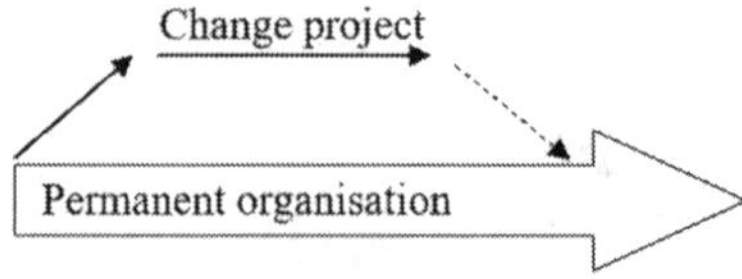

FIGURE 6.2 Change project; permanent organisation.

group housing, develop and adjust the working methods for the staff in the new housing, and improve the opportunities for participation and co-determination of those living in the homes. The project's main activities were to coordinate relocation planning, conduct training to prepare staff for work in the new group housing, and write a manual describing the new work methods. The project was carried out over a number of training days for all employees, wherein staffs were asked to develop their own way of working and formulate goals for group housing. This resulted in a systematic manual for the work. The residents were invited to participate in the so-called migratory circles, which were meant to be partly social training and practical preparation for the move to new accommodations.

Before the project, the activities were characterised by a social service care logic that governed the work of the group housing. The work primarily focused on the individual needs of the residents, which meant that the various homes developed different working methods. This variation in working methods made it difficult to maintain common working methods in all the group homes and ensure that it was good quality. There was also a variety of values about what constituted good care, which resulted in different group homes developing different daily routines for their work.

The implementation of the project contributed to the development of a more professional and systematic way of working. The professional logic was based on services that follow with standardised and approved practices (cf. Arman et al., 2014; Reay, Goodrick, Waldorff, & Casebeer, 2017). Similar routines were developed in all accommodations. It was during the training days that new working methods were discussed. The creation of the work manual improved the staff's knowledge about which laws and rules guide the operations, and provided information about future work in the new group housing. The participants also implemented most ideas in the manual immediately rather than waiting until after the project was terminated, which was suggested in the project plans. They found no reason to postpone implementation of such ideas, since all parties involved already knew what had been proposed and decided. Thus, the implementation of the new work methods was undramatic because the project was so closely integrated with the permanent organisation, and the existing social service care logic was not at all challenged by the professional logic, but smoothly integrated. The different logics shared fundamental values, including the goal of the client's well-being. This facilitated the introduction of the professional logic, which instead of challenging the current social service care logic was mixed within it (cf. Fincham & Forbes, 2015). The professional logic instead offered a clearer order for work at the group housing and was consistent with the operations idea and organisational goals. Neither of the two logics challenged the notion of the activities of those who worked there, but became part of the new professional logic, which was integrated and aligned to the organisation's goals (Besharov & Smith, 2014).

The second example is a change project in collaboration between the social insurance agency, social services, primary care, and psychiatry, where the target group was people with mental health problems who needed vocational rehabilitation. The project aimed to improve the rehabilitation chain between medical treatment and vocational rehabilitation (Löfström, 2010). It developed a working method with a rehabilitation team (with social workers, district doctors, psychiatrists, and social insurance officers) that planned, coordinated, and followed up with the rehabilitation programmes for people with psychiatric diagnoses. The social welfare service office, which is the focus of the example, developed a clear relationship with the project during the project period. This was an advantage because it meant that the team was given the opportunity to work independently and develop a way of working. The downside was that the working methods the team developed were not favourably received by their colleagues in the permanent organisations. While the separation supports the project, it also created difficulties in relation to the social welfare service office. The project and the team became more and more separated from the permanent organisations, and finally the project ended without the project team's work being implemented in the social welfare service office. One reason why the work was not implemented was that the methodology developed in the project was an expression of a professional logic that was a combination of different actors' logics. This logic was characterised by a clear focus on the client and the resources gathered around the client's needs in a common assessment, rather than assessing each actor's potential contributions (cf. Kyratsis, Atun, Phillips, Tracey, & George, 2017). Moreover, the logic was not consistent with the managerial logic, with its stronger demands for prioritising efficiency, cost savings and measurable efficiency developed by the local government management (cf. Currie & Spyridonidis, 2016). When the demand for efficiency and standardised services is introduced, these expressions of leadership logic challenge the possibility for independent professional assessments (Arman et al., 2014). This resulted in a conflict in which professional logic representatives tried to contest the managerial logic by showing the results of their work, but in spite of that decisions were made to focus on another part of the operations (Besharov & Smith, 2014).

Finally, we can reasonably assume that project will be even more difficult to carry out if there is a combination of multi-organisational relationships tasked with creating new activities or new organisations. In these types of projects, several local authorities come together in order to both increase their operational capacity to act and create joint operations to solve specific new problems. The main challenge in these projects, regardless of whether it is experimental or changing, is threefold: (1) to deal with inter-organisational challenges based on spreading shared responsibilities (which could include various types of governance structures, regulations, financial conditions, operational responsibilities, and organisational cultures); (2) to create a vital and clearly shared responsibility (considering that organisations generally tend to primarily protect their own interests); and (3) to scale up the experiment and create permanent conditions for collaboration.

Running Projects in the Shadow of Human Service Organisations

In the previous section, we tried to illustrate the conditions for running different kinds of projects in human service organisations. Our empirical cases show the importance of understanding the sources and prehistories of each project, and of examining the relationships between permanent human service organisations and temporary project organisations during their life cycles. The cases also examine how project organisations were terminated and dissolved, and the possible impacts they created on the ongoing permanent organisations. With regard to public policy makers they are not always aware of the fundamental difference between spectacular and big infrastructural technical projects, and all these experimental and change projects that are continuously run in hospitals, schools, and social service agencies – all in the shadow of recurrent operations. Some policy makers believe that public human service organisations operations are likely determined by rational political decisions and budget allocations, but in reality, the current and following years' operations are usually determined by the previous year's operations and their institutional logics (DiMaggio & Powell, 1983). Although there could be changes in political majorities, public policies, and budget allocations, institutional logics in human service organisations remain and are not easy to change.

These cases show the importance of adapting and translating to the existing logics in the organisation. The different logics must meet and blend, which happens throughout project work. However, there is a need for this to happen to some extent even between the change projects and permanent organisations, otherwise there is a risk that new logics will find it difficult to coexist or take over (Thornton, Ocasio, & Lounsbury, 2012). The probability of a project having a long-term and sustainable effect on the host organisations' permanent activities will increase if the project does not challenge the current dominant institutional logic or blend into a new logic, and can therefore integrate into the host organisations' core operations. What our empirical cases also show is what Besharov and Smith (2014) call compatibility, in other words to what extent the different logics are compatible and reinforce organisational actions. This means that a high degree of compatibility between different logics, for example values, increases the possibility that the projects succeed in contributing to a long-term change in the permanent organisation.

Although many projects live in the shadow of human service organisations, they are not powerless and can sometimes achieve profound change in permanent organisations. In many cases there is dissatisfaction with the ongoing permanent operations, and in such cases projects offer a promise, a hope, and thus a possible threat to the ongoing operations (Sahlin-Andersson, 2002). Generally speaking, project organising appears to be an appropriate strategy when implementing ambiguous policy, since the rationale behind using projects is that it is often wiser to begin with and learn from a small experiment before broadening the action to drive change across an entire organisation or an entire societal sector (Matland, 1995; Jensen et al., 2018). Another reason could be a wish to involve actors from different professions and organisations that otherwise does not work together.

Project organisations can also be used when implementing policy with conflicting interests (Matland, 1995; Jensen et al., 2018) since projects can be used to establish a compromise, wherein the different actors reduce the level of conflict via negotiations. Here, there is a big risk that the project will not succeed in achieving change in the permanent operations nor will be transformed to a permanent organisation after it is terminated (Jensen et al., 2018). Even if this is the case, the project may have played an important role in the public administration and thus has been a useful project.

Conclusions

The purpose of this chapter is to identify problems and challenges that project managers and public administrations face when handling relationships between temporary project organisations and permanent public human service organisations, since these relationships influence the long-term outcome of change work and public policy implementation. We outline that there is a need to understand the importance of the different basic conditions of the routines-based public human service organisation versus the time-based project organisation, and the meaning and importance of institutional logics when trying to integrate experiences and practices from the temporary organisation into the permanent public human service organisation.

The importance of the concept of institutional logic is shown in a lot of previous research on human service organisations (e.g., Garrow & Hasenfeld, 2010) and is also relevant in our examples of typical project organisations that operate in human service organisations. However, our main contribution is the obvious need to understand the relationships between temporary project organisations and permanent public organisations, as the former often operate in the shadow of the latter. As our examples in the previous sections have shown, there is a common denominator in the projects that had long-term and lasting impacts on the permanent organisations. These projects did not focus only on their own objectives and time schedules, but focused just as much on what was going on in their host organisations. The projects that had a more limited impact on the host organisations seemed to be too oriented towards the project's internal work and goals, and did not succeed in fitting into the existing institutional logics in their host organisations. These findings should be given more attention in the literature on project organisation and policy implementation, and also among public policy makers.

Note

1 *Acknowledgments:* Christian Jensen was supported by Mistra Urban Future.

References

Arman, R., Liff, R., & Wikström, E. (2014). The hierarchization of competing logics in psychiatric care in Sweden. *Scandinavian Journal of Management*, 30(3), 282–291.

Besharov, M. L., & Smith, W. K. (2014). Multiple institutional logics in organizations: Explaining their varied nature and implications. *Academy of Management Review*, 39(3), 364–381.

Buttner, S., & Leopold, L. (2016). A "new spirit" of public policy? The project world of EU funding. *European Journal of Cultural and Political Sociology*, 3(1), 41–71.

Coombs, C. R. (2015). When planned IS/IT project benefits are not realized: A study of inhibitors and facilitators to benefits realization. *International Journal of Project Management*, 33(2), 363–379.

Currie, G., & Spyridonidis, D. (2016). Interpretation of multiple institutional logics on the ground: Actors' position, their agency and situational constraints in professionalized contexts. *Organization Studies*, 37(1), 77–97.

Dille, T., & Söderlund, J. (2011). Managing inter-institutional projects: The significance of isochronism, timing norms and temporal misfits. *International Journal of Project Management*, 29(4), 480–490.

DiMaggio, P. J., & Powell, W. W. (1983). The iron cage revisited: Institutional isomorphism and collective rationality in organizational fields. *American Sociological Review*, 48(2), 147–160.

du Gay, P., & Lopdrup-Hjorth, T. (2016). Fear of the formal. *European Journal of Cultural and Political Sociology*, 3(1), 6–40.

Fincham, R., & Forbes, T. (2015). Three's a crowd: The role of inter-logic relationships in highly complex institutional fields. *British Journal of Management*, 26(4), 657–670.

Fred, M., & Hall, P. (2017). A projectified public administration: How projects in Swedish local governments become instruments for political and managerial concerns. *Statsvetenskaplig tidskrift*, 1(119), 185–205.

Garrow, E., & Hasenfeld, Y. (2010). Theoretical approaches to human service organizations. In Y. Hasenfeld (Ed.), *Human services as complex organizations* (2nd ed., pp. 33–57). Los Angeles, CA: Sage Publications.

Godenhjelm, S., Lundin, R. A., & Sjöblom, S. (2015). Projectification in the public sector: The case of the European Union. *International Journal of Managing Projects in Business*, 8 (2), 324–348.

Grabher, G. (2002). Cool projects, boring institutions: Temporary collaboration in social context. *Regional Studies*, 36(3), 205–214.

Greenwood, R., Raynard, M., Kodeih, F., Micelotta, E. R., & Lounsbury, M. (2011). Institutional complexity and organizational responses. *Academy of Management Annals*, 5(1), 317–371.

Hasenfeld, Y. (2010). The attributes of human service organisations. In Y. Hasenfeld (Ed.), *Human services as complex organizations* (2nd ed., pp. 9–32). Los Angeles, CA: Sage Publications.

Hietajärvi, A.-M., Aaltonen, K., & Haapasalo, H. (2017). Managing integration in infrastructure alliance projects: Dynamics of integration mechanisms. *International Journal of Managing Projects in Business*, 10(1), 5–31.

Hill, C. J. & Lynn, L. E. Jr. (2005). Is hierarchical governance in decline? Evidence from empirical research. *Journal of Public Administration Research and Theory*, 15(2), 173–195.

Hodgson, D. E. (2004). Project work: The legacy of bureaucratic control in the post bureaucratic organization. *Organization*, 11(1), 81–100.

Jacobsson, M., Lundin, R. A., & Söderholm, A. (2015). Researching projects and theorizing families of temporary organizations. *Project Management Journal*, 46(5), 9–18.

Jalocha, B. (2012). Projectification of the European Union and its implications for public labour market organisations in Poland. *Journal of Project, Program & Portfolio Management*, 3(2), 1–16.

Jensen, C., Johansson, S., & Löfström, M. (2006). Project relationships: A model for analyzing interactional uncertainty. *International Journal of Project Management*, 24(1), 4–12.

Jensen, C., Johansson, S., & Löfström, M. (2013). The project organization as a policy tool in implementing welfare reforms in the public sector. *International Journal of Health Planning and Management*, 28(1), 122–137.

Jensen, C., Johansson, S., & Löfström, M. (2018). Policy implementation in the era of accelerating projectification: Synthesizing Matland's conflict-ambiguity model and research on temporary organization. *Public Policy and Administration*, 33(4), 447–465.

Johansson, S., Löfström, M., & Ohlsson, Ö. (2007). Separation or integration? A dilemma when organizing development projects. *International Journal of Project Management*, 25(5), 457–464.

Jones, C., & Lichtenstein, B. B. (2008). Temporary interorganizational projects: How temporal and social embeddedness enhance coordination and manage uncertainty. In S. Cropper, M. Ebers, C. Huxham, & P. S. Ring (Eds.), *Handbook of interorganizational relations* (pp. 231–255). London, England: Oxford University Press.

Kreiner, K. (1995). In search of relevance: Project management in drifting environments. *Scandinavian Journal of Management*, 11(4), 335–346.

Kyratsis, Y., Atun, R., Phillips, N., Tracey, P., & George, G. (2017). Health systems in transition: Professional identity work in the context of shifting institutional logics. *Academy of Management Journal*, 60(2), 610–641.

Löfström, M. (2010). Inter organizational collaboration projects in the public sector: A balance between integration and demarcation. *International Journal of Health Planning and Management*, 25(2), 136–155.

Lundin, R. A., Arvidsson, N., Brady, T., Ekstedt, E., Midler, C., & Sydow, J. (2015). *Managing and working in project society: Institutional challenges of temporary organizations*. Cambridge, England: Cambridge University Press.

Lundin, R. A., Söderholm, A., & Wilson, T. (2001). On the conceptualization of time in projects. Paper presented at the 16th Nordiska Företagsekonomiska Ämneskonferensen, Uppsala University, Sweden.

Marsden, T., Sjöblom, S., Andersson, K., & Skerratt, S. (2012. Introduction. Exploring short-termism and sustainability: Temporal mechanism in spatial policies. In S. Sjöblom, K. Andersson, & T. Marsden (Eds.), *Sustainability and short-term policies: Improving governance in spatial policy interventions* (pp. 1–14). Farnham, England: Ashgate.

Matland, R. E. (1995). Synthesizing the implementation literature: The ambiguity-conflict model of policy implementation. *Journal of Public Administration Research and Theory*, 5(2), 145–174.

Maurer, I. (2010). How to build trust in inter-organizational projects: The impact of project staffing and project rewards on the formation of trust, knowledge acquisition and product innovation. *International Journal of Project Management*, 28(7), 629–637.

Mintzberg, H. (1980). Structure in 5s: A synthesis of the research on organization design. *Management Science*, 26(3), 322–341.

Nytrø, K., Saksvik, P. Ø., Mikkelsen, A., Bohle, P., & Quinlan, M. (2000). An appraisal of key factors in the implementation of occupational stress interventions. *Work & Stress*, 14(3), 213–225.

Olsson, N. O. E. (2006). Management of flexibility in projects. *International Journal of Project Management*, 24(1), 66–74.

Ramus, T., Vaccaro, A., & Brusoni, S. (2017). Institutional complexity in turbulent times: Formalization, collaboration, and the emergence of blended logics. *Academy of Management Journal*, 60(4), 1253–1284.

Reay, T., Goodrick, E., Waldorff, S. B., & Casebeer, A. (2017). Getting leopards to change their spots: Co-creating a new professional role identity. *Academy of Management Journal*, 60(3), 1043–1070.

Reay, T., & Hinings, C. R. (2009). Managing the rivalry of competing institutional logics. *Organization Studies*, 30(6), 629–652.

Røvik, K. A. (1998). *Moderna organisationer: trender inom organisationstänkandet vid millennieskiftet* [*Modern organizations: Trends in organizational thinking at the turn of the millennium*]. Malmö, Sweden: Liber.

Sahlin-Andersson, K. (2002). Project management as boundary work: Dilemmas of defining and delimiting. In K. Sahlin-Andersson & A. Söderholm (Eds.), *Beyond project management: New perspectives on the temporary–permanent dilemma* (pp. 241–260). Malmö, Sweden: Liber.

Sundström, P., & Zika-Viktorsson, A. (2009). Organizing for innovation in a product development project combining innovative and result oriented ways of working: A case study. *International Journal of Project Management*, 27(8), 745–753.

Sydow, J., & Braun, T. (2017). Projects as temporary organizations: An agenda for further theorizing the interorganizational dimension. *International Journal of Project Management*, 36(1), 4–11.

Thornton, P. H., & Ocasio, W. (1999). Institutional logics and the historical contingency of power in organizations: Executive succession in the higher education publishing industry, 1958–1990. *American Journal of Sociology*, 105(3), 801–843.

Thornton, P. H., & Ocasio, W. (2008). Institutional logics. In R. Greenwood, C. Oliver, K. Sahlin-Andersson, & R. Suddaby (Eds.), *Sage handbook of organizational institutionalism* (pp. 100–129). London, England: Sage.

Thornton, P. H., Ocasio, W., & Lounsbury, M. (2012). *The institutional logics perspective: A new approach to culture, structure and process*. Oxford, England: Oxford University Press.

7

PILOTS AS PROJECTS

Policy Making in a State of Exception[1]

Simon Bailey

UNIVERSITY OF KENT

Damian Hodgson and Kath Checkland

UNIVERSITY OF MANCHESTER

Projectification in the public sector is associated with a wide range of developments, but a particularly influential stream of project working in this area results from the increasing prevalence of public policy pilots, organised and structured in line with project forms. Situated within macro-political trends towards de-centralised and "post-bureaucratic" organisational arrangements (see Introduction, this volume), pilots can be seen as a pragmatic means of reducing the inherent uncertainty and "ungovernability" of policy making. At the same time they afford opportunities to practitioners and localities in shaping emergent policy agendas. However, pilots bring with them a set of political tensions associated with their mobilisation of project rationalities, and the organisational processes upon which their operation depends. In this chapter we examine the promise and dangers of pilots, drawing upon an empirical case of a pilot programme in the United Kingdom (UK). We begin by situating policy piloting in context.

Public policy pilots have been deployed in the UK since the 1960s (Burch & Wood, 1983), but their use has become increasingly common since the election of the New Labour government in 1997 (Sanderson, 2002). Since this time their use has been situated within a broader rhetoric of "evidence-based policy" (EBP), a movement which sought to replace ideologically-driven policy making with a more rationalist, scientific approach where decision making is driven instead by clear empirical questions of "what works" and "how" (Martin & Sanderson, 1999; Sanderson, 2002). From this perspective, policy must be piloted in order for evidence of its effectiveness to be collected and objectively assessed. In this way, policy piloting is presented as self-evidently rational, allowing policy makers to test the validity of policy promises through scientific evaluation of their success or otherwise before decisions are made on the wider implementation of policy.

In a clear articulation of this logic, an official report produced in 2003 suggests that "the term 'pilot' should ideally be reserved for rigorous early evaluations of a policy ... before that policy has been rolled out nationally and while it is still open to adjustment" (Jowell, 2003, p. 11). This agnostic stance represents an attempt to be impartial and disinterested, which is seen to be essential for true experimentation. This also explicitly couples pilots with their evaluation, the process of "testing" a theory in practice, although it is noted that this coupling results in "frequent conflicts between the demands of the policy cycle on the one hand and rigorous evaluation on the other" (Jowell, 2003, p. 27). Nonetheless, for proponents of EBP, this practical challenge does not detract from the essential scientific rigour of policy piloting; when done correctly, objective evaluation is essential to ensure that policies are judged on their effectiveness alone, quite separate from party ideologies and the vagaries of political debate. In the process, the generation and adoption of policy may be de politicised, in the sense that it should be based on judgements of rational criteria such as effectiveness or cost rather than on ideological preferences.

However, such robust commitments to rationalism and rigour in policy piloting have been challenged by various streams of research. One line of early research into policy pilots in the UK highlights the politicised definition of "evidence" in pilots and looks critically at how such "evidence" is generated and used in policy making (Mackenzie, Blamey, & Hanlon, 2006; Martin & Sanderson, 1999; Sanderson, 2002). More recent research on policy pilots seeks to move beyond the rhetoric of experimentation and the putative identification of "what works", asking instead what "multiple purposes" pilots might serve beyond those made explicit in official documents (Ettelt, Mays, & Allen, 2014). In looking beyond the rationalist veneer, this work explores associated issues of meaning and power (Nair & Howlett, 2016), recognising that policy pilots are involved in actively "framing or projecting the future" (p. 1). Based on case studies of three pilot programs, Ettelt et al. (2014) identify four purposes of piloting; not only experimentation but also piloting as a mode of implementation, demonstration, and for learning. They also note how these multiple purposes are often conflated, highlighting the tendency for policy makers to assume that "these divergent purposes can be managed in such a way as to be complementary" (p. 329). Ettelt et al. (2014) conclude that piloting should be seen as a policy making "tool" which is "mostly about making policy 'work' in accordance with the wishes of their political masters". Extending this line of argument, Bailey et al. (2017) demonstrate how piloting carries out policy work, mobilising processes, and resources in order to enrol actors in the process of policy generation, at the possible expense of political debate and deliberation.

This repositions piloting within a broader conception of policy development and implementation as a mode of power, or "rationality of government" (Foucault, 1991) and as an instrument with which to effect a kind of de-politicisation (c.f. Hall, Chapter 2, this volume). This resonates with Harrison & Wood's (1999) description of policy making as "manipulated emergence", as policy makers move away from detailed top-down planning through exhaustive policy "blueprints" to the deliberate spread of a more generic and flexible "bright idea". The "blueprint" approach, it is argued, requires policy makers to specify in advance the endpoint of a policy and the means of achieving it, while the "bright idea" approach entails presenting a general philosophy or direction, rather than a specific vision for policy. This shift implies a change in the means by which policy ideas are translated into local practices; the blueprint specifying institutional arrangements, defining roles and responsibilities in advance, and the bright idea leaving considerable space for "translation by incentivised local actors … into specific organisational arrangements which accord with the philosophy behind the original idea" (Harrison & Wood, 1999, p. 752). This implies that policy objectives might be described in vague terms, and lacking concrete details of appropriate institutional and organisational arrangements. These details and arrangements are placed in the hands of incentivised local actors.

This is an approach that has come to shape policy making in the UK and elsewhere over the past three decades, notably, the European Union (EU) (see Büttner, Chapter 9, and Fred and Mukhtar-Landgren, Chapter 10, this volume). In the UK, a seemingly endless line of "programmes", "demonstrators", "vanguards", "pathfinders", and other synonyms for policy pilots testify to the ongoing attraction of this strategy to enrol local practitioners and frontline workers in a particular policy direction. What can be seen in this strategy, therefore, is a recognition of the limits of top-down rational planning and an attempt to enrol local insights and bottom-up enthusiasm to produce a more fluid and adaptive implementation of policy. To be effective, this approach needs to navigate between two extremes related to autonomy and control: affording local actors too much autonomy risks divergence from the core objectives of policy makers; defining policy aims too narrowly risks stifling innovation and deadening the enthusiasm for local empowerment upon which the approach depends. This dilemma of autonomy and control is one of the core problems of organisational theory, producing the need for what Peters and Waterman (1995) promoted as the "simultaneous loose-tight properties" of "excellent" organisations, which maximise both central direction and individual autonomy.

One specific approach to square this circle, widely adopted and with particular relevance for the policy debates discussed above, is the turn to project organising, which offers in principle both strategic (or policy) direction along with localised accountability for innovation and delivery. At the same time, this implies a decentralised policy making process, with the potential to empower localities, but also to bypass the institutional structures which are designed to govern political decision making. As projects supply the practical means according to which these ideas and dangers might be materialised, we conceive of projects as both a "technicalisation" and "instrumentalisation" of policy making enabling innovation but in the process detaching projects from the democratic political process (Fred & Hall, 2017; see Ettelt and Mays, Chapter 1, and Hall, Chapter 2, this volume). Below, then, we consider the parallels and differences between policy pilots on one hand and project organising on the other. This requires a wider framing of policy pilots within broader societal shift described by some as "projectification" (Lundin & Söderholm, 1998), and a consideration of the proliferation of these and other projects within the public sector (Jensen, Johansson, & Löfström, 2013; Sjöblom, Löfgren, & Godenhjelm, 2013).

Our aim is to examine empirically the process according to which project rationalities become enmeshed in local policy making, through an example of a pilot scheme in the UK health sector. In our discussion we consider the implications this has for political and organisational decision making beyond our empirical setting. We begin by introducing relevant literature on projects.

Projects and Project Organisations

Identifying an activity as a project is an act which carries with it significant consequences (Hodgson & Cicmil, 2006). First and foremost, it specifies that the activity is time-bounded, that is, it has a defined beginning and end, even if these are not yet specified. It also denotes the activity as non-routine (see Jensen et al., Chapter 6, this volume); although often lying within standard organisational "business as usual", it is separate, indeed deliberately separated, from on-going and persistent routine work (Morris, 1997). This presents a particular advantage; it allows the project a degree of focus that many other organisational activities lack. This is typically emphasised by the appointment of the project manager, who formally holds responsibility for the delivery of the project as intended and may have exclusive responsibility for the project, being able to deliver this without distractions or conflicting external priorities. For the duration of the project, all activities within the project may be directed towards a specific, and clearly specified, goal. The result, at least in principle, is an organisational form which promises to deliver both "controllability and adventure", in the memorable phrase of Kerstin Sahlin-Andersson (2002). Frequently, however, the creation of a project carries with it much more substantial implications insofar as it frames an activity in terms of a particular lexicon and set of practices, tools and methodologies associated with the field of project management (Hodgson, 2002; see Shaw et al., Chapter 12, this volume). The project's progress can then be subject to project management technologies, making it possible for project progress to be monitored against a plan and a schedule, maximising transparency (see Löfgren and Allen, Chapter 5, this volume).

There is a great deal of writing on projects which celebrates their emancipatory potential, as summarised by Lindgren et al. (2014, p. 1386); it is claimed that projects

> are what modern and desirable jobs are all about ... with success and joy being built on passion and dedicated teamwork ... and where individuals are unleashed from the iron cages of bureaucracy and tradition and can build their interpersonal relations on trust, loyalty and shared values.

Only recently has critical research paid serious attention to the political consequences of project work; for example, through the pressure of precarious and discontinuous employment (Eskinsmyth, 2002; Koch, 2004), the transfer of organisational and managerial responsibilities onto individual workers (Hodgson, 2002), and the larger political consequences of the rise of project management (Clegg & Courpasson, 2004; Lindgren et al., 2014; see Shaw et al., Chapter 12, this volume).

Concern regarding these dysfunctional consequences of projects is increased by the growing reliance on projects across sectors, a process described as "projectification", and the public sector across nations has experienced a similar proliferation of the processes and forms of projects (Jensen et al., 2013; Sjöblom et al., 2013). Both government and politics have become increasingly "projectified", which has been associated with "the imperative for strategic change that has characterised public sector reform policies in recent decades" (Sjöblom et al., 2013, p. 3). As such strategic change is typically driven by policy initiatives in the public sector (see Godenhjelm et al., Chapter 8, this volume), it is no surprise to see projectification increasingly adopted as the vehicle for policy change, as policy makers seek to drive a change from one state of affairs to another. That is, in order to mobilise the necessary financial and human resources necessary to deliberate, design, and disseminate a new policy, an entity must be created which carries the strategic objectives of the policy and differentiates it from the present – a role fulfilled by the project form. The future is therefore a key concern for these policy actors – the ability to predict and "project" the future might be the key to the success or otherwise of a set of policy goals (Nair & Howlett, 2017). Projects thus provide the temporary organisational vehicle necessary to deliver long term sustainable policy change, with a temporal desynchronisation between ongoing public sector activities and the intensive, transformational work of the policy project. We conceptualise this desynchronisation here through the concept of the "state of exception" (Agamben, 2005; Gregg, 2011) to capture the distinctive (and frequently intensified) temporality of projects with heightened time and resource pressures.

The state of exception is a concept drawn from legal philosophy, and is commonly attributed to the work of Carl Schmitt. Schmitt (1985) was concerned with the paradox that he saw at the heart of state legal proceedings, which is that there will always be times when the state must be able to make decisions outside the law, such that the law is able to adapt over time to changing social conditions. The justification for this action is the "state of emergency" or "state of exception" – that is, exceptional times call for exceptional action. The central concern then becomes legally defining the conditions which might give rise to the suspension of normal legal restraints. He also notes the potential for the legitimate use of these powers to be extended over time in response to changing conditions. Picking up on this point, Agamben (2005) calls attention to the contemporary capacity of governments to normalise the state of exception, such that this apparently exceptional and temporary power becomes part of the routine disciplinary apparatus of government. Drawing on Foucault's (1991) concept of governmentality, and illustrating with reference to the passing of the Patriot Act in the USA, following the 9/11 terrorist attacks, Agamben's argument is that the state of exception becomes a powerful tool for imposing an open-ended restrictive regulation and control at the population level.

In a similar way, organisations may seek to create conditions where the normal rules of work are suspended (Gregg, 2011) such that more extreme demands are made of employees – to stave off a crisis, say, or to generate a technological leap. In some situations – or indeed, in some industries, such as digital and media sectors – this intensive mode of work becomes normalised as a semi-permanent condition, and as Gregg (2011) suggests, this shift is often supported by the reliance of such industries on deadline-driven project work. In these and other sectors, then, temporary organisations offer a route to creating a space, embedded within a normal organisation, where extreme working behaviours are demanded, in terms of both intensity of work commitment and extensity of work (in the form of very long working hours), as Lindgren et al. (2014) observe. Where temporary organisations are ubiquitous, what ought to be provisional and exceptional measures ("just for this critical project") can represent a permanent or enduring condition, indeed, a "rationality of government" (Foucault, 1991). It can be argued that the ability of projects to generate a "state of exception", and thereby elicit exceptional behaviours from project employees, represents a key driver behind the phenomenon of projectification across industries and sectors.

Our interest in this chapter is to examine the relationship between the state of exception as a rationality of government and projectification as an instrument of policy making through policy pilots. Piloting seeks to mobilise exceptional conditions of time and space, and human and financial resource, as a mechanism for "making real" the future projection of policy. Piloting can thus be seen as a mechanism of coordination and control, which promotes both stability and change – a tool for "achieving change and for reducing complexity in situations where setting goals is difficult" (Sjöblom et al., 2013, p. 6). The question which arises from this is the sustainability of policy changes "tested" through policy pilots, and the relationship between such pilots, often forged in a "state of exception", and the permanent service or organisation which they seek to transform. In turn these questions give rise to further concerns about the place of projectification and exceptional measures within the domains of policy and public administration as well as their implications for broader conceptions of organisational life.

Projectification of Health Policy

This chapter draws on a "policy ethnography" (Dubois, 2009) of a pilot programme located in the National Health Service (NHS) in England. We present an empirically grounded narrative which explores the implementation of the pilot. This initiative was situated in a policy climate of austerity across the UK, which strengthened the longstanding state trend of withdrawal from direct funding and directing of public services, including healthcare. The policy trajectory within healthcare is complex and contradictory. In particular two core tensions sit at the heart of current healthcare policy in England. The first of these tensions is between the desire to make the health service more responsive to local needs, and the concurrent need to maintain accountable national standards of care. The second tension is between the objectives of competition and collaboration within health service provision. These two tensions are intertwined through the policy trajectory that began with the first White Paper produced by the Conservative-Liberal Democrat Coalition Government of 2010–2015: "Greater autonomy will be matched by increased accountability to patients and democratic legitimacy, with a transparent regime of economic regulation and quality inspection to hold providers to account for the results they deliver" (Department of Health, 2010).

This became law two years later through the 2012 Health and Social Care Act (HSCA). The HSCA represented a massive structural reorganisation of the NHS, abolishing two tiers of regional planning organisations (Strategic Health Authorities and Primary Care Trusts) and replacing them with an "arms-length" national commissioning body, "NHS England" (NHSE), and local, clinically-led planning and purchasing organisations, called Clinical Commissioning Groups (CCGs). In so doing, the HSCA expanded the existing market within the English NHS, with a firm division between purchasers and providers of care, by increasing the role of the private sector in the delivery of health care. Notably, the HSCA intensified the competition law to which the NHS in England was subject, thus, in principle, preventing anti-competitive collaboration between providers or collusion between purchasers and providers of services. The intended effect of these changes was to "liberate" the NHS from top-down direction and bureaucracy and generate a genuine market based on local decision-making and competition.

Only two years after the HSCA had been passed into law, however, the challenges posed by fragmentation were already apparent. Making use of its strategic independence from the Department of Health and the government, NHS England (2014) released a new strategy document called the Five Year Forward View (FYFV). Running directly contrary to the competitive spirit of the HSCA, the FYFV envisaged "new models of care" which would require commissioners and providers of care to collaborate to create new care organisations at a local level. This stood in contradiction not only to the HSCA, but almost three decades of health policy since the 1991 Health and Community Care Act which had established competition at the heart of the NHS by creating the split between "purchasers" and "providers" of health and social care. In order to provide "new models of care", providers were being asked to form regional partnerships with would-be competitors. Often commissioners were involved in setting up these "place-based" collaboratives, and then expected to commission these single composite local providers of health care. While this placed all parties at risk of breaching competition law, this was seen by some to be necessary to reintegrate a system fragmented by extreme competition and localism (Gore, Hammond, Bailey, Checkland, & Hodgson, 2018).

In order to encourage provider organisations to engage in this "creative" and "disruptive" work (Checkland, Parkin, Bailey, & Hodgson, 2018), NHS England attached lucrative, time-bound, and conditional funding arrangements through a national programme for "vanguards" who were prepared to experiment and innovate. Alongside national programmes, regional teams of NHS England were given flexibility in their allocation of resources towards "transformation" programmes and projects. The resulting funding programmes mobilised project rationalities in a bid to normalise new ways of working and organising. Despite concerns about the sustainability of the resulting pilots, they have proliferated on the basis of the social and financial capital attached to becoming a successful "pioneer", and the multiple interests and purposes that policy piloting can serve (see Ettelt and Mays, Chapter 1, and Li, Chapter 3, this volume).

Access to Care

The objective of the programme which comprises the empirical setting for this chapter was to extend access to health care. The term "access" to care can be understood in several different ways and has been disaggregated into three elements; "physical" access (the geographical distribution of services and their resulting proximity for users in different areas); "timely" access (the speed with which users can access a particular service, that is, the service responsiveness and availability of appointments); and "choice" (the ability of the service user to choose where and from whom to access a particular service) (Boyle, Appleby, & Harrison, 2010). Each of these elements, when emphasised, foregrounds a particular set of social and political concerns. Historically, socially deprived areas have had poorer *physical* access to General Practitioners (GPs), also known as family doctors in other contexts, for example. This inequality has endured despite repeated policy attempts to address it by incentivising individuals to establish surgeries in particular areas. More recently, *timeliness* of access has been emphasised, not only due to consumerist expectation of responsiveness but also based on arguments that timely access to care, and faster diagnosis time, affects the efficacy of treatment for some conditions, such as cancer. The principle of *choice* has had great rhetorical appeal for policy makers over the last two to three decades in the UK and elsewhere; however, in practice it relies on there being more than one option to the user, which is dependent on many other considerations – the other two dimensions of access, for example, and the resources available to the user, among others. Taken together, this evidence suggests that "access" is not a "technical" matter of simply increasing supply of services, but rather at a conceptual level signifies finding an appropriate "fit" between the needs of users and the capacity of services (Levesque, Harris, & Russell, 2013), which in turn involves deeply political decisions to be made about resource allocation and service design.

Building upon an historical policy analysis in the UK, Simpson et al. (2015) argue that "timely" access has increasingly come to dominate the definition of access mobilised within policy, which aims to provide "advanced access", "same day access", and more recently a "24/7 NHS". In part, this focus reflects the fact that increasing timely access does not generally demand major capital investment in comparison to the other two types – addressing either physical access or choice requires the costly establishment of new services, practices and premises. Timely access on the other hand can be addressed through a reorganisation or extension of existing services. Another reason why timely access has come to dominate political attention is the relative ease with which it can be rendered measurable and such changes communicated to voters.

The Pilot Programme

Our argument concerns the mobilisation of project rationalities through policy pilots and the practical and political consequences this brings. We build our argument drawing upon qualitative data collected as part of a mixed-methods study of one of the transformation programmes launched in 2013 by a regional NHSE team in an area of England.

A competitive invitation was sent out to every provider across the region, inviting them to submit a proposal for extending access to care for a defined population of at least 30,000 people. Initially the programme was allocated £2 million, which was divided between six pilot projects, ranging from £50,000 to £500,000 per project. Pilots were initially given six months to implement services; however, approximately three months in to the programme, the timeline was extended to one year and budgets were doubled. In the words of the programme designer, speaking at a launch event for the programme, the purpose of the programme was to "challenge the usual bureaucracy" that stood in the way of innovation.

Our research began with the launch of the programme, and combined a quantitative impact evaluation with a qualitative process evaluation. The former sought to measure retrospectively the impact of the new services upon health service use. The latter explored the process according to which implementation unfolded, and sought to answer the questions of how services developed in the manner they did, and why some were taken up and became embedded, while others either stalled or failed to start at all. The process evaluation involved 89 interviews with a total of 109 pilot participants, beginning with the leads in each pilot area, and moving on to other key project management and service provider roles. In addition researchers observed key events such as strategy and operational groups and scrutinised documentation relating to the proposals and their implementation. Lastly, the research team participated in quarterly action learning events throughout the duration of the programme, where emerging findings were shared and collective "lessons learned" drawn. In this way the qualitative evaluation can be described as a critical form of "policy ethnography" (Dubois,

2009), in which an active and participatory relationship was established between the research team and the pilot teams. The following discussion builds upon the contextual description already provided, presenting a description which combines findings with reflection upon those findings and upon the experience of "being there" with the pilot teams as they attempted to enact change. The narrative is organised according to the themes that interest us in this chapter: *the access programme and temporality*, and *piloting and project rationalities*, which we then discuss in relation to projectified conceptions of policy and organisation.

Findings

The Access Programme and Temporality

Launched in 2013, in the immediate wake of one of the most significant restructures in the history of the NHS, the access programme capitalised on a moment of transition in a turbulent policy environment. Among the changes that came with the HSCA 2012 was the creation of "NHS England", a quasi-independent institution formed as an intermediary between the Department of Health (DH) and healthcare providers, to develop a national strategy and administer the budget provided by the DH. Initially it was proposed that NHS England would function as a central, national body with the regional teams acting as "spokes" for the central function. However, in 2013 NHS England was still in the early stages of working out what the "national way" of doing things might be, while the CCGs, who were the statutory commissioners of care, were still in the process of becoming established, meaning that the regional "spokes" had a moment of relative autonomy.

This devolved a certain level of autonomy to regional teams, who were able to act with some flexibility in relation to their transformation budgets. However, individual areas had to be prepared to take a risk – to fund innovation from within their existing budgets in order to develop novel solutions which may result in larger reductions in excessive expenditure elsewhere. For example, regional teams were encouraged to work on finding "innovative" solutions to the perceived problem of "inappropriate" health service use among deprived populations. In line with this, launching their programme around "access to care", the regional team in question (hereafter: RT) expressed an interest in finding ways to encourage patients to make more use of primary care rather than going directly to hospital emergency departments with everyday healthcare issues. It had been widely suggested, in media and in government pronouncements, that the recent rise in hospital attendances reflected difficulties patients faced making timely appointments with their GP, forcing them to turn to other, more expensive, acute services. This is a rhetorical narrative that is widely accepted in the health sector in the UK and elsewhere (Kringos, Boerma, van der Zee, & Groenewegen, 2013; Simpson et al., 2015).

The decision was then made to set aside funding to improve access to primary care, and thus save money on secondary care. This was a risky strategy, involving significant financial investment but with the possibility that this expenditure might not be recouped through cost reductions in the usage of acute services. This points to the favourable relationship between political uncertainty and projectification within a context of competitive public service planning and provision. Project and market rationalities here work together, with the RT making a strategic market speculation in an attempt to make substantial budgetary savings. The risk/return relationship here was based upon autonomy granted from the central organisation to the regions, while the policy direction itself was very much in line with the "bright ideas" at the national level; indeed, the programme caught the attention of the Health Secretary and the Prime Minister, who promoted it as an example of pioneering local innovation before the programme had been officially launched.

The RT in question then further transferred this autonomy onto local service providers, by putting out a competitive call for innovative proposals. The RT adopted a permissive approach to the programme, writing the call for proposals in very broad terms, leaving space for interpretation and experimentation by providers. In addition to explicitly encouraging pilots to move quickly and "challenge bureaucracy", the RT also sent the proposal directly to providers, rather than relying on the standard bureaucratic process which would have been to cascade down through local commissioners (CCGs). Further, in allowing individuals just two weeks to put bids together, the RT ensured that only particular individuals, those with ideas and networks that could be mobilised quickly, would be able to submit proposals. The temporal structure of the programme itself was similarly intense, with pilots given four weeks to launch services – which in many cases required the development of an entirely new way of working, including the creation of new organisations or inter-organisational collaborations, using new technologies, sharing patient data – often for the first time – and requiring new governance arrangements to be drawn up from scratch. The short timescales were combined with regular reporting requirements, through which pilots were encouraged to focus upon outputs from the very beginning. These timescales can be seen as the RT "hedging" their bet by forcing pilots to regulate the degree to which they could experiment and instead focus upon those things most likely to show demonstrable, quantifiable results in a short amount of time.

We therefore see temporal dynamics operating at several different levels through the establishment and initiation of the programme as well as within the broader context:

1. Institutional level; the turbulent policy environment, where major structural change led to a temporary and situated "liminality" (Henfridsson & Yoo, 2014), which was perceived by some as an opportunity to do something different;
2. Meta-organisational level; the opportunism of the regional team in taking advantage of this liminality by initiating a pilot programme with short lead

in times, vague objectives, and bypassing the usual bureaucratic chain of command;

3. Local level; individuals and organisations at the local level incentivised by the financial and symbolic capital (e.g. status) associated with the programme mobilise quickly through existing networks;
4. Project level; once the programme begins, the temporal apparatus of the project form directs action towards the timely accumulation of quantifiable outputs (Koch, 2004).

We now move to explore the project level in more detail, in particular, measurement and its effects within the pilots.

Piloting and Project Rationalities

The programme brief emphasised in general the aim of "extending access". We suggest that this general wording was in part meant to encourage a productive sense of ambiguity for pilots, encouraging local creativity and experimentation (c.f. Ettelt et al., 2014). This capitalised upon the complexity and ambiguity inherent in the term "access" itself (see above).

Within the short time frames of the access programme studied here, timely access very quickly emerged as the dominant understanding of access to be pursued in the majority of the projects. Four out of six projects incorporated timely access as the main component of their project from the start, mirroring national policy debates. So while in principle, the ambiguity of the term "access to care" offers scope for diversity of responses from the pilot teams, the regulative effect of project rationalities, both in terms of short timelines and emphasis on measurable delivery, effectively delimits the imaginative scope of the projects.

With regards to timely access, the outcome data of most interest to the RT, and therefore the pilots, was a shift in the number of service users attending acute services to instead attend the newly extended GP services. This was the core assumption upon which the speculation of the RT had been made; that an increase in the supply of provision in one health sector could lead to reduced demand, and consequent cost saving, in another. Focussing on the quantification of the service from the start meant that the need to establish a working service quickly – ensuring that service users were attending the extended access service instead of going to acute services – was the dominant concern. In order to save time and money, each pilot joined several existing practices together in order to create a "hub" organisation through which the extended service could be provided. However, this required each component practice to share their patient data with the hub, in order for the extended service at the hub to mirror the service a patient would receive at their home practice. Both technical and governance challenges were encountered when seeking to share patient data, reflecting a lack of technical inter-operability that existed between the IT systems in use in each practice, and legal governance issues concerning the sharing of confidential data outside of patients' home practice. In light of the pressure upon them to demonstrate measurable outcomes in a short space of time, each pilot sought temporary solutions to these problems. In some cases this involved elaborate technical and governance "workarounds", which are adaptive practices designed to make something work in context, either by adapting the intervention or by adapting the situation to which it is being applied (Cresswell, Mozaffar, Lee, Williams, & Sheikh, 2017; Gasser, 1986). Although they could be effective in terms of achieving the immediate goal, workarounds often made the operation of the services extremely complex and time-consuming – with clinicians working across several platforms, each with their own security protocols, to draw information from separate systems in the course of a consultation. Despite short-term effectiveness, such workarounds meant that the pilot itself represented poor preparation for sustainable long-term delivery of the service. Moreover, workarounds are very often comprised of informal and unsanctioned work practices (Star, 1991). This enacts a rupture between project work and routine work by rendering invisible the work necessary to coordinate the new practice; again, with implications for the adoption and sustainability of innovation (see Jensen et al., Chapter 6, this volume). Beyond this practical organisational concern, the potentially unsanctioned nature of workarounds presents problems for the bureaucratic delimitation of authority and accountability and this can lead to questionable standards being adopted. In our case, for example, the work that was undertaken to create a clinical record that could be seen and edited by all relevant clinicians was achieved at the expense of a comprehensive process for informing patients of the proposed changes and gaining their consent.

The ingenuity displayed in developing such workarounds, and the willingness of service providers to tolerate not only complexity but also bureaucratic and ethical ambiguity in pursuit of the pilot goals, exemplifies the intensive effort, passion and commitment generated in the exceptional conditions of a pilot – with teams "responsibilised" (Rose, 1989; see also Hall, Chapter 2, this volume) through the project form to "deliver" in the face of significant challenges. Moreover, the enforced technical rationality of the project, itself an effect of the intense temporal order of the project and the need for quantifiable output, meant that the service that got delivered was not necessarily "what worked", but what could be "made to work" within the time available, in spite of any problems encountered. This signals a problem with the state of exception invoked through the mobilisation of project rationalities within policy pilots, which we will now discuss in more detail.

Discussion: Policy Making in a State of Exception

The intensity of resource expenditure within the access programme was evidenced in the substantial financial investment made by the RT, the temporal mechanisms they built into the design and implementation of the pilot programme, and the intensive human effort that this generated. This combined with the attempt by the RT to suspend the ordinary state of things, in bypassing bureaucratic channels, and to create the "state of exception" within which the pilots operated. This requirement was passed on to pilot teams, who were required to suspend in part their own "day jobs", as well as suspend what might be considered "routine" considerations of formal health care organisation; detailed bureaucratic procedures for addressing quality, operability and accountability. More intensive and extensive working was demanded within the pilot projects to establish new arrangements, solve problems and deliver against a demanding timescale. However, the strategy was at least partially "successful" for the RT, as they were able to demonstrate measurable success against a key metric (reduced hospital activity in the areas where extended access was implemented), which led to a push for the spread of extended access, as timely access, across the region.

The mobilisation of project rationalities through piloting via the state of exception has several implications for theories of policy making and public organisation. Our case suggests firstly that policy formulation and implementation through piloting can become shaped by the need to deliver measurable outputs in a short space of time. Questions of what "should" be done, which might ordinarily be subject to lengthy deliberation, become relegated behind the question of what can be delivered quickly, what can be rendered measurable in this timescale, and practical questions of how it might be implemented. This would appear to support arguments that projectification entails a kind of de-politicisation (see Ettelt and Mays, Chapter 1; Hall, Chapter 2; Li, Chapter 3; Chaib, Chapter 4; and Lofgren and Allen, Chapter 5, all this volume) where deliberation over policy orientation, or the political implications of how the problem and goals are defined, are squeezed out in favour of technical questions of delivery. While the case offers evidence of this tendency, at the same time, piloting also appears to give influence in shaping policy to non-political actors. While scope is limited, not all of the pilots followed the same route or interpreted the question of access in the same way, and some drew on the funding to pursue other local policy priorities, demonstrating a kind of "street-level" policy entrepreneurship (Bailey et al., 2017). We suggest that further work is therefore needed to tease out the relationship between politicisation, de-politicisation and implications of the projectification of policy on local actors and practitioners.

Secondly, in addition to the enforcement of a technical rationality that regulated pilot efforts, the exclusive focus on quantifiable outputs also excluded components of pilots that demonstrated only qualitative benefit. This means that services that either did not show any measurable success within the time given, or had only qualitative data to support their success, struggled to achieve recognition from the RT and were thus poorly placed to access future funds. Consequently, there is a sense of "myopia" (Nair & Howlett, 2017) produced through piloting, and a consequent failure to learn from both success and failure. If policies are spread after piloting, as in our case, then it is likely that this myopia would result in a failure to understand and accommodate the heterogeneity among different areas and providers. This could likely have several effects at the spread phase, such as fragmentation, resistance and the potential to produce or reproduce inequalities between regions. Further work is needed on what happens in the policy process *after* piloting to understand the effects of this myopic vision.

Thirdly, the intensity of work in this "state of exception" and the propensity to rely on workarounds in our case left substantial question marks over the long term sustainability of the service as piloted. This was true even in those pilots that demonstrated success against key metrics. If piloting can be seen as a kind of policy experiment (Campbell, 1969; Jowell, 2003), then this raises questions over the "validity" of the experiment, because the object that was formed out of the process was shaped not only by the project rationalities imposed upon the programme, but by the contingencies and circumstances encountered through the experiment itself. In this instance, projectification appears to produce both uncertainty and precarity, as temporary, intense, and risky working arrangements shape the experience of policy recipients, and the policy objects they form (Bailey et al., 2017). One consequence is an undermining of the logic of evidence-based policy through "piloting for experimentation" (c.f. Ettelt et al., 2014). A further danger is that this intensified working becomes routinely expected as the pilot becomes mainstream, or at least there is the risk that this shapes over-optimistic calculations about the likely effect of rolling-out arrangements piloted in this way.

Lastly, the extremely tight time frames through which the programme was designed and launched worked to exclude all but the most motivated, ambitious and well connected participants. This questions the "reliability" of the experiment, as both the existing capital endowments and the "entrepreneurial zeal" of the pilot leads was an important mediator in the enthusiastic uptake and commitment to the programme within the time-limited terms offered by the funders. Projectification in this instance appears to constitute the reproduction of political and social capital. Once again this works to undermine the logic of evidence-based policy through piloting, in this case appearing to more closely resemble what Ettelt et al. (2014) describe as "early adoption".

These points prompt reflection on what might be considered a "success" or "failure" when it comes to policy piloting, which following the logic of experimentation ought to be a key concern for policy makers. Following McConnell (2010), we might think about the judgement of policy success or failure as comprised of three elements: policy, process and politics. Policy relates to the overarching policy goal, process to the means adopted to achieve that goal, and politics to broader successes or failures such as boosts to reputation or legitimacy. Reflecting on how these play out in this case, it can be argued that there was some limited policy success against the key metric of shifting activity away from hospitals. Process success, however, in this case is much harder to define. On the one hand we have shown the productive effects of the process, for example, in the temporal mechanisms mobilised by the funders. However, we have also demonstrated the wider concerns that are brought into play by the mobilisation of such processes. It is therefore not simply that processes worked for some and not others, or in some circumstances and not others (c.f. Pawson, 2009), but rather that these processes were simultaneously productive *and* "dangerous" (Foucault, 1996). The funding of the programme built upon a risky and opportunistic investment of funds by one of the "spokes" of a centralised national organisation. This process demonstrated some success, but one does not imagine such a process would become widely or overtly promoted by the central administration. Subsequent policy changes which have removed power from these "spokes" by combining local teams into larger regions and cutting their budgets is perhaps indicative of a concern over degrees of devolved autonomy. This brings us to the last concern – political success. For the programme designers, the limited success of the programme was capitalised upon in external communications, and the programme was widely understood, locally and nationally, to have "succeeded". The policy goals themselves were pushed across the region (with a fraction of the funding received under the pilot conditions), and the chief architect of the programme engineered a significant career move on the back of this.

These points serve to underline the problems outlined here and elsewhere with evidence-based policy in power-saturated contexts, where interventions are not just composed of practical (re)arrangements, but perform a social order, and the success or otherwise of a project relates to more than just technical mastery.

Conclusion

Our case suggests that policy pilots can be seen as a peculiar type of project with a distinct logic of continuity–discontinuity, which separates them from a more conventional managerial understanding of piloting as an "initiation phase" in the implementation trajectory (Van de Ven, Angle, & Poole, 2000). The effects discussed above, in terms of the production and reproduction of political and social capital, lead us to the claim that the state of exception enacted through policy piloting acts as a mechanism of authorisation through which contestable policy objects can be formed and disseminated and a new class of political elites can emerge (du Gay, 2008). This makes piloting potent in a political context described in terms of flattened hierarchies and an absence of traditional bureaucracy as formal and effective authority (Clegg, Harris, & Höpfl, 2011). In our case, the "state of exception" authorised novel action, by mobilising disparate network resources around the emergence of a shared goal, encouraging opportunism and competition which act as levers in flattened hierarchies, and, imposing a technical rationality on entrepreneurial actors drawn by the promise of experimentation, innovation, autonomy and influence.

This suggests that projectification can be seen as a kind of substitute for traditional bureaucracy, which is not just about enabling action, but about managing uncertainty in the attempted projecting of the future which policy making undertakes. Against this practical utility is the somewhat dangerous informality through which policy piloting can proceed. Bureaucratic authorisation proceeds according to the assumption that limits must be placed upon executive freedom to act in order for collective work to be undertaken in an effective and accountable manner (du Gay, 2005; du Gay & Vikkelsø, 2016). If projectification through piloting results in authorisation governed not by ethics or effectiveness but by a highly situated and technical rationality, then further attention is required to the possible relegation of the values and practices of formal organisation in the business of state.

Note

1 *Acknowledgements:* This research was funded by the National Institute for Health Research (NIHR) Collaboration for Leadership in Applied Health Research and Care (NIHR CLAHRC Greater Manchester). The views expressed in this article are those of the authors and not necessarily those of the National Health Service (NHS), the NIHR, or the Department of Health and Social Care.

References

Agamben, G. (2005). *State of exception*. London, England: University of Chicago Press.

Bailey, S., Checkland, K., Hodgson, D., McBride, A., Elvey, R., Parkin, S., Rothwell, K., & Pierides, D. (2017). The policy work of piloting: Mobilising and managing conflict and ambiguity in the English NHS. *Soc Sci Med*, 179, 210–217.

Boyle, S., Appleby, J., & Harrison, A. (2010). *A rapid view of access to care*. London, England: The King's Fund.

Burch, M., & Wood, B. (1983). *Public policy in Britain*. Oxford, England: Martin Robertson.

Campbell, D. T. (1969). Reforms as experiments. *American psychologist*, 24(4), 409.

Checkland, K., Parkin, S., Bailey, S., & Hodgson, D. (2018). Institutional work and innovation in the NHS: The role of creating and disrupting. In *Managing improvement in healthcare* (pp. 237–254). Basingstoke, England: Palgrave Macmillan.

Clegg, S., & Courpasson, D. (2004). Political hybrids: Tocquevillean views on project organizations. *Journal of Management Studies*, 41(4), 525–547.

Clegg, S., Harris, M., & Höpfl, H. (2011). *Managing modernity: Beyond bureaucracy?*Oxford, England: Oxford University Press.

Cresswell, K. M., Mozaffar, H., Lee, L., Williams, R., & Sheikh, A. (2017). Workarounds to hospital electronic prescribing systems: A qualitative study in English hospitals. *BMJ Quality & Safety*, 26(7), 542–551. doi:10.1136/bmjqs-2015-005149

Department of Health (2010). *Equity and excellence: Liberating the NHS*. London, England: Stationary Office

du Gay, P. (2005). *The values of bureaucracy*. Oxford, England: Oxford University Press.

du Gay, P. (2008). Keyser Süze elites: Market populism and the politics of institutional change. *The Sociological Review*, 56(1 suppl), 80–102. doi:10.1111/j.1467-954X.2008.00763.x

du Gay, P., & Vikkelsø, S. (2016). *For formal organization: The past in the present and future of organization theory*. Oxford, England: Oxford University Press.

Dubois, V. (2009). Towards a critical policy ethnography: Lessons from fieldwork on welfare control in France. *Critical Policy Studies*, 3(2), 221–239. doi:10.1080/19460170903385684

Eskinsmyth, C. (2002). Project organization, embeddedness and risk in magazine publishing. *Regional Studies*, 36(3), 229–243.

Ettelt, S., Mays, N., & Allen, P. (2014). The multiple purposes of policy piloting and their consequences: Three examples from National Health and Social Care Policy in England. *Journal of Social Policy*, 44(02), 319–337.

Foucault, M. (1991). Governmentality. In G. Burchell, C. Gordon, & P. Miller (Eds.), *The Foucault effect: Studies in governmentality* (pp. 87–104). Chicago, IL: University of Chicago Press.

Foucault, M. (1996). Talk Show (L. Hochroth & J. Johnston, Trans.). In S. Lotringer (Ed.), *Foucault live: Collected interviews 1961–1984* (pp. 146–170). New York, NY: Semiotext(e).

Fred, M., & Hall, P. (2017). A projectified public administration: How projects in Swedish local governments become instruments for political and managerial concerns. *Statsvetenskaplig tidskrift*, 119(1), 185–205.

Gasser, L. (1986). The integration of computing and routine work. *ACM Trans. Inf. Syst.*, 4(3), 205–225. doi:10.1145/214427.214429

Gore, O., Hammond, J., Bailey, S., Checkland, K., & Hodgson, D. (2018). Not every public sector is an institutional field: Evidence from the recent overhaul of the English National Health Service. *Public Management Review*. doi:10.1080/14719037.2018.1503703

Gregg, M. (2011). *Work's intimacy*. Cambridge, England: Polity.

Harrison, S., & Wood, B. (1999). Designing health service organization in the UK, 1968 to 1998: From blueprint to bright idea and "manipulated emergence". *Public Administration*, 77(4), 751–768.

Henfridsson, O., & Yoo, Y. (2014). The liminality of trajectory shifts in institutional entrepreneurship. *Organization Science*, 25(3), 932–950. doi:10.1287/orsc.2013.0883

Hodgson, D. E. (2002). Disciplining the professional: The case of project management. *Journal of Management Studies*, 39(6), 803–821.

Hodgson, D. E., & Cicmil, S. (2006). *Making projects critical*. Basingstoke, England: Palgrave Macmillan.

Jensen, C., Johansson, S., & Löfström, M. (2013). The project organization as a policy tool in implementing welfare reforms in the public sector. *The International Journal of Health Planning and Management*, 28(1), 122–137. doi:10.1002/hpm.2120

Jowell, R. (2003). *"Trying it out": The role of "pilots" in policy making*. London, England: Stationery Office.

Koch, C. (2004). The tyranny of projects: Teamworking, knowledge production and management in consulting engineering. *Economic and Industrial Democracy*, 25(2), 277–300.

Kringos, D., Boerma, W., van der Zee, J., & Groenewegen, P. (2013). Europe's strong primary care systems are linked to better population health but also to higher health spending. *Health Affairs*, 32(4), 686–694. doi:10.1377/hlthaff.2012.1242

Levesque, J. F., Harris, M. F., & Russell, G. (2013). Patient-centred access to health care: Conceptualising access at the interface of health systems and populations. *International Journal for Equity in Health*, 12(18). doi:10.1186/1475-9276-12-18

Lindgren, M., Packendorff, J., & Sergi, V. (2014). Thrilled by the discourse, suffering through the experience: Emotions in project-based work. *Human Relations*, 67(11), 1383–1412. doi:10.1177/0018726713520022

Lundin, R., & Söderholm, A. (1998). Conceptualising a projectified society: Discussion of an eco-institutional approach to a theory on temporary organizations. In R. Lundin & C. Midler (Eds.), *Projects as arenas for renewal and learning processes* (pp. 13–23). Boston, MA: Kluwer.

Mackenzie, M., Blamey, A., & Hanlon, P. (2006). Using and generating evidence: Policy makers' reflections on commissioning and learning from the Scottish Health Demonstration Projects. *Evidence & Policy*, 2(2), 211–226.

Martin, S., & Sanderson, I. (1999). Evaluating public policy experiments: Measuring outcomes, monitoring processes or managing pilots? *Evaluation*, 5(3), 245–258.

McConnell, A. (2010). Policy success, policy failure and grey areas in-between. *Journal of Public Policy*, 30(3), 345–362. doi:10.1017/S0143814X10000152

Morris, P. W. G. (1997). *The management of projects*. London, England: Thomas Telford.

Nair, S., & Howlett, M. (2016). Meaning and power in the design and development of policy experiments. *Futures*, 76, 67–74. doi:10.1016/j.futures.2015.02.008

Nair, S., & Howlett, M. (2017). Policy myopia as a source of policy failure: Adaptation and policy learning under deep uncertainty. *Policy & Politics*, 45(1), 103–118. doi:10.1332/030557316x14788776017743

NHS England (2014). *Five year forward view*. London, England: Stationery Office.

Pawson, R. (2009). *Evidence-based policy: A realist perspective*. London, England: Sage.

Peters, T. J., & Waterman, R. H. (1995). *In search of excellence: Lessons from America's best-run companies*. London, England: HarperCollins.

Rose, N. (1989). *Governing the soul: The shaping of the private self* (1999, 2nd ed.). London, England: Routledge.

Sahlin-Andersson, K. (2002). Project management as boundary work: Dilemmas of defining and delimiting. In K. Sahlin-Andersson & A. Söderholm (Eds.), *Beyond project management: New perspectives on the temporary–permanent dilemma* (pp. 241–260). Copenhagen, Denmark: Copenhagen Business School Press.

Sanderson, I. (2002). Evaluation, policy learning and evidence-based policy making. *Public Administration*, 80(1), 1–22.

Schmitt, C. (1985). *Political theology*. Cambridge, MA: MIT Press.

Simpson, J. M., Checkland, K., Snow, S., Voorhees, J., Rothwell, K., & Esmail, A. (2015). Access to general practice in England: Time for a policy rethink. *British Journal of General Practice*, 65(640), 606–607. doi:10.3399/bjgp15X687601

Sjöblom, S., Löfgren, K., & Godenhjelm, S. (2013). Projectified politics: Temporary organisations in a public context. *Scandinavian Journal of Public Administration*, 17(2), 3–12.

Star, S. L. (1991). The sociology of the invisible: The primacy of work in the writings of Anselm Strauss. In D. Maines (Ed.), *Social organization and social process: Essays in honor of Anselm Strauss* (pp. 265–283). New York, NY: Aldine de Gruyter.

Van de Ven, A. H., Angle, H. L., & Poole, M. S. (2000). *Research on the management of innovation: The Minnesota studies*. Oxford, England: Oxford University Press on Demand.

8

PROJECT GOVERNANCE IN AN EMBEDDED STATE

Opportunities and Challenges[1]

Sebastian Godenhjelm and Stefan Sjöblom

UNIVERSITY OF HELSINKI

Christian Jensen

UNIVERSITY OF GOTHENBURG

Projectification, interpreted as an increasing reliance on project-related principles, techniques, and procedures, is a consequence of several challenges facing the modern welfare state. Torfing and colleagues summarise the essential challenges in arguing that:

> We have seen a gradual widening of the temporal and spatial horizons for strategic action in the field of public policymaking. As such, it is becoming increasingly clear that many policy problems are ill-defined and that public problem-solving involves a growing number of choices about who to involve, when, where and how.
>
> *(Torfing, Peters, Pierre, & Sorensen, 2012, p. 229)*

In response to these challenges, civil servants, politicians, and managers increasingly perceive the use of projects as an organisational solution to strengthen the problem-solving capacity of public sector organisations. Furthermore, new policy fields such as IT policies, innovation policies, regional policies, and climate policies have emerged. As many scholars have observed, projects are important tools for implementing these policies and as a consequence, responsible organisations use norms, rules, and the vocabulary associated with project management in order to describe and make sense of organisational practices (Cicmil & Hodgson, 2006; Fred, 2018; Godenhjelm, 2016; Jacobsson, Pierre, & Sundström, 2015, p. 12; Sjöblom, Löfgren, & Godenhjelm, 2013).

We take these observations as a starting point for our analysis and argue that projectification might provide at least partial solutions to the aforementioned governance problems but may also generate new challenges to public policy making and problem solving. This is mainly because public sector projects are embedded in a complex institutional context. Administrative agencies and organisations follow an operational logic based on permanency, coordination, and continuity. Ideal perceptions of the project rationality, on the contrary, depict project organisations as valuable devices for responding to the need for adaptation and "just-in-time" delivery (Hodgson, 2004; Sjöblom et al., 2013). In other words, there are contradictory forces pulling in different directions when it comes to adopting project principles and procedures in public policy making. In doing so, governments thus face a twofold problem. Governments have to maintain their capacity to coordinate policy development and implementation while enhancing collaborative capacities, by engaging municipalities, regions, civil society, and market organisations in the policy making process (cf. Christensen & Laegreid, 2007, p. 1063).

With respect to public policy making, "embeddedness" is thus essentially about the complex interaction between numerous actors, administrative levels, ideals, and organising principles through which policy processes evolve. As a consequence, public sector projects – more distinctly than in the private sphere – are organisational hybrids combining various operational forms of logic, inter-organisational patterns, and policy goals (cf. Johanson & Vakkuri, 2018). They rest on multiple sources of legitimacy and they provide multiple opportunities for legitimising and evaluating their performance.

According to governance theory, favourable restructuring, innovation, and change are conditional on the institutional and collaborative qualities of the actors involved (cf. Ansell & Gash, 2007). Following this line of reasoning, projectification may affect key institutional qualities of the politico-administrative system in ways that either strengthen or weaken governments' capacities to develop and implement policy. The purpose of this chapter is to specify the institutional factors through which projectification may affect the making of public policy. We argue that these factors fall under three dimensions especially pertinent to embedded public structures. In the next section, we specify the dimensions with reference to key features of public sector projectification. The dimensions will also structure the reminder of this chapter.

The aim of our study is to develop a framework for analysing how projectification may affect government capacities for policy development and implementation in embedded public contexts, thereby also contributing to a more pluralistic understanding of projects beyond the traditional project management heritage.

Analysing Projectification in Embedded Public Structures: Three Dimensions

The growing projectification of the public sector coincides with a combination of several societal developments, such as new social challenges that create fiscal, social, and political pressures. These challenges include ageing populations, jobless growth, and growing social inequalities, but also the problem of implementing new ideas and solutions such as sustainability, resilience, or innovation. Such multifarious policy concepts reflect the increasingly "wicked" or ungovernable character of societal problems, but especially in a public context, they also show that building institutional capacity for dealing with demands and expectations require both short and long-term perspectives. As further elaborated below, we argue that in assessing the options for strengthening government capacities by means of projects, three key dimensions of organisational life are particularly essential to bear in mind. These are: (a) the *context*, that is, the wider organisational and institutional environment of public sector projects; (b) *temporality*, that is, the temporal fit between projects and permanent organisations; and (c) *strategy*, or how policymakers act and react in response to project ideals and activities.

The three dimensions are also important because reform agendas of Western bureaucracies since the 1980s have had a considerable impact on the context, the temporal scope, and the strategic alternatives of public sector organisations in a wider sense. As a result of the decentralised New Public Management (NPM) and New Public Governance (NPG) reforms of recent decades, new institutional structures in which horizontal governance ideals supplement traditional vertical problem-solving capabilities have emerged. Furthermore, different forms of international, national, and local fund and support systems supplement or replace the existing tax-based financial structure (Büttner & Leopold, 2016; Sulkunen, 2006). Examples of such funding systems are the European Union (EU) structural funds, national innovation systems, and development programs, as well as large infrastructure projects carried out as public–private partnerships. By means of temporary funding, policies at supranational as well as national levels translate and convert high political ambitions concerning sustainability, inclusion, growth, and innovation into various types of development actions and interventions. Public sector projects have thus become symbols of flexibility, innovation, and something post-bureaucratic, which resonates well with the values and ideals of the aforementioned reform agendas (Fred, 2018, p. 32; Godenhjelm, 2016, p. 23).

However, although NPM and NPG reforms have pushed central governments to decentralise decision making, in the 2000s they have especially strengthened their coordinative capacities by means of Whole-of-Government approaches and other means for accountability and control (Christensen & Laegreid, 2007). When assessing the effects of public sector projectification, it is thus important to bear in mind the wider structural and institutional context of the project. Reforms and management principles do not affect all policy fields, administrative levels, and organisations alike. The *context* – our first key dimension – is important, especially for revealing possible contradictory effects of projectification on capacities for policy development and implementation.

Furthermore, capacities for policy development and implementation is not a question of either short-term or long-term ability, but both. As a consequence, *temporality* is a second key dimension of embedded public structures. Defining the temporal scale is important, as projects can be means for acceleration, thus affecting the initiation, implementation, and termination of the project as such. However, temporality is also a matter of synchronisation, that is, the temporal relationship between societal institutions. Supranational institutions, national governments, policy programs, funding systems, and comprehensive evaluation frameworks may operate according to diverse time frames.

Finally, contextual and temporal features affect the third important dimension, namely *strategy*. Strategies are not only a matter of how project leaders seek to reduce temporal and contextual uncertainties and to increase the discretion of the project organisation, but also of how authorities at different levels act as financiers and specifiers when they fund projects with the intention of achieving long-term effects. Policymakers have to manage potentially contradictory strategies, management principles, and policy recommendations simultaneously. In other words a multitude of strategies are available but not all strategies necessarily enhance capacities for policy development and implementation. In the following sections, we further elaborate on the specific institutional factors related to the three dimensions through which projectification is likely to affect government capacities for policy development and implementation.

The Contextual Dimension: Projects in Embedded Public Environments

The environmental – or contextual – impact on organisations is one of the classical issues in organisational theory. The idea that external factors may have a strong impact on the internal behaviour of an organisation is more or less a truism and countless studies have shown that contingencies such as uncertainty, complexity, and the allocation of authority and resources affect the inner workings of organisations (e.g., Mintzberg, 1979). Furthermore, institutional theory emphasises that institutional aspects of the environment such as traditions, norms, values, and procedures affect the organisation (e.g., Scott, 2008). Lately, the concept of embeddedness has increased in importance, stressing that the organisation and its context is not only a matter of internal–external relationships. In fact, all organisational actions take place in a more or less complex societal web of structures, resources, actors, and values (Engwall, 2003; Jacobsson et al., 2015). Given the increasing speed that organisational transformations are facing today, project research focus should be broadened beyond the projects isolated from their contexts (Lundin & Steinthórsson, 2003).

From an explicitly institutional point of view, Sydow and Staber (2002) refer to embeddedness as both the simple presence of particular institutions necessary for survival, innovation, and change, and the forms through which meaning is constructed, trust is built and knowledge is exchanged. Perceived as being dependent on the reproductive actions of agents, such institutions can be formal organisations such as training institutes, associations, and state agencies, but also formal standards and regulations as well as informal rules, shared norms, and taken-for-granted beliefs (Sydow & Staber, 2002, p. 218).

Recently Jacobsson et al. (2015) have added an important dimension to a conventional understanding of institutional embeddedness by emphasising the embeddedness of the state as such, thereby drawing attention to the capacities of the core executive for governing by organising, that is, steering by means of institutional design. A common assertion has been that once coordinative institutions are in place, no additional steering is necessary (Jacobsson et al., 2015, p. 4). Such an assertion, however, neglects variations in the capacity of government institutions to operate within collaborative structures. What are the most important factors from a contextual point of view, and which are likely to affect government capacities for project-driven policy development and implementation?

The Interface Between Project Organisations and Government Agencies

According to ideal conceptions, project organisations are able to operate more efficiently in complex environments compared to traditional bureaucratic structures (e.g., Wirick, 2009). Through a decoupling of issues and a strong focus on outputs, they are attractive tools for action. They also imply an element of order in complex and at times "wicked" environments. The potential strengths of project organisations not only include their ability to generate new products, procedures, practices, or new ways of thinking but they also provide opportunities to create new organisational capabilities within highly institutionalised structures.

However, the practices and mechanisms for interaction between project organisations and permanent structures are thus essential not only for the effectiveness but also for the democratic qualities of public policy making. Although previous research suggests that many projects fail to create value and support learning beyond their own context (e.g., Godenhjelm, 2016; Jensen, Johansson, & Löfström, 2017; Sjöblom, Andersson, Marsden, & Skerratt, 2012), we have limited knowledge of the interactions between projects and permanent organisations and the extent to which they actually facilitate problem solving and long-term policy development. Particularly the significance of government institutions and agencies in these embedded processes is a rather neglected issue in both contemporary project management literature and in the extensive governance debate.

In order to enhance agency, renewal, and change, government institutions cannot solely facilitate at arm's length or by following a hands-off strategy. Neither can they restrict their role to that of a collaborative actor among others (cf. Jacobsson et al., 2015, p. 4). Government agencies have to enhance trust in values that support the desired direction of the policy processes in question. Furthermore, government agencies should be able to meta-govern the processes by affecting the institutional design in ways that support the direction of change. They are also expected to facilitate the micro-level implementation of policies, that is, to enhance the capacity for change of individual agencies and collaborating actors within the partnerships, projects and networks through which individual policies are implemented, thereby also facilitating the long-term utilisation and consolidation of specific changes and innovations. Means for micro-level facilitation can include information, participatory procedures, collaborative practices, and evaluation. The notion of microsteering is especially important for defining and assessing the effects of inter-linking mechanisms between temporary and permanent organisations in a public context.

There is a considerable body of research showing that managing common pool resources can benefit from actors agreeing on common rules and practices and from building common knowledge (Carlsson & Berkes, 2005; Gardiner, Ostrom, & Walker, 1990). However, comprehensive reviews of the literature, particularly on natural resource management, also indicate that no structural characteristics such as density of relations, degree of cohesiveness, or interconnectivity between actors present a monotonically increasing positive effect on processes of importance for resource governance (Bodin & Crona, 2009, p. 366). Favouring one characteristic is likely to occur at the expense of others. This is also likely to be the case concerning projects in a more general sense.

Although it is common to view change as an organisational response to exogenous forces, complexities also emerge endogenously as government institutions and other actors have partially new roles to play in the collaborative governance game (Pierre, 2012; Schneider, 2012). Even though projects and other collaborative forms of organising are sources of strong synergetic potential, they also run the risk of contributing to diversity and fragmentation due to competing values and interests among the actors involved and a lack of facilitation mechanisms at the interface of politico-administrative and collaborative structures. Transferring knowledge gained from EU-funded Leader or Regional Conservation Partnership Program (RCPP) projects to permanent organisations and achieving institutional change that lead to sustainable results have been deemed particularly challenging (Munck af Rosenschöld, 2017, p. 59). Godenhjelm, Lundin and Sjöblom (2015, p. 342) argue that traditional sequencing concepts frequently used in private sector projects lack a final sequence that would enable effective mechanisms for the knowledge transfer required in a public sector setting. This highlights the need for contextually sensitive interlinking mechanisms in the final phases of the project so that long-term outcomes from temporary outputs can be created, successful project ventures can be identified and implemented, and unsuccessful ventures buried (Godenhjelm, 2016, p. 70).

Strength of Coordinative Actions

Another crucial contextual factor follows from variations between policy fields that coevolve with projects or project-based organising (cf. Sydow, Lindkvist, & Defilippi, 2004, p. 1478). Policy fields vary in terms of policy styles and traditions. As a consequence, project forms of organising also vary in significance. As the state was "rolled back" by neoliberal reform, or "rolled out" by outsourcing public governance (Rhodes, 2017, p. 214), new policy fields such as innovation policies, regional development policies, sustainability policies, and climate policies emerged, resting on strong demands for resources from different societal sectors. These developments have undoubtedly been an important driver behind projectification in these particular policy fields (cf. Fred, 2018; Godenhjelm, Munck af Rosenschiöld, Kuokkanen, Andersson, & Sjöblom, 2012).

Since the financial crisis of the early 1990s, there has been a constant need for increased strategic agility (OECD, 2010) and for securing a flexible adaptation of the governance systems to external and internal challenges. The multi-functional and cross-sectoral nature of policy problems has emphasised the need for coordination at all administrative levels by means of approaches such as program management, "Whole of Government" and comprehensive models of evaluation (Bouckaert, Ormond, & Peters, 2000). The purpose is to provide flexible instruments for eliminating contradictions and tensions between different policies but also a means for de-politicising decisions by making them a matter of operational management (Sjöblom & Godenhjelm, 2009). Programs, networks, and working-groups serve as inter-organisational and cross-sectoral instruments in order to provide political and administrative support for strategic initiatives (cf. Bouckaert et al., 2000). Not only will the strength of governmental coordinative actions cause differences between policy fields. What is more important, they also affect the discretion of government agencies for engaging in projects on a collaborative basis as well as the discretion of the individual projects.

In other words, coordinative actions are likely to affect the inclination and the strategies of government agencies for meta-governing and micro-steering project-based policy development and implementation. Embedded public sector projects are thus continuously coupled and decoupled to government structures by means of numerous mechanisms for interaction and coordination. Only multi-dimensional conceptualisations can capture the complexity of the contextual embeddedness that characterise contemporary project-based policy development and implementation (cf. Sydow et al., 2004, p. 1479). The two key contextual factors identified above – the interface between project and permanent structures and the strength of coordinative actions – are further affected by the temporal features of the institutional environment in which projects operate.

The Temporal Dimension: Tensions Between Temporary and Permanent Organisations

The Project Management Institute's (2004, p. 5) Body of Knowledge, as well as its Government extension (Project Management Institute, 2006, p. 5), define projects as "a temporary endeavour undertaken to create a unique product, service, or result". The European Court of Auditors (2009, p. 7) present a similar definition, stating that a project is a "non-divisible operation, delimited in terms of schedule and budget, and placed under the responsibility of an organisation which implements, closest to the field, the resources allocated to the intervention". Time and temporality are thus central elements in most operational project definitions. The definitions also raise the question of whether these operational definitions can take into consideration the wide spectrum of sectors and societal complexity in which projects operate.

In their seminal work on the theory of the temporary organisation Lundin and Söderholm (1995, p. 438) state that time, and time horizons that limit the temporary organisation, are crucial for the project and fundamental in order to understand temporary organisations. They convey a sense of urgency about the task, signalling that action is necessary. The authors argue that time can be viewed either as linear, cyclical, or spiral. According to their view, permanent organisations generally follow a linear perception of time that represents something eternal. On the other hand, temporary organisations are always running out of time. Despite this temporal limitation, according to project ideals, the projects are a superior way of organising due to their ability to foster evolutionary learning by means of their cyclical or spiral perception of time (Lundin & Söderholm, 1995, p. 440). Project organisations handle uncertainties associated with their tasks by organising them into sequences or phases, which enable efficient action in order to complete the task before the project ends (see Bailey et al., Chapter 7, this volume). Given the fact that citizens pose more individualised and utility-driven demands and taking into account the increased pressure on governments to take tangible actions and produce quick outputs, it is unsurprising that the use of projects in the public sector has gained momentum when addressing contemporary policy problems (Godenhjelm, 2016, p. 15).

Neither the notion of time as cyclical or spiral, nor the belief in structuring the project into phases, are without their critics. The short-cyclical nature of projects is especially challenging. Research on the interdependencies between projects and firms, networks localities and institutions, and the "learning orthodoxy" in industrial and regional contexts shows the importance of long-term relationships for the generation of trust as a necessary precondition for successful innovation and learning (Grabher, 2002, pp. 205–206). A lack of long-term relationships can also lead to opportunistic and short-sighted behaviour among actors (Söderlund, 2012, p. 48).

The ability to place temporary organisations in a broader context is of particular importance in a public sector environment in which well-institutionalised structures are prerequisites for cooperation and flexible adjustment in public governance (Torfing et al., 2012, p. 104). The increased temporality portrayed by projects is particularly challenging in a public sector setting and there has been little methodical analysis of the inherent temporal features of current organisational forms, especially in relation to current governance systems (Sjöblom et al., 2013, p. 4). The following sections highlight two key challenges.

Securing Long-term Outcomes by Means of Democratic Procedures

Projectification of the public sector represents a paradoxical situation in which the number of temporary organisations is increasing, while long-term policies and objectives are being emphasised more than ever (Sjöblom, 2009, p. 166). Objectives and policies that attempt to reduce long-term effects such as climate change highlight the need to take quick and innovative action, for which projects are believed to be ideally suited (Brady & Hobday, 2011, p. 273). Projects are also expected to increase the problem-solving capabilities of the executive systems (Sjöblom et al., 2013, p. 3). However, successful outcomes might require a generational time perspective in contrast to the limited time perspective portrayed by projects (Marsden, Sjöblom, Andersson, & Skerratt, 2012; Munck af Rosenschöld, 2017, p. 52). Successful and innovative outcomes would also require a reduction of steering and control as over-institutionalisation and strong structural dependencies might reduce the flexible and integrative capacities associated with temporary organisations (Sjöblom et al., 2013, p. 7).

Public-sector projects usually involve multiple organisations and have an effect on a significantly wider range of stakeholders than private sector projects (Wirick, 2009, p. 57). Ideally, stakeholder participation and management in particular should enable diverse interests and expertise to be organised on a just-in-time basis. When managed in a non-hierarchical way, they are expected to create spaces where collaborative action emerges (Sjöblom et al., 2013, p. 3). Research on EU-funded regional development innovation projects, however, shows that while the number of stakeholders included in projects has a positive effect on project innovations, interlinking project stakeholder membership does not (Godenhjelm & Johanson, 2016, p. 13).

There is a shortage of systematic knowledge on how flexible management capabilities and temporary outputs can contribute to long-term outcomes and especially of how political responsibility and accountability for long-term outcomes can be secured. In situations in which the system of governing is subject to continuous change, the effects of new procedures and policy devices should also be assessed in relation to core democratic values such as participation, transparency, and accountability (Sjöblom, 2009, p. 167). Accountability might become a highly situational relationship based on the nature of the actor, or the conduct, rather than the democratic nature of the obligation (cf. Bovens, 2007, p. 461).

The Temporal Fit Between Public Institutions

In a public sector context, research on complex adaptive systems (CAS) shows that contemporary governance processes operate on different spatial and temporary scales that have become increasingly non-linear and unpredictable (Axelrod & Cohen, 2001; Duit & Galaz, 2008, pp. 311–312; Torfing et al., 2012, p. 229). Adaption in complex governance systems is not only a matter of relationships between differentiated organisational forms representing different rationales (i.e., public vs. private sector); it also requires the capacity to manage differentiated and sometimes competing time frames. Large-scale EU Cohesion policy for instance operates over a seven-year period, EU parliaments are elected every fifth year, while national and municipal parliaments are elected (in Finland) every four years, not to mention national and regional policy programmes that vary considerably. The question of synchronisation between different public policy time frames is thereby highly relevant and brings into question both the perception of permanent organisations in the public sector as representing linear time, as well as the ability to utilise the results from projects that follow a cyclical and/or spiral conception of time.

Numerous studies have suggested that research on project management should extend its temporal scope beyond the single project for analysing: (a) how project practices evolve through history over prior, present, and future projects, but also (b) for analysing the temporal fit or misfit between institutions, actors, and policies affecting the activities of the single project. In an embedded politico-administrative structure, the latter is highly important (Engwall, 2003; Munck af Rosenschöld, Honkela, & Hukkinen, 2014). Laux (2011, p. 232) argues that societies are characterised by a massive desynchronisation between the tempo of political decisions and that of social evolution. Desynchronisation can thus be interpreted as a consequence of three parallel developments. The extended *temporal scale* of societal problems demands increasingly open-ended and long-term processes. An essentially unchanged *temporal logic* of parliamentary systems means that decisions placed under time pressure are increasingly incompatible with democratic time structures. By consequence there is an enforced need to fortify the capacities of the executive systems as for *strategic agility* and just-in-time action (cf. Laux, 2011; Sjöblom et al., 2013).

It is thus important to recognise that the complexity characterising contemporary governance systems is not only a structural matter. It is also a consequence of the fact that democratic institutions and other societal actors may operate according to very diverse time frames, which makes it important to assess the temporal fit or misfit between involved actors and institutions. Organisations and instruments operating in a short-term context are also vulnerable to asymmetric power relations, making integration into frameworks for democratic institutions difficult (Voss, Smith, & Grin, 2009, p. 287). From a temporal point of view, institutionalisation reflects both the delicate balance between over-institutionalisation in order to secure coherence and synchronised activities as well as the high degree of autonomy needed for pursuing experimental, innovative, and decisive actions (Sjöblom et al., 2013, p. 7). Given the magnitude of projects funded by the EU, and the increasing reliance on project outcomes in contemporary public policy implementation, projectification could have far-reaching consequences that affect the states' ability to exert control. This stresses the need to ensure the correct temporal fit between projects, democratic institutions, and the regulative frameworks. The two key temporal factors identified above – the contribution to long-term goals and opportunities for synchronisation in terms of temporal fit – in addition to the contextual factors described above, affect the significance of various strategic alternatives in the highly institutionalised environment in which projects operate.

The Strategic Dimension: Operating in a Highly Institutionalised Environment

In the previous sections, we have described a number of strategic considerations without being explicit about strategy. Considerations about contextuality and temporality thus affect the terms of action and what it is possible to do when using a project as a policy tool. But projectification as a strategy may also change the wider institutional setting. In particular, one may pay attention to the strategic implications that projectification has in terms of increasing the adaptive capacities of the public sector.

The business literature is unequivocal about strategy – it is the essence of competitive success. The strategy concept is well articulated, and a plethora of techniques, approaches, and perspectives exist (Rosenberg Hansen & Ferlie, 2014). However, in the public sector, the claims for the benefits of strategy are historically more low-key. Similar activities in the public sector relate to policies, programmes, reforms, campaigns, and plans of various kinds, concepts that all have similarities with the notion of intended strategy, captured in the motto "think before you act". This is unsurprising since public administration is more concerned with functions and broader legal and political responsibilities than with narrow objectives (Alford & O'Flynn, 2009).

However, with the NPM-doctrine having been introduced in the public sector, public service organisations were made less distinctive from private sector firms, and concepts such as strategy and objectives have become more common and usable (Ferlie, 2003; Johanson, 2009). Generic management models and different project management techniques have thereby strengthened their role and importance. Based on public sector NPM reforms, Brunsson and Sahlin-Andersson (2000) identify how new organisational ideals were constructed and introduced, ideas that emphasise identity (being unique and special), hierarchy (management and control) and rationality (setting objectives, measuring results, and allocating responsibility). NPM reforms have thus streamlined public organisations, which has several implications. Managers at different levels must be able to influence professionals' understanding of their role and the task of their organisation to a larger extent than previously. The increased need to manage knowledge and understanding has also led to the development and use of more indirect management techniques in the public sector, such as visions, values, culture, etc. To solve societal challenges, NPG reinforces this trend by stipulating broad and comprehensive collaboration and corresponding dialogue-based leadership with other strategically guided organisations (Osborne, 2007; Torfing & Ansell, 2014). Project management as a practice has had a significant role in this development.

However, neither strategy nor projects are neutral organisational tools helping to re-organise and restructure workflows and working conditions. They are also new managerial practices (Rose & Miller, 2008) which establish new hierarchies and relations of social control in public organisations (Diefenbach, 2009), such as senior managements' desire to control professionals and other experts that traditionally dominate and have discretion over public services (Llewellyn & Tappin, 2003). In a review of the research on strategic planning and management in the public sector, Poister, Pitts, and Edwards (2010) concluded that the linkages between strategic planning and organisational outcomes or performance improvements are sparse, and perhaps the same holds true for PM, at least with respect to infrastructure development megaprojects (Cicmil & Hodgson, 2006; Flyvbjerg, 2014).

Today, strategies have become a way for public agencies to authenticate their sense of purpose and long-term direction. Although this is largely in line with an administrative rationale, it does not facilitate the agile management that many have called for (Crawford & Helm, 2009). It is a delusion to argue that the world stops while the plans are drawn up and implemented. In a fast-changing world, one needs to be more responsive to signals from the environment, and reflect, learn, and experiment by continuously testing alternative actions in small steps. The idea of temporary projects gains approval in this context and enters the public sector as a new and more flexible policy instrument (see Introduction, this volume).

More recent research has identified three reasons why projectification is such a popular strategy and implementation instrument within the public sector (Jensen et al., 2013). The reasons can be *political*, meaning that political actors have an interest in showing initiative and innovation in high-profile policy areas, in particular if they receive media attention. There are also *administrative* reasons, due to which EU and national authorities need an organisational form that allows appropriation control, governance, and monitoring. Finally, *organisational* reasons force local actors to find flexible organisational forms through which they are able to manage and control policy development and implementation more freely than within traditional structures.

Below, we will briefly discuss some precarious considerations when using projects as an overall umbrella strategy to pursue public sector development and change. The first challenge concerns projectification in the public sector as such, and the time pressure and irregularity that it creates in an otherwise relatively legally regulated public environment. The second challenge concerns what happens after the project ends; how to scale-up and implement lessons learned, and how to introduce new methods and solutions in existing structures or within emergent structures created by the project.

Time Pressure and Irregularity in a Legally Regulated Public Environment

When working with projects in the highly regulated public sector, the detachment of specific tasks and goals from multi-goal activities permeated by legality, transparency, and rule of law is challenging. Through the use of projects, policymakers introduce new concepts of change and urgency into a system usually emphasising coordination and continuity (Bason, 2010; Marchi & Sarcina, 2011). Quick changes in strategic direction are challenging as they can lead to irregularity, increased ambiguity as well as opportunism (Söderlund, 2012, p. 48). When project funding is applied in competition, it can be tempting to be optimistically biased in order to get projects approved (Lovallo & Kahneman, 2003). Asquin, Garel, and Picq (2010) argue that a positive funding decision can lead to high expectations, which can be difficult to fulfil, and can reinforce pre-existing project fatigue.

In dealing with complex problems, it is also important to consider how the actors involved perceive irregularities and ambiguities, that is, tensions in terms of what can be done (Head & Alford, 2015; Tsoukas & Chia, 2002). As mentioned in previous sections, projects are established to solve non-routine tasks that have a high degree of complexity and interdependence between involved actors. Lundin and Söderholm (1995, p. 452) also acknowledge that theories associated with planning techniques entail major disadvantages. They argue that such planning techniques are common in construction type projects where projects are repetitive and isolated rather than arenas for learning. Although project management methods and techniques can help to facilitate public sector projects, they may not be fully adequate for projects in complex settings.

However, the project organisation can be an appropriate tool for policy implementation also in such settings, since the rationale behind using projects is that it is often wiser to begin with and learn from a small experiment before broadening the action towards changing an entire organisation or an entire societal sector (see Bailey et al., Chapter 7, and Ettelt and Mays, Chapter 1, this volume). However, such projects are contextually sensitive. Actors involved in the projects have to engage in power structures and politics in order to build trustful relations between the project and its stakeholders (Jensen et al., 2017). Thus, using traditional rationalistic and normative project management tools, which presuppose high predictability and good planning conditions, can be difficult within policy fields in which challenges are "wicked" in ways that may even counteract learning. As proposed by Weick (2002), in a world of ambiguity, managing should be seen as a process of continually rearranging the contradictions of organisational life. Strategy unfolds over time, not as a process of deliberate planning but as a "self-referential process of discovery and self-clarification that is never complete because things are always turning away" (Chia & Holt, 2011, p. 5). Duffiels and Whitty (2016) claim that the traditional project management model should be supplemented with a project-learning model through which fragmentary experiences are rearranged into temporary patterns, which are subject to change in more or less continuous processes.

Upscaling and Implementation in Existing or Emergent Structures

Many public-sector projects operate in the context of highly institutionalised politico-administrative rule-based silo structures, and not within traditionally project-based organisations in which a project mind-set, vocabulary, and techniques dominate (i.e., pharmaceutical or construction industry). Therefore, temporary development work is often conducted in parallel with existing permanent activities. The specific processes occurring when projects cease to exist have been deemed open questions (Söderlund, 2012, p. 58). Consequently, one major challenge of organising development and change as temporary organisations is to know what will happen after the project ends: how to upscale and implement lessons learned, and how to introduce new methods and solutions in existing structures or within emergent structures created by the project. This requires individual policymakers and permanent organisations to have a capacity to absorb the results derived from the project, but also to deal with competing values and conflicts of interest.

A significant aspect of the built-in parallelism is the problem of veto power. Is it a representative of the project or of the regular activities who has the veto power? This parallelism between permanent and temporary organisations representing different institutional rationales concerning change and development is frequently put to the test when the projects are completed and when lesson learned should be scaled up and have impact on established practices (see Jensen et al., Chapter 6, this volume). To act strategically under these circumstances is a relational achievement, meaning that project outcomes require negotiations in order to be transformed into something that someone else considers necessary and valuable. Brulin and Svensson (2012) have stated that a lack of negotiation prevents mutual learning and exchange, a situation which can be harmful to wider capacity building. This not only highlights the significance of understanding the different institutional rationales of the actors involved, but also stresses the need to take into account strategic incentives for implementation beyond the project itself.

Summing up, projectification raises the question of actors' awareness about the complexity within which the project operates. There are always circumstances, underlying causal relationships, and system characteristics related to time, context, and strategy that are relevant. Although there are different, more specific strategic challenges, the overall and general challenge concerning institutional capacity building is to manage various institutional barriers and existing power relationships that can inhibit the transfer and use of knowledge and results. Thus, it is important to extend the understanding of projectification in the public sector by emphasising how different perceptions of context, time, and strategy affect its capability.

Concluding Discussion

In this chapter, we have presented a theoretical discussion about the key institutional factors through which projectification may affect public policy development and implementation, especially factors that may strengthen or weaken governments' policy making capacities. Our main argument is that these factors fall under three key dimensions especially pertinent to embedded public structures: namely, *context*, *temporality*, and *strategy*. We furthermore argue that the outcome of the specific institutional factors associated with the three dimensions will affect the predictability and operational rationales of the policy processes, but also the opportunities for long-term implementation of project-driven achievements.

It is important to recognise that structural "*embeddedness*" is not only about internal–external relationships. Contemporary organisational actions take place in a complex societal web of time frames, operational rationales, structures, and resources, where it may be hard to determine what is "internal" and what is "external". Due to differences in resources, policy styles, and traditions, these webs vary from one municipality, region, or state to another. With respect to the *contextual dimension*, it is thus essential to expand the organisational context beyond those actors immediately involved in the projects. In public policy making, structural dependencies are especially important with respect to the capacities and inclination of government agencies for meta-governing at one extreme and micro-steering project-based activities on the other. The conditions under which such efforts support or counteract project-driven actions is an increasingly important field of research. From a contextual point of view, we have emphasised the significance of the interface in terms of interlinking mechanisms between projects and government organisations as a means for capitalising on project achievements beyond the immediate project context. However, the interface is sensitive. If government organisations want to maintain the initiative by means of strong coordinative actions, this may restrict the discretion of the actors involved in ways that are detrimental to project driven policy development and implementation.

Factors related to the *temporal dimension* further highlight the complexities between over-institutionalisation to secure coherence and synchronised activities on the one hand, and the high degree of autonomy needed for pursuing project-driven experimental and decisive actions on the other hand. The challenge is finding the correct temporal fit between the actors involved and institutions, as well as to achieve balance between innovative action and coherence and control. Inability to align the results from projects that follow a cyclical and/or spiral concept of time with the permanent organisations linear conception of time could have severe consequences and could pose an inherent risk of projects producing fragmented and desynchronised policy outcomes. The temporal fit between projects, programs, policies, and government institutions on the one hand, and democratic procedures through which involved actors can be held accountable on the other, are thus essential factors for fostering sustainable change and innovation by means of project driven action.

In terms of *strategies* in a highly institutionalised environment, the results highlight that strategies matter, but that institutions do also. We have particularly emphasised two challenges in these respects. The first one concerns irregularities that projectification may create in an otherwise relatively legally regulated public environment. The second challenge is a matter of the "post-project" sequence of the policy process, that is, the opportunities for upscaling project outcomes and implementing lessons learned. Issues of complexity, different forms of logic, and preferential right of interpretation are here of paramount importance and need to be observed.

Our chapter emphasises the need for a more pluralistic understanding of projects beyond traditional project management heritage by discussing the institutional characteristics that may favour or impede policy development and implementation in a projectified public sector. It highlights the repercussions that projectification may have in terms of capacity of government institutions to operate within collaborative structures and to coordinate policy development. In summary, project governance in an embedded state requires *multi-dimensional conceptualisations of embeddedness*, an awareness of the delicate balance between *over-institutionalisation and autonomy*, as well as an understanding of the *different rationales that permanent and temporary organisations follow*.

Note

1 The research done in relation to this chapter was conducted as a part of the research project on Promoting capacities for innovation and change: Project driven innovations in a Nordic context (2017–2018), which was funded by The Joint Committee for Nordic research councils in the Humanities and Social Sciences (NOS-HS). Christian Jensen was in addition supported by Mistra Urban Future.

References

Alford, J., & O'Flynn, J. (2009). Making sense of public value: Concepts, critiques and emergent meanings. *International Journal of Public Administration*, 32(3–4), 171–191.

Ansell, C., & Gash, A. (2007). Collaborative governance in theory and practice. *Journal of Public Administration Research and Theory*, 18(4), 543–571.

Asquin, A., Garel, G., & Picq, T. (2010). When project-based management causes distress at work. *International Journal of Project Management*, 28(2), 166–172.

Axelrod, R., & Cohen, M. D. (2001). *Harnessing complexity: Organizational implications of a scientific frontier*. New York, NY: The Free Press.

Bason, C. (2010). *Leading public sector innovation: Co-creating for a better society*. Bristol, England: The Policy Press.

Bodin, Ö., & Crona, B. I. (2009). The role of social networks in natural resource governance: What relational patterns make a difference? *Global Environmental Change*, 19(3), 366–374.

Bouckaert, G., Ormond, D., & Peters, G. B. (2000). *A potential governance agenda for Finland: Turning 90 in the administration's tasks and functions*. Helsinki, Finland: KU Leuven.

Bovens, M. (2007). Analysing and assessing accountability: A conceptual framework. *European Law Journal*, 13(2), 447–468.

Brady, T., & Hobday, M. (2011). Projects and innovation: Innovation and projects. In P. Morris, J. Söderlund, & J. Pinto (Eds.), *Oxford handbook of project management* (pp. 273–296). Oxford, England: Oxford University Press.

Brulin, G., & Svensson, L. (2012). *Managing sustainable development programmes: A learning approach to change*. Farnham, England: Glover.

Brunsson, N., & Sahlin-Andersson, K. (2000). Constructing organizations: The example of public sector reform. *Organization Studies*, 21(4), 721–746.

Büttner, S. M., & Leopold, L. M. (2016). A "new spirit" of public policy? The project world of EU funding. *European Journal of Cultural and Political Sociology*, 3(1), 41–71.

Carlsson, L., & Berkes, F. (2005). Co-management: Concepts and methodological implications. *Journal of Environmental Management*, 75(1), 65–76.

Chia, R., & Holt, R. (2011). *Strategy without design*. Cambridge, England: Cambridge University Press.

Christensen, T., & Laegreid, P. (2007). The whole-of-government approach to public sector reform. *Public Administration Review*, 67(6), 1059–1066.

Cicmil, S., & Hodgson, D. E. (2006). New possibilities for project management theory: A critical engagement. *Project Management Journal*, 37(2), 111–122.

Crawford, L. H., & Helm, J. (2009). Government and governance: The value of project management in the public sector. *Project Management Journal*, 40(1), 73–87.

Diefenbach, T. (2009). New public management in public sector organizations: The dark sides of managerialistic "enlightenment". *Public Administration*, 87(4), 892–909.

Duffiels, S., & Whitty, S. J. (2016). Application of the systemic lessons learned knowledge model for organisational learning through projects. *International Journal of Project Management*, 34(7), 1280–1293.

Duit, A., & Galaz, V. (2008). Governance and complexity: Emerging issues for governance theory. *Governance. An International Journal of Policy, Administration, and Institutions*, 21(3), 311–335.

Engwall, M. (2003). No project is an island: Linking projects to history and context. *Research Policy*, 32(5), 789–808.

European Court of Auditors (2009). *The sustainability and the Commission's management of the Life-Nature Projects*. Luxembourg: European Communities.

Ferlie, E. (2003). Quasi-strategy: Strategic management in contemporary public sector. In A. Pettigrew, H. Thomas, & R. Whittington (Eds.), *Handbook of strategy and management* (pp. 279–298). London, England: Sage.

Flyvbjerg, B. (2014). What you should know about megaprojects and why: An overview. *Project Management Journal*, 45(2), 6–19.

Fred, M. (2018). *Projectification: The Trojan horse of local government*. Öresund, Sweden: All Media.

Gardiner, R., Ostrom, E., & Walker, J. E. (1990). The nature of common-pool resource problems. *Rationality and Society*, 2(3), 335–358.

Godenhjelm, S. (2016). *Project organisations and governance: Processes, actors, actions and participatory procedures*. Helsinki, Finland: Unigrafia.

Godenhjelm, S., & Johanson, J. E. (2016). The effect of stakeholder inclusion on public sector project innovation. *International Review of Administrative Sciences*, 84(1), 42–62.

Godenhjelm, S., Lundin, R. A., & Sjöblom, S. (2015). Projectification in the public sector: The case of the European Union. *International Journal of Managing Projects in Business*, 8 (2), 324–348.

Godenhjelm, S., Munck af Rosenschiöld, J., Kuokkanen, K., Andersson, K., & Sjöblom, S. (2012). The democratic implications of project organisations: A case study of leader-projects in Finland. In S. Sjöblom, K. Andersson, T. Marsden, & S. Skerratt (Eds.), *Sustainability and short-term policies. Improving governance in spatial policy interventions* (pp. 55–80). Surrey, England: Ashgate.

Grabher, G. (2002). Cool projects, boring institutions: Temporary collaboration in social context. *Regional Studies*, 36(3), 205–214.

Head, B., & Alford, J. (2015). Wicked problem: Implications for public policy and management. *Administration and Society*, 47(6), 711–739.

Hodgson, D. E. (2004). Project work: The legacy of bureaucratic control in the post-bureaucratic organization. *Organization*, 11(1), 81–100.

Jacobsson, B., Pierre, J., & Sundström, G. (2015). *Governing the EMBEDDED STATE: The organizational dimension of governance*. Oxford, England: Oxford University Press.

Jensen, C., Johansson, S., & Löfström, M. (2013). The project organization as a policy tool in implementing welfare reforms in the public sector. *The International Journal of Health Planning and Management*, 28(1), 122–137.

Jensen, C., Johansson, S., & Löfström, M. (2017). Policy implementation in the era of accelerating projectification: Synthesizing Matland's conflict–ambiguity model and research on temporary organizations. *Public Policy and Administration*, 33(4), 447–465.

Johanson, J. E. (2009). Strategy formation in public agencies. *Public Administration*, 87(4), 872–891.

Johanson, J. E., & Vakkuri, J. (2018). *Governing hybrid organisations: Exploring diversity of institutional life*. New York, NY: Routledge.

Laux, H. (2011). The time of politics: Pathological effects of social differentiation. *Time and Society*, 20(2), 224–240.

Llewellyn, S., & Tappin, E. (2003). Strategy in the public sector: Management in the wilderness. *The Journal of Management Studies*, 40(4), 955.

Lovallo, D., & Kahneman, D. (2003). Delusions of success: How optimism undermines executives' decisions. *Harvard Business Review*, 81(7), 56–63.

Lundin, R. A., & Söderholm, A. (1995). A theory of the temporary organization. *Scandinavian Journal of Management*, 11, 437–455.

Lundin, R. A., & Steinthórsson, R. S. (2003). Studying organizations as temporary. *Scandinavian Journal of Management*, 19(2), 233–250.

Marchi, S., & Sarcina, R. (2011). Temporariness in appreciative reflection: Managing participatory and appreciative, action and reflection projects through temporary organisations. *Reflective Practice*, 12(2), 159–177.

Marsden, T., Sjöblom, S., Andersson, K., & Skerratt, S. (2012). Introduction. Exploring short-termism and sustainability: Temporal mechanisms in spatial policies. In S.

Sjöblom, K. Andersson, T. Marsden, & S. Skerratt (Eds.), *Sustainability and short-term policies: Improving governance in spatial policy interventions* (pp. 1–15). London, England: Ashgate.

Mintzberg, H. (1979). *The structuring of organizations: A synthesis of the research*. Englewood Cliffs, NJ: Prentice-Hall.

Munck af Rosenschöld, J. (2017). *Projectified environmental governance and challenges of institutional change towards stability*. Helsinki, Finland: Unigrafia.

Munck af Rosenschöld, J., Honkela, N., & Hukkinen, J. I. (2014). Addressing the temporal fit of institutions: The regulation of endocrine disrupting chemicals in Europe. *Ecology and Society*, 19(4), 0–9.

OECD (2010). *Value for money in government: Public administration after "New Public Management"*. Paris.

Osborne, S. P. (2007). Editorial. New public governance? *Public Management Review*, 8(3), 377–387.

Pierre. (2012). Governance and institutional flexibility. In D. Levi-Faur (Ed.), *The Oxford handbook of governance* (pp. 187–214). Oxford, England: Oxford University Press.

Poister, T. H., Pitts, D. W., & Edwards, L. H. (2010). Strategic management research in the public sector: A review, synthesis, and future directions. *American Review of Public Administration*, 40(5), 522–545.

Project Management Institute (2004). *A guide to the project management body of knowledge* (3rd ed.). Newton Square, Pennsylvania: Project Management Institute.

Project Management Institute (2006). *Government extension to the PMBOK* (3rd ed.). Newton Square, Pennsylvania: Project Management Institute.

Rhodes, R. A. W. (2017). *Network governance and the differentiated polity. Selected essays, Volume I*. Oxford, England: Oxford University Press.

Rose, N., & Miller, P. (2008). *Governing the present: Administering economic, social and personal life*. Cambridge, England: Polity.

Rosenberg Hansen, J., & Ferlie, E. (2014). Applying strategic management theories in public sector organizations: Developing a typology. *Public Management Review*, 18(1), 1–19.

Schneider, V. (2012). Governance and complexity. In D. Levi-Faur (Ed.), *The Oxford handbook of governance* (pp. 129–142). Oxford, England: Oxford University Press.

Scott, R. W. (2008). *Institutions and organizations: Ideas interests and identities*. Thousand Oaks, CA: Sage.

Sjöblom, S. (2009). Administrative short-termism: A non-issue in environmental and regional governance. *Journal of Environmental Policy & Planning*, 11(3), 165–168.

Sjöblom, S., Andersson, K., Marsden, T., & Skerratt, S. (2012). *Sustainability and short-term policies: Improving governance in spatial policy interventions*. S. Sjöblom, K. Andersson, T. Marsden, & S. Skerratt (Eds.). London, England: Ashgate.

Sjöblom, S., & Godenhjelm, S. (2009). Project proliferation and governance: Implications for environmental management. *Journal of Environmental Policy & Planning*, 11(3), 169–185.

Sjöblom, S., Löfgren, K., & Godenhjelm, S. (2013). Projectified politics: Temporary organisations in a public context introduction to the special issue. *Scandinavian Journal of Public Administration*, 17(17), 3–11.

Söderlund, J. (2012). Theoretical foundations of project management: Suggestions for a pluralistic understanding. In P. W. G. Morris, J. K. Pinto, & J. Söderlund (Eds.), *The Oxford handbook of project management* (pp. 37–64). Oxford, England: Oxford University Press.

Sulkunen, P. (2006). Projektiyhteiskunta ja uusi yhteiskuntasopimus. In K. Rantala & P. Sulkunen (Eds.), *Projektiyhteiskunnan kääntöpuolia* (pp. 17–38). Helsinki, Finland: Gaudeamus.

Sydow, J., Lindkvist, L., & Defilippi, R. (2004). Project-based organizations, embeddedness and repositories of knowledge: Editorial. *Organization Studies*, 25(9), 1475–1489.

Sydow, J., & Staber, U. (2002). The institutional embeddedness of project networks: The case of content production in German television. *Regional Studies*, 36(3), 215–227.

Torfing, J., & Ansell, C. (2014). Collaboration and design: New tools for public innovation. In C. Ansell & J. Torfing (Eds.), *Public Innovation through collaboration and design* (pp. 1–18). London, England: Routledge.

Torfing, J., Peters, G. B., Pierre, J., & Sorensen, E. (2012). *Interactive governance: Advancing the paradigm*. Oxford, England: Oxford University Press.

Tsoukas, H., & Chia, R. (2002). On organizational becoming: Rethinking organizational change. *Organization Science*, 13(5), 567–582.

Voss, J. P., Smith, A., & Grin, J. (2009). Designing long-term policy: Rethinking transition management. *Policy Sciences*, 42, 275–302.

Weick, K. E. (2002). Essai. Real-time reflexivity: Prods to reflection. *Organization Studies*, 23(6), 893–898.

Wirick, D. W. (2009). *Public-sector project management: Meeting the challenges and achieving results*. Hoboken, NJ: John Wiley & Sons.

9

THE EUROPEAN DIMENSION OF PROJECTIFICATION

Implications of the Project Approach in EU Funding Policy[1]

Sebastian M. Büttner

UNIVERSITY OF DUISBURG-ESSEN

Projectification in contemporary public policy has many different faces of which one is distinctly European. During the past two to three decades, the European Union (EU) has strongly fostered projectification in public policy. Starting from a few pilot projects in the early 1980s, project funding has become a major instrument of EU policy making. Through multi-annual programming and project funding, the European Commission aims to implement its own policy agenda and EU-specific policy goals throughout the EU territory and even beyond. Project funding plays a central role in many policy areas of the European Union – from the funding of numerous smaller local development initiatives and larger infrastructure projects in the field of cohesion policy, to the funding of entrepreneurial and scientific research and numerous other initiatives in the EU's neighbourhood policy. This has not only fostered the proliferation of certain notions and practices of project management in the public sector (Kovách & Kučerová, 2009; Sjöblom, Löfgren, & Godenhjelm, 2013; Godenhjelm, Lundin, & Sjöblom, 2015; Fred, 2018); it has also contributed to the development of a distinct sphere of professional practice, a particular "project world" of EU funding policy so to speak (Büttner & Leopold, 2016), with its own standards and logics of policy implementation.

In this chapter, I examine why projectification has become so prominent in the context of EU policy making and discuss major sociological implications of the EU's move to project funding since the 1980s. I argue that projectification constitutes an attractive tool for the European Commission, the major executive agent of EU policy making, in order to gain political influence in a position of limited political authority. Accordingly, the European Commission expended huge efforts in developing project funding as a policy tool when it first established its own approaches towards European policy implementation. However, as I will show, while project funding was mainly designed to bring

European policy initiatives "closer to the citizens"[2], the project approach in EU funding policy comes at the cost of increased standardisation and specialisation of policy implementation. As a result, it has brought about a complex and highly structured system of policy implementation that strongly regulates almost all actions and procedures within this system. It has also fostered the emergence of new types of occupations and groups of professionals offering services to citizens and potential "beneficiaries" of EU funding and mitigating between the requirements of the European Union and the demands of local actors. This increasing "expertisation" of EU funding, as will be discussed towards the end of this chapter, creates new social distinctions and new hierarchies within the current system of EU policy implementation: while it brings new opportunities for numerous local actors and professionals, it also fosters the expansion of unstable and sometimes precarious projectified jobs in the local structures of EU policy implementation.

This chapter starts with a short discussion of the role of EU funding in the current system of EU policy making and some basic information on the beginnings of EU funding, before presenting major organisational features of EU funding. The aim is to show the effort the European Commission has expended developing and standardising project funding as a major tool of European policy implementation. The final section displays major areas of employment and categories of expertise relating to EU project funding. It will be shown that EU funding has created new jobs and new types of private services in public policy, propelling the specialisation and expertisation of EU policy implementation.

Making Sense of EU Governance: European Policy Making Under the Condition of Limited Authority

The nature of EU government and the actual political authority of the European Union are matters of ongoing dispute and contestation in EU studies. Numerous authors have stressed the growing dominance of EU politics in many policy making areas over the past decades, especially since the introduction of the Single Market at the beginning of the 1990s (Stone Sweet et al., 2001; Kauppi, 2005; Fligstein, 2008; Münch, 2010; Vauchez, 2015). It has been highlighted that the EU has gained increasing regulatory power in many policy areas that have long been strongholds of the individual European nation states (Majone, 1996; Hooghe, 2001; Featherstone & Radaelli, 2003; Haller, 2008; Beck & Grande, 2007; Bernhard, 2011). Through rulings by the European Court of Justice (ECJ), and in combination with legislation introduced by the European Commission to establish common European standards, the EU has substantially increased its relative governing power compared to member states over the past three decades (Sandholtz & Stone Sweet, 1998; Scharpf, 1999; Münch, 2010; Vauchez, 2015, 2016). Other observers have challenged this interpretation. Even though Europe and the world have seen extensive economic, political, and social integration over recent decades, they still see a striking dominance of national interests in EU politics and a lack of joint decision making (Moravcsik, 1998; Habermas, 2015, pp. 3–28).[3]

No matter which interpretation one follows, there is no clear-cut answer to the question of the EU's actual political authority, and apparently the answer crosses the binary distinction between "European" versus "national" authority (Beck & Grande, 2007). The EU is certainly not a classical "state" – if one compares the EU with the classical model of sovereign territorial state, at least. However, the EU is much more than just an intergovernmental agency or a simple derivate of nation-state power; it is a supranational political authority in its own right, with distinct political competences, resources, and governmental tasks. Beyond that, it is a distinct bureaucratic order widely reaching into the EU member states, affecting both politics and everyday social life all around the EU territory (Hooghe & Marks, 2001; Featherstone & Radaelli, 2003; Münch, 2010; Büttner, 2012). Accordingly, the governance system of the EU is often described as a "multi-level governance system" (Hooghe & Marks, 2001; Münch, 2010). Moreover, it is also described as a "transnational administrative space" (Stone Sweet et al., 2001; Shapiro, 2001; Hofmann, 2008) in order to capture the far-reaching "Europeanisation" of national bureaucracies and the increasing dominance of EU regulations and regulatory agents in contemporary Europe.

In line with these considerations – but remembering that modern "government" is by no means only propelled by state agents and administrative bodies (Hood, 1995, 1998; Power, 1997; Rose & Miller, 2008; Djelic & Sahlin-Andersson, 2008) – the system of EU governance is conceptualised here as a distinct field of professional practice. Hence, it is regarded as a distinct "social field" that establishes its own logics and standards within the existing structures of policy making and policy professionalism and widely reaches into local structures of EU member states and even beyond, such as prospective EU member states (so called "candidate countries") and even other neighbouring areas.[4] This field is more than just an administrative space, since it widely exceeds the boundaries of classical state bureaucracies and interlinks policy experts and professionals from different areas of society, who all deal with EU affairs and EU policy making in their day-to-day working lives (Büttner et al., 2015). Since EU policy making produces its own logics, standards, regulations, and policies in the form of legal texts, policy proposals, reports, and official political proclamations, it requires special knowledge and expertise from those who are linked to EU activities or interested in profiting from them. In addition, the paradigmatic shift from "government" to "governance" and the introduction of new organisational routines under the heading of "new public management" (NPM) has brought about new organisational standards, new policy approaches, and new types of actors in EU politics and policy making. Hence, the notion of a social field captures the growing "professionalisation" of EU policy making (in the sense of a growing codification of European policy objectives and practices of policy making) and the multiplicity of actors, occupations and forms of expertise which have emerged within and beyond the institutional core of EU policy making in the past few decades. Based on this perspective, the establishment of the political authority of the EU is considered an open struggle over the enforcement and establishment of European rules and standards of policy making through and within the field of EU affairs.

In addition to law making and standards setting, project funding indeed represents an important element of the EU's struggle for governmental authority. Accordingly, it represents an important feature of the "field of EU affairs" as well (Büttner et al., 2015, p. 583f.). The European Commission has expended great effort developing its own policy agenda based on standardised conceptions of project management (PM), fostering the proliferation of "projectification" (Fred, 2018) all around the EU territory and beyond. About half of the EU budget is allocated to funding projects in one way or another: from funding the EU's cohesion policy and rural development to funding research projects under the umbrella of "Horizon 2020", or activities funded for external partners under the umbrella of neighbourhood policy.[5] Consequently, PM practices have gained huge prominence in the EU's system of policy implementation. What is more, since the end of the 1980s, the entire organisational structure of the EU system of policy making has been based on major tools and techniques deriving from PM and strategic planning. Today, the logic of PM permeates almost all administrative layers of EU policy implementation. All areas of EU policy making, in which project funding or grant giving play an important role, are fundamentally structured in accordance with principles of PM. EU funding has strongly fostered the emergence of a sophisticated pan-European system of project-based policy implementation, overlaying and subtly transforming established national and local structures of policy making. Thus, EU project funding represents a distinct area of practice within the larger field of EU affairs, with procedural rules, standard practices, and rules of play which actors must know and take into account, if they aim to be part of this particular arena of policy making.

From Pilot Projects to the Europe 2020 Strategy: The Rise of Projectification in EU Governance

The practice of project funding is not exclusive to EU policy making or contemporary public policy; it has a much longer history. It has long been common practice in public policy, when public money was allocated to external contractors and service providers to fulfil certain predefined tasks or achieve clearly defined policy outcomes. As outlined by Garel (2013, p. 666), the concept of project funding emerged between the 1940s and 1960s in the context of larger publicly financed projects, such as military and aerospace projects, or huge state-funded construction projects. In this context, many tools and techniques of PM that are still used today were developed (Hodgson, 2002; Garel, 2013). However, the public sector itself was not directly affected by projectification during this era. The approach to project funding mainly affected external contractors, who were responsible for the appropriate management and implementation of projects. The public authorities just controlled the fulfilment of a project and the correct spending of the allocated funds. Beyond that, however, apart from these larger national investment programmes, project funding was also developed long ago in the context of international development policy – especially by international agents of development cooperation, such as the World Bank or the Organisation for Economic Co-operation and Development (OECD). It has been shown that as early as the 1970s, the World Bank was promoting its own PM techniques and tools in international development practice and supervised their application in specific local settings (Ika, Diallo, & Thuillier, 2010; Landoni & Corti, 2011; Ika & Hodgson, 2014).[6]

By the beginning of the 1980s, project funding techniques that had been established in international development policy were also adopted by the European Commission and incrementally introduced into the emerging system of EU policy implementation. This marks a fundamental turn in the history of European policy making and the beginning of policy coordination at the European level. Until the end of the 1970s, the policy making power of the European Commission was quite limited. Although the European Commission had its own budget and funds, such as the European Social Fund (ESF), the European Agriculture Guidance and Guarantee Fund (EAGGF), and the European Regional Development Fund (ERDF), there was no distinct European approach to policy making until the end of the 1970s. The Commission simply allocated funds to its member states based on pre-determined criteria. Due to growing dissatisfaction and scepticism about the effectiveness of this structural policy approach, however, the European Commission aimed to establish its own European framework of policy coordination, one that would ensure tighter control over spending while simultaneously fostering local forces of development (European Commission, 2008, p. 29). Consequently, by the beginning of 1980s, the Commission started to experiment with new concepts and models of "conditional" project funding that were already put in place and regularly applied in international development policy (Mellors & Cooperthwaite, 1990, p. 102). In this way, project funding and development programming made their way into EU policy making.

The experimentation with the policy instruments of project funding in European politics began with the funding of two pilot projects in the field of regional development policy, the so-called "Integrated Development Operations" (IDOs) in Naples (Italy) and Belfast (Northern Ireland). Shortly afterwards, another three IDOs were set in place in the Lozère region (France), in the Western Isles (Scotland) and in southeast Belgium within the framework of agricultural policy (Mellors & Cooperthwaite, 1990, p. 102; European Commission, 2008, p. 10). These initial attempts of European project funding were further developed in the following years through the funding of IDOs in other policy fields and introducing the so-called "Integrated Mediterranean Programmes" (IMPs) in Greece, Italy, and France in 1986.

Ultimately, these IMPs served as blueprints for the development of the EU's cohesion policy, which was officially introduced in 1989 in the run-up to the establishment of the Common Market at the beginning of 1990s. This not only marks the beginning of a new approach towards spatial development in European politics in the wake of the introduction of the Common Market; it also marks a fundamental turning point in the history of EU politics and the starting point for the establishment of the current system of EU policy making. For the first time, the European level gained its own competences in policy coordination and policy implementation. Principles and procedures developed in the pilot projects in structural policy making during the 1980s – such as multi-annual programming, strategic planning, project-based funding – still constitute fundamental principles and practices of EU policy making in many different policy fields today. This has given techniques of social organisation, which were largely specified in the context of management studies and related disciplines, a central place in the current system of EU policy making.[7]

The 1988/89 reforms also transformed the then existing budgeting system of the European Communities from annual budgeting to so-called "Multiannual Financial Frameworks" (MFFs) in order to overcome annual budget battles (Matthijs, 2010, p. 22). This fostered an enormous streamlining of all areas of EU policy making, with the so-called "programming periods" of individual policy areas being synchronised with the timespan of the multi-annual financial frameworks.

Since the 1988/89 reforms, principles and practices of strategic planning have gained increasing importance in the programming of EU policy making. With the introduction of the Lisbon strategy in 2000, the strategic approach was made central to the EU's governance system. Since then, and especially since the beginning of the fourth MFF in 2007, the "aims" and "objectives" of the EU's overarching ten-year development strategies have been the focus and major priority of all EU policy making activities. Consequently, a major part of EU project funding is currently dedicated to fulfilling the "Europe 2020 strategy", the current EU growth strategy for the period 2010–2020. Programming within each policy field and all projects and activities financed by EU funds must correspond, in one way or another, with the aims and objectives outlined in the Europe 2020 strategy: that is, the promotion of a "smart, sustainable and inclusive economy" with "high levels of employment, productivity and social cohesion".[8] Hence, the practices of PM and project programming[9] were directly built into the overall system of strategic planning of EU policy making. Strategic development planning, project programming, and project funding have become a strong liaison in EU governance. The system of EU governance strongly relies on these practices.

The Logics and Major Organisational Features of EU Project Funding

As highlighted above, the projectification of EU funding was originally borne out of dissatisfaction with the status quo. Policymakers in the European Commission aimed to gain a stronger role in policy coordination and tighter control over spending EU funds while simultaneously mobilising local initiatives in order to drive forward policy initiatives with a distinctly "European" scope. Against this backdrop, project funding based on strategic policy programming seemed like an ideal policy instrument for European policymakers, since it promises controlling and supervision as well as mobilising bottom-up self-organisation in similar ways. Beyond that, the instrument of project funding also seemed to correspond well with public spending requirements and limited public budgets. Since projects are usually established to pursue specific tasks and goals within a clearly defined timespan, the project approach seemed well-suited to effective implementation of clearly defined policy goals. For a governmental body with a very limited budget and limited autonomous policy-making capacity, such as the European Commission, conditional project funding was particularly attractive, promising tangible outcomes while keeping resource use manageable (European Commission, 2008, pp. 26–36).

Thus, project funding seems to be well-matched to the requirements of "governing" in advanced liberal societies, which have been described by proponents of Foucauldian governmentality studies as the "liberal art of government" (Rose & Miller, 2008; see also Mackenzie and Barratt, Chapter 13, this volume). The approach to project funding, however, is neither self-evident nor something which can be created from whole cloth. On the contrary, it is embedded in a broad set of standards and standardised practices of PM. In fact, modern PM is a distinct area of professional practice with an almost global reach, decisively affecting the organisation of work in many areas of professional life (Hodgson, 2004; Bröckling, 2016, pp. 170–195). It was defined as a management technique by project engineers and project managers during the second half of the 20th century (Garel, 2013). Scientists, consultants, and professional organisations such as the Project Management Institute or the Association of Project Management have promoted and popularised PM as a standard management technique and as an own field of professional expertise (Hodgson, 2002; Paton, Hodgson, & Cicmil, 2010). Consequently, numerous standards and techniques of PM have been developed and spread into professional work all over the world.[10] Thus, there are numerous PM tools and models of varying degrees of sophistication on the market, ranging from simple hands-on management schemes, such as the famous "Gantt charts", or the concept of a "project lifecycle", to more comprehensive computer-based planning and simulation tools (Morris, 1997; Stevens & Johnson, 2002; Cleland & Gareis, 2006; Nokes & Kelly, 2011; Lock, 2013; Project Management Institute, 2013).[11]

Compared to the amount of reflection on "project management" in the business world and adjunct management studies, however, PM techniques in the context of EU policy making have remained rather rudimentary and underspecified. The project approach of EU funding mainly rests upon fundamental principles of development planning and on the concept of a "project lifecycle", as developed and promoted in international development cooperation during the 1970s (Ika et al., 2010, pp. 65ff.). Thus, the specification of standards and standard procedures in policy-related fields has developed relatively uncoupled from management studies and developments in PM research. Nonetheless, the "project world of EU funding" (Büttner and Leopold, 2016) certainly constitutes a distinct area of expertise and professionalism with own EU-specific standards, notions and a whole set of standardised procedures. Moreover, during the past three decades the European Commission has expended huge effort in promoting these standards through EU funding and EU-funded project implementation. Hence, the entire concept of EU funding policy rests upon the notion of "appropriate" and "effective" PM. Only actors who are able to plan, develop, and implement projects according to rules and regulations specified in EU funding schemes and within a predefined timeframe are eligible to receive EU funds. Successful policy implementation in EU funding policy essentially means effective PM. This idea has led to the emergence of a complex multi-layered system of policy planning and policy implementation (Büttner, 2012; Godenhjelm, Lundin, & Sjöblom, 2015; Fred, 2018).

Since the entire structure of EU funding is quite complex, it is not possible to go into every detail on all existing programmes in this chapter.[12] In general, however, EU funding is mostly provided by the following five structural and investment funds: (1) the European Regional Development Fund (ERDF), (2) the European Social Fund (ESF), (3) the Cohesion Fund (mainly for larger infrastructure investments in less-developed EU member states), (4) the European Agricultural Fund for Rural Development (EAFRD) and (5) the European Maritime and Fisheries Fund (EMFF).[13] Other funds are provided for specific projects in individual policy areas and for particular "community initiatives", such as the seven "flagship initiatives" linked to the Europe 2020 strategy. The European Union does not usually provide full funding for projects and policy implementation measures. All projects co-funded by the Structural Funds – especially within the framework of cohesion policy – have to be partly co-funded by the recipients themselves or by the respective local or regional authorities.

Most of the EU's policies, funds and funding programmes are planned and compiled by employees of the Directorate-Generals (DGs) of the European Commission that are responsible for the respective policy area, albeit in close cooperation with local and national experts, stakeholders, and policymakers. Moreover, all policies, funds, and funding programmes are outlined in accordance with the duration of the overall budgetary framework of EU policy making for a period of seven years. Hence, every seven years all funding schemes and programmes come to an end and are subject to readjustment, renegotiation, and reorientation. Some programmes are abandoned. Others are continued and readjusted according to new aims, objectives, and challenges of EU policy making as set out in the overall action plans and strategies of EU policy, such as the former Lisbon strategies and the current Europe 2020 strategy. Beyond that, all programmes pass through the official political processes of EU policy making, including official committees, the Parliament, and the European Council. Thus, preparing funding schemes and programmes for a new period takes several years before the programmes are officially set up.

When the individual funds and programmes are officially adopted and set up, the overall strategic aims and visions are reduced to concrete "operational programmes" (in the context of cohesion policy) or "work programmes" (in the context of EU research funding) displaying concrete "aims", "objectives", and "scopes" of funding to which potential beneficiaries must relate when applying for EU funding. Technically, all programmes and funding schemes are administered at the European level by the DGs and specialied executive agencies. In addition to compiling the programmes, the DGs of the Commission and adjunct executive agencies are also responsible for the overall programme management, selecting projects, and monitoring project implementation.[14]

Hence, EU funding policy is a highly structured and standardised system of policy making. It is organised as a multi-layered governance system that aims to mobilise numerous local and national project-based initiatives within a given European framework (see also Fred and Mukhtar-Landgren, Chapter 10, this volume). The entire system of EU policy implementation – from the European to local government level – is pervaded by the notions, logics, and standards of PM and related techniques and practices. This has directly affected the terminology of EU policy making, including the emergence of a particular "vocabulary" of EU funding policy, that is, a set of notions, technical terms, and abbreviations that are distinctive to EU policy implementation (Büttner et al., 2018). It has also fostered the emergence of new actors and new tasks in the administrative system of EU policy implementation, a stronger role for private actors in processing public policies, an enormous expansion of professional practices that are closely linked with PM (e.g., auditing, monitoring, and controlling), and a stronger emphasis on fundraising, professional project acquisition, reporting, and so forth. These professional structures of EU funding and the drive towards stronger specialisation and expansion of related practices will now be outlined in more detail.

The Professional Core of EU Funding: Insights into the Project World of EU Funding

European Union funding has fostered the rise of specialised experts and professionals at various levels of policy making and at different stages of policy implementation. In order to give an impression of the wide range of employment in the system of EU funding and to provide an overview of the various tasks and jobs linked with EU project funding and EU project implementation, we distinguish three major areas of employment: (a) *specialised administrative units* and *managing authorities* at various levels of government; (b) the so-called *beneficiaries* of EU funding applying for funding and implementing the projects in specific local settings; and (c) *specialised service providers* who support, advise, and monitor the aforementioned groups and bodies in their day-to-day business. These three areas of employment together make up the professional core of the project world of

EU funding; they are the major areas of activity of the numerous professional agents of EU policy implementation (for an overview, see also Figure 9.1).

In the following, I briefly discuss three major developments in the professional structure of EU funding. I start with a short overview of the two main areas of employment: the "specialised administrative units" and the so-called "beneficiaries" of EU funding. They are fundamental because they are generally the core actors of EU funding policies. The administrative units are the administrative backbone of EU funding, planning, controlling, and monitoring the process of policy implementation. The beneficiaries have to apply for project funding and deliver appropriate project proposals. However, since the acquisition and management of EU-funded projects are all but self-evident practices, huge effort is expended on informing potential beneficiaries about EU funding opportunities and the basics of project acquisition and management.

EU funding has also paved the way for the emergence of numerous private consultancies and private companies providing services to beneficiaries and administrative units related to the acquisition, administration, monitoring, or execution of EU-funded projects. The emergence of a private market of services is one of the most striking expressions of the increasing specialisation and professionalisation of EU funding. It supports the interpretation of a growing privatisation of policy making in contemporary governance systems and a strong tendency towards profit-seeking in the acquisition of EU funds.

Specialised Administrative Units: Planning, Administering, and Monitoring EU Funding

In the current system of EU funding policy, numerous *administrative units* at different levels of government are engaged with programming, managing, and monitoring EU funding programmes. The different programmes are usually managed and coordinated by the DGs and specialised *executive agencies*. In the case of cohesion policy, they are managed by so-called "management authorities" at national and regional levels of administration. These *managing authorities* typically have overall responsibility for managing and coordinating the implementation of a certain operational programme. They are usually located in a ministry of national or regional governments or in similar administrative units. They are often supported by additional technical offices and secretariats organising the calls for project proposals, selecting the participants and monitoring the implementation of individual projects, especially the legal and financial aspects of project implementations.

The management of EU programmes, and more particularly the implementation of each EU-funded project, is also routinely accompanied by comprehensive auditing, accounting, and evaluation activities. Thus, there is a strong drive to expand "rituals of verification" (Power, 1997) and "quantification" (Porter, 1995) in EU funding, practices that have arisen in the past three decades in many areas

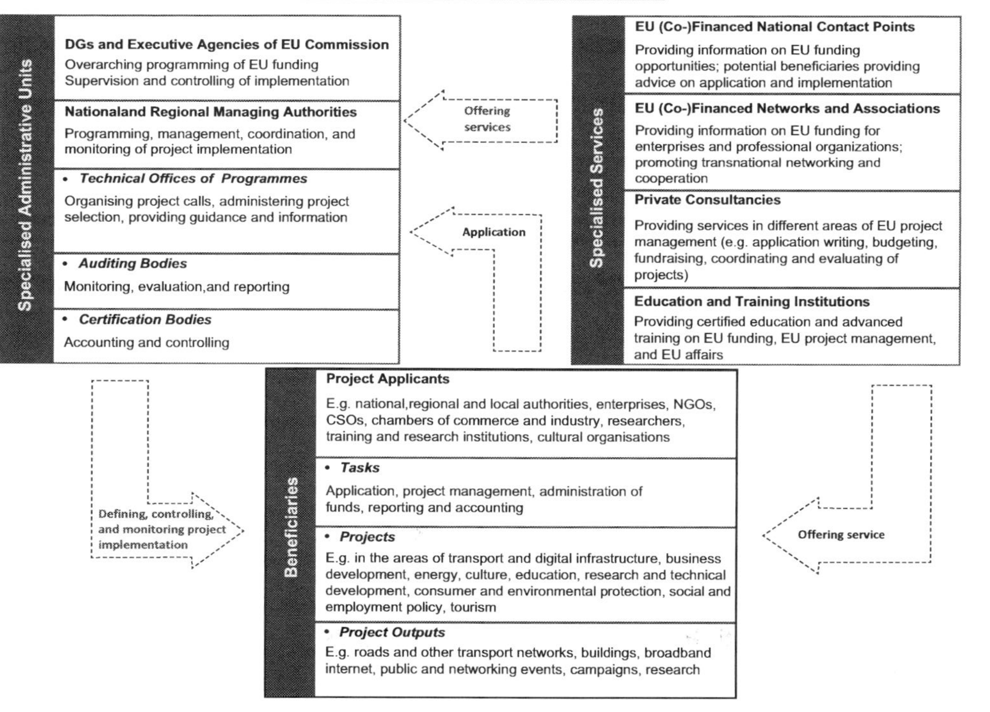

FIGURE 9.1 Project world of EU funding.

of public policy. Since the budgeting for projects is very strict, and the evaluation requirements are clearly fixed in the legal regulations of EU funding, the EU Commission outlines highly specific "evaluation guidelines" and publishes detailed evaluations of the "performance" of individual projects and programmes, or even an entire policy area.

Therefore, the administration of EU funding programmes is accompanied by an increasing number of auditing, monitoring, and controlling practices. In the current implementation system of EU cohesion policy, for instance, accounting and controlling of project expenditures are carried out by specialised *certification bodies*. Evaluation of the "effectiveness" and "efficiency" and reporting on the "impact" of individual projects is mainly monitored and coordinated by specific *auditing bodies*. In addition, numerous external experts and specialised consulting companies are hired on special-order contracts to monitor and evaluate the proper implementation of projects.

Beneficiaries: Adapting the Logics of Projectification

European Union funding provides resources to numerous actors, organisations, and institutions to support initiatives and policies that correspond as much as possible with European targets, aims, and values. Accordingly, many different types of actors and organisations can be *beneficiaries* of EU funding, in one way or another. They can be national, regional, and local authorities from both EU countries and non-EU countries[15], other public or private organisations, enterprises, associations and chambers, research institutions and individual researchers, non-governmental organisations (NGOs), educational and training institutions, regional development agencies, and many other regional and local organisations and networks. In addition, the size and scope of projects can vary significantly, ranging from setting up websites and information platforms, to publications, infrastructure, public events, personnel, academic studies, and research projects, to larger construction projects in infrastructure development and transportation, to name just a few examples.

First and foremost, however, in order to be "eligible" of EU funding, it is essential for beneficiaries to meet the aims and objectives outlined in a certain programme or scheme of funding. Beneficiaries must therefore link their planned activities with the aims and objectives put forward in the grant programmes. They need to explain precisely how and why their project will implement the objectives of the programme, calculate all future expenditures and set up "milestones", "outputs", and their own "evaluation criteria". Thus, in addition to fulfilling the administrative rules of project applications, a major challenge for beneficiaries is to present their activities as a contribution to achieving the general strategic aims of EU policy making (those outlined in the 2020 strategy, above all). Accordingly, beneficiaries must fully adapt to this rhetoric when applying for project funding. They often hire external specialists, such as private consultants and service providers, to help them in preparing the application and managing running projects. Many beneficiaries, especially those with some experience in EU funding, also employ their own EU funding specialists or even establish entire departments dedicated to EU project management. In these offices, specialist staff complete all necessary tasks, from project acquisitions and applications to project implementation and project administration or hire and cooperate with external specialists. These specialists are usually employed on limited contracts for the duration of project funding.

Hence, EU funding has paved the way for the expansion of jobs and occupations that correspond strongly with more general descriptions of the ethics of the *cité par projects* described by Boltanski and Chiapello (2005, p. 125). This means that many people within the project world of EU funding are not employed permanently, but depend on constantly acquiring new projects and continuous project funding. Accordingly, beneficiaries – and especially project workers – dealing with EU projects "on the ground" have to be "entrepreneurial" to a certain extent, and they must constantly look for new networking partners and funding opportunities (Bröckling, 2016). This fundamentally structures the logic of EU funding and the orientations of many local agents who are concerned with project acquisition and management. In order to prolong their employment, people are constantly obliged to acquire new funding opportunities and new projects. Since it is important to stay in contact with potential project partners, the ongoing search for further project opportunities and project partners is as important as being informed about current developments in EU funding. This creates a strong drive for the expansion of PM practices and fosters the expansion of projectified work and working conditions in the public sector and beyond.

The Rise of a Market of Specialised Services Around EU Funding and EU Project Management

It has already been highlighted how the current system of project-based policy implementation in the context of EU policy making produces a huge demand for consulting, advice, and information services. Accordingly, we can find a wide range of both public and private information offices, service providers, and training centres that inform potential beneficiaries about the basics of EU funding and the "*dos*" and "*don'ts*" of EU project management. First and foremost, there are about 500 Europe Direct Centres across every major city all around the EU territory, offering educational material and information about Europe and the EU in general, but also on basic aspects of EU funding. In addition, there are European Enterprise Networks offering advice to small and medium-sized enterprises on EU funds, related standards, and potential international cooperation partners (http://een.ec.europa.eu/). The increasing need for advice has also triggered a huge expansion in a private market of specialised service providers and consultancies. While public advisory services are usually free of charge and offer basic advice on technical details and general application procedures, these private consultancies offer more in-depth advice and support to current and potential beneficiaries. This has become a relatively big and vivid market in the past two decades.

Hence, the system of EU funding generates employment opportunities for people with expertise in areas like EU fundraising, managing funds, and implementing, evaluating, and coordinating EU funded projects. There seems to be a demand for advice, specialised training, and practical knowledge about how to acquire and manage EU funding, and there is an increasing need for specialists with particular practical knowledge of "how to do things" and the right kind of "EU literacy".[16] This goes hand-in-hand with a process of standardisation and codification of knowledge about EU funding and EU project management, which can also be seen in the expansion of specific academic and non-academic curricula and training programmes and the establishment of related professional associations at both European and national levels of policy making. The past two decades have seen an enormous increase in graduate studies offering degrees in "European Studies", "European Affairs", "European Law", and "European Management". While most of these study programmes focus on EU politics and the historical and cultural dimensions of European integration, some study programmes also explicitly include specialist educational schemes and training programmes on EU funding and EU project management. The most prestigious educational institute in the field of EU affairs, the College of Europe located in Bruges, offers special training courses and further education programmes on EU funding tailored to the needs of practitioners and specialists, including a one-week training course on "EU Project Management" which teaches how to raise EU funds, how to implement EU projects, and how to evaluate them.[17]

In addition to study programs and training courses provided by academic institutions, there is also a wide range of advanced training and further education on EU funding offered by private consultancies and educational institutes. Thus, professional training courses and certificates are offered for who would like to specialise in "EU project coordination", and special courses and training programmes are offered on specific EU funds and EU programmes (e.g., the European Social Fund, ERASMUS+, or "Creative Europe", the new EU support programme for Europe's cultural and creative sectors). Beyond that, in four-week training program provided by private service providers, one can also obtain a certificate in "EU Fundraising", which entails courses on the overall structure of EU funds and programmes, the particular "application lyrics" which are required when applying for project funding, and how to conceptualise and run potential projects.[18] Consequently, the emergence of certificates has fostered the creation of new occupational profiles in the area of EU funding. This increase in training and certification is also accompanied by the emergence of specific professional associations, such as the EU Fundraising Association.[19] These associations seek to "professionalise EU fundraising and EU project management" by setting "quality standards" and "codes of conduct" for this area of employment (http://eu-fundra

ising.eu/). They promote EU fundraising and project management as distinct "occupations" and serve as a platform for members to exchange information and experience and find potential collaboration partners. These new occupations can be seen as prototypical agents of projectification in contemporary public policy. Hence, in sum, there is a dynamic process of "professionalisation" within the project world of EU funding, in which different institutions, both public and private, provide professional training in tasks which are typical for the project world of EU funding. This fosters the standardisation and codification of EU project funding. Whether this helps reduce barriers to participating in EU funding, however, is highly debatable.

Final Remarks

This chapter has outlined the rise of projectification in EU policy making and major organisational features of the project world of EU funding. It has been argued that project funding was introduced at the European level to strengthen the capacity of policy making in times of very limited policy making competences. Indeed, along with the introduction of the European Single Market, the introduction of project funding has, overall, substantially transformed the nature of European governance and certainly strengthened the policy making capacity of the European Commission within the EU member states and beyond. However, as has been shown, the EU funding policies were introduced at the cost of strong standardisation of EU policy making and a strong emphasis on "efficient" and "effective" project management. Moreover, EU funding has become a highly distinctive field of practice requiring special knowledge and competences for those who are or who want to be "eligible" for receiving EU funding. Thus, EU funding policy has brought about a strong drive towards specialisation in EU policy implementation, in the sense that EU funding and EU project management have become a playing field for professionals and experts. These experts offer different kinds of professional services relating to EU project funding and EU project implementation, and in this way propel the expertisation of EU policy implementation. Hence, although EU funding centres around the idea that EU funding policies bring Europe "closer to the citizens", EU funding is mainly expert-driven.

Beyond that, EU funding fosters the emergence of notions, organisational standards, and practices and that are closely linked with rise of projectification: (a) an expansion of projectified jobs and working conditions in the public administration, especially in those areas that depend most on EU project funding, and (b) an enormous expansion of "rituals of verification" and "quantification" in the public sector (Porter, 1995; Power, 1997), for example, standards and practices of accounting, monitoring, and evaluating policy implementation which substantially determine the timing of policy making and the way public services are currently administered. Thus, practices of auditing, accounting, and controlling have gained huge significance in EU funding policy. These expert systems are a major driving force in the project world of EU funding, fostering the ongoing specification of standards and practices of EU project implementation.

Overall, two major distinctions become obvious within the current structures of EU funding. First, the distinction between professionals who have to apply for project funding and "deliver" policy outcomes and those who plan, control, and monitor the process of project funding. This distinction usually differentiates "beneficiaries" from people employed in the administrative offices of EU funding policy. The second distinction divides those who are employed relatively securely in permanent positions and those who are employed temporarily on limited contracts or as self-employed independent consultants for the duration of a particular task or project. The second distinction is not as clear-cut as the first, since it is strongly dispersed among the different areas of employment within the project world of EU funding. In general, however, it can be said that employees in public offices which plan, monitor, and control EU funding are more likely to be employed permanently than those whose jobs and positions are mainly dependent on project funding. In addition, a huge proportion of service providers are self-employed, offering their services as independent contractors on a fee basis. Hence, the projectification of public policy in the context of EU funding has a dual effect: while it creates new funding opportunities for numerous local actors and opens up job opportunities for a number of professionals, it also establishes new hierarchies within the existing structures of public policy among different kinds of professionals and fosters the expansion of generally unstable and, in part, precarious jobs and working conditions within and at the vicinity of the public sector.

Notes

1 The data and empirical insights used in this article derive from the research project "Professionalization of EU policymaking? A qualitative study of EU expertise". The project was a sub-project of the research group "Horizontal Europeanization", funded by the German Science Foundation (DFG) from 2012 to 2018. Most data were gathered between 2014 and 2016. They derive from content analyses of webpages, funding programs, related policy papers and from qualitative interviews with experts working in the field of EU funding. I am grateful to Lucia Leopold and Matthias Posvic for their contribution to data collection and for their input on earlier drafts of this chapter. Some results presented here have already been published in Büttner, S. and L. Leopold (2016). A "new spirit" of public policy? The project world of EU funding. *European Journal of Cultural and Political Sociology, 3*(1), pp. 41–71 copyright © European Sociological Association reprinted by permission of Taylor & Francis Group on behalf of European Sociological Association.

2 This is a prominent notion that is often used in the context of EU policy making, and especially with regards to EU cohesion policy and regional development funding.

3 This point of view is fuelled by observations of a resurgence of nationalist sentiments in international politics over the past few years. This has been epitomised by more recent political manoeuvres of the current U.S. administration, but also echoed by the Brexit

referendum in the United Kingdom in 2016 or in the ongoing quarrels over the redistribution of refugees and asylum seekers in EU politics (Outhwaite, 2017; Krastev, 2017).

4 The field-analytical approach draws on Pierre Bourdieu's conflict-theoretical conception of field analysis (see, for instance, Bourdieu & Wacquant, 1992). According to Bourdieu, social fields are socially constructed social spaces in which social relations are structured in terms of struggles for social recognition and social positioning. In social fields, distinct rules of play are established, fundamentally defining and determining legitimate actions within the field. Accordingly, Bourdieu distinguishes a variety of fields, such as the arts, bureaucracy, politics, and so forth. In more recent times, the field concept has also found its way into European studies (Fligstein, 2008; Georgakakis & Weisbein, 2010). Our conception of a transnational field of EU affairs follows this tradition (see Büttner et al., 2015).

5 The EU's current multi-annual budget from 2014 to 2020 amounts to EUR 1.082bn. About 30 percent of this budget is provided to farmers and businesses linked to the agricultural and fisheries industries in the form of direct payments. Another six percent is earmarked for financing the staff and the administrative apparatus of EU institutions. The remaining 64 percent, approximately EUR 690 bn, is allocated for the period 2014 to 2020 to fund different EU-initiated policies, of which the majority (about 70 to 80%) are subject to project funding of one sort or another.

6 Ika, Diallo and Thuillier (2010, pp. 63ff.) described the development of a distinct knowledge corpus of PM in international development. They call it international development PM (IDPM).

7 For similar interpretations, see also: Sjöblom, Löfgren & Godenhjelm (2013); Godenhjelm, Lundin, & Sjöblom (2015); Fred (2018); Godenhjelm et al., Chapter 8, Fred and Mukhtar-Landgren, Chapter 10, and Jałocha and Ćwikła, Chapter 11, all this volume.

8 For an overview, see http://ec.europa.eu/europe2020/index_en.htm (last accessed, September 2018).

9 Programming is a fundamental planning tool within PM. It allows a larger number of individual projects to be coordinated within a common framework. In this sense, there is a close link between the practice of programming and strategic planning. See: Maylor et al. (2006).

10 Since the 1960s thousands of books and articles – both practical guides and scientific reflections – have been published specifying the methods, techniques, and practices of PM and reflecting upon major caveats and pitfalls of various PM techniques and methods. A famous example from the numerous publications of this kind is the *Guide to the Project Management Body of Knowledge (PMBOK© Guide)* edited by the Project Management Institute (2013).

11 Also on this topic, see: Shaw, Hughes and Greenhalgh, Chapter 12, this volume.

12 For an overview of all existing EU funding programmes, see: https://ec.europa.eu/info/funding-tenders/funding-opportunities/funding-programmes/overview-funding-programmes_en (last accessed, September 2018).

13 For an overview see: http://ec.europa.eu/regional_policy/en/funding/ (last accessed, September 2018).

14 The only policy area in which the programming and management of EU funding is divided amongst different layers of policy making is cohesion policy and the related structural funds for rural development. In these areas, national and regional authorities compile and manage their own so-called "Strategic Reference Frameworks" (SRFs) and "Operational Programmes" (OPs), albeit in close accordance with the overall strategic visions and funding regulations of the EU cohesion policy (see Büttner, 2012).

15 Administrations and official state authorities from outside the area of the European Union can obtain EU funds, for instance, from pre-accession assistance or from the funds provided by the EU Neighbourhood Policy and Development Cooperation. The funding provided by EU cohesion policy, especially in the area of Territorial Cooperation, may also include beneficiaries from outside the EU.

16 For some examples of the services offered by consulting providers, see the following webpages: www.open-europe-consulting.eu/en, www.clerens.com/eu-project-management.html, or www.eucore.eu/ (last accessed, September 2018).
17 See at: http://do.coleurope.eu/prof/EUProjectManagement/ (last accessed, September 2018).
18 See, for example, the offers provided by consulting businesses in Germany at: www.eufrak.eu/weiterbildungen.html, or at: www.emcra.eu/akademie/qualifizierung-zum-eu-fundraiser/ (last accessed, September 2018).
19 See: www.efa-net.eu/ and for the equivalent at the national level in Germany, see: http://eu-fundraising.eu/ (last accessed, September 2018).

References

Beck, U., & Grande, E. (2007). *Cosmopolitan Europe*. Cambridge, England: Polity Press.

Bernhard, S. (2011). Beyond constructivism: The political sociology of an EU policy field. *International Political Sociology*, 5(4), pp. 426–445.

Boltanski, L., & ChiapelloE. (2005). *The new spirit of capitalism*. New York, NY: Verso.

Bourdieu, P., & Wacquant, L. (1992). *An invitation to reflexive sociology*. Chicago, IL: University of Chicago Press.

Bröckling, U. (2016). *The entrepreneurial self: Fabricating a new type of subject*. London, England: Sage.

Büttner, S. (2012). *Mobilizing regions, mobilizing Europe: Expert knowledge and scientific planning in European regional development*. London, England: Routledge.

Büttner, S., & Leopold, L. (2016). A "new spirit" of public policy? The project world of EU funding. *European Journal of Cultural and Political Sociology*, 3(1), pp. 41–71.

Büttner, S., Leopold, L., Mau, S., & Posvic, M. (2015). Professionalization in EU policy-making? The topology of the transnational field of EU affairs. *European Societies*, 17(4), pp. 569–592.

Büttner, S., Mau, S., Zimmermann, K., & Oeltjen, O. (2018). Benennungsmacht und vokabular der EU-governance. *Österreichische Zeitschrift für Soziologie*, 43(S1), pp. 37–63.

Cleland, D. I., & Gareis, R. (2006). *Global project management handbook: Planning, organizing and controlling international project*. New York, NY: McGraw-Hill.

Djelic, M. L., & Sahlin-Andersson, K. (Eds.) (2008). *Transnational governance: Institutional dynamics of regulation*. Cambridge, England: Cambridge University Press.

European Commission (2008). EU cohesion policy 1988–2008: Investing in Europe's future. *Inforegio panorama*, 26, June 2008. Luxembourg: Publications Office. Retrieved from http://eustructuralfunds.gov.ie/files/Documents/InvestinginEuropesFuture.pdf

Featherstone, K., & Radaelli, C. M. (Eds.) (2003). *The politics of Europeanization*. Oxford, England: Oxford University Press.

Fligstein, N. (2008). *Euro-clash: The EU, European identity, and the future of Europe*. Oxford, England: Oxford University Press.

Fred, M. (2018). *Projectification: The Trojan horse of local government*. Malmö, Sweden: Malmö University.

Garel, G. (2013). A history of project management models: From pre-models to the standard models. *International Journal of Project Management*, 31, pp. 663–669.

Georgakakis, D., & RowellJ. (Eds.) (2013). *The field of Eurocracy: Mapping EU actors and professionals*. Basingstoke, England: Palgrave Macmillan.

Georgakakis, D., & Weisbein, J. (2010). From above and from below: A political sociology of European actors. *Comparative European Politics*, 8(1), pp. 93–109.

Godenhjelm, S., Lundin, R. A., & Sjöblom, S. (2015). Projectification in the public sector: The case of the European Union. *International Journal Managing Projects in Business*, 8(2), pp. 324–348.

Habermas, J. (2015). *The lure of technocracy*. Cambridge, England: Polity Press.

Haller, M. (2008). *European integration as an elite Process: The failure of a dream?*London, England: Routledge.

Hodgson, D. E. (2002). Disciplining the professional: The case of project management. *Journal of Management Studies*, 39, pp. 803–821.

Hodgson, D. E. (2004). Project work: The legacy of bureaucratic control in the post-bureaucratic organization. *Organization*, 11, pp. 81–100.

Hofmann, H. C. H. (2008). Mapping the European administrative space. *West European Politics*, 31(4), pp. 662–676.

Hood, C. (1995). Contemporary public management: A new global paradigm? *Public Policy and Administration*, 10(2), pp. 104–117.

Hood, C. (1998). *The art of the state: Culture, rhetoric, and public management*. Oxford, England: Oxford University Press.

Hooghe, L. (2001). *The European Commission and the integration of Europe: Images of governance*. Cambridge, England: Cambridge University Press.

Hooghe, L., & Marks, G. (2001). *Multi-level governance and European integration*. Lanham, MD: Rowman & Littlefield.

Ika, L. A., Diallo, A., & Thuillier, D. (2010). Project management in the international development industry: The project coordinator's perspective. *International Journal of Managing Projects in Business*, 3(1), pp. 61–93.

Ika, L. A., & Hodgson, D. (2014). Learning from international development projects: Blending critical project studies and critical development studies. *International Journal of Project Management*, 32(7), pp. 1182–1196.

Kauppi, N. (2005). *Democracy, social resources and political power in the European Union*. Manchester, England: Manchester University Press.

Kovách, I., & Kučerová, E. (2009). The social context of project proliferation: The rise of a project class. *Journal of Environmental Policy & Planning*, 11, pp. 203–221.

Krastev, I. (2017). *After Europe*. Philadelphia, PA: University of Pennsylvania Press.

Landoni, P., & Corti, B. (2011). The management of international development projects: Moving toward a standard approach or differentiation? *Project Management Journal*, 42(3), pp. 45–61.

Lock, D. (2013). *Project management* (10th ed.). Farnham, England: Gower.

Majone, G. (1996). *Regulating Europe*. London, England: Routledge.

Matthijs, H. (2010). The budget of the European Union. IES Working paper series. 4/2010. Retrieved from www.ies.be/node/1062

Maylor, H., Brady, T., Cooke-Davies, T., & Hodgson, D. (2006). From projectification to programmification. *International Journal of Project Management*, 24(8), pp. 663–674.

Mellors, C., & Cooperthwaite, N. (1990). *Regional policy*. London, England: Routledge.

Moravcsik, A. (1998). *The choice for Europe: Social purpose and state power from Messina to Maastricht*. Ithaca, NY: Cornell University Press.

Morris, P. W. G. (1997). *The management of projects*. London, England: Thomas Telford.

Münch, R. (2010). *European governmentality: The liberal drift of multilevel governance*. London, England: Routledge.

Nokes, S., & Kelly, S. (2011). *The definitive guide to project management: The fast track to getting the job done on time and on budget*. Harlow, NY: Financial Times/Prentice Hall.

Outhwaite, W. (ed.) (2017). *BREXIT: Sociological responses*. London, England: Anthem Press.

Paton, S., Hodgson, D. E., & Cicmil, S. (2010). Who am I and what am I doing here? Becoming and being a project manager. *Journal of Management Development*, 29, pp. 157–166.

Porter, T. M. (1995). *Trust in numbers: The pursuit of objectivity in science and public life*. Princeton, NJ: Princeton University Press.

Power, M. (1997). *The audit society: Rituals of verification*. Oxford, England: Oxford University Press.

Project Management Institute (2013). *A guide to the project management body of knowledge (PMBOK® Guide)* (5th ed). Newton Square, Pennsylvania.

Rose, N., & Miller, P. (2008). *Governing the present*. Cambridge, England: Polity Press.

Sandholtz, W., & Stone Sweet, A. (1998). *European integration and supranational governance*. Oxford, England: Oxford University Press.

Scharpf, F. (1999). *Governing in Europe: Effective and democratic?*Oxford, England: Oxford University Press.

Shapiro, M. (2001). The institutionalization of European administrative space. In A. Stone Sweet, W. Sandholtz, & N. Fligstein (Eds.), *The institutionalization of Europe*. Oxford, England: Oxford University Press, pp. 94–112.

Sjöblom, S., Löfgren, K., & Godenhjelm, S. (2013). Projectified politics: Temporary organisations in a public context. Introduction to the special issue. *Scandinavian Journal of Public Administration*, 17(2), pp. 3–12.

Stevens, M., & Johnson, B. (2002). *Project management pathways*. Wycombe, England: The Association for Project Management.

Stone Sweet, A., Sandholtz, W., & Fligstein, N. (Eds.) (2001). *The institutionalization of Europe*. Oxford, England: Oxford University Press.

Vauchez, A. (2015). *Brokering Europe: Euro-lawyers and the making of a transnational polity*. Cambridge, England: Cambridge University Press.

Vauchez, A. (2016). *Democratizing Europe*. New York, NY: Palgrave Macmillan.

10

AGENTS, TECHNIQUES, AND TOOLS OF PROJECTIFICATION

Mats Fred

MALMÖ UNIVERSITY

Dalia Mukhtar-Landgren

LUND UNIVERSITY

Over the last couple of decades, *the project* as an organisational solution has been observed as a widespread practice in sectors as diverse as IT, housing, social services, education, and culture. This "projectification" of the public sector is characterised not only by an increase in number of projects (see Bergman et al., 2013; Brady & Hobday, 2011; Maylor et al., 2006) but also by more substantial processes of change (Mukhtar-Landgren & Fred, 2018; Packendorff & Lindgren, 2014). When project management (PM)-inspired language, as well as PM techniques and tools, permeate public sector organisations, it affects not only how specific projects are run but also how "ordinary" public service day-to-day activities are organised and executed (cf. Fred, 2018; Büttner, Chapter 9, this volume). In this regard, public sector projectification is characterised by processes of adaptation and transformation: individual and organisational agents change, adjust, match, or simply facilitate the use of project organisations and PM techniques. Previous research on projectification has documented the phenomenon of the increasing use of projects and PM techniques (see e.g. Godenhjelm, 2016; Lundin et al., 2015; Maylor et al., 2006; Grabher, 2002), as well as showing how it occurs in various sectors of society (Munck af Rosenschöld, 2017; Sanderson & Winch, 2017; Kuokkanen, 2016; Murray, 2016). While this research tends to focus on *why* processes of projectification emerge and in *what* contexts, we use the example of EU project funding in Swedish local government to analyse and understand *how* processes of projectification unfold in terms of transformation and adaptation. This is in addition to analysing and understanding what types of agents facilitate this development – in other words, the *who* and the *how* of public sector projectification.

In this chapter, we use the empirical example of EU social cohesion policy[1] as a case study for how processes of projectification unfold. On the European Commission's website, the social cohesion policy is described as "the EU's main investment policy" with the ambition "to support job creation, business competitiveness, economic growth, sustainable development, and improve citizens' quality of life" (European Commission, 2018). Almost a third of the total EU budget – €351.8 billion – has been allocated to the cohesion policy for 2014–2020, making it "the policy behind the hundreds of thousands of projects all over Europe" (ibid.). As cohesion policies are prevalent in almost all EU countries and organised in similar ways, they make a good case study for the dynamics of the *who* and the *how* of projectification. Project funding is the main policy instrument used to implement the social cohesion policy. In this chapter, the perspective of EU funding as a policy instrument, or a tool of government, is placed centre stage.

The EU social cohesion policy is implemented by creating incentives for local governments to participate by seeking project funding. This means that its success is dependent upon the EU's ability to spark the local will to join common policy goals (cf. Bruno et al., 2006). However, before any project funding is awarded, this potential local willingness must be paired with the competence to organise the work according to the EU's objectives (Carlsson & Mukhtar-Landgren, 2018). This governing technique is often referred to as soft governing (cf. Borrás & Jacobsson, 2004, p. 188; Trubek & Trubek, 2005; Bruno et al., 2006, p. 521). *Soft governing* is a concept used to describe governance based on *voluntary* participation and agreements. It is characterised by vague goal formulations, thus providing a certain local autonomy in terms of levels of interpretation (cf. Andone & Greco, 2018, p. 79; Borrás & Jacobsson, 2004). Here we apply the policy instrumentation perspective to argue that policy instruments are not demarcated tools but rather processual and contextual tools that initiate local processes as they are implemented as tools of government (Lascoumes & Le Galès, 2007). This implies that project funding within the implementation of EU cohesion policy unfolds on the local level in continuous processes of interpretation and adaptation.

We will argue that the degree of local discretion, and the need to facilitate and enable project funding, generates new (project-supporting) roles for older organisations as well as generating completely new agents of projectification active in each stage of the process – from the initial application to the final evaluation of EU projects – constituting what we describe as a project market. These agents will not be seen as mere intermediaries transferring knowledge from the EU to local government but as active *mediators* (Latour, 2005) involved in processes of transformation and adaptation (Czarniawska & Sevón, 2005). We see them as bridges in interpreting, transforming, and translating the substance of what is being mediated. They construct, and are themselves constructed in, local processes of change at the same time as they change and affect ideas and practices (Mukhtar-Landgren & Fred, 2018). We understand projectification in terms of the ongoing mediation of EU project techniques and tools into everyday local government practices. We refer to the agents involved in these processes as *mediators* and *agents* of projectification, and we refer to the strategies and policy instruments as *techniques* and *tools* of projectification.

The aim of this chapter is to conceptualise and analyse EU funding as a policy instrument, specifically, in terms of how processes of projectification are mediated, by whom, and with what techniques and tools. Using the example of EU project funding in Swedish local government, our guiding research questions are:

1. Who are the key mediators involved in the context of local government EU projects?
2. How do these mediators engage local government in EU projects, and with what techniques and tools?

Our main theoretical concepts of policy instrumentation and mediation are clarified in the proceeding section. Thereafter, a description of our methodological approach and empirical material follows. The remainder of the chapter is then devoted to a theoretically-informed empirical analysis of who the key mediators are and how they operate. The chapter concludes with a summary of our findings.

EU Funding as a Governing Tool: Processes of Policy Instrumentation and Mediation

We approach and analyse EU project funding in its capacity as a *policy instrument*. The policy instrumentation perspective reveals a theorisation of the relationship between governing and the governed, and each policy instrument "constitutes a condensed and finalized form of knowledge about social control and ways of exercising it" (Lascoumes & Le Galès, 2007, p. 11). Therefore, we regard policy instruments not as purely technical instruments or rational and discrete tools but rather as contextual and processual, generating effects that are materialised in different and often unexpected ways. This means that a policy instrument, such as EU funding, uses a variety of techniques and tools that produce specific effects of their own, independent of their stated objectives or the aims ascribed to them (cf. Lascoumes & Le Galès, 2007, p. 10; Büttner & Leopold, 2016). Lascoumes and Le Galès (2007) differentiate between instrument, techniques, and tools. An *instrument*, they argue, is a type of social institution at the macro level (in our case, "EU project funding"), a *technique* is a concrete device at the meso level that operationalises the instrument, and a *tool* is a micro device within a technique. In our case, the policy instrument used to implement EU policy is project funding, the techniques are the local and regional strategies and processes that "open up" and/or create content as well as form for EU projects, and the tools are the instruments and practices of management used in the day-to-day practices of local government organisations.

Following Lascoumes and Le Galès typology of different policy instruments, EU funding can be regarded as a "new" public policy instrument. In contrast to the more traditional policy instruments based on legislation or economic and fiscal motives, the new policy instruments offer "less interventionist forms of public regulation" (Lascoumes & Le Galès, 2007, p. 13) and are based either on "agreement and incentives", "information and communication" or "de facto standards and best practices" (ibid., p. 12). These new sets of policy instruments are all prevalent in the implementation of EU project funding, based on soft governing techniques and "lend themselves to organizing a different kind of political relations, based on communication and consultation" (ibid, p. 13; cf. Büttner & Leopold, 2016; Godenhjelm et al., 2015).

The skills and infrastructure needed to implement EU cohesion policy has led to an emerging field of EU expertise – what Büttner and Leopold describe as the "EU project world" – where a wide range of private and public agents engage "with the acquisition, implementation, management, evaluation and monitoring of EU-funded projects" (Büttner & Leopold, 2016, p. 54; cf. Mukhtar-Landgren & Fred, 2018; Chapter 9, this volume). EU funding initiates a number of simultaneous yet overlapping local processes, thus opening up for a "proliferation of actors" (Lascoumes & Le Galès, 2007, p. 2) with diverging initiatives and actions. In regard to agents, policy instruments, such as EU funding, can be seen as forms of institutions "partly determin[ing] the way in which the actors are going to behave" (Lascoumes & Le Galès, 2007, p. 9). In this sense, the capacities for action of different agents of EU project funding, ranging from civil servants to consultants, differ widely depending on local interpretations by different public and private agents – a testament to the importance of studying who these agents are and how they operate.

Processes of Mediation

When EU policies are implemented in local government, they are not merely transferred from the EU to the local level but rather are continuously developed and changed with their application in new contexts (see, for example, Czarniawska, 2008; Czarniawska & Sevón, 2005; Clarke et al., 2015; Munday, 2016). In other words, they are translated in a simultaneous process of movement and transformation (Suarez & Bromley, 2015, p. 145). Agents involved in these processes of change each add to the proliferation of ideas as they materialise into concrete forms of local government practice (cf. Czarniawska & Joerges, 1996). However, the materialisation of ideas is not only expressed in *ideational* changes in policy content but also in *organisational* change, such as the embodiment of new organisations, new roles for old organisations, or the emergence of new divisions, subunits, or lines of demarcation (cf. Latour, 1986; Lavén, 2008, p. 32; Czarniawska & Joerges, 1996). As a result of the combination of the policy instrumentation perspective and theories of mediation and translation, projectification is not only to be regarded as an increase in the number of projects within an organisation or organisational field but also as processes of transformation and adaptation. This entails changes influenced by PM techniques and tools in the practices of individual and organisational agents (cf. Fred, 2018).

The agents involved in local government EU project work are thus not passive links "simply diffus[ing] a fixed set of ideas and practices" but rather mediators (cf. Söderholm & Wihlborg, 2013, p. 268). For Bruno Latour, the concept of *mediators* highlights how actors, by necessity, "transform, translate, distort, and modify the meaning or the elements they are supposed to carry". The concept of the mediator developed in contrast to the concept of *intermediary* agents, or those who simply "transport[s] meaning" without changing it (Latour, 2005, p. 39). Mediators act upon ideas which are translated and acted upon in the process. They transform and translate the ideas by adapting and adjusting them to regional and local circumstances, thus involving continued local and regional processes of change (Latour 1986). Mediators are also often associated with specific agents within or around organisations, where they appear as bridges in interpretations and contextualisation (Söderholm & Wihlborg, 2013). Yet, from a theoretical perspective, mediators are not actors that proceed or act "outside" processes of mediation; instead, these actors emerge and take form in the mediating processes. In the case of EU project funding, a number of new actors, roles, and organisations are not only produced but also constantly reproduced in processes of projectification through the instrumentation of EU policy (cf. Chapters 9, 11, and 12, this volume).

The Swedish Case, Research Design and Empirical Material

Our empirical focus has been on Skåne, Sweden's southernmost region and a successful region in regard to EU applications. Skåne consists of 33 local governments, or municipalities,[2] where the largest (in terms of number of inhabitants) is Malmö, with a population of approximately 330,000, and the smallest is Perstorp, with around 7,000 inhabitants. Compared to most other countries, local self-government is strong in Sweden. Each municipality has great freedom to make decisions about its own activities and organisation including independent powers of taxation (Montin & Granberg, 2013; Larsson & Bäck, 2008). The responsibilities and activities of Swedish municipalities are comprehensive: They employ roughly 770,000 people (almost 20% of the entire workforce of Sweden) and are major applicants for, and recipients of, EU funds.

Our empirical material consists of 32 semi-structured and transcribed interviews conducted with local government civil servants and regional EU coordinators between 2015–2017 as well as official EU documents from all 33 municipalities and several regional governmental bodies and networks. The analysis of both the interviews and the documents was done in two steps. First, we located key agents in local government EU work in Skåne, meaning the key individuals, organisations, and networks commonly referred to by civil servants, websites, reports, or policy documents. This step had the characteristics of a qualitative and lighter type of social network analysis (Wassermann & Faust, 1994) where, instead of statistical data or techniques, we used a snowball sampling approach. One statement or person led to another, generating a map with key connections of people in Skåne related to EU projects. The second step was to investigate how the identified agents work to enable or promote local government EU projects. Here, we used the distinction made by Lascoumes and Le Galès (2007) between instrument, techniques, and tools, with a particular focus on the latter two and how they incentivise local government project organisations.

The chapter builds on previous research on how EU project funding not only supports but also accelerates the tendencies of public sector projectification (see for example Godenhjelm, 2016; Büttner & Leopold, 2016). The context of local government EU projects is a fruitful area to study mediators in processes of public sector projectification for a number of reasons. First, the context involves several tiers of government, creating "space to manoeuvre" for the initiation and/or installation of mediators. Second, as the implementation of EU project funds is based on a voluntary coordination at a sub-national level (Bruno et al., 2006, p. 52), it creates incentives for local and regional governments to comply with and join common policy goals thus installing functions or engaging in processes to do so (see Sørensen & Triantafillou, 2015; Carlsson & Mukhtar-Landgren, 2018). Third, and more generally, "the EU project world" (Büttner & Leopold, 2016) is important to study on the local and practical level because EU projects are widely implemented and affect thousands of European civil servants, organisations, and citizens.

The *Who* and the *How* of Projectification

European structural and investment funds have been described as the "home turf" of multilevel governance (Marks, 1992), with their strong emphasis on implementation in levels ranging from the European to the local city district. This is reinforced in practice through the partnership principle. The modus operandi of the partnership principle is to involve the most relevant actors in regional development (Bache, 2004, p. 119), including both public, private, and civil society actors with local knowledge and insights in regional preconditions and prerequisites for success (Klijn & Koopenjan, 2000; Sørensen & Torfing, 2011). Or, as stated on the home page of the European Social fund: "Working in partnership is the best way to ensure that spending is as effective and efficient as possible and meets the needs of the region or community concerned" (ESF, 2018a).

The structural funds and the social cohesion policy are thus implemented through multi-actor negotiations in vertical and horizontal partnerships (Dabrowski et al., 2014 p. 355). The multi-actor character permeates every level of the implementation process – from the formal organisation of the decision-making bodies to the singular projects which are expected to be collaborative and network-based (Carlsson & Mukhtar-Landgren, 2018). In Sweden, different EU funds are organised in different ways, but one re-occurring aspect is the prevalence of regional organisations. For instance, The Social Fund, the Region Development Fund, and Leader all function primarily on the regional level. As a result, our empirical mapping focused on the regional and local levels of implementation, while keeping in mind that several of these funds also have a formal national body.

Today, the European Structural and Investment Funds finance 27 different programmes "in which Swedish organisations, government agencies and enterprises can participate" (SAERG, 2016, p. 1). From our policy instrumentation perspective, the EU funding applied in these schemes initiates processes of implementation that unfold continuously on the regional and local level. Below, we describe this process through an initial section that maps and analyses (a) the mediating agents of projectification in Skåne and (b) the techniques and tools applied in the processes of instrumentation and mediation.

The Agents of Projectification

Swedish municipalities engage with the EU social cohesion policy when they apply for funding from the structural and investment funds (Carlsson & Mukhtar-Landgren, 2018). It is through the application process that they enter the project world of formal EU institutions. When entering this world, they interact with three different forms of organisations which, although they are separated and specified here, are much more interlinked in practice. First, the implementation of the EU funds is channelled through formal, top-down public agencies as part of the EU project funding architecture, meaning regional, often decision-making, offices. Secondly, and parallel to the establishment of formal EU organisations, municipalities have, as a result of EU funding opportunities, developed a number of bottom-up organisations and networks engaged in different aspects of EU project work. Third, and finally, in tandem with these developments, a field of EU-related expertise has emerged in Skåne, including a range of consultancy firms that, in various ways, promote the use of projects and EU funding in local government. Municipalities navigate between these three types of organisations in all processes of the EU project funding cycle – from project ideas to project application and project evaluation.

Starting with the first group, the formal project funding architecture of the EU has generated a number of new institutions in Skåne. Regulated by the EU (Regulation [EU] nr 1303/2013, L 347/321), these "new" institutions lay down, amongst other rules, the common provisions for a number of EU funds including CF, EAFRD, EMFF, ERDF, ESF, and.[3] In the regulation, it is stated that member states are to form partnerships to implement the funds. The organisation of the partnerships differ somewhat between countries and funds but have in common the fact that they entail the incidence of new forms of regional organisations acting as mediators between the EU and municipalities, and as such, are also agents of projectification. One example is the ESF council, a state authority responsible for EAFRD and ESF, which is an organisation with eight regional offices throughout Sweden (ESF, 2018b). Another example is the SAERG

Council in Skåne[4] working to "ensure that EU funds are invested in projects that promote regional growth and employment" (SAERG, 2018) or the seven Leader offices[5] in Skåne that explicitly work with project support (Leader in Skåne, 2018). These organisations, initiated top down, all have regional strategies for the implementation of the different EU funds: they administrate them and provide a number of project-supporting functions. Together with the five *Europe Direct* offices in Skåne that provide individuals and organisations with information about the EU, they are the foundation of the EU's partnership-based multilevel system mediating between the EU and the regional and local governments.

In addition to the emergence of these "new" EU organisations, existing institutions at different levels take on new roles as a consequence of EU multilevel governance (cf. Stephenson, 2013, p. 828). The formal political organisation, Region Skåne (the county council), is one example of an organisation that has taken on new functions in the processes of implementing EU funding. It has an important role in setting up regional goals for the ESF and the ERDF and has a staffed office in Brussels.

We also find several regional *bottom-up* partnerships installed by the municipalities in Skåne. One example is the Skåne Association of Local Authorities (KFSK), a regional collaborative organisation initiated and governed by the 33 municipalities in Skåne and staffed with a sub-division focused solely on municipal EU issues. KFSK's activities are financed through membership fees from the municipalities, fees from the courses and conferences they organise, and through external project funding (KFSK, 2018a). Two similar organisations are *Skåne Northeast* and *Southeastern Skåne* (SÖSK). The explicit purpose of these organisations is to support municipalities' EU-related work. One example is SÖSK, which supports the municipalities by providing *project developers* whose roles are to "actively work with project advice to the member municipalities" (SÖSK EU Strategy, 2015, p. 7).

When civil servants in the smaller municipalities were interviewed, they spoke of difficulties in keeping up with EU-related policies, thus rendering the regional support an important part of EU-related work. As a result, the regional bottom-up organisations have great legitimacy within the municipalities (cf. Mukhtar-Landgren & Fred, 2018). However, legitimacy also comes in terms of output, in terms of the ability to enable funding and initiate projects: *Skåne Nordost*, for instance, state on their website that they "have been able to facilitate the acquisition of SEK 280 million (approx. €27 million) through different [EU] projects" (Skåne Nordost, 2018).

Where the regional level is emphasised in the governance architecture of the EU cohesion policy and in the EU structural and investment funds, the local level is more diffuse, and municipalities lack a formal role therein (Carlsson & Mukhtar-Landgren, 2018). As a result, municipalities not only seek information and support from the aforementioned top-down organisations or engage in bottom-up organisation but also employ their own EU experts. All 33 municipalities employed at least one EU expert, and in some cases, several. They have titles such as EU Coordinators or EU Strategists, and in some municipalities, EU work is delegated to a Business Developer. These EU experts are usually employed in central administration, which has close links with the city council and management. Their mediating roles differed somewhat depending on municipality. Some describe their role as providing information about possible EU funds, while others talked about how the work would enable others to apply for funding. Also, several describe how their sole purpose was to enable different departments to increase their work with EU-funded projects. An example of the latter is in Östra Göinge, where the EU coordinator is described as a person working to guide the municipality's activities "by matching their needs with external funding opportunities, supporting them in developing project ideas and seeking external funding for projects" (Östra Göinge, 2018). In Malmö, as well as in Kristianstad, we found not only several EU coordinators but also a network of coordinators working to build the organisational capacity to handle future EU projects.

In addition to these *public* top-down and bottom-up organisations and initiatives, our mapping revealed that *private* companies play an important role in promoting the initiation of EU projects. The use of consultancy firms is common in Skåne, primarily in relation to different kinds of EU and project training courses, seminars, evaluations, and audits. The consultancy firms range from local consultants with just a few employees to larger internationally recognised enterprises with regional offices. The municipal will to participate in EU projects along with their relative lack of EU knowledge and project skills have made Skåne an attractive place for consultancy firms with EU and/or project expertise.

Finally, it is important to emphasise that the boundaries between different agents of projectification are often blurred and that actors tend to move around and assume different roles. During our research, we also noticed that it was common for individual agents to move between these different positions. For instance, we found one EU coordinator who works part time as an EU consultant from "within" local government to promote EU projects, but who also worked from "outside" to promote the same. Another civil servant initially worked as a regional EU facilitator to later work for a municipality as an EU coordinator. Yet another civil servant moved in the opposite direction; after having spent some time in Brussels, this person went from a municipality to the regional office.

To summarise, a wide range of projectification agents divide, share, and assemble what we regard as a regional market of EU project funding. At this market, different roles are taken that come into play. Those that are initiated top-down and embedded within the formal decision-making procedures of the EU have the ascribed purpose of managing the funds, informing about funding and supporting organisations with an interest to participate and apply for EU funding. Others are formed bottom-up and emerge from a lack of EU knowledge and expertise, a willingness to engage in EU work, and the attraction of external funding. In addition to these top-down and bottom-up initiatives, there is also a considerable market share available for consultancy firms facilitating local government EU projects through consultation, training courses, and audits. Processes of projectification are thus facilitated bottom-up as well as top-down and within the confinements of a sizable market, where many agents appear to know each other or at least know about each other. In the next section, we describe and analyse how these mediating agents work in practice when adjusting, appropriating, and transforming EU knowledge and information to municipalities.

Techniques and Tools of Projectification

Within the regional market of EU project funding, the different agents use a number of techniques and tools that have been developed to enable the acquisition of EU funding. As the implementation of social cohesion policy is based on incentives for project funding through local alliances and regional networking, a number of softer policy techniques have been developed in Skåne. After surveying our empirical material, we have categorised the techniques and tools used by the aforementioned mediating agents and place them accordingly into five sections: (i) information, (ii) collaborations and meetings, (iii) courses and training, (iv) road maps and EU strategies, and finally, (v) consultation. These are presented and exemplified below in terms of techniques (i.e. the strategies and processes that "open up" and/or create the content and form of EU projects) and tools (i.e. the day-to-day practices and micro devices of local government organisations).

Information

> By using EU funding, the municipality can raise the ambition level of local development projects and also become a more attractive employer who, with the help of EU funding, can strengthen staff skills in a number of areas.
>
> *(Kristianstad, 2018)*

This quotation taken from a municipal website is a typical example of how actors use information as a technique of government (exemplified here with the internet as a policy tool). The mediating agent chooses what to emphasise and what not to emphasise, or even include at all about the EU. Our mapping revealed that the information on the municipal websites is directed primarily at two target groups; (i) citizens, regarding what the EU "is" and what it "does" for the municipality and (ii) organisations or civil servants in search of EU funding. In addition to this general information, descriptions of ongoing and/or completed EU projects are common. Related to the project descriptions is another frequently-used EU policy tool, *best practices*, which refers to projects that are presented to other organisations as successful and inspiring examples. The ongoing projects are often described in terms of future "success" and worded in terms of the future results of the project. Best practices are also found on the regional level. KFSK, for instance, has a special web page devoted to "The EU project of the month", where successful EU projects are presented (KFSK, 2018b), a platform also used by municipalities to showcase their best projects.

In addition to websites, all agents, with the exception of consultants, produce and disseminate brochures, booklets, or pamphlets about the EU in general or their own organisations' EU-related work, including individual EU projects. One example of a widely distributed brochure in Skåne is "Your guide to EU funding" (KFSK et al., 2018).[6] In the foreword, it states that the purpose of the publication "is to showcase the possibilities of the EU's programs and funds". Other examples are the reports from the ESF council and the SAERG Council intended to inform about and inspire potential EU project applications.

While these techniques and tools of information could be defined as an attempt of neutral provision of factual information, the extent to which it is used and the volume of information acts to promote engagement. In addition, some of the material goes beyond the provision of information to adopt a more explicit promotional tone.

Collaboration and Meetings

> My Europe 2018 – What does the EU do for the Municipalities of Skåne?
>
> On 3 May, the municipalities of Skåne opened the doors to visitors to the My Europe 2018 event. The purpose of the day was to highlight and demonstrate how EU investments create positive local effects by giving visitors concrete examples of how the EU creates development opportunities in their neighbourhood.
>
> *(KFSK, 2018c)*

All mediators are inherently collaborative in their organisational structure. The bottom-up organisations all comprise a number of collaborating municipalities. Yet, as the KFSK website quotation shows, collaboration is also an important policy instrument or technique. Meetings and conferences are important tools, as they combine the ambitions to inform and promote with an ambition to network; hence, it can be understood in terms of a "deliberate choice to govern" (Vangen et al., 2015, p. 1239) by bringing organisations together to attain certain political goals. At the meeting presented in the quotation, the visitors were given the opportunity to "[m]ingle and network with around 15 projects in Skåne [… and] opportunities to learn more about the EU's policy processes where provided" (KFSK, 2018c). These events enable EU projects by bringing possible project collaborators or stakeholders together, showcasing good examples of past projects, and directing potential stakeholders and municipalities to where EU funding is available. Another example is the "European Day" which is "celebrated" every year on 9 May. In 2017, a range of organisations[7] co-organised an event on this day to highlight projects and give municipalities the opportunity to meet and learn from each other as well as receive information about where and how they can apply for further EU funding (Hässleholm, 2018).

In addition to arranging meetings and conferences, the regional bottom-up organisations coordinate several networks, including a Horizon 2020 network, a Brussels network, a network coordinating EU funding, and a network designated for strategical EU issues (KFSK, 2018d). But it is not solely the bottom-up organisations that use these networking tools: The formal EU organisations, ERDF and ESF, also organise conferences to bring together potential project partners and showcase successful past projects. They also organise learning networks of EU project managers and project evaluators.

The techniques and tools of collaboration and meetings open up for EU funding possibilities and generate incentives by providing access to funding opportunities and project partners, as well as best practices to choose from. However, they also create a sense of community where agents know and learn from each other; at the same time, a certain measure of competition is detected along the lines of "if they initiated such a project, perhaps we could or should too".

Courses and Training

Regions and consultants, and to some extent municipalities, arrange courses related to EU funding. These were not only general PM courses but also courses targeting EU projects or EU funding more specifically. The courses are the result of mediating processes where the agents present not only what the municipalities can apply for funding towards but also which types of PM are preferred and recommended by EU organisations. KFSK, as one of the bottom-up organisations, offers a range of EU-related courses including "Economics in EU applications and the management of EU projects" and "EU projects 3.0 – for optimal use of EU funding" (KFSK, 2018d). In contrast, SÖSK works to continually train new *project developers* in each municipality so that new projects can be developed locally and regionally. Thus, the regional bottom-up organisations take on the role of showing the municipalities how to initiate and manage EU projects as well as assuming the role of developer by designing appropriate EU projects for its members.

In several municipalities, we found consultants who were involved in the training courses and in the development of municipal project models to be used in EU projects – models that also demanded further training for the employees. In Eslöv municipality, for instance, a consultancy firm was involved in the development of a project model as well as in several project management and project methodology courses to civil servants as well as to politicians. Similar, but with a specific EU focus, Malmö continuously works to train their EU coordinators in areas relating to the EU, EU funding, and PM.

Although we do not have a full picture of who attends these courses, it is clear that there are more people taking PM and EU-related courses than there are people involved in EU projects in Skåne. Initiated from within the municipalities as well as from outside, the training courses aim to equip civil servants and organisations with tools and techniques to handle (future) projects in general and EU projects in particular. They work to construct a particular understanding of the EU and EU projects, and in doing so, shape legitimacy for the participation in EU funding processes, among other things, through EU strategies or road maps.

Road Maps and EU Strategies

Several municipalities have specific policies or official strategies related to either externally funded projects in general or towards EU projects in particular. These policies and strategies reveal how municipalities want to work; furthermore, they reflect the municipalities' will and direction, as it is here where they demonstrate their view of EU work. As a typical example, Hässleholm has an "EU strategy" with the purpose of "strengthening EU knowledge and access to EU funding through project funding" (Hässleholm, 2016).[8] Lomma has an "internationalisation policy", in which EU projects are specified as an important tool in the pursuit "of achieving better results for the municipality" (Lomma, 2018). These roadmaps can be seen as a methodology to "de-silo" organisations (cf. Brandtner et al., 2017) and gather different actors around joint ventures, encouraging employees to apply for EU funding and providing them with the legitimacy to do so. We found yet another, more far-reaching example of EU strategy in Kristianstad. Here, the city management has adapted the municipal budget to fit the concepts and structure of "Europe 2020" (Kristianstad budget, 2017) with the purpose of increasing the possibilities to receive EU funding.

Although initiated top-down, the road maps and the EU strategies are less of an interventionist form of techniques and tools and more of incentivising approach that enables and gives civil servants and municipal organisations legitimacy to act upon and engage in EU funding processes.

Consultation

Consultation comprises techniques and tools used by mediators to advise and consult in relation to EU-related work. As mentioned, some EU coordinators describe their role as consulting others to apply for EU funding or ensure the organisations increase their use of EU funding. However, the regional bottom-up organisations, as well as some private consultancy firms, also use consultation techniques and tools to increase the use of projects. One such tool utilised broadly in Skåne is the EPA (EU Project Analysis). These analyses are offered to municipalities by the aforementioned regional bottom-up agents. The purpose of an EPA is to "map how municipalities can use EU funding in local development planning" (KFSK, 2018e). In practice, this entails a process in which municipal documents (e.g. budgets and visionary/development plans) are reviewed by a coordinator and local development priorities are "matched" with EU project-funding opportunities. The EPA method is described as an "in-depth analysis" in order to "give each individual municipality a clear picture of how to make use of EU funding in their development" (ibid.). In relation to an identified problem (e.g. the integration of newly arrived immigrants), the municipality is presented with a "smörgåsbord" of funding opportunities, and suggestions on how the policy problem at hand could be reformulated into an EU project to receive funding. This can include describing "education" in terms of "life-long learning" or long-term unemployment in terms of "social exclusion" (cf. Mukhtar-Landgren & Fred, 2018). The EPA analysis was developed by KFSK, but we found similar tools (although under different names) conducted and sold by other regional agents in Skåne, like the aforementioned Leader organisations, for instance.

Another example of consultation comes from consultancy firms. Municipalities regularly use these firms to audit EU projects and how the municipalities work with and organise EU projects. In the conclusions of these written audit reports, more EU projects are generally strongly encouraged. As a typical example, the consultants involved in Lund recommended that the municipality acquire more knowledge of EU funding and also apply for more project funding than was then the case:

> The fact that not all subunits examined have applied for funds from the EU is a testament, according to our assessment, of the fact that the municipality does not make optimal use of the opportunities that comes with EU funding.
> *(Öhrlings, 2008, p. 1)*

Although the audit reports are something that the municipality does not necessarily have to consider in their future work, they do encourage municipalities to engage in more EU projects, and this seems to make a difference in practice. A few years ago, in certain municipalities that were audited, we could trace project activities back to the audit reports. In Eslöv, for instance, the EU coordinator claims that he was hired, that their EU policy was implemented, and that several EU applications were completed as a result of the audit (Interview, EU coordinator, 2016).

The audit reports may thus be important as tools to legitimise and support the further use of EU projects. It should be noted that some consultancy firms also provide the service of reviewing EU projects as well as a service they call "audit as a basis for successful projects". These consultants act as mediating "EU experts", auditing local government EU activities to map what the municipalities do and could do with EU funding. These audits generally result in the recommendation to apply for more EU funding and engage in more EU projects.

Summarising Discussion

The aim of this study was to contribute to the understanding of how processes of projectification unfold in local government through processes of instrumentation and mediation – with an empirical focus on the questions, "by whom?" and "with what techniques and tools?". Our analysis was divided into two sections. In the first section, we located key projectifying agents in local government EU work in Skåne, and in the second section, we investigated how they worked and which techniques and tools they used to enable and promote local government EU projects. We found three separate but interrelated categories of agents of projectification: *formal (EU-associated) decision-making agencies, bottom-up organisations and networks initiated by the municipalities themselves*, and *a range of consultancy firms*. Taken together, these agents develop and utilise a number of techniques and tools resulting in processes of projectification.

The mapping of agents and their practices indicates a strong prevalence of soft governing techniques, based not on sanctions or binding legislations but rather on incentives and mutual agreements (cf. Andone & Greco, 2018). The purpose of the policy instruments employed in relation to the structural and investment funds can thus be said to enable, facilitate, and promote the use of EU funding. In this regard, EU agents (including institutions, authorities, and consultancy firms) make EU projects possible and pave the way for agents eager to engage in local government EU work.

In this chapter, EU project funding has been described as a process of policy instrumentation unfolding in ongoing and continuous processes of projectification. While Büttner and Leopold (2016) describe how these processes materialise in an "EU project world", we conceptualise the day-to-day practices of that world in terms of an EU project funding market held together by mediators and their application of policy techniques and tools of information, roadmaps/policies, collaborations/networks, courses, and consultation. Several of the techniques and tools (training courses, project support) are sold to the municipalities as services on a market. In this regard, the policy instrumentation of EU funding has generated a regional market in which municipalities can acquire project techniques and expertise as well as collaborating partners that are necessary to get funding. Even the networking activities, conferences, and meetings have the characteristics of being part of a market: project funding is "available" for your choosing, different agents are presented or constructed as possible project collaborators or stakeholders, and you may also "shop" for best practices as solutions to the many problems your municipality struggles with.

Within the EU project funding market, transactions are made between different public and private agents and the goods "available to purchase" are not only EU funding and EU expertise but also project courses, project partners, best practices, and network activities. This echoes the argument of Aron Buzogány (2013), who describes the public sector as developing "into consultancy-like companies with rather symbiotic relationships towards donor agencies" (p. 81) due to the policy instrumentation of EU funding. Even though some agents, primarily the formal, decision-making agencies, partake in the EU project funding market in order to inform, others (including bottom-up organisations and consultancy firms) are there to promote and increase the use of EU funding in local government, albeit with different motives.

The local and regional (public and private) agencies are inhabited by a number of different individuals. Our empirical analysis indicated that these individuals often moved between the different types of agencies. They often changed positions, roles, and organisations – but they continued working within the same market of EU funding. In the words of Kovách and Kučerová (2009), these individuals can be seen as part of a larger societal development – the rise of a "project class". The emphasis on projects and the demand for local expertise and managerial skills strengthen the legitimisation of the project class, thus "making it not only a class of experts, but also a managerial category that is part of the implementation of project programmes" (Kovách & Kučerová, 2006, p. 4). So, what do these actors do? The techniques and tools used by these agents – information, collaboration and meetings, courses and training, road maps and EU strategies, and consultation – are all soft policy techniques based on creating local incentives for the municipalities to engage in EU projects. The soft governing approach gives local governments a certain autonomy when it comes to interpreting, adapting, and transforming the content and the practical outlet of the social cohesion policy. While some of the techniques imply a mere distribution of information, we argue that they all serve a promotional purpose, but some are used to more explicitly and thoroughly transform and adapt local policies and strategies to match the aim and objectives of the social cohesion policy and the specific funds. We found that the bottom-up organisations as well as some consultants do not only facilitate or help out when asked or commissioned to do so but also explicitly promote the use of EU funding and design and propose specific projects for the municipalities.

So, how do processes of projectification unfold? We argue that they unfold through the workings of different agents sharing, at the same time as constructing, a project funding market in which they mediate between EU funding and possible EU projects. The mediators are situated between the "available" EU funds on one side and possible local government EU projects on the other. At this market, some mediators inform about possible funding. Others enable funding opportunities and project activities through networks, training courses, and meetings. And yet some promote and "sell" projects and project ideas through courses, best practices, or the transformation and adaptation of local government strategies and policies to those of EU funding requirements. Processes of projectification are triggered by project-supporting incentives created top-down at the same time as several bottom-up initiatives trigger the same phenomenon. Also, processes of projectification are triggered regardless of whether there are or ever will be any EU projects. The municipalities not only employ EU strategists and engage in EU bottom-up organisations and EU networks but also train staff in PM and project methodology and develop project models to handle possible forthcoming projects. The result is that they future-proof the organisation in terms of agents of projects and PM techniques and tools.

Notes

1 Sometimes described as the EU's Regional Policy.
2 In total, Sweden has 290 municipalities.
3 The European Social Fund (ESF), the European Regional Development Fund (ERDF), the Cohesion Fund (CF), the European Agricultural Fund for Rural Development (EAFRD) and the European Maritime and Fisheries Fund (EMFF).
4 The office of Swedish Agency for Regional Development in Skåne is one of nine Swedish offices.
5 Leader (*Liaison Entre Action de Dèveloppement de 'l'Èconomie' Rurale*). The offices promote collaboration and local development through project organisation. Leader is a local development method that is based on project support with funding from the European Structural and Investment Funds. There are 48 Leader offices in total in Sweden.
6 Available online: https://kfsk.se/eu/eus-fonder-och-program/, last accessed 28 June 2018.
7 The municipality of Kristianstad, Europe Direct Hässleholm, EU Office Skåne Nordost and Region Skåne.
8 In their strategy, the municipality also describes how it participated in close to 20 projects between 2010–2015 and received almost EUR 42 million from the EU. Thus, the strategy also serves as documentation of past successful EU applications, perhaps to inspire further applications.

References

Andone, C., & Greco, S. (2018). Evading the burden of proof in European Union soft law instruments: The case of commission recommendations. *International Journal for the Semiotics of Law*, 31(1), 79–99.

Bache, I. (2004). Multi-level governance and European Union regional policy. In I. Bache & M. Flinders (Ed.), *Multi-level governance*. Oxford: Oxford University Press.

Bergman, I., Gunnarsson, S., & Räisänen, C. (2013). Decoupling and standardisation in the projectification of a company. *International Journal of Managing Projects in Business*, 6 (1), 106–128.

Borrás, S., & Jacobsson, K. (2004). The open method of co-ordination and new governance patterns in the EU. *Journal of European Public Policy*, 11(2), 185–208.

Brady, T., & Hobday, M. (2011). Project and innovation: Innovations and projects. In P. Morris, J. Pinto, & J. Söderlund (Eds.), *The Oxford handbook of project management*. Oxford, England: Oxford University Press.

Brandtner, C., Höllerer, M. A., Meyer, R. E., & Kornberger, M. (2017). Enacting governance through strategy: A comparative study of governance configurations in Sydney and Vienna. *Urban Studies*, 54(5), 1075–1091. doi:10.1177/0042098015624871

Bruno, I., Jacquot, S., & Mandin, L. (2006). Europeanisation through its instrumentation: Benchmarking, mainstreaming and the open method of co-ordination…toolbox or Pandora's box? *Journal of European Public Policy*, 13(4), 519–536. doi:10.1080/13501760600693895

Büttner, M. S., LeopoldM. L. (2016). A "new spirit" of public policy? The project world of EU funding. *European Journal of Culture and Political Sociology*, 3(1), 41–71.

Buzogány, A. (2013). Stairway to heaven or highway to hell? Ambivalent Europeanization and civil society in central and eastern Europe. In H. Kouki & E. Romanos (Eds.), *Protest beyond borders: Contentious politics in Europe since 1945*. New York, NY: Berghahn.

Carlsson, V., & Mukhtar-Landgren, D. (2018). Styrning genom frivillig koordinering? En studie av europeiska socialfondens genomförande i lokal förvaltning [*Governing through voluntary coordination*]. *Statsvetenskaplig tidskrift*, 120(5), 137–161.

Clarke, J., Bainton, D., Lendvai, N., & Stubbs, P. (2015). *Making policy move: Towards a politics of translation and assemblage*. Bristol, England: Policy Press.

Czarniawska, B. (2008). *A theory of organising*. Cheltenham, England: Edward Elgar.

Czarniawska, B., & Joerges, B. (1996). Travels of ideas. In B. Czarniawska-Joerges & G. Sevón (Eds.), *Translating organisational change*. Berlin, Germany: Walter de Gruyter.

Czarniawska, B., & Sevón, G. (2005). Translation is a vehicle, imitation its motor, and fashion sits at the wheel. In B. Czarniawska & G. Sevón (Eds.), *Global ideas: How ideas, objects, and practices travel in the global economy*. Fredriksberg, Denmark: Liber, and Copenhagen Business School Press.

Dabrowski, M., Bechtler, J., & Bafoil, F. (2014). Challenges of multi-level governance and partnership: Drawing lessons from European Union cohesion policy. *European Urban and Regional Studies*, 21(4), 355–363.

ESF (2018a). *How the ESF works*. Retrieved from http://ec.europa.eu/esf/main.jsp?catId=525&langId=en

ESF (2018b). *Myndigheten* [*The Agency*]. Retrieved from www.esf.se/sv/Om-ESF-radet/Organisation/

European Commission (2018). *The European main investment policy*. Retrieved from http://ec.europa.eu/regional_policy/en/policy/what/investment-policy/

Fred, M. (2018). *Projectification: The Trojan horse of local government*. Lund, Sweden: Statsvetenskapliga Institutionen.

Godenhjelm, S. (2016). *Project organisations and governance: Processes, actors, actions, and participatory procedures*. Publications of the Faculty of Social Sciences 11.

Godenhjelm, S., Lundin, R., & Sjöblom, S. (2015). Projectification in the public sector: The case of the European Union. *International Journal of Managing Projects in Business*, 8(2), 324–348.

Grabher, G. (2002). Cool projects, boring institutions: *Temporary collaboration in social context' in production in projects: Economic geographies of temporary collaboration*. Gernot Grabher (Ed.), *Regional Studies, Special Issue*, 36(3), 205–215.

Hässleholm (2016). EU-strategi för Hässleholms kommun 2016–2020 strategier. [*EU strategy for Hässleholm*]. Retrieved from www.hassleholm.se/download/18.70700e471590eb638507a3de/1482143693617/EU-strategi%202016-2020.pdf

Hässleholm (2018). Välkommen till Europadagen 9 maj på rådhus skåne i Kristianstad [*Welcome to the celebration of the Europeand day in Kristianstad*]. Retrieved from www.hassleholm.se/nyheter/alla-nyheter/nyheter/2017-04-13-valkommen-till-europadagen-9-maj-pa-radhus-skane-i-kristianstad.html

KFSK (2018a). Skåne association of local authorities. Retrieved from https://kfsk.se/english/

KFSK (2018b). Månadens EU-projekt [*The EU project of the month*]. Retrieved from https://kfsk.se/eu/nyheter-event-2__trashed/kommunforbundets-eu-projekt/

KFSK (2018c). Mitt Europa 2018 – vad gör EU för skånes kommuner? [*My Europé 2018 – What do the EU do for the municipalities in Skåne?*] Retrieved from https://kfsk.se/eu/nyheter/mitt-europa-2018-vad-gor-eu-for-skanes-kommuner/

KFSK (2018d). Om oss [*About KFSK*]. Retrieved from https://kfsk.se/eu/om-oss-2/

KFSK (2018e). EU projektanalys [*EU project analysis*]. Retrieved from https://kfsk.se/eu/skane/eu-projektanalys-epa/

KFSK *et al.* (2018). Din guide till EU-finansiering. För individen, kommunen och din region. [*Your guide to EU funding*]. Retrieved from www.google.com/url?sa=t&rct=j&q=&esrc=s&source=web&cd=1&cad=rja&uact=8&ved=2ahUKEwj0w4Ka54rfAhUGXCwKHSxkA6YQFjAAegQIChAC&url=https%3A%2F%2Fkfsk.se%2Fwp-content%2Fuploads%2F2018%2F05%2FEU-programguide2018_digital_komprimerad.pdf&usg=AOvVaw3Kw3pPA1c0WNp74XYxaWxJ

Klijn, E. H., & Koppenjan, J. (2000). Interactive decision making and representative democracy: Institutional collisions and solutions. In O. V. Heffen, W. J. M. Kickert, & J. A. Thomassen (Eds.), *Governance in modern society: Effects, change and formation of government institutions*. Dordrecht: Kluwer Academic.

Kovách, I., & Kučerová, I. (2006). The project class in central Europe: The Czech and Hungarian cases. *European Society for Rural Sociology*, 46(1), 3–21.

Kovách, I., & Kučerová, I. (2009). The social context of project proliferation: The rise of a project class. *Journal of Environmental Policy and Planning*, 11(3), 203–221. doi:10.1080/15239080903033804

Kristianstad (2018). EU – sammarbete [*EU collaboration*]. Retrieved from www.kristianstad.se/sv/kommun-och-politik/internationellt-arbete/eu-samarbete/

Kristianstad budget (2017). Budget 2017 flerårsplan 2018-2019 [*The budget for Kristianstad 2017*]. Kristianstad kommun.

Kuokkanen, K. (2016). *Developing participation through projects? A case study from the Helsinki metropolitan area*. Helsinki, Finland: University of Helsinki.

Larsson, T., & Bäck, H. (2008). *Governing and governance in Sweden*. Lund, Sweden: Studentlitteratur.

Lascoumes, P., & Le Galès, P. (2007). Introduction. Understanding public policy through its instruments: From the nature of instruments to the sociology of public policy instrumentation. *Governance*, 20(1), 1–21.

Latour, B. (1986). *Science in action: How to follow scientists and engineers through society*. Cambridge, MA: Harvard University Press.

Latour, B. (2005). *Reassembling the social: An introduction to actor-network-theory*. Oxford: Oxford University Press.

Lavén, F. (2008). *Organising innovation: How policies are translated into practice*. Göteborg, Sweden: BAS Publishing.

Leader in Skåne (2018). Leader i Skåne – lokalt ledd utveckling genom leadermetoden [*Leader in Skåne – local development through the Leader method*]. Retrieved from www.leaderskane.se

Lomma (2018). Policy för internationella frågor [*Policy for international issues*]. Retrieved from https://lomma.se/kommun-och-politik/eu-och-internationellt-arbete/policy-for-internationella-fragor.html

Lundin, R. A., Arvidsson, N., Brady, T., Ekstedt, E., Midler, C., & Sydow, J. (2015). *Managing and working in project society: Institutional challenges of temporary organizations*. Cambridge, England: Cambridge University Press.

Marks, G. (1992). Structural policy in the European Community. In A. Sbragia (Ed.), *Europolitics: Institutions and policy making in the "new" European Community* (pp. 191–224). Washington, DC: The Brookings Institution.

Maylor, H., Brady, T., Cooke-Davies, T., & Hodgson, D. (2006). From projectification to programmification. *International Journal of Project Management*, 24(8), 663–674.

Montin, S., & Granberg, M. (2013). *Moderna kommuner* [*Modern municipalities*]. Stockholm, Sweden: Liber.

Mukhtar-Landgren, D., & Fred, M. (2018). Re-compartmentalizing local policies? The translation and mediation of European structural funds in Sweden. *Critical Policy Studies*, 1(19). doi:10.1080/19460171.2018.1479282

Munck af Rosenschöld, J. (2017). *Projectified environmental governance and challenges of institutional change toward sustainability*. Helsinki, Finland: University of Helsinki.

Munday, J. (2016). *Translation studies: Theories and applications* (4th ed.). London, England: Routledge.

Murray, L. T. (2016). Governing rural Indonesia: Convergence on the project system. *Critical Policy Studies*, 10(1), 79–94.

Öhrlings (2018). Revsionsrapport. Granskning av kommunens EU-arbete. Lunds kommun. [*Audit report of EU work in Lund*]. Sweden: Öhrlings.

Östra Göinge (2018). EU arbetet [EU work]. Retrieved from www.ostragoinge.se/kommun/externt-finansierade-projekt/eu-arbete/

Packendorff, J., & Lindgren, M. (2014). Projectification and its consequences: Narrow and broad conceptualisations. *South African Journal of Economic and Management Sciences*, 17(1), 7–21.

Sanderson, J., & Winch, G. (2017). Public policy and projects. *International Journal of Project Management, Special Issue*, 35(3), 221–223.

Skåne Nordost (2018). EU-kontoret [*The EU office*]. Retrieved from www.skanenordost.se/eu-kontoret/

Söderholm, K., & Wihlborg, E. (2013). Mediators in action: Organizing sociotechnical system change. *Technology in Society*, 35(4), 267–275.

Sørensen, E., & Torfing, J. (2011). Enhancing collaborative innovation in the public sector. *Administration and Society*, 43(8), 842–868.

Sørensen, E., & Triantafillou, P. (2015). Governing EU employment policy: Does collaborative governance scale up? *Policy & Politics*, 3(34), 331–347. doi:10.1332/030557315X14351553104423

SÖSK EU Strategy (2015). EU-strategi för sydöstra Skåne [*EU strategy for south east of Skåne*]. Sydöstra Skåne.

Stephenson, P. (2013). Twenty years of multi-level governance: "Where does it come from? What is it? Where is it going?" *Journal of European Public Policy*, 20(6), 817–837.

Suarez, D., & Bromley, P. (2015). Institutional theories and levels of analysis: History, diffusion, and translation. In J. Schriewer (Ed.), *World culture re-contextualised: Meaning constellations and path-dependencies in comparative and international education research* (pp. 139–159). London, England: Routledge.

Swedish Agency for Economic and Regional Growth (SAERG) (2018). Swedish agency for economic and regional growth. Retrieved from https://tillvaxtverket.se/english.html

Trubek, D. M., & Trubek, L. G. (2005). Hard and soft law in the construction of social Europe: The role of the open method of co-ordination. *European Law Journal*, 11(3), 343–364.

Vangen, S., Hayes, J. P., & Cornforth, C. (2015). Governing cross-sector inter-organizational collaborations. *Public Management Review*, 17(9), 1237–1260.

Wassermann, S., & Faust, K. (1994). *Social network analysis: Methods and applications*. Cambridge, England: Cambridge University Press.

11

OBSERVING THE PROCESS OF CULTURE PROJECTIFICATION AND ITS AGENTS

A Case Study of Kraków

Beata Jałocha and Małgorzata Ćwikła

JAGIELLONIAN UNIVERSITY IN KRAKÓW

Kraków is a city vibrant with culture. For centuries, artists and other professionals involved in creative activities have been forging its unique atmosphere. With dozens of cultural organisations and hundreds of projects every year, it is a place where we may observe several organisational trends exemplifying processes of more general nature. In this chapter, we want to focus on one of these trends: project-based work that leads to the projectification of culture.

A special momentum for the development of a project approach to culture management in Kraków was the implementation of the European City of Culture (ECoC) Kraków 2000 project. It was the first such a large, complex, international cultural project after 1989, that is, after the fall of communism in Poland. It was also the first event of this type in the history of cultural management in the city that forced local authorities and artists to understand the mechanisms of financing and managing European projects. In our deliberations, accepting ECoC Kraków 2000 project as a turning point in the way cultural activities were implemented, we do not want to focus solely on the cause-and-effect aspects of the projectification phenomenon. Our intention is to pay attention to what and who makes the projectification of culture in Kraków so rapid, appearing now as a solution that has no alternatives. Therefore, we will focus on the so-called "agents of projectification" (Fred, 2018), entangled in various ways in project work.

Despite the rapid development of projectification studies, Fred and Mukhtar-Landgren (2017) in their reflections on the projectification of local government in Sweden aptly observe that studies on projectification processes usually focus on the reasons and consequences of projectification. Thus, they turn their attention to the "black box" of projectification, asking questions of how processes of projectification occur in practice and who facilitates and promote these processes (Fred & Mukhtar-Landgren, 2017). Although projectification is attracting more and more attention from researchers, and we understand some of the roots and repercussions of the phenomenon itself, we still do not know much about who strengthens it and how (Packendorff & Lindgren, 2014; Fred, 2018). Therefore, it is important to take a closer look at the actors involved in projectification processes and to understand their motivations, expectations, and capacity to make choices while being involved in project work. Mats Fred (2018, p. 139) writes that besides the explicit understanding of projectification (e.g. the growing number of projects), there are "more subtle aspects of projectification." He claims that projectification processes manifest themselves through *inter alia* "practices and agents that promote the project logic." Hence, understanding the complex nature of projectification may not be possible without understanding the actions undertaken by "agents" supporting or advocating processes of projectification. Our goal is, therefore, using the case of Kraków, and particularly the ECoC Kraków 2000 project as a starting point, to show how the network of "agents" is strengthening and legitimising the projectification of culture. The example of the European City of Culture Kraków 2000, embedded in the contexts of changes in Poland after 1989, offers a unique perspective for observation of the proliferation of the project-based activities development in the city. We are interested in who the "agents" of projectification are and how they act in order to (consciously or unconsciously) make projects a framework for cultural events in Kraków. We define agents as people and/or organisations who start, encourage, and maintain activities that support or advocate project organising. Thus, we claim that agency is connected with the ability to act, make things happen and change ideas into actions (Gell, 1998). Serving as frameworks for undertakings rooted in the logic of time, omnipresent projects urge people to act on both small and large scale. We argue that the projectification of culture in the city, as a broad phenomenon, is provoked and maintained by a wide network of organisational and individual agents. Before we go into the research results where we analyse the role of chosen agents, we will provide an overview of the research context and theoretical basis for this paper: projectification and the history of arts funding.

Research Design

After the above brief introduction to the issues we wish to reflect upon in this chapter, we go on to present a description of the research we conducted with the aim of understanding the activities of Kraków's agents of culture projectification.

To understand how Kraków has become a projectified city of culture, who the agents of projectification are, and what projectification means to them, we carried out qualitative research based on literature review and in-depth interviews. Our inquiry was driven by a research question: how do agents of projectification promote and maintain the reliance on project organisation and project management techniques, strengthening the projectification of culture in Kraków? For this purpose, we identified some of the actors in the process who are in our opinion the most important fundaments of projectification in Kraków at the local level. Among them, there are those who participate indirectly in the process of the projectification of culture in Kraków: European Union (EU) institutions (which define areas of financing), ministries and local government (which distribute funds for competitions), cultural institutions (which conduct projects), the artists (who "deliver" art in form of various projects), and inhabitants of Kraków (who demand cultural projects adapted to their expectations).

For our analysis, we will take into consideration a group of six selected representatives of this process whom we regard as local agents of projectification. As a starting point, we chose the organisers of the ECoC in 2000. It was the first such large cultural project coordinated in Kraków that triggered the project-based organisation of culture in the city. Hence, the manager of this project was our first interviewee. Based on the interview with him, using snow-ball sampling inspired approach, we identified further interlocutors: a clerk from the culture department of the City Hall, a manager of the gallery partly financed from the city's funds, an artist cooperating with public, private, and non-governmental institutions (NGOs), an academic teacher from the first Polish cultural management programme offered at the university (established 1994 at the Jagiellonian University in Kraków) who teaches future culture managers, and a culture management studies graduate who works as a freelancer on numerous projects carried out by public institutions and NGOs. There are many more "agents" of the projectification of Kraków's culture; however, we deliberately chose the above people, since they represent a variety of groups involved in the creation and management of the culture of Kraków. Although several cultural institutions are benefiting from the international and national funds, the main decisions concerning culture are made at the local level. This includes most of the European Union Structural Funds and Cohesion Funds. Thus, all our interviewees are representatives of the local network. An additional argument to take this perspective is the fact that the management of public funds in Poland has been established at the local level pursuant to the act from December 1990 about communities' income and the way of subsidising public expenses (Szulborska-Łukaszewicz, 2015). This opened the way for local governments to take responsibility for culture in the city, after decades of centralisations during communism.

Three of the respondents have been engaged in Kraków's culture management processes for 20 years, the others are younger and innate in project reality which they take for granted. All of them told us how projects affected the current artistic activity of the city. This selection was also aimed at reaching two generations of people partaking in the making of culture in Kraków, some of them being strongly involved in ECoC Kraków 2000 development. As a result, we were also able to learn more about the change that had occurred in the organisation of culture and to conclude that the status quo of culture "projectification" that we believe we are dealing with now is completely natural and obvious to younger people, who do not have any other solutions to compare it with. Here, we deliberately omit the role of spectators, who are often unaware of the organisational mechanisms underlying an event, and the aim of our research was to examine these mechanisms. At the same time, it should be added that we are aware of the limitations of our research caused by selective sampling.

Partly structured in-depth interviews were conducted by us personally in June 2017. The interviews lasted for over two hours each and were then transcribed and analysed using the NVivo software. The analysis of Kraków's current cultural offer from the organisational standpoint was a springboard for the interviews. However, for people involved in the ECoC Kraków 2000, we also focused on what happened before and during the preparations for this historic project. Main features included the one-off nature of events, grant-based financing, temporary engagement of artists, and following the priorities specified in cultural policies. This explicitly indicates the project logic revealed in defining the time frames of projects, creating task-oriented teams, setting goals, and in specific forms of financing. Therefore, during the designing and conducting of the interviews, we did not shun using the term "project." In the process, we noticed that our interlocutors tended to naturally replace certain words like "exhibition" or "performance" with a semantically broad "project." On the other hand, during the interviews, we intentionally avoided the term "projectification," as it could have evoked negative connotations with something that imposes limitations or unification. At this point, it should be pointed out that the Polish word "*projektyzacja*," being the translation from the English "projectification," sounds similar to "*biurokracja*" (bureaucracy) and "*technokracja*" (technocracy). It can, therefore, be interpreted as a pejorative concept. Only in the final interviewing phase did we mention the word "projectification" as a kind of summary. To our interlocutors, it was not an everyday, common term, although they understood its legitimacy. During the entire research, we were very careful about the language we used and sensitive to the emerging terms. Our reflections on this are included in the summary part of the research.

Projectification

In order to outline the background and illustrate the space in which the agents operate, first we will discuss the development and current understanding of projectification phenomena.

The process of projectification results from the changes occurring in the organisational world, which are forced by the new life and work paradigm and organisational changes of the postmodern society (Midler, 1995; Lundin et al., 2015; Sjöblom et al., 2013; Jensen et al., 2016). The concept devised by Christophe Midler (1995) serves as the usual starting point for coining definitions of what projectification is. To Midler, based on his research at Renault factory, projectification has been a positive phenomenon showing the transformation of the company's processes towards greater innovation. Therefore, projectification was originally interpreted as the intensified use of projects and as the departure from repetitive production to non-routine work with temporary projects (Bredin & Söderlund, 2011). Ekstedt (2009) also points out that projectification can be understood in three ways: as the expansion of project-based organisation; as an increased use of projects in traditional organisations; and as greater inter-organisational cooperation through projects. In all of these forms, there have been attempts to define projectification as a phenomenon occurring within the organisation's space and limited to changes in management styles.

A breakthrough in how the concept of projectification was understood ensued when several new concepts appeared, including the Project-Oriented Society (Gareis, 2002). What followed was the division into the three "levels" of projectification – societal, organisational, and personal (Maylor et al., 2006; Kuura, 2011), that can also be described as the macro, meso, and micro levels of projectification. The next most important moment was when the researchers of critical project studies joined the discussion on the consequences of projectification (e.g., Lindgren & Packendorff, 2003; Hodgson & Cicmil, 2008). It became clear that "projectification is more than a formalisation of project management" (Aubry & Lenfle, 2012), and that perhaps what we are experiencing now is the "projectification of everything" (Jensen et al., 2016). Over the last few years, the understanding of this concept has begun to expand to include its undoubtedly deeper and richer context. Packendorff and Lindgren (2014) argue that projectification may be explained from the two perspectives: narrow and broad. Furthermore, projectification may also be construed as a tendency in which the lives of individuals, as well as the activities of organisations, are subject to continuous transformation (Kalff, 2017) based on various projects. The notion of projectification merely as narrow organisational phenomenon is slowly fading away from the scholarly debate. As emphasised by Cicmil, Lindgren, and Packendorff (2016, p. 59), "projectification is a complex ethical problem with consequences for long-term sustainability of organisations and society." Therefore, projectification may be interpreted as a kind of multidimensional cultural and discursive phenomenon (Packendorff & Lindgren, 2014) that influences people, organisations, and societies in general. It offers a framework for discussing current organisational trends from several perspectives, especially in sectors such as culture, where projects constitute the modus operandi of organisational daily routines and activities.

The Creating and Financing of Culture: Historical Contexts

In this part of the chapter, we discuss the history of creating and funding culture. We briefly show how the culture was financed in the past and to what kind of pressures artists have been exposed to since centuries. The section is divided into two parts. In the first one, we present a long-term perspective in which we discuss the development of culture financing in western countries in general. In the second part, we focus on the specificity of culture financing in Poland. Outlining the background of culture financing will allow us to further indicate the beginnings of the processes of culture projectification in Kraków.

Origins of Culture Financing

"My God! How terrible these money questions are for an artist!" Paul Gauguin allegedly said. Despite reluctance to financial issues frequently displayed by artists, their profession has always been connected with the necessity of acquiring funds for their own activities. In the context of European art, since the Renaissance (XIV–XVII century), a crucial role has been played by patrons, who have surrounded themselves with artists, requiring from them the provision of specific services in return for financial support. The relationship between a patron and an artist was like a contract specifying the cost, material, size, and content of the ordered work. Often, donors had specific expectations. For example, in the painting *The Virgin and Child with Canon van der Paele* (Jan van Eyck, 1436), the founder Joris van der Paele is kneeling before the Virgin Mary, while Raphael Santi (1483–1520) and Sandro Botticelli (1445–1510) intentionally beautified their patrons in their paintings to make them look better than in reality. Furthermore, the relations between patrons and artists were often tense, especially when there was too much intervention in the ordered work of art. It should be added, however, that patronage as a form of art support led to the creation of valuable works of art, fostered conditions for artistic exploration that resulted in the development of aesthetic sensitivity, and also played a significant role in the context of education. During the Renaissance, patronage was associated with religious issues. Many wealthy families treated paintings as manifestations of tangible culture and a spiritual sacrifice at the same time and thus used to order them to be hung in churches. Another vital function was the political one. The members of aristocracy frequently ordered portraits of their rulers in the hope of winning favour with them in this way (Gombrich, 1960). The fate of artists was also influenced by the advancement of technology (Gombrich, 1960). With the invention of print (*c.* 1440), the circle of patrons expanded, and the ordering of works that could be duplicated became less expensive. Years later, the Reformation (1517–1648) stripped the churches of exuberant decorations, once again forcing artists to seek new ways of support. It was the time when the culture of artistic salons emerged. Artists began to be invited to entertain representatives of the upper class. In order to cater for the prevailing needs and tastes, they started to represent everyday topics and sell their works at markets. This shift in the thematic layer is perfectly illustrated by the works of the Dutch masters, including Jan Vermeer (1632–1675) and Rembrandt (1606–1669), who worked for the emerging bourgeois class. The rise of cultural policies attributing the role of an artistic patron to public authorities is a 20th-century invention, particularly widely applied in Europe (Throsby, 2010).

Financing of Culture in Poland

For many centuries the supporting of artists in Poland was similar to the solutions in Western Europe. There were many attempts to adopt the Western European models locally. At the end of the 18th century, there emerged a specific trend influenced by political fate: during partition (1772–1918) most of the artists were in exile; the interwar period was too short for any permanent solutions to be worked out; and the Second World War, for obvious reasons, halted any development of cultural policies whatsoever. Under the communist regime (1945–1989), the Polish culture was subordinated to the interests of the state and was mainly a propaganda tool. The state's intention was to manipulate the artists' expression in such a way that it rationalised the party doctrine and at the same time maintained an appearance of artistic freedom (Fik, 1996). Polish artists had to choose between either abiding by the requirements imposed on them by the authorities or emigration. Many opted for the latter. At that time, Poland experienced so-called "sovietisation of culture" (Fik, 1996), and artists were associated in trade unions, where their activities were under constant scrutiny. Art was financed from public funds and local governments began to set up units which controlled whether creative activities were consistent with the party line. Making artists financially dependent was a clever way to thwart any potential acts of rebellion. The entire system of social benefits and rewards provided artists with the means to live. The income guarantee was supposed to shape attitudes of obedience, rendering any initiative contrary to the state policy too risky. What is more, it is safe to say that such a solution exempted artists from the need to seek funds, and all artistic operations were planned in advance and were part of an intricate, well-thought-out plan in which there was no room for creativity or imagination. The revolution of 1989, resulted in the end of communism in Poland, definitely changed the situation of artists, who suddenly had to become managers responsible not only for creative ideas but also for gaining funds and providing the organisational base. Values such as individualism, changeability, independence, and speed of action finally began to matter. At this moment we can observe the latent beginning of projectification in the country, driven for example by aid programmes (delivered in form of projects) and an intensive development of the Third Sector after 1989 operating on project-based funding (Makowski, 2015), most of them in the field of culture (Ilczuk, 2001). This process was additionally strengthened when Poland joined the EU 2004 and new programmes became available.

Today, the state still orders works from artists but now in the form of an open competition or public procurement, where the funding is allocated to specific projects. What counts, however, is not only the finished work as a result of artistic endeavours but the entire process, including presentation of the idea at the stage of applying for funds, control over expenditures at the creation stage, and post-completion reporting. The control, which was so far politically oriented, has turned into bureaucratic control, performed by projects. This is not just a trend present in the financing of culture. It is only a reflection of the current mega trends, such as the processes of control in the distribution of EU funding. According to Büttner and Leopold (2016, p. 63), project funding in the context of EU policy implementation does not seem to deviate much from the former command-and-control structures of classical Weberian bureaucracies. This places artists in a new role, making them co-responsible for the way public funds are spent, but at the same time expanding the network of dependencies, which now includes state institutions, public cultural institutions mediating between artists and officials, and, finally, artists themselves. This new network of people involved in the organisation of culture coincides with the group of projectification agents we selected. The financing of artistic activities in the form of projects resulted in the growth of roles necessary in the process of artistic projects implementation. In cultural institutions, the process resulted in creating professions, so far absent – specialists in raising funds for projects, accountants specialised in project accounting, specialists for project promotion, etc.

The Background of Culture Projectification in Kraków and the European City of Culture 2000 Project

Following the brief summary of historical perspective on culture funding, in this part of the chapter we will explain projectification's genesis in the city. To explain how the process began, we will use a breakthrough project for Kraków's culture – the ECoC 2000 – as a starting point.

The first signs of forthcoming intense projectification of Kraków's culture we may probably trace to the mid-1990s, when city clerks, politicians, and local artists started expressing aspirations to become the European City of Culture[1] – Kraków 2000 (K2000). The ECoC initiative was developed in 1985 and has, to date, been awarded to more than 50 cities across the European Union.[2] Its broad aim, in general, was to, according to the European Commission, foster relations between "the peoples" of the EU member states (Wåhlin et al., 2016). In the last thirty years, the ECoC has grown into one of the most ambitious cultural programmes in the world. It promotes cultural diversity across Europe and fosters intercultural dialogue among citizens. Cities interested in participating in the competition must submit a proposal for consideration several years before the title-year. Kraków, although Poland was not an EU member at this time, was entitled to apply for the title of ECoC, and the application was prepared and sent in 1995. Kraków was chosen, along with other eight European cities, to become ECoC in 2000.

The year 2000 and the earlier preparations to win the title of the European City of Culture were a prelude to the new, project-based forms of activity. This overlapped with the technological development, particularly with the growing popularity of the Internet, which was not yet widely available when the K2000 project was launched. Web-supported real-time remote work in dispersed virtual teams appeared to be a sign of tempting and sophisticated modernity. Modernity, innovativeness, and cooperation – these words recur like a mantra in the reports concerning the beginning of Kraków 2000. The projectification of Kraków's culture was much more profound than a mere adoption of a specific form of administration of funds that were slowly beginning to flow from the EU. It was a dream of the modern city full of art and artists. It was also a specific manifestation of breaking away from the old political system and the post-communist mechanisms of management of cultural organisations (Szulborska-Łukaszewicz, 2017). Projects were not only aimed at the facilitation of management, but they were to be a prelude to the future and a harbinger of capitalistic welfare. The longing for modernity and for being part of the West as well as the feeling of backwardness and stagnation resulting from the country's communist history became the catalysts for the culture projectification processes in Kraków. Almost everyone could become an agent of the new project era.

A wave of fascination with project management as a universal method of the fulfilment of goals resulted in many proposals to make use of this approach also in culture. These suggestions concerned, for example, an increased probability of success of a film (Farrell, 1994), measurement of the quality of an artistic project mainly based on the audience feedback (Ashrafi et al., 1994), and protection of cultural heritage (Báez & Herrero, 2012). Projects have become an integral part of the process of creating a culture in cities. The need to increase scrutiny over the implementation of tasks in culture might have acted as a catalyst for the development of project work, also in Kraków. The first calls for cultural project proposals were announced in Kraków in 1994 – shortly before Kraków started preparations for the ECoC. However, the very idea of project competitions was so abstract in the Poland of those days that the first attempts to implement it failed. The then Polish Minister of Culture Kazimierz Dejmek (1993–1996) annulled the first call for projects, regarding this form of culture financing as inappropriate (interview with Kazimierz Dejmek; Gierat-Bieroń, 2009). Initially, cultural institutions and the people responsible for the shaping of cultural policies expressed resistance towards project work, which was also mentioned by two of our older interlocutors. Thus, at the end of the 1990s, Kraków was a place that would hardly be said to have reached "project maturity." People responsible for culture at the political level kept sticking to communist schemes and the deep-rooted yet out-dated solutions based mainly on the fulfilment of central institutions' recommendations and predictability. Nobody in Kraków was aware of the project procedures, there were no adequately trained staff, and no entity on the local level that could manage cultural projects and support institutions which might have wanted to enrich their programmes in this way (for a more complex description of the circumstances in Kraków in which ECoC 2000 was planned see: Gierat-Bieroń & Sonik, 2011). The ECoC project became the turning point with regard to the development of the city's cultural offer, the intensified projectification of culture, and the implementation of new ways of organisational thinking. Clerks, artists, and organisers began to gain first project experiences, laying foundations for a new structure of how culture functioned in the city. According to official reports of the ECoC, in order to be able to implement the ECoC, the culture management structure in the city was reorganised, a special unit responsible for the project was created, and detailed rules for recruitment, implementation, and settlement of projects were set (Biuro Kraków 2000/2001). These were necessary actions for Kraków to benefit from EU funds allocated for the implementation of the project. As Büttner and Leopold (2016) (see also Büttner, Chapter 9, this volume) rightly notice – only actors who are able to adapt and reproduce EU's managerial standards, based essentially on projects, can participate within the world of EU funding. Projectification spread rapidly, inspiring enthusiasm in the context of new procedures and changing the language of culture description. At the website of the gallery whose manager was included in our research, there is a special sub-page devoted only to projects. Almost every cultural institution in Kraków has re-organised webpages in order to inform explicitly about projects. The City Hall established a new unit only to manage cultural projects and at the curriculum of cultural management studies from where one lecturer we have interviewed the subject "management of cultural projects" is present at the BA as well as at the MA level. Virtually everything – from theatre plays to bookstore book promotions and community workshops – became a project.

Since the programmes dedicated to supporting cultural initiatives in the form of projects have been introduced in Kraków, there is ongoing discussion whether the city should support more projects allocating lower grants or less with a higher budget (Program Rozwoju Kultury). From year-to-year, this tendency is changed causing conflicts between the city and the cultural organisations and among cultural managers leading particular organisations themselves who are never sure if they get support and in what amount. The main tendency, however, is to support great festivals organised by the Kraków Festival Office, a municipal institution continuing work of the office of European City of Culture 2000. The small initiatives are thus often excluded (Szulborska-Łukaszewicz, 2017). Besides this, grants organisations may also apply for funds at the provincial, national, and international levels which increase the chances for project-based support and generates more project-oriented work.

In 2018, Kraków is a city that boasts two sizeable entertainment arenas with modern equipment, a new opera building, and modernised museums, including a number of brand-new facilities. All of these places were created as a result of projects co-financed with EU funds granted for two purposes: infrastructural projects and soft projects aimed at creating new events. The most significant role in the city is played by large public cultural institutions. They have the final say when defining the artistic activities of Kraków, although the city's artistic milieu is characterised by dispersion and fragmentariness (Jach et al., 2016). On the artistic level, it is believed that modernity is still dominated by historical narrations – "moving around this city physically and mentally resembles functioning within a relatively conservative museum" (Jach et al., 2016, p. 8). Kraków has failed to become a cultural melting pot that brings forth brand new artistic ideas. Projects keep piling up and projectification is expanding, but this is not necessarily accompanied by the exploration of the space of artistic experiment and artistic bravery.

Culture in Kraków as Seen by the Agents of Projectification

In this section, we give voice to our interlocutors whom we have identified as agents of projectification. Our interviewees sketch a picture of a city that has changed rapidly over the last three decades. The modification of the way in which cultural events are carried out is a crucial part of this process of change.

Kraków's actors entangled in projectification processes see projects as something mainly positive which denies several arguments by scholars representing a critical approach to the projectification in the field of culture (Lindgren & Packendorff, 2006; Szreder, 2016). However, some reflect on how a project may limit artistic activity. For example, the manager of an art gallery says:

> Artistic activities are limited by certain technical requirements resulting from grant procedures – that a project always has to bring something visible, measurable, or countable in the end. I think that this is often very stressful to artists, but also to the people dealing with contemporary institutions – because we produce not only exhibitions but also knowledge, reflection, a series of intangible things, and we work on the basis of interpersonal relations that are not countable.
>
> *(Art gallery manager)*

The measurability of results is sometimes perceived as the limitation of artistic freedom and the lack of conformity with the logic of artistic activities (Glinkowski, 2012). However, the concern about projects possibly limiting artistic activity was not particularly evident in most of the statements we received from our interlocutors. Instead, they indicated a different aspect frequently brought up in the 1970s and 1980s by the artists and researchers affiliated with Institutional Critique (Alberro & Stimson, 2009), a social and artistic movement trying to democratise artistic institutions: a lack of continuity of artistic endeavours. Nowadays, the lack of continuity in the performance of tasks is understood by our interlocutors as a consequence of projectification, rather than Institutional Critique inspired.

Undoubtedly, the continuous project "race," manifesting itself through grant competitions and rivalry between cultural institutions in Kraków, focuses on short-term activities and single initiatives. Perhaps, this single, ephemeral kind of expression is quite natural and neutral in many fields of art. However, there are probably types of culture that need a long-term approach:

> When I observe theatre, for example, I can say that it is experiencing a deep collapse as an art. I am saying this as a man who sees and knows it – also from the inside. I have been observing this for at least 30 years now. … Theatre has become a client of everyday life. To me, this is a result of certain projectification. It is one of the forms where clientelism appears.
>
> *(Lecturer)*

Clientelism may be here understood as a modern form of the patron–artist relationship and an abuse of public functions. Managers of cultural organisations are involved in the political tensions as the financing of culture is often subject of individual decision of politicians. Good relations to them may be thus beneficial. Short-term projects are suitable tools to strengthen this situation and to limit the independence of artists and organisations. At the same time, the agents of projectification mention innovativeness as one of the main motives behind their actions. Innovativeness and flexibility are repeated by both clerks and artists. It seems that, in most of the cases, our interlocutors showed that they had accepted the project-based mode of action in Kraków's cultural space. The initial rebellion and resistance of institutions towards projectification that appeared in the mid-1990s turned into a sort of forced acceptance. As we have mentioned before, the managers of cultural institutions were in the early 1990s against project-based funding. However, this model was forced by the organising committee of the ECoC, as the 1994 so-called "task budget" was introduced initiating institutions and NGOs to make projects already counted to the ECC 2000 programme (Szulborska-Łukaszewicz, 2017). Now, to employees of these institutions, particularly to those with few years of service, project activity is completely natural, because it is the only form of action in a culture that they know. In order to survive, municipal cultural institutions have to go after grants and carry out even more projects. Subsidies received from the city help to cover mainly current expenses – costs of employment and infrastructure maintenance:

> 24/25 from the city budget is granted for the maintenance of institution, and only 1/25 is set aside for the programme. … We are financially dependent on projects and various grants. Our project calendar is subject to various funds without which we are unable to function.
>
> *(Art gallery manager)*

In this gallery, nearly 1/3 of the yearly budget is thus collected through grants from different programmes (based on financial reports for 2016 and 2017). The situation of Kraków's cultural institutions reflects a broader trend connected with the projectification of all sectors of the economy. Until recently, the uncertainty about future existence and the lack of long-term safety were typical of the sector of NGOs. Currently, apart from the budget year, the rhythm of public cultural institutions in Kraków is dictated by the cycle of applications in various grant calls. Agents of projectification adapt to local conditions. However, there are also some attempts to divert away from and reject the projectified method of making culture.

Local agents of projectification sometimes differ in their attitudes towards the projectification of culture: they participate in the reinforcement of projectification, but they also form a specific resistance movement against the mechanisms it imposes. Because they constitute a diversified group, they become involved in the processes of culture projectification in many different ways.

One of the groups of agents of the projectification of Kraków's culture includes *artists*. Their role is not as obvious as it might seem. They sometimes join the process unconsciously, as if art was a certain element in a stretched web of projects:

> The artist is at the end of this chain. He performs something, does something. I can imagine the situation when someone may not even know that he/she is taking part in a project. As for a music band, they play a concert, they are invited by an organisation. They do not have to realise that this is part of a larger project.
>
> *(Artist)*

The question of whether a work of art is created under any formalised project financed from various sources seems to be of secondary importance to those who create it. At the same time, presumably, not every artist can afford the luxury of being "above" and not having to deal with project-related red-tape; therefore, some of them develop project management skills. Also, individual support for artists in form of scholarships has in Kraków project-based work. In the call for proposals for the "Kraków's Scholarships for Creatives 2018" we can read that the requirements to get funds as an individual artist are focused on "goals of the project", "justification for the project support", "schedule of realisation", and "two letters of recommendation with evaluation of the project proposal" (Public Information Bulletin, online[3]). This shows how much artists are pulled into the project worlds. However, the main role in the cultural project administration is played by clerks and managers.

The role of *clerks* in the current system is reduced mainly to the performance of recommendations from above, without interfering in the content of cultural programmes. The themes of such programmes are dictated by programme authors, who are affiliated with political elites. Therefore, discrepancies can be seen on various administrative levels. Ministerial schemes devised by the representatives of the current government focus on historical policy and national values; on the level of provinces and cities, there is often larger thematic freedom and diversity. There is also another issue worth noting. As our interlocutor remarked, clerks have a decreasing knowledge of culture. Within structures of the city office, they wander between various departments without the profound expertise in the subject area of a given department but with excellent knowledge of project procedures. Another problematic issue is the evaluation of submitted ideas. Commissions responsible for the allocation of funds to various initiatives are often façades, and individuals are entangled in a network of employment relations. Our clerk talks about this without hesitation:

> Apart from that, employees and their superiors always sign the same documents. Employees award the same number of points as someone above them does. If there is such a dependency.
>
> *(Clerk)*

Undoubtedly, the work of clerks is facilitated by and organised around the planned call for project proposals, adherence to time limits for settlements and reporting, and the predictability of partner institutions' behaviour.

Universities offering project management courses to arts managers are part of this cultural ecosystem too. Thus, another group of agents of Kraków's cultural projectification includes *academic lecturers* who prepare students for accommodating themselves to project methods. In Kraków, the culture management programme is implemented at a number of universities in the form of courses and studies. As we have mentioned before, when looking at the culture manager education programme on the university level, we may get the impression that the subject "project management" is of extremely high importance. However, a more profound study of the programmes leads us to conclude that the teaching of project management usually involves the uncritical replication of certain classic project management rules that have often been regarded as imperfect in progressive research in this field (Hodgson & Cicmil, 2008). Projects are presented as the optimal and indispensable formats that have to accompany various kinds of cultural initiatives in the modern world. Moreover, there is usually no coverage of polemical literature that presents projectification from other viewpoints.

The graduates of cultural management programmes implement projects on a daily basis. They are increasingly well prepared for management in culture, for instance, thanks to the availability of a broad educational offer. Undoubtedly, as a result of the educational process to which they are subjected and which does not question project work at all – on the contrary, it prepares graduates to participate in grant competitions – culture managers form a key group among the agents of projectification in Kraków. This generates the following opinions, whose authors see no alternative to the projectification of culture:

> If we talk about a project that is understood in the space of visual arts, almost every multi-factor task consists of various factors. We can ask: how can a cultural institution operate today without being a projectified institution?
>
> *(Art gallery manager)*

Moreover, the project is also perceived by culture managers as an opportunity to experiment and as a source of cooperation. It offers Kraków's institutions the possibility of going beyond orthodox activities and establishing external relations with other cultural institutions both from Kraków and from abroad. Thus, when looking at Kraków's culture only from the angle of municipal cultural institutions, we can see a unified system of organisations that, on the one hand, have a public status and, on the other hand, have entered the cycle of project culture (originally regarded as an area reserved for NGOs) in order to survive (Ilczuk, 2002). However, Kraków's culture encompasses not only the dominant tycoon organisations but also small institutions, NGOs, and individuals who implement their own ideas without any public support. Our interlocutor referred to this group as "the underground," and we call them "partisans of projectification":

> Apart from institutions, there is the entire underground, which acts very openly. Cultural or educational events prepared not on a project basis, but in such a way that someone has an idea, goes to a place, asks if he/she may do it, posts an event on Facebook, and it turns out that people are interested and come along. Well, there are many such things … I mean summer cinema shows, social media Thursdays, exhibitions in bars, vernissages hosted in places other than museums or galleries, or concerts given by unknown bands in various small pubs.
>
> *(Culture manager)*

This indicates that the cultural life of Kraków exists also outside the main institutional stream, which is dependent on municipal funds and project grants. At the same time, it can be noticed that this form of creation of art involves, as one culture manager said, "self-exploitation": sacrificing one's own private time and funds in order to make the idea happen. This is the price paid for being independent of grants.

Discussion

Projectification covers various professional groups that reinforce the potential for projectification by remaining in a system built of projects and by permanently expanding it with new structural elements. Taking into account the absence of unequivocally negative opinions among our respondents, we can assume that projects evoke some sort of fascination. Projectification is not a "virus" that has disseminated in an uncontrolled manner; it is rather something alluring, charming, accepted, and desired; something that is addictive and, therefore, may be dangerous.

Agents of projectification are constantly active, by which they foster the further growth of the said phenomenon in the field of culture. They are influenced by various macro processes (e.g. mega narrations of the EU, the clientelism of culture recipients). Nevertheless, they also often have a lot of possibilities of acting freely and independently, which makes them believe they are outside of the processes happening in the city. What our research has shown is the notion of a project as a symbol of organisational and artistic freedom is undermined only sporadically. In a discourse on the creation of art, some opinions voiced by artists and curators challenge the primacy of project work. For example, Kuba Szreder (2016) points out the precarious conditions of artists' work, mainly in the field of visual arts. He also explains how cultural institutions fall into the trap of networking, believing that they will survive thanks to intense cooperation. Even though expressed very rarely, these opinions, aimed at sparking off a discussion on other organisational solutions, do not change the fact that Kraków reinforces its projectification; in any case, Kraków does not lag behind other Polish cities that are subject to similar processes. Politicians want the agents to be active, and, paradoxically, the partisans are also part of the cultural ecosystem from which the city benefits – it has more projects showing Kraków as an active cultural city, without paying a penny.

Attempting to comprehend why none of our interviewees displayed resistance to the use of projects as a basic form of creating culture has urged us to reflect that, in this way, agents of projectification try to legitimise their own actions. As Lindgren and Packendorff (2003) write, people legitimise their work in a variety of ways. Employees try to build sets of shared beliefs, where they explain (to themselves and others) why and how they work. By doing so, they somehow try to give meaning to their own actions. They need it in order to maintain a sense of rationality and validity of the work they perform. It seems that in the case of our respondents we are dealing with the situation of giving meaning to the project work and rationalising its mechanisms. The oppressiveness emphasised by the researchers of critical project studies becomes rationalised, the principles are accepted, and the overall concept of project work as an effective way to implement culture-related tasks is validated. One example includes the attitude of cultural clerks in Kraków – they do not question the relevance of projectification, because this system gives them a sense of comfort, and also the possibility of controlling subordinate institutions and artists, who have to obey the rules imposed on them in order to exist professionally. The projectification of culture in Kraków is an ongoing fact. Although project work has been embedded in cultural activities for a long time, the professional, managerial way of "doing the culture" started about 30 years ago. The most important trigger, at the end of the 1990s, was a large, EU-funded project – ECoC Kraków 2000. The implementation of large, international projects, such as ECoC, not only causes a "cultural turn" (Wåhlin et al., 2016) in the management of the city's culture. In the case of Kraków, it was a contribution to fundamental changes in the way of managing the artistic offer of the city. Implementation of this particular project formalised project management activities, catalysing at the same time the projectification process. Nowadays it is reinforced both by the method of acquisition of new funds for organisations and individual artists and by the adopted paradigm of thinking about a culture where the theatrical project has replaced the premiere and the musical project has replaced the concert. The city of Kraków itself perceives short-term actions as a justified part of its own development strategy which is being implemented by the network of local projectification agents. The most significant legacy of the ECoC project seems to be the change of the paradigm of thinking about managing culture in the city – towards a totally project-based approach.

Final Conclusions

In this chapter, we drew attention to the phenomenon of projectification of culture in the city. On the example of Kraków, we showed how political changes after 1989 and first of all the implementation of a large project – the European City of Culture 2000 – triggered the process of massive projectification. The changes, whose prelude was the preparation of the ECoC, resulted in a different, project-based way of managing culture in the city, and created a space for a number of new actors in the area of culture (mainly cultural and project managers, experts assessing projects proposals). Our purpose was also to show, how the work of "agents" evokes actions strengthening and legitimising the projectification of culture in Kraków. In order to reach this purpose, this chapter used a qualitative oriented approach targeting, through interviews, professionals involved in art activities, who for us constitute a group of projectification agents at the local level.

The agents of culture projectification in Kraków constitute a diverse group of people involved in the creation and management of the city's culture. The group consists of artists, academic lecturers, art managers, and clerks acting on behalf of politicians. They represent different types of organisations and sectors. They have created a specific ecosystem of projectified culture: they need to cooperate in order to pursue their plans within the project-oriented cultural policy of the city. Based on the conducted research our conclusions are:

- Agents are completely entangled in the project "whirl". They are making projects constantly, at the same time applying for more projects and thinking about new ideas to be implemented in the form of projects. There is no "no-project" time.
- Agents experience some sort of project fascination, which may make them become addicted to this form (Szreder, 2016; Rowlands & Handy, 2012). This helps them strengthen projectification processes and legitimise their activities.
- At the language level, agents talk about projects instead of movies, performances, etc. They use a specific language. Today, the term "project" serves as an equivalent of various creative and organisational activities. At the same time, the term "projectification" seems to be used in scientific circles and is rarely encountered in the context of practical activities.
- Agents involved in grass-roots initiatives without public support are still making projects. The city may benefit from that without any effort because an active artistic scene makes the city attractive to inhabitants and tourists.
- Agents of projectification are forced to adapt themselves to project work, but the flexibility of projects guarantees them a lot of leeway. They do not feel oppressed by the project work. Quite the contrary – they enjoy project work and value the freedom that project work gives them.
- Agents do not believe in de-projectification. The idea of not working in projects is completely abstract to them. They see de-projectification as a utopia that simply cannot happen.

In Kraków there are plenty of projects experts who replace experts from the field of the arts during decision making processes concerning cultural funding. We may thus assume that the formal side of the project application, including detailed project description using managerial language, not necessarily corresponding with the artistic value are of great importance for the groups deciding who will get grants.

Based on our observations, we may conclude that what is symptomatic is the fact that the actors of the process in question are reluctant to seek alternative ways of performing their activities. Perhaps, assuming that projectification is a phenomenon from which there is no escape, it is worth launching a discussion not on whether or not to carry out projects at all, but on how to conduct projects in a manner that never overshadows the aesthetic values of art. This consideration could be elaborated on during further research on agency in the projectified world of culture.

Notes

1 The name "European Capital of Culture" was introduced in 1999. Nevertheless, Kraków used the earlier version of the title, "European City of Culture," in 2000.
2 European Union Commission, 2008: https://ec.europa.eu/programmes/creative-europe/actions/capitals-culture_en
3 Public Information Bulletin, City of Kraków, Call for Proposals (Krakow's Scholarships for Creatives) www.bip.krakow.pl/?dok_id=93585 (accessed: 30.07.2018).

References

Alberro, A., & Stimson, B. (Eds.) (2009). *Institutional critique: An anthology of artists' writings.* Cambridge, MA: The MIT Press.

Ashrafi, R., Hartman, F., & Jergeas, G. (1998). Project management in the live entertainment industry: What is different? *International Journal of Project Management*, 16(5), 269–281.

Aubry, M., & Lenfle, S. (2012). Projectification: Midler's footprint in the project management field. *International Journal of Managing Projects in Business*, 5(4), 680–694.

Báez, A., & Herrero, L. C. (2012). Using contingent valuation and cost–benefit analysis to design a policy for restoring cultural heritage. *Journal of Cultural Heritage*, 13(3), 235–245.

Biuro Kraków (2000/2001). *Program KRAKÓW 2000 Europejskie Miasto Kultury. Raport końcowy*. Kraków, Poland: Biuro Kraków 2000.

Bredin, K., & Söderlund, J. (2011). Projectification on the way. In *Human resource management in project-based organizations* (pp. 1–22). London, England: Palgrave Macmillan.

Büttner, S., & Leopold, L. (2016). A "new spirit" of public policy? The project world of EU funding. *European Journal of Cultural and Political Sociology*, 3(1), 41–71.

Cicmil, S., Lindgren, M., & Packendorff, J. (2016). The project (management) discourse and its consequences: On vulnerability and unsustainability in project-based work. *New Technology, Work and Employment*, 31(1), 58–76.

Ekstedt, E. (2009). A new division of labour: The "projectification" of working and industrial life. In M. A. Moreau, S. Negrelli, & P. Pochet (Eds.), *Building anticipation of restructuring in Europe* (pp. 31–54). Brussels, Belgium: Peter Lang.

Farrell, L. M. (1994). Risk management and the evaluation of entertainment investment projects. *Project Management Journal*, XXV(2), 37–43.

Fik, M. (1996). Kultura polska 1944–1956. In J. Otwinowska & J. Żaryn (Eds.), *Polacy wobec przemocy 1944–1956*. Warsaw, Poland: Editions Spotkania.

Fred, M. (2018). *Projectification: The Trojan horse of local government*. Doctoral dissertation. Lund University/Malmo University.

Fred, M., & Mukhtar-Landgren, D. (2017). Un-packing the black box of local government projectification in the EU. Paper presented at IRSPM 2017 in Budapest.

Gareis, R. (2002). *Management in the project-oriented society [Forschung für Wirtschaft und Gesellschaft]*. Vienna: WU-Jahrestagung. Retrieved from http://epub.wu-wien.ac.at/

Gell, A. (1998). *Art and agency: An anthropological theory*. Oxford: Clarendon Press.

Gierat-Bieroń, B. (2009). *Ministrowie kultury dobry transformacji, 1989–2005 (wywiady)*. Kraków, Poland: Universitas.

Gierat-Bieroń, B., & Sonik, B. (2011). *Kraków 2000: Po 10 latach [Kraków 2000: 10 years after]*. Kraków, Poland: Krakowskie Biuro Festiwalowe, Instytut Dziedzictwa.

Glinkowski, P. (2012). Artists and policy-making: The English case. *International Journal of Cultural Policy*, 18(2), 168–184.

Gombrich, E. H. (1960). The early Medici as patrons of art: A survey of primary sources. In E. F. Jacob (Ed.), *Italian Renaissance studies* (pp. 279–311). New York, NY: Barnes & Noble.

Hodgson, D., & Cicmil, S. (2008). The other side of projects: The case for critical project studies. *International Journal of Managing Projects in Business*, 1(1), 142–152.

Ilczuk, D. (2001). *Cultural citizenship: Civil society and cultural policy in Europe*. Amsterdam: Boekmanstudies, Circle.

Ilczuk, D. (2002). *Polityka kulturalna w społeczeństwie obywatelskim*. Kraków, Poland: Wydawnictwo Uniwersytetu Jagiellońskiego.

Jach, A., Kownaka, M., & Ziółkowska, M. (Eds.) (2016). *Widok publiczny*. Kraków, Poland: Krakowskie Biuro Festiwalowe.

Jensen, A., Thuesen, C., & Geraldi, J. (2016). The projectification of everything: Projects as a human condition. *Project Management Journal*, 47(3), 21–34.

Kalff, Y. (2017). The knowledge worker and the projectified self: Domesticating and disciplining creativity. *Work Organisation, Labour and Globalisation*, 11(1), 10–27.

Kuura, A. (2011). Policies for projectification: Support, avoid or let it be? Discussions on Estonian Economic Policy. Retrieved from https://ssrn.com/abstract=1884204

Lindgren, M., & Packendorff, J. (2003). Deconstructing projects: Towards critical perspectives on project theory and projecticised society. Conference paper, Making Projects Critical: A Crisis of Instrumental Rationality?, April 10–11, 2003, Bristol Business School, Bristol, UK.

Lindgren, M., & Packendorff, J. (2006). *Projects and prisons*. In D. Hodgson & S. Cicmil (Eds.), *Making projects critical*. New York, NY: Palgrave Macmillan.

Lundin, R., Arvidsson, N., Brady, T., Ekstedt, E., Midler, C., & Sydow, J. (2015). *Managing and working in project society*. Cambridge, England: Cambridge University Press.

Makowski, G. (2015). Rozwój sektora organizacji pozarządowych w Polsce po 1989 r. *Studia BAS*, 4(44), 57–85.

Maylor, H., Brady, T., Cooke-Davies, T., & Hodgson, D. (2006). From projectification to programmification. *International Journal of Project Management*, 24(8), 663–674.

Midler, C. (1995). "Projectification" of the firm: The Renault case. *Scandinavian Journal of Management*, 11(4), 363–375.

Packendorff, J., & Lindgren, M. (2014). Projectification and its consequences: Narrow and broad conceptualisations. *South African Journal of Economic and Management Sciences*, 17, 7–21.

Rowlands, L., & Handy, J. (2012). An addictive environment: New Zealand film production workers' subjective experiences of project-based labour. *Human Relations*, 65(5), 657–680.

Sjöblom, S., Löfgren, K., & Godenhjelm, S. (2013). Projectified politics: Temporary organisations in a public context. *Scandinavian Journal of Public Administration*, 17(2), 3–12.

Szreder, K. (2016). *ABC Projektariatu*. Warsaw, Poland: Bęc Zmiana.

Szulborska-Łukaszewicz, J. (2017). O europeizacji miasta na przykładzie Krakowa, Europejskiego Miasta Kultury. *Zarządzanie w Kulturze*, 18(4), 527–548.

Szulborska-Łukaszewicz, J. (2015). Trends in cultural policy and culture management in Poland (1989–2014). *Zarządzanie w Kulturze*, 16(3), 221–240.

Throsby, D. (2010). *The economics of cultural policy*. Cambridge: Cambridge University Press.

Wåhlin, N., Kapsali, M., Näsholm, M. H., & Blomquist, T. (2016). *Urban strategies for culture-driven growth: Co-creating a European Capital of Culture*. Cheltenham, England: Edward Elgar.

12

STANDARDISATION AND ITS CONSEQUENCES IN HEALTH CARE

A Case Study of PRINCE2 Project Management Training

Sara Shaw, Gemma Hughes, and Trish Greenhalgh

UNIVERSITY OF OXFORD

> What strikes me as I listen and watch is the number of diagrams, graphics, categories and bulleted lists that make up the course. These are symbolic of the PRINCE2 approach – we're not only supposed to see them, learn them and internalise them, but then also reproduce them (and certainly not critique them). By doing the course the intention is that I *become* a PRINCE2 project manager, au fait with the language, the flow diagrams, the bullets, the categories, and roles and then accredited to take them, use them and circulate them out in the 'real world'.

The above quote is taken from an autoethnographic account of training for PRINCE2 – or **PR**ojects **IN** **C**ontrolled **E**nvironments – a structured project management methodology tool developed by the United Kingdom (UK) government. It captures the universal approach to project work that characterises PRINCE2 ("the number of diagrams, graphics, categories, and bulleted lists that make up the course"), which typically sees projects as discrete work packages within wider organisational programmes. The overarching task in PRINCE2 is to clearly define the project and direct the work of the project manager ("learn them and internalise them … reproduce them", "use them and circulate them") towards the most efficient use of resources. Varied techniques ("the language, the flow diagrams, the bullets, the categories, and roles") help to construct the project plan that, if followed, delivers the desired outcomes.

This approach to project management requires management practices and tools that assure an efficient use of resources. It has expanded relentlessly over the past 80 years: tools have emerged (e.g. the Gantt Chart), project organisation structures have become formalised (e.g. the use of "temporary organisations" to integrate activities and people across different settings), and project management has emerged as an academic discipline (Fred, 2014; Morris, 2011; Hodgson & Cicmil, 2008;

Morris et al., 2011a, 2011b). The appeal of careful planning and control of critical variables (e.g. resources) has enabled expansion, initially from military planning and operations research, to other sectors including information technology (IT), finance, pharmaceuticals, and, more recently, finance and health care (Hodgson, 2004; White & Fortune, 2002).

The promotion of such universal models of project management reflects the enduring impact of Fordist rationalisation on contemporary management, with its focus on instrumental rationality, predictability, and control (Hodgson & Cicmil, 2007; Shenhav, 1999) and a strategic focus on developing the future perfect (Morris et al., 2011a). It raises questions about the work that such standardised models do, generally or in specific areas of work such as health care (our interest), and concerns about the potential knock-on effect on the use of discretion and value-based judgements. It is these questions and concerns that are the focus of our chapter.

Limited attention has been given to project management in the context of health care. Notable exceptions include recent work on the projectification of patients through self-management (Glasdam et al., 2015), and studies documenting the rise of projects in emergency response situations in developing countries (e.g. Lotte & Susan Reynolds, 2014). There has been some work describing the use of specific project management techniques in health care settings (e.g. use of Six Sigma in hospital radiology (Benedetto, 2003)) and documenting a rise in the use of external consultancies (e.g. to implement Total Quality Management (Badrick & Preston, 2002); see also Büttner, Chapter 12, this volume) in health care. Yet to our knowledge, little research has been conducted examining the evolution of project management in health care, the approach to managing projects and the way in which this might shape health care.

The apparent lack of critical interest in project management is surprising. Health care is a moral activity, involving complex legal, organisational, financial, cultural, professional, medical, ethical, and personal perspectives. The promotion of universal models of management holds the potential to downplay the human issues and organisational politics that account for how and why projects evolve. Yet little is understood about the consequences of project management – and projectification more broadly – on this activity. We therefore critically examine the significance of project management for public sector health care, drawing on a case study of PRINCE2 to examine how the idea of project management is constructed, the discourses and categories in play, and the implications for public sector health care. We adopt an interpretive approach that takes issues of morality, equality, and ethics to be at least as important as concerns of organisational efficiency and effectiveness; recognises that the process of managing projects is a struggle over the realisation of ideas; and acknowledges that projects are mediated by a range of settings, actors, language, and artefacts (Cicmil, 2006; Fournier & Grey, 2000; Hodgson & Cicmil, 2008). Our main argument is that the categories and language underpinning PRINCE2 emphasise standardised, technical procedures and market logic and elevate universal, abstract rationality in projects in ways that potentially constrain the action of individuals who work within and manage such public sector projects, and detract from the values underpinning a public health service that has human experience and emotion at its heart.

The Rise of Public Sector Project Management

We develop our argument in the context of increasing reliance on projects in public sector organisations, and the use of a range of associated project management tools and methods as fundamental building blocks in the public sector. In the past 20 years there has been a significant rise in the number of projects being undertaken in the public sector (Fred, 2014; Wald, 2016; Büttner & Leopold, 2016). Precise estimates are hard to come by but recent work suggests that projects form over 30% of the work of public administration (Wald, 2016), and that the workforce is expected to grow significantly in the next ten years (Project Management Institute, 2017). These figures provide only a partial view of the public sector. However, they suggest that the project form is increasingly being applied to public sector tasks and settings.

Health care is not typically thought of as a project-intensive industry. That is changing with health care now regarded by the project management industry as "lead[ing] the pack in terms of growth between 2010 and 2020", with a projected 30% global increase in project management roles during that period (Project Management Institute, 2013). In the UK formal figures on the number of project managers working in the National Health Service (NHS) are not available. In September 2017, NHSjobs – a dedicated online recruitment service – offered 410 project management positions (around 3%) of a possible 14,763 clinical, executive, and administrative positions in the NHS, with many requiring specialist training and/or certification (e.g. PRINCE2). NHS England – the body that sets the overall priorities and direction of the NHS – now actively supports set up and delivery of projects (e.g. NHS England, 2016) and 'project manager' is one of the roles explicitly identified in health careers by Health Education England, the body that oversees education and training for health staff in England. These figures suggest that there is a significant amount of project-based work in health care undertaken by individuals with specialist expertise and a distinct set of competencies. Those responsible for managing and delivering projects in health care continue to use tools, like PRINCE2, that situate project management as a process involving a series of decisions, plans, and actions that are undertaken to achieve specific (often pre-articulated and pre-agreed) goals (Packendorff, 1995; Cicmil, 2006; Morris et al., 2011b).

The steady rise in the use of projects has been characterised as projectification – a social process in which, at its extreme, all aspects of life are colonised by project-related principles, rules, techniques, and procedures (Hodgson & Cicmil, 2008). Contemporary industrialised society is characterised by contingency, unpredictability, and rapid change (Mautner, 2013). Projects are one way in which public sector organisations have sought to handle these challenges, providing "adaptability and contingency considered to be a superior way of reacting to unanticipated and irregular situations" (Sjöblom et al., 2013, p3). Fuelled by increasing use of information and communications technology (ICT) and a wealth of programmes and tools intended to make projects easier and more efficient to manage (Cicmil, 2006; Morris et al., 2011a), projects are thought to provide flexibility, accelerate decision-making processes, increase problem-solving capabilities and innovativeness, and deliver strategic goals (Sjöblom et al., 2013).

For those involved in developing and delivering project management, tools such as PRINCE2 provide a structured approach to managing work that is now commonplace in public sector organisations. Such tools are thought to provide a universal, standardised approach to delivering (i.e. implementing) effective public policy. As such they might be thought of as naturalised objects (Bowker & Star, 1999) bringing people together through a process of "learning by membership" through which the procedures, tools, and practices of project management become taken-for-granted and the conditional nature of the standards they embody becomes lost. This is the aspiration of organisations such as the US-based Project Management Institute (PMI), the International Standards Organization (ISO), and the UK-based Office of Government Commerce. All have sought to develop universal standards for project management (i.e. structured bodies of knowledge specifying the competencies and methodologies needed to be a project manager) and a range of professional certifications. However, despite efforts to develop a universal body of knowledge with universal standards for project management, progress has been patchy (Hodgson & Cicmil, 2007) with limited international integration across professional bodies and discrepancies across bodies of knowledge (Hodgson, 2005).

For others, including many working in the public sector, the project-related principles, rules and procedures underpinning PRINCE2 and other project management tools form a new iron-cage (cf. Weber) of project rationality by which their work is organised. Long-term thinking and strategic planning, as well as innovation and creativity, tend to be trumped by short-term delivery of technical tasks within restricted timeframes and budgets (Midler, 1995; Fred, 2014), and particular forms of knowledge and interests become privileged – and others excluded – in the process of managing projects (Bowker & Star, 1994, 1999; Timmermans et al., 1995). This clearly has consequences. As Bowker and Star (1999) say: "every successful standard imposes a classification system, at the very least between good and bad ways of organising actions or things" (p. 15). Through this lens the principles underpinning project management – visibility, predictability, and control – are not only based on a set of standards (i.e. agreed-upon rules for the production of textual or material objects [Bowker & Star, 1999, p. 14]), but are also oriented to means rather than ends (i.e. being concerned with identifying the most efficient method of getting the job done and not the appropriateness of the job itself) and so risk moral blindness (Sayer, 2011).

The challenge is to uncover and illuminate the efforts that underpin and construct these apparently universal standards and ways of working. This is clearly a difficult challenge given the tendency for standards to "disappear from sight" (Hodgson & Cicmil, 2007, p. 436). We take up that challenge here by focusing on the kinds of knowledge that are privileged in PRINCE2, the language and categories used, and the ways in which they structure and make sense of project work.

Studying Projects in Controlled Environments

Individuals are often the target and carriers of project management discourse. To our knowledge this has rarely been explored through reflective methodologies. Hence this paper is an attempt to look more closely at the content of public sector project management training and how it is experienced. We undertook a case study of PRINCE2 training. We deliberately used an *n* of 1 case study design to enable us to generate an empirically-rich and holistic account of project management methodology and hone in on the particularity of a specific methodology from which we could inform theoretical generalisations about the nature of project management (Stake, 1995). We used critical case sampling (Patton, 2001), an approach that involves selecting one or more cases that hold important information for in-depth study. We choose PRINCE2 as our critical case for two reasons. Firstly, it is widely used in the UK and internationally, in public and private sectors, and is commonly referred to as "the industry standard" (the PRINCE2 manual now being published in over ten languages and the foundation exam reportedly having being taken by over one million people). Secondly, PRINCE2 originated in the public sector; hence, for instance, participants in previous research undertaken by our team focused on two government-led technology programmes (see Greenhalgh et al., 2010) frequently used it in their work. On this basis, PRINCE2 seemed likely to "yield the most information [about project management methodologies] and have the greatest impact on the development of knowledge" (Patton, 2001, p. 236).

We used auto-ethnography as our primary means of collecting data, supplementing this with analysis of key documents. Auto-ethnography is a form of qualitative research which uses self-reflection and writing to describe and systematically analyse personal experience in order to understand cultural experience (Chang, 2008; Anderson, 2006). It is distinct from other forms of self-narrative (e.g. personal essays) in that it moves beyond the personal story into analysis that connects with wider cultural, political, and social meanings (Ellis et al., 2010). In this sense, auto-ethnographers "excavate rich details [and] bring them onto the examination tables to sort, label, interconnect, and contextualise them in the sociocultural environment" (Chang, 2008, p. 51). Our approach was informed by the principles of analytic auto-ethnography (Anderson, 2006), features of which include being a full member in the setting, visible as such in published texts, and committed to developing theoretical understandings of broader social phenomena.

Sara Shaw (SS) wrote the auto-ethnography while undertaking PRINCE2 training over ten months from April 2016 to January 2017. SS is a social policy academic, with training in business finance. She had previously undertaken a PhD and postdoctoral work in health research policy before co-leading an interdisciplinary research unit (along with Trish Greenhalgh, a senior academic and primary care doctor) focused on undertaking social science-informed research on health, care, and technology. Gemma Hughes (GH) is a university-based researcher interested in the organisation and delivery of health and social care and who, at the time of writing, previously worked as a senior NHS commissioner with varied exposure to projects (and project management). All authors are part of a Wellcome Trust-funded programme exploring the role of technologies in health and care (www.scals.org), which provided an opportunity to come together and reflect on the ways in which different kinds of technologies do (and don't) shape health care work. It is under the umbrella of this programme that we conducted the auto-ethnography.

Data collection began when SS began searching for PRINCE2 training. A Google search for "prince2 course" resulted in 536,000 hits, ranging from the PRINCE2 website through to companies providing training for PRINCE and PRINCE2, recruitment consultants providing additional training for employees, and training providers with a range of courses in more focused areas (e.g. project or time management). We focused on companies providing PRINCE2 training and elected to go with a provider who supplied on-line training to enable SS to engage with the course over an extended period of time. We then randomly selected a provider from the list, who described themselves as "a project and programme management training organisation bringing best practice learning to individuals and organisations via flexible course options, supporting documents and media". SS initially signed up for a six-month course with the stated aims of understanding "the PRINCE2 project management methodology", gaining "sufficient knowledge to pass the PRINCE2 Foundation…and Practitioner Examination[s]", and appreciating "how to tailor and apply PRINCE2 to achieve successful project outcomes". This was subsequently extended for a further six months.

SS worked systematically through each of 22 modules, performing exercises (at the end of each module) and referring to the allied PRINCE2 manual and course materials. Auto-ethnographic field notes were taken throughout, recording experiences and reflections of the training in textual and graphical form (e.g. screen capture of the training). This resulted in an in-depth, 36-page (11,612 word) account of engaging with PRINCE2.

As noted above, our intention was to critically examine the categories and language underpinning PRINCE2. We therefore identified supporting documents for analysis, including PRINCE2 manuals (from 2005 and 2009) and academic publications (since 1989 when PRINCE was first launched) explaining and/or defending PRINCE2.

Our methodological approach was grounded in linguistic ethnography, an approach that typically takes language as its prime point of analytic entry (Snell et al., 2015) and that guided us to examine the formal descriptions and underlying assumptions behind PRINCE2. Analysis began with repeated close readings of the data by SS, GH, and Trish Greenhalgh (TG). Through discussion we identified a tension between the highly structured approach incorporated within PRINCE2 (focusing largely on processes and procedures), and the people, experiences, and perspectives that make up contemporary health care. Take, for instance, the definition of a project as: "a temporary organisation that is created for the purpose of delivering one or more business products according to an agreed Business Case" (Office of Government Commerce, 2009, p. 8), in which projects are framed in the language of the market ("business products"), follow a structured process ("temporary organisation", "agreed Business Case"), and appeared to rarely engage with people, their values, morals, emotions, or experiences or to acknowledge inherent uncertainties in providing health care.

We explored this tension further by unpacking the assumptions underpinning PRINCE2, the language and categories used, how they are constructed, and how contradictions are negotiated and defended. We identified four themes that we thought worthy of more detailed examination: establishing a project management system, generating order through standardisation, substitution of technical for moral responsibility, and redefining projects as business. Within each of those themes, we then focused on prominent or puzzling emphases, moving between elements of our data to examine the language and categories that make up project management work in PRINCE2.

This process raised questions about the ways in which projects are categorised and codified, the role of language in guiding management processes, and the role that categories and symbolic visions play as "actors" that contribute to the evolution of project management. This led us to undertake more detailed analysis, paying attention to the framing of the texts, rhetorical claims, and the evolution of related documents over time and through various versions, and looking for potential explanations for particular categories and the language and practices that might support them. Analysis was informed by our theoretical interests in language and classification (see above), the techniques and procedures allied to contemporary project management, and our research on technology and health care delivery (e.g. Greenhalgh et al., 2010)

Our study did not require ethics approval. Given our focus on the content of PRINCE2, we elected to anonymise details of the training provider.

Establishing a Project Management System

PRINCE2 is described as "a principle based method" (Office of Government Commerce, 2009), providing knowledge to support project management professionals using universally accepted criteria developed in collaboration with external experts and reviewed regularly via an in-built system of accreditation. The idea is that a set of seven universal principles (Box 12.1) provides a framework for "best practice", allowing PRINCE2 projects to be applied "regardless of project scale, type organisation, geography or culture" (Office of Government Commerce, 2009, p. 11). These principles, and the accompanying text, are delivered in an impersonal tone with, for instance, little (if any) use of first or third person (despite the acknowledgement that "projects involve people" (Office of Government Commerce, 2009, p. 13)), those managing projects referred to in terms of their job title (e.g. Project Manager), and use of technical language and graphics throughout manuals (e.g. in relation to "manage by exception" or "chronological flow"). Across versions of the PRINCE2 manual, and on associated websites, the language used has discursive affinity (Hajer, 2006) with that used in official documents, emphasising objective knowledge ("universal principles") and an authoritative definition of project management.

BOX 12.1 OVERVIEW OF PRINCIPLES UNDERPINNING THE PRINCE2 METHODOLOGY*

1. *Continued Business Justification* – A PRINCE2 project must make good business sense, with justified use of time and resources.
2. *Learn from Experience* – PRINCE2 project teams should learn lessons from their experience of previous projects.
3. *Define Roles and Responsibilities* – Everyone involved in a PRINCE2 project should know what they and others are doing, with roles and responsibilities agreed.
4. *Manage by Stages* – A PRINCE2 project should be "planned, monitored and controlled" through each stage.
5. *Manage by Exception* – A PRINCE2 project involves defining "distinct responsible for directing, managing and delivering" the project and defining accountability and tolerances throughout.
6. *Focus on Products* – PRINCE2 project focus on "the definition and delivery of products".
7. *Tailor to the Environment* – Projects need to adapt PRINCE2 to the environment, size, complexity, importance, capability and risk.

** These principles are adapted from the 2009 version of PRINCE2 manual which, in contrast to earlier versions of the manual, explicitly describe PRINCE2 as a principle-based method. In earlier versions of the manual principles are visible but not explicitly documented in the same way.*

The use of official language is unsurprising. PRINCE was established in 1989 by the Central Computer and Telecommunications Agency (CCTA, since renamed the Office of Government Commerce). It was originally based on

PROMPT, a project management method created by Simpact Systems Ltd in 1975, and adopted by CCTA in 1979 as the standard to be used for all Government information system projects. Based on PROMPT, PRINCE was launched in 1989 and became the project management methodology of choice for government projects. Initially focused on the IT sector, it was subsequently refined to broaden its appeal in other sectors. PRINCE2 was published in 1996. This second iteration was reviewed by various external experts (21 "individuals and organisations" being listed in the 2005 manual, growing to 14 "reference group" members, and 87 "reviewers" in the 2009 version and accounts of input from a consortium of 150 European organisations (ILX Marketing Team, 2017)), adding a further layer of authority by drawing on a coalition of experts (Hajer, 2006) to maintain and promote the concepts, ideas, and practices allied to PRINCE2. This is reinforced though the use of PRINCE2 Foundation and Practitioner certification (relying on simple exams, with re-registration required to maintain Practitioner level), which further legitimates the expert knowledge and standard processes underpinning PRINCE2.

PRINCE2 does not exist independently. It has been shaped and reshaped over time in response to expert review (see above), feedback from users, and developments in the project management community. Project Management Professional (PMP), offered by the US-based Project Management Institute, is a competitor of PRINCE2. Each acknowledges the other's existence in allied material. For PRINCE2 this has involved review of the PMI Body of Knowledge (PMBOK), reviewing the level of flexibility and adaptability offered and changing their own offering in similar ways. For instance, the second version of PRINCE offered a broader methodology applicable to projects of varying size and complexity (specifying "tailoring" as an underpinning principle, Box 12.1), in response to changes in PMBOK. More recently the ownership rights to PRINCE2 were transferred to AXELOS Ltd (a joint venture, with the Cabinet Office and Capita owning 49% and 51% respectively and bringing together a range of "best practice methodologies" alongside PRINCE2) leading to a "PRINCE2 2017 Update" that focused on linking with other methodologies (notably Agile) and, much as PMI, promoting scalability and flexibility,

The mutual shaping across project management has the effect of at least espousing to generate universal knowledge and standards underpinning project management practice. This idea, that there exists a core set of knowledge and practices, is a key component in arguments for standardisation across projects that underpins the PRINCE2 methodology.

Generating Order Through Standardisation

Since its inception PRINCE2 has been promoted as moving towards a more adaptable project management methodology, characterised by flexibility and network relationships. However, our analysis indicated that the way in which

PRINCE2 is designed is remarkably rigid, evoking notions of standardised and technocratic models of scientific management (e.g. Taylor, 1911). This rigidity was evident in the way projects were intended to move though a structured and pre-determined life cycle. The combination of pre-defined principles, themes, processes, and variables within the PRINCE2 methodology (Figure 12.1) required technical processes and procedures to be followed by all projects.

Take the following extract from SS's journal as she was first introduced to PRINCE2, which describes a prescribed, linear process for managing all projects:

> We shift to focus on the project management method which is about "planning, delegating, monitoring and control of all of the aspects of the project, and the motivation of those involved to achieve the project within the expected performance targets for time, cost, quality, scope, benefits and risks" (*Managing Successful Projects with PRINCE2*, p. 4). Again the language stands out, this time as quite technocratic – the focus is on targets, deliverables, control techniques, planning; the assumptions are about [a] linear process, working through stages, standardised processes. Do we all need to control all aspects of a project in this way?
>
> *(Journal, p. 4)*

Project management methodologies like PRINCE2 necessarily use heuristics as a way of simplifying processes and communicating the (often complex) nexus of tasks and relationships that need negotiating and managing in projects. But the language of PRINCE2 was more than straightforward simplification: the focus was on maintaining procedural control through prescribed linear stages ("linear process", "working through stages", "standardised processes"), symbolised by models, boxes, and categories (e.g. Figure 12.1). Take the example of "directing a project" – a key process in the PRINCE2 methodology. In the PRINCE2 manual (Office of Government Commerce, 2009, p. 135), this process was depicted using 29 boxes and multiple arrows, suggesting compartmentalised stages of work (from initiation, through authorisation and direction to closure) that flow neatly from one to the other. This standardised process was framed positively: the aspiration is that all projects are directed in the same way, undertaking the same tasks ("initiation notification", "stage authentication", and so on), using the same terminology, performed by the same roles (the "Project Manager", for instance, having responsibility for organising and controlling the project, selecting people to do the project work, and drawing up project plans to describe what the project team will do and when) and irrespective of the political and policy contexts in which they take place. Uncertainty, mess and disorder were "controlled" out, with unpredictable events ("exceptions") predicted and managed as part of the PRINCE2 process. In this way, the process of "directing a project" was made to appear "neat and smooth" (Journal, p. 12).

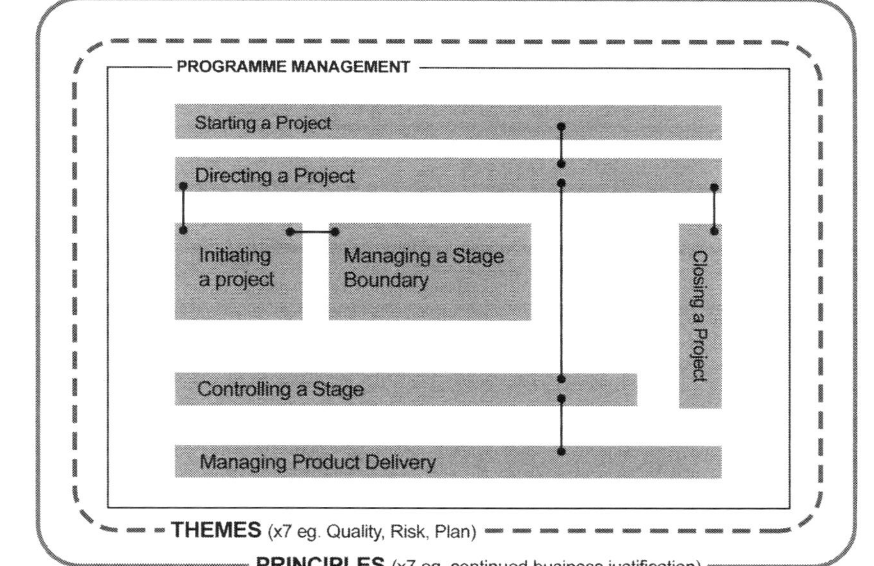

FIGURE 12.1 Overview of PRINCE2 process (derived from *Managing Successful Projects with PRINCE2*, Office of Government Commerce, 2009).

There were hints in the PRINCE2 methodology that project management is not always quite so neat and tidy and that standardisation can be difficult to achieve. Values and emotions crept in and order was challenged. For instance, following user feedback and wider developments in project management (see above), the Office for Government Commerce added an additional section on "tailoring" in the "PRINCE2: 2009 Refresh". This new section sat uncomfortably in the wider training programme. On the one hand it resituated PRINCE2 as a series of "interlinked elements" that can be adjusted or scaled to the project at hand and the environment that the project takes place in, on the other hand it fell back on standardised processes and pre-determined procedures to do so:

> So the idea of tailoring is less about omitting any of [the elements of PRINCE2] … and more about applying an appropriate level of project management (e.g. "adapting the method to external factors", "using it with a 'lightness of touch'") … tailoring is not something that is embedded in the PRINCE2 method, simply something to be thought about at one of the key stages. And tailoring follows the same approach: carving work up into sections and stages, and documenting and reviewing everything.
>
> *(Journal, p. 31)*

This kind of slippage (e.g. between prescribed stages and unplanned work) was rarely acknowledged or dealt with in PRINCE2. It emerged here and there (when, for instance, a degree of flexibility was required in the management process), but was then side-lined or negotiated in ways that appear to fit better with the standardised PRINCE2 methodology. Take the example of giving "ad hoc" direction, an integral part of directing a project. "Ad hoc" suggests an informal approach that recognises that "stuff happens" (i.e. it is impossible to pre-determine everything). However, the recognition surfaced by use of the term "ad hoc" was quickly put to one side with categories requiring:

> "ad hoc direction" pre-defined as: "result[ing] from requests, reports, external influences, project board members individual concerns, informal requests for advice and guidance, an issue report, an exception report, a highlight report or in response to advice and decisions from corporate or programme management".

This finite list carefully sets out the things that can prompt "ad hoc direction" in a PRINCE2 project and, with pre-determined roles and processes flowing from each category, the people and procedures to follow. The finality of the list and informality of the term jarred. "Even here", it seemed, "they want[ed] to control, predict and standardise everything" (Journal, pp. 24–25). In other words, even where a more flexible and informal approach was acknowledged within PRINCE2 – one where meaning was constructed in the process of managing – the approach to managing followed the same standardised and technocratic approach outlined above.

Prioritising Technical Over Moral Responsibility

PRINCE2 methodology employs a technocratic form of rationality: one that uses specific models, procedures, and techniques to enhance calculability and increase visibility of those engaged in project work. In PRINCE2 training the methodology tended to be presented as value-free: "the way in which everything is sectioned off into neat blocks … comes across as a simple way of managing projects that is neutral and neat. People, mess, concerns, muddles, emotions and so on do not feature" (Journal, p. 11). PRINCE2 was underpinned by the principles of instrumental rationality, a concern with the most efficient or cost-effective means to achieving (in this case) successful delivery of a project, and limited scope for reflection on the value of that project or its delivery. In other words, PRINCE2 methodology encourages users to focus on the means rather than the end, to substitute moral and ethical concerns with technical procedures.

Project management methodology is based on the ability to read, interpret, and apply rules and procedures, relying on people to respect the rules and, in turn, impose these rules on others (Clegg & Courpasson, 2004). In our analysis of PRINCE2 people were characterised in terms of fixed, pre-specified roles and with little (if any) sense of people's interests, agendas, or jobs. Project management roles and positions were ever-present (e.g. "Project Manager", "Team Manager", "Senior Supplier", "Project Support"), and situated in terms of their position in the project management hierarchy ("Corporate or Programme Management" being at the top of the hierarchy and "Team Members" and "Project Support" being at the bottom). Values, interests, and emotions remained hidden. There was little (if any) sense of experiential learning or self-organisation, with project managers framed as "automatons who simply internalise and implement PRINCE2" (Journal, p. 12). This was reflected in the experience of *doing* PRINCE2 training:

> Having got to the end of the course, I feel relieved. It's not a fun or engaging course and the language and focus on processes and procedures has felt like an oppressive weight bearing down on me. It's fair to say that I never want to use PRINCE2 and find the approach stifling. I suspect any of the projects I'm involved in would grind to a halt if this is the approach we used and can only imagine that those using it in health and social care – also the wider public sector – feel no sense of freedom, creativity or invention in undertaking and managing projects.

This extract captures the repetition, monotony, weariness, and rigidity experienced in learning PRINCE2 in which processes and procedures (order) take precedence over creativity and judgement in the management of projects. The image conjured up in materials was of a confident project manager exuding predictability, assurance, and reliability and delivering the desired project outcomes in the most effective and efficient ways possible. And yet, trainees were intended to "internalise the discipline" undergoing months of technical training, immersion in the PRINCE2 body of knowledge (Box 12.1), and gaining certification, to submit to the structure rather than control it. Certainty and reliability were valued with limited (if any) scope for bringing in human judgement, creativity, or emotion in *doing* projects.

In our analysis, we found that a significant part of the work of PRINCE2 project teams involved documentation: "business case", "project plan", "stage plan", "product description", "risk register", "issue register", "quality register", "risk management strategy", "milestone charts", and more all featured in PRINCE2 project management. The emphasis was on planning, reporting, storing, and auditing documents allied to specific tasks and roles. The textual flow felt onerous, and the need to record and monitor was paramount. On the one hand, this appeared to serve the purpose of enabling users to make sense of the PRINCE2 methodology. On the other hand, the extent of documentation, and on breaking project management down into textual components, appeared to reconfirm the underlying concern of PRINCE2 with maintaining order through "products", rather than through personal autonomy and oversight.

Documenting appeared deeply embedded within PRINCE2 methodology. Technical rationality – expressed through documentation and the bureaucratic procedures that goes with it – promoted a sense of legitimacy for those managing projects, making "calculation and choice redundant" and "established patterns of action virtually unassailable" (Bauman, 1991, p. 164), absenting critical reflexivity (Adams & Balfour, 2009; Arendt, 2003) and negating the need to engage with social or ethical concerns. Take the following examples, drawn from field notes:

> There is undoubtedly a need for planning … but for me this process divorces "senior users" or "team managers" from the realities of peoples everyday lives and instead immerses them in a technocratic process more concerned with frameworks, stages and tasks than, for instance, what it means to be living with multiple chronic conditions.
>
> It seems to me that any sense of practical reasoning (and the judgements, emotions or morals that entails) is completely irrelevant in the PRINCE2 process. The focus is on instrumental rationality and institutional procedures. "Early warning indicators", "risk budgets" … all speak of the technocrat applying principles to their work and … of devolving any sense of responsibility for the whole of the project.
>
> *(Journal, p. 26)*

Our analysis of PRINCE2 suggested that the methodology substitutes moral and ethical responsibility (e.g. for team members, patients and their families, or the equitable distribution of resources) with technical concerns. This substitution is made possible through meticulous separation of tasks and procedural routines, and through a "hierarchy of command" (Bauman, 1991) in which appreciation of the wider aspects of project management are removed from the field of vision of team members. In the PRINCE2 methodology the project managers' act becomes an end in itself. What matters is whether the act has been performed according to the best available technological know-how, and whether the task or project is successful (i.e. doing the thing right, rather than doing the right thing). The result (in theory at least) is that moral standards are side-lined in the interests of securing the success of a project. There was no mention in the PRINCE2 methodology of ethics or morals, or of reflexivity or active questioning on the part of those responsible for managing projects. And, turning to health care, there appeared little scope for acknowledging the plasticity of patients' personal circumstances and lived experience.

Action borne out of moral (rather than technical) responsibility might include arguing for a preferred decision, advocating on behalf of service users, or arguing to deviate from procedure, none of which appear permissible in the PRINCE2 methodology. The inclusion of a category of "unplanned events" hinted at the possibility of moral concerns and judgements. However, as elsewhere, such unplanned events were subject to technical procedures: being categorised as a "request for change", an "off specification", or a "problem/concern" and then "simply…controlled out of the management process" (Journal, p. 18).

Redefining Public Sector Projects as Business

Market logic (informed by the exchange of goods and services) appeared to be a guiding principle underpinning PRINCE2 methodology. Terms such as "suppliers", "business", "business case", "continued business justification", "product", "commercial sensitivity", "investment appraisal", "overspends", and "increases in revenue" featured regularly and suggested the potential for the substitution of products over experiences.

Such language was deeply rooted in PRINCE2 methodology. Linguistic choices repeatedly defined projects as business, with "suppliers" and "users" focused on value for money (or profit) and development of products. Take the following extract from fieldnotes about PRINCE2's quality theme (Figure 12.1), which describes how "quality" is redefined in terms of tangible products:

> John [my online tutor] tells me that "Quality, in a PRINCE2 environment, is focused on a projects' products". All of these products are defined and described, with quality criteria assigned to each. Quality methods are then outlined, agreed and tracked. The focus is then on developing quality standards and procedures, quality planning, quality control and quality assurance in order to ensure a good and successful product. There is little sense of things other than products: people, caring, depression, happiness do not cut the mustard here and are not featured in the PRINCE2 manual.
>
> *(Journal, p. 11)*

This extract suggests not simply that market logic is appropriated into the PRINCE2 methodology, but that market language holds the potential to colonise lifeworlds (Chouliaraki & Fairclough, 1999; Mautner, 2013). While terms such as "product" or "customer" might be fitting in the context of a market relationship (e.g. between shopkeeper and purchaser), they appear reductive when applied to non-business and non-productive relationships that typically characterise the public sector (e.g. that between health care provider and patient). They add particular semantic features and connotations (e.g. implying freedom for everyone to access and purchase "care" – the product), but lack others (e.g. the complex web of rights, duties, and collective rather than individual interests). We found repeated examples of similar linguistic choices throughout our data, with such language implying that care was available in the form of material objects or products (rather than, say, experiences and interactions).

Discussion

Our concern in this chapter has been to draw attention to the tensions inherent in standardised project management methodologies in health care and the potential for moral blindness. This reflects a move in the literature that is concerned to uncover the roots of project management in ideas of contemporary society characterised by standardisation, large-scale operations, and bureaucracy (Cicmil et al., 2009; Hodgson & Cicmil, 2006, 2007, 2008). To date there has been limited critical (i.e. theoretically informed) analysis of project management, the social and ethical territory that project management occupies, or the consequences of project management practice and the specific tools and techniques employed (Hodgson & Cicmil, 2008; Morris et al., 2011a). We have sought to add to this literature by undertaking a case study of PRINCE2 training. In doing so we have provided insights into the ways in which this particular project management methodology is structured, the appeal it offers in terms of organising (often value-laden and emotionally wrought) health care work, the potential it holds to guide project work in particular ways, and the propensity to obscure (if not disregard) ethical and moral concerns. We have chosen to focus on a project management tool that has been widely used in health care and study it in depth using auto-ethnography, the strengths of which lie in its combined ethnographic, cultural, and autobiographical orientation (Chang, 2008). However, PRINCE2 is one of a range of tools and we have not engaged with the social and interpretive work (e.g. the tacit knowledge possessed by managers and how this shapes use of PRINCE2) that takes place in translating PRINCE2 methodologies into everyday practice. While we have elected not to focus on the day-to-day use of PRINCE2 we are not suggesting that the standards and texts allied to PRINCE2 are absorbed uncritically by users, rather that the body of knowledge underpinning PRINCE2 holds potential to guide users to emphasise market logic and instrumental rationality in ways that detract from the values underpinning a public health service. It is also quite possible that methodologies like PRINCE2 offer important mobilising metaphors, prescribing as well as describing possible approaches and offering one of a range of tools that managers can use and adapt to their everyday work.

Our findings do suggest that PRINCE2 methodology – and projectification more broadly – is characteristic of neo-liberal managerialism that substitutes organisational for professional values; prioritises bureaucratic, hierarchical, and managerial controls over collegial relations; and emphasises budgetary restrictions and rationalisation, performance targets, accountability, and increased political control (Preston-Shoot, 2011; Mautner, 2013). Projects are assumed to be the same (and project tasks to be clearly defined and unambiguous, the focus being on efficient use of resources and techniques) with matters of conduct, ethical judgement, and decision-making obscured and removed from the contexts in which they take place. The emphasis is on organisational (over occupational) professionalism with control resting with (in this case) the project or temporary organisation, and priorities manifest in the form of managerial procedures and techniques (Evetts et al., 2011). While there are some who feel that by rigorously adopting project management methodologies we can achieve more effective and efficient project management work (not least those responsible for developing and implementing PRINCE2, PMA, and similar project management tools), we argue that by prioritising standardised techniques and procedures such an approach holds the potential to reshape the perception and/or design of health care work (Mautner, 2013); lose independent critical thought and reflection (Arendt, 2003); separate decision-making from the organisational politics in which its takes place (Preston-Shoot, 2011; Li, chapter 3, this volume); and distance people as cogs (non-humans) in the project management machine (Adam, 2011; Bauman & Donskis, 2013). This critique of project management resonates with wider analyses that situate such managerial rationality as "the unquestioned pacemaker of modern social order" (Shenhav, 1999, p. 3), shaping various technocratic devices from Taylorism onwards.

The classification and ordering of project work in PRINCE2 makes some aspects of work (and workers) visible over others. Our findings show how the structured approach underpinning PRINCE2 (in theory) diffuses individual responsibility and moral accountability, requiring compartmentalised accomplishment of tasks undertaken in pre-specified roles (project manager, team leader, and so on). The danger lies in the potential for moral blindness (Bauman & Donskis, 2013), where professionals and administrators are encouraged to step into a morally neutral role of project manager to carry out their duties and conform to organisational policies consistent with the norms of bureaucratic procedure and technical rationality, while at the same time participating in administrative evil-doing (Adams & Balfour, 2009). As Bauman (1991) put it: "cruelty is not committed by cruel individuals, but by ordinary men and women trying to acquit themselves well of their ordinary duties" (p. 154). Temporary organisations like PRINCE2 projects are characterised by diffused and scattered information. The point Bauman (and others) makes is that no one in the organisation may have a complete enough picture to acknowledge, comprehend, or address the destructive activity potentially embedded in project work. However, care should be taken in imposing the idea that use of PRINCE2 methodologies in health care will inevitably result in administrative evil. Indeed, the way in which project management methodologies like PRINCE2 are used in health care likely also reproduces the culture of the NHS and offers scope for redefinition.

In the mainstream project management literature projects are considered suitable ways to avoid inefficiency, address risk, and control project work by employing standardised work procedures and engaging project workers in the delivery of a new product or event. Little is mentioned of the emotional labour involved in such work. Our findings suggest the work of PRINCE2 projects requires submission to monotonous conditions and managerial control. Such findings are reflected in recent critical literature on project management (e.g. Lindgren et al., 2014) and suggest that there is likely a recursive relationship between the PRINCE2 discourse (of standardised procedures) and project workers subjective experience (of monotony and control).

PRINCE2 is all about the successful delivery of projects. On the face of it this might seem a straightforward and uncontested ambition. However, our findings have shown that PRINCE2 offers a standardised approach to managing projects, grounded in instrumental rationality, and drawing on technocratic values, unified models, and pre-determined sets of procedures that bring a natural order (Douglas & Wildavsky, 1980; Douglas, 1984) to the process of managing projects and take little account of the values and experiences of those involved in, or subjected to, the PRINCE2 process. It is tempting to view the rationalising practices of PRINCE2 methodology as objective and value-free; however, as our findings have shown, the representation of project management as a neutral, transferable body of knowledge with specialised terminology and universal appeal has potentially far-reaching consequences.

References

Adam, G. B. (2011). The problem of administrative evil in a culture of technical rationality. *Public Integrity*, 13(3), 275–286. doi:10.2753/pin1099-9922130307

Adams, G. B., & Balfour, D. L. (2009). *Unmasking administrative evil* (3rd edition). Armonk, NY: M. E. Sharpe.

Anderson, L. (2006). Analytic autoethnography. *Journal of Contemporary Ethnography*, 35(4), 373–395. doi:10.1177/0891241605280449

Arendt, H. (2003). Personal responsibility under dictatorship. In I. Kohn (Ed.), *Responsibility and judgment* (pp. 17–48). New York, NY: Schocken Books.

Badrick, T. C., & Preston, A. P. (2002). Role of external management consultants in health-care organizations implementing TQM. *Clinical Leadership & Management Review*, 16(5), 281–286.

Bauman, Z. (1991). *Modernity and the Holocaust.* Cambridge, England: Polity Press.

Bauman, Z., & Donskis, L. (2013). *Moral blindness: The loss of sensitivity in liquid modernity*. Cambridge, England: Polity Books.

Benedetto, A. R. (2003). Six Sigma: Not for the faint of heart. *Radiology Management*, 25(2), 40–53.

Bowker, G., & Star, S. L. (1994). Knowledge and infrastructure in international information management: Problems of classification and coding. In L. Bud-Frierman (Ed.), *Information acumen: The understanding and use of knowledge in modern business* (pp. 187–213). London, England: Routledge.

Bowker, G., & Star, S. L. (1999). *Sorting things out: Classification and its consequences*. Cambridge, MA: MIT Press.

Büttner, S. M., & Leopold, L. M. (2016). A "new spirit" of public policy? The project world of EU funding. *European Journal of Cultural and Political Sociology*, 3(1), 41–71. doi:10.1080/23254823.2016.1183503

Chang, H. (2008). *Autoethnography as method*. Walnut Creek, CA: Left Coast Press.

Chouliaraki, L., & Fairclough, N. (1999). *Discourse in late modernity: Rethinking critical discourse analysis*. Edinburgh, Scotland: Edinburgh University Press.

Cicmil, S. (2006). Understanding project management practice through interpretative and critical research perspectives. *Project Management Journal*, 37(2), 27–37.

Cicmil, S., Hodgson, D., Lindgren, M., & Packendorff, J. (2009). Project management behind the facade. *Ephemera: Theory and Politics in Organization*, 9(2), 78–92.

Clegg, S., & Courpasson, D. (2004). Political hybrids: Tocquevillean views on project organizations. *Journal of Management Studies*, 41(4), 525–547. doi:10.1111/j.1467-6486.2004.00443.x

Douglas, M. (1984). *Purity and danger: An analysis of concepts of pollution and taboo*. London, England: ARK Paperbacks.

Douglas, M., & Wildavsky, A. (1980). *Risk and culture: An essay on the selection of technical and environmental dangers*. Berkeley, CA: University of California Press.

Ellis, C., Adams, T. E., & Bochner, A. P. (2010). Autoethnography: An overview. *FQS*, 12(1). doi:10.17169/fqs-12.1.1589

Evetts, J., Muzio, D., & Kirkpatrick, I. (2011). A new professionalism? Challenges and opportunities. *Current Sociology*, 59(4), 406–422. doi:10.1177/0011392111402585

Fournier, V., & Grey, C. (2000). At the critical moment: Conditions and prospects for critical management studies. *Human Relations*, 53(1), 7–32. doi:10.1177/0018726700531002

Fred, M. (2014). Projectification of public health: Social investment funds in Swedish municipalities. Paper presented at JIBS, October 2014.

Glasdam, S., Oeye, C., & Thrysoee, L. (2015). Patients' participation in decision-making in the medical field: "Projectification" of patients in a neoliberal framed healthcare system. *Nursing Philosophy*, 16(4), 226–238. doi:10.1111/nup.12092

Greenhalgh, T., Stamer, K., Bratan, T., Byrne, E., Russell, J., Hinder, S., & Potts, H. (2010). *The Devil's in the detail: Final report of the independent evaluation of the Summary Care Record and HealthSpace programmes*. Retrieved from http://citeseerx.ist.psu.edu/viewdoc/citations;jsessionid=B0147DAB02061C33F5824EE324FEC7FD?doi=10.1.1.395.983

Hajer, M. (2006). Doing discourse analysis: Coalitions, practices, meaning. In M. van der Brink & T. Metze (Eds.), *Words matter in policy and planning: Discourse theory and method in the social sciences*. Utrecht, Netherlands: Netherlands Graduate School of Urban and Regional Research.

Hodgson, D. (2004). Project work: The legacy of bureaucratic control in the post-bureaucratic organization. *Organization*, 11(1), 81–100. doi:10.1177/1350508404039659

Hodgson, D. (2005). "Putting on a professional performance": Performativity, subversion and project management. *Organization*, 12(1), 51–68. doi:10.1177/1350508405048576

Hodgson, D., & Cicmil, S. (2006). *Making projects critical*. New York, NY: Palgrave Macmillan.

Hodgson, D., & Cicmil, S. (2007). The politics of standards in modern management: Making "the project" a reality. *Journal of Management Studies*, 44(3), 431–450. doi:10.1111/j.1467-6486.2007.00680.x

Hodgson, D., & Cicmil, S. (2008). The other side of projects: The case for critical project studies. *International Journal of Managing Projects in Business*, 1(1), 142–152.

ILX Marketing Team (2017). *The history of PRINCE2*. Retrieved from www.prince2.com/blog/the-history-of-prince2/

Lindgren, M., Packendorff, J., & Sergi, V. (2014). Thrilled by the discourse, suffering through the experience: Emotions in project-based work. *Human Relations*, 67(11), 1383–1412.

Lotte, M., & Susan Reynolds, W. (2014). Epidemic projectification: AIDS responses in Uganda as event and process. *Cambridge Journal of Anthropology*, 32(1), 77–94. doi:10.3167/ca.2014.320107

Mautner, G. (2013). *Language and market society*. London, England: Routledge.

Midler, C. (1995). "Projectification" of the firm: The Renault case. *Scandinavian Journal of Management*, 11(4), 363–375.

Morris, P. W. G. (2011). A brief history of project management. In P. W. G. Morris, J. Pinto, & J. Söderlund (Eds.), *The Oxford handbook of project management*. Oxford, England: Oxford University Press.

Morris, P. W. G., Pinto, J., & Soderlund, J. (2011a). Introduction: Towards the third wave of project management. In P. W. G. Morris, J. Pinto, & J. Söderlund (Eds.), *The Oxford handbook of project management*. Oxford, England: Oxford University Press.

Morris, P. W. G., Pinto, J., & Soderlund, J. (2011b). *The Oxford handbook of project management*. Oxford, England: Oxford University Press.

NHS England (2016). *Supporting sustainable general practice: A guide to initiating and managing a project (Vol. NHS England (South))*. Bristol, England.

Office of Government Commerce (2009). *Managing successful projects with PRINCE2™*. Norwich, England: The Stationery Office.

Packendorff, J. (1995). Inquiring into the temporary organization: New directions for project management research. *Scandinavian Journal of Management*, 11(4), 319–333.

Patton, M. Q. (2001). *Qualitative evaluation and research methods* (3rd ed). Newbury Park, CA: Sage.

Preston-Shoot, M. (2011). On administrative evil-doing within social work policy and services: Law, ethics and practice. *European Journal of Social Work*, 14(2), 177–194. doi:10.1080/13691450903471229

Project Management Institute (2013). *Industry growth forecast – Project management between 2010 + 2020*. Retrieved from www.scribd.com/document/323515178/PMI-Industry-Growth-Forecase-2010-2020

Project Management Institute (2017). *Pulse of the profession: 9th global project management survey*. Retrieved from www.pmi.org/-/media/pmi/documents/public/pdf/learning/thought-leadership/pulse/pulse-of-the-profession-2017.pdf

Sayer, A. (2011). *Why things matter to people*. Cambridge, England: Cambridge University Press.

Shenhav, Y. A. (1999). *Manufacturing rationality: The engineering foundations of the managerial revolution*. Oxford, England: Oxford University Press.

Sjöblom, S., Löfgren, K., & Godenhjelm, S. (2013). Projectified politics: Temporary organisations in a public context. Introduction to the special issue. *Scandinavian Journal of Public Administration*, 17(2), 3.

Snell, J., Shaw, S. E., & Copland, F. (2015). *Linguistic ethnography: Interdisciplinary explorations*. Basingstoke, England: Palgrave Macmillan.

Stake, R. (1995). *The art of case study research*. London, England: Sage.

Taylor, F. W. (1911). *Principles of scientific management*. New York, NY: Harper.

Timmermans, S., Bowker, G., & Star, S. L. (1995). Infrastructure and organisational transformation: Classifying nurses work. In W. Orlikowski, G. Walsham, M. R. Jones, & J. I. DeGross (Eds.), *Information technology and changes in organizational work* (pp. 334–370). London, England: Chapman & Hall.

Wald, A. (2016). Projectification, innovative capacity and flexibility: Macro- and micro-level perspectives. Paper presented at the Concept Symposium: Governing the Front-End of Major Projects, Sola Strand Hotel.

White, D., & Fortune, J. (2002). Current practice in project management: An empirical study. *International Journal of Project Management*, 20(1), 1–11. doi:10.1016/S0263-7863(00)00029–00026

13

THE FREELANCE PROJECT MANAGER AS AN AGENT OF GOVERNMENTALITY

Evidence from a UK Local Authority

Ewan Mackenzie

NEWCASTLE UNIVERSITY

Edward Barratt

UNIVERSITY OF ESSEX

The deployment of project management (PM) expertise in United Kingdom (UK) local government, and the public sector more generally, has been widely noted. The "corporate professions" of management consultancy and PM, or the "consultocracy" (Hodge & Bowman, 2006), critics argue (Kipping et al., 2006; Hodgson, 2007; Muzio et al., 2011), have prioritised "marketisation strategies" to inculcate this professional knowledge base in the UK public sector. Hodgson (2007) likewise argues that PM has emerged through a more general demand for "responsive" and efficient organisational structures, financial accountability, fixed-term contracts, and private-public partnerships, especially in information and communication technology (ICT) service provision. PM thus represents not only a form of knowledge and practice by which managers and consultants are expanding their influence in the public sector (Boltanski & Chiapello, 2005), but also a key form of market-led and state-endorsed knowledge and practice that neatly aligns with more centralised political aims.

This chapter sets the experience of a UK local authority, given the pseudonym here of "Northern County", in a field of power relations amid the politics of economic austerity in the 2010s. We examine the efforts of political actors and diverse "governmental" authorities (Foucault, 1982; Dean, 1999; Rose, 1999) to normalise PM knowledge and practice as a solution to the struggles of local government. Drawing on data derived from a participant observation study conducted during 2011 and 2012, supplemented by interviews and access to relevant local authority documents and reports, we illustrate how attempts to encourage PM are reliant on the work of freelance consultants of PM expertise. As agents of projectification, these subjects were contracted project managers with significant experience in ICT transformational change and management consultancy in both private and public sectors. Crucial to a council wide programme for enhancing PM expertise across this local authority, we comment on the identities and practices of five freelance PM consultants, showing them to be advocates of their own distinctive understandings and ways of enacting PM expertise. We go on to address the consequences and effects of this programme, illustrating how certain forms of tactical yet limited "resistance" are defined by the key targets of this intervention; local government workers increasingly involved in project work at the local authority.

Inspired by Foucauldian scholarship (Dean, 1999; Munro, 2012) we go on to argue that PM knowledge and practice constitutes an exemplary technology of "governmental" power; an inconspicuous bundle of concepts, techniques, and professional competencies that aims to effect control "at a distance" (Dean, 1999; Rose, 1999; Munro, 2012). We reflect on the diverse programmatic objectives and ambiguities at play in the messy implementation of this particular scheme of rule (McKinlay et al., 2012). In doing so the implications and dangers for democracy in local government in the UK are addressed (Du Gay, 2000, 2008; Newman, 2014). We begin, however, with an account of the course of change at the local authority and the role that PM was intended to play in that process.

The Case of "Northern County": An Introduction

Since the early 1980s local government in the UK has been subject to a series of political and economic reforms intended to make it more receptive to the requirements of central government (Forsyth, 1980; Miller, 2005; Newman, 2014). In the 1980s and 1990s the Conservative government considered local government to be wasteful, excessively bureaucratic, and acting in its own interests (Du Gay, 2000). Political autonomy was curtailed and funding was significantly reduced. Contracting out was imposed, decreasing the power of trade unions operative in the provision of local services (Brooke, 1991). There is a long history of the deployment of management techniques in local government encouraged by the requirements of central government in this period. In general terms, however, local government became increasingly associated with contracting out, the performance monitoring of contracted out services, deteriorating employment conditions, and work intensification (Patterson & Pinch, 1995).

"New Labour", coming to power in 1997, though hybrid in its programmatic ambitions for local government (Bevir, 2016), is commonly associated with the application of a more intensive management and monitoring regime. In particular, the system of audit and inspection associated with the Best Value programme was deployed to enhance quality and cost savings in the provision of local services (Power, 2004). This approach delimited autonomy for decision-making, on the one hand, and tied resource allocation to narrow dimensions of performance, on the other. Contract-relations and budgetary accountability substituted direct managerial authority as a primary organising principle (Hebson et al., 2003).

In the second decade of the 21st century, however, local government in the UK witnessed unprecedented public expenditure and employment cuts, compounding the struggle to meet the needs of local services (Newman, 2014). Following the formation of the Conservative and Liberal Democrat coalition government in 2010, the UK was subject to the most severe public spending cuts since the Second World War (Yeates et al., 2010). The coalition's "Big Society" programme, despite professing to "liberate" communities and public service workers, emphasised a conservative communitarianism that sought to decentralise "duty and responsibility" while radically reducing local government funding (HM Treasury, 2010b; Cameron, 2011).

Yet, at the Labour controlled "Northern County", while cost saving measures would certainly be made in the months that followed, there would be no simple acquiescence to the politics of austerity. Statements of policy at Northern County affirmed the need for "transformational change to the operating culture of the Council" (Northern County, 2010c). There was to be a new emphasis on the sharing of services, information sharing, and collaborative working to address the root causes of social problems and to improve "customer" service. If cuts were necessary, citizens were to have a greater say over how they were to be made and, "community" would, it was claimed, be strengthened. Local business enterprise would be encouraged to promote growth for the jurisdiction and play a part in the "rebalancing" of the local economy that would see a significant reduction in public sector employment (Northern County, 2010a).

A strategic programme outlined changes to the management of the local authority. By early 2011, a severance scheme was in place and voluntary redundancy was offered to local government workers who qualified. Identifying potential candidates for redundancy took place in combination with a broader restructuring programme. Permanent members of staff across the local authority were required to re-apply for their positions. The expectation was that remaining staff should become more "responsive" to the needs of their clients by displaying "ownership" of policies, programmes, and projects. Corporate themes alluding to the heightening of individual responsibility were addressed in subtle terms in an interview with Julia, the Deputy Chief Executive. Staff should not simply take responsibility, they should also become proactive in relation to the needs of their clients. As she stated, this was a matter of taking "initiative" and of being "flexible, responsive, customer focused".

These statements should be understood in the context of the changing priorities for local government associated with "New Labour" during its final year in government, and in response to the repositioning of their opponents on the economy and "austerity" (Seldon & Lodge, 2010). Inspired by new thinking in local government, and given the support of both the UK Government's Leadership Centre for Local Government and the Treasury's Operational Efficiency

Review (Grint and Holt, 2011), the "Total Place" initiative sought to bring local authorities, their partners, and local citizens together in an effort to align service provision with the needs of the local population. Notions of the horizontal "joining up" of public service policy and provision inspired an array of interventions during the years of "New Labour": measures to promote economy and efficiency, to tackle complex, "wicked", and costly social problems in a system of government understood to have been fragmented by the Conservatives. The objective was to enhance "customer" experience through more seamless and integrated systems, and to address the multiple economic, social, and environmental conditions that may enhance the quality of existence in a place (Cowell & Martin, 2003; Downe & Martin, 2006; Lyons, 2006). The report on the "Total Place" pilot projects launched in 2009, in effect, gave a new salience and coherence to these diverse practices of "joining up" (HM Treasury/Communities and Local Government, 2010), intimating a new way of framing the strategic "leadership" role of local government, of renewing local democracy, and supposedly enhancing local autonomy and choice. The "Total Place" pilot projects, it was claimed, had shown what was possible with "strong and coordinated local leadership". All public service providers in a local area, including third-sector organisations, it was professed, could work more effectively together. The pilot projects had allowed for the identification of areas of overlap and duplication in back office and support functions, thereby promoting "efficiency". They had allowed local partners to collocate services, to align budgets, and implement joint outcomes with the aim of preventing difficult and costly social problems. The pilot projects had also included citizens in the collaborative planning of services to help to identify priorities and enhance "joined up" service provision, emphasising the "customer's" point of view. The UK government budget statement of March 2010 (HM Treasury, 2010a) announced an array of measures in support of this "whole area" approach to local government. Nevertheless, as the programmatic statement of the leaders of the Labour controlled Northern County in 2010 confirmed, "Total Place" survived the demise of "New Labour" in May 2010. The expertise of project management was then considered to be an essential means to the accomplishment of Northern County's objectives.

Project Management in the Era of Austerity

Historically, the local authority as a whole had established its own PM methodology based on the government sponsored PRINCE2™ framework, first released through the UK Civil Service in 1996 (UK Cabinet Office, 2016). PRINCE2™ is an iteration of the project management method known as **PR**ojects **IN** **C**ontrolled **E**nvironments (PRINCE), designed to separate projects into controlled stages while maintaining clear lines of accountability. Building on the earlier framework, PRINCE2™ was conceived as a generic cross sector methodology, designed to be applicable to any project in the public or private sectors. At Northern County the goal had been to "standardise the basic processes of project management" (Northern County, 2009) in the aftermath of the establishment of the new unitary local authority in 2009, formed out of various district councils and the old county council. In taking PRINCE2™ as the norm, albeit adapted in the interests of simplicity and cost effectiveness, Northern County was following a familiar pattern in local government during the "New Labour" years. During the 1990s the Improvement and Development Agency (IDeA), promoting "best practice" and private/public partnerships, encouraged the development of this variant of project management expertise (de Groot, 2006). After 2003, efforts to enhance delivery and service procurement (Byatt, 2001) reinforced a new concern with the "capacity" of local government. The joint LGA/Central Government Capacity Building initiative, supported by the inspection regime of the Audit Commission, further encouraged the advancement of PM expertise as PRINCE2™ became accepted "best practice" (DCLG, 2008; Audit Commission, 2009). A host of experts and authorities thus championed a methodology that defined financial, quality, and risk control throughout the project "lifecycle" as a primary organisational competency (CCTA, 1997; OGC, 2009). The key priorities were the "continual business justification" of programmes and projects, clear alignment with corporate objectives (OGC, 2009, pp. 21–28), and due attention to "continuous improvement" in the deployment of PM capabilities (Cicmil & Hodgson, 2006).

Following the news of substantial budget cuts in June 2010 (HM Treasury, 2010b) the local authority was seeking to expand the provision of PRINCE2™ training (for details on PRINCE2™ training, see Shaw et al., Chapter 12, this volume). For the ICT unit in particular there were additional pressures to expand provision. In late summer 2010, sanctioned and compiled by senior management, an independent assessment by a leading professional services firm criticised the ICT unit as lacking the necessary efficiency and effectiveness (Northern County, 2010b). A new investment programme was called for to install the technical infrastructure and encourage the necessary approach for the sharing of services, information sharing, project management, and organising.

Within the ICT unit further training in PRINCE2™ was offered at various levels of professional competence: "professional", "practitioner", and "foundational". It was anticipated that a small team of contracted freelance consultant project managers in the Corporate Programme Office (PO), as agents of projectification, would provide the impetus for extending know how. In line with the local authority's new competency programme, staff would be expected to adopt a proactive approach to project organising. It should become the norm, as one of our senior interviewees put it, that "we constantly reflect on all our actions and activities and become more self-aware" (Marcus, Authority Learning and Organisational Development Manager). Those experienced with PRINCE2™ at a higher level of proficiency would thus be encouraged to "champion" the technology as proactive educators. Change, in this view, was an "opportunity" for staff to learn best practice skills that would be needed, and a means for enhancing employability at a time of employment insecurity. The expectation was that staff, with expert guidance, would come to "embody" the required practices such that little in the way of management would be required for the application of "joined up" working and efficient and integrative systems in line with "Total Place".

Enacting Project Expertise "with Intelligence"

The PO had been set up as a physically isolated office space within which ICT programme activities were managed. Here the programme manager, Paula, oversaw freelance consultants and permanent project managers authorising and overseeing projects. The freelance consultants were agency personnel brought in on six-monthly contracts to encourage the required approach to projects and support programme activities. They had significant experience in PM and PRINCE2™ through delivering ICT change projects and management consultancy work in both private and public sectors. Some members of the PO group were also associated with the UK (APM) and US professional associations (PMI). Paula oversaw the process using a portfolio manager, making visible and reportable work activity within a PRINCE2™ framework. The status of all projects in the department were thus mapped through a "RAG" (red, amber, green) projection, resembling the traffic light system favoured by the UK Government's Office of Government Commerce (Bourn, 2004, p. 6) throughout the project lifecycle. Half hour project meetings took place weekly at which time the freelancers reviewed the RAG status of each project with senior managers.

Encountering these expert freelance consultants in the early stages of the change programme, we found them to be advocates of a know-how intended to "empower" others to govern themselves. These subjects assumed no requirement for high level proficiency among the targets of their intervention. Rather, a lower level of "awareness" of PM's underlying principles was expected. In the discourse of "awareness" phrases such as "always get sign off", "flag waving", "auditability of the project", and "the only thing that matters is getting the job done" appeared to constitute fundamental rules of engagement. Above all there was an obligation to document and inscribe every decision and every action taken. Paula, for example, reiterated the PM canon of "completed as defined" when asked to define what she meant by "success". Another, Darren, repeatedly used the terminology of putting "walls" around a project.

Nonetheless, for the freelance consultants governing through "awareness" was construed as different in kind from the true nature of PM expertise. They described their professional histories in the private sector as management consultants, project managers, and ICT managers as constitutive of their professional practice and self-understanding. These subjects framed their relationship to projects in terms of "ownership", denoting the achievement of personal goals and an expertise only available to the experienced practitioner. As evidenced in both the interviews and project meetings we attended, project "ownership" extended to identifying strategic targets among organisational actors proactively, with a view to building a community of interest. Acting to secure this community meant that one must actively campaign to achieve the PM canon of stakeholder "buy in".

The tactical character of these practices was something that these freelance consultant project managers identified with in their work and life. Paula, for example, described a fusion of personal and work relationships as business like conversations, where it becomes "hard to get out of the mode of 'what can I get out of this? what is at stake here?'". They appeared to "own" their projects to the point at which they would deploy combative mechanisms to secure and protect delivery. Suggesting an expertise without formal programmatic status, to "own" a project was ultimately to manipulate its course in accordance with appropriate, "intelligent" tactics of alliance building.

As custodians of expertise, the freelance consultants appeared to envision themselves as being at odds with their senior sponsors at Northern County. Paula, for example, commented that senior managers felt threatened by her professionalism. These subjects tended to query the use of PRINCE2™ in the public sector as "used simply as a process", as contrasted with their own practice of "using PRINCE2™ with intelligence". Though there were few indications of outright contestation, the difficulties that local government staff were experiencing in adapting to their new project roles early in the programme, and demonstrating "responsiveness", was a theme to which the consultants often returned. As one of our interviewees, Theo, commented while indicating that he was viewed as a threat by ICT project staff: "They [ICT project staff] seem to tolerate a lack of progress … there is no traction on projects … they just seem to live with it … if we [freelance consultants] can get you [ICT staff] doing your projects better, you are more likely to be retained than released".

The Identities of the Freelance Project Experts

Though working lives were reported as intensive, involving long hours and regularly responding to emergencies, all the freelance project managers we interviewed generally judged freelance project work to be a "solution" through which one could learn to manage better, earn more, and lead a more satisfying life. Satisfaction for all the freelancers derived in part from a pastoral and supportive relationship with those who were understood to lack PM expertise at the local authority. These subjects were concerned to frame their work as a matter of caring for others, with their best interests and wellbeing in view. John, one of the freelance project managers in the Corporate Programme Office, explained in an interview that his care for others meant that staff "have a much better ability to see what is coming over the horizon".

In a distinctive way, life was addressed by these freelance project experts as something of a project in itself. In such instances the potential application of PM's processes of rationalisation, such as in the "risk management" of one's career, were seemingly "empowering" and "productive". In the case of John, making himself up as a freelance project manager relied on a discourse of self-actualisation. His own career was addressed as an adventurous journey and a vehicle for continual learning. As he stated,

> There must be certain character traits that make a contractor. I was always left alone to do my own thing, so was everyone I know who was successful that I went to school with... I had a completely different upbringing to the kids I hung around with.

Similarly, Darren described his work as a means to actively care for and generate respect for himself through continually changing and developing. Notable in this case was an account of more intimate personal relationships, articulated as coming second to his working life. It was "fickle, enjoyable relationships" that took precedence from this perspective. Furthermore, despite sympathising with the plight of staff at Northern County, vulnerable at the early stages of a restructuring programme, Darren constructed an identity in opposition to the working culture at the local authority and in response to what he judged to be an insensitivity towards the sovereign customer: "You've got a culture that is being indoctrinated, to protect your job, protect your pension, protect everything around you. And the customer? ... You kind of wonder, well, why are you there to do that job?"

Notions of giving all of oneself, and then "grieving" for a project on its completion were also evident, calling upon discourses of self-realisation as projects were posed as all-encompassing personal experiences. These themes would be emphasised further as ideas of independence were linked to continual stimulation and learning in project work. As Paula reflected:

> Oh, it's quite interesting, 'cause I've been doing an operational role for the last 18 months. And we came to a major milestone ... I walked into the office, day one, and thought, "Okay, what do I do now?" Cause I'd delivered my work, you know? My project is now finished, even though I was in an operational role that goes on for the next 30 years, my brain says, "I've now delivered my project. What do I do now?" So, I resigned.

Ambivalence and Insecurity: The Experience of Local Authority Staff

The targets of the change programme were local government managers and lower level administrators set apart from the corporate programme office and increasingly involved in project work within a PRINCE2™ framework. The majority had been trained formally in PRINCE2™. Most had already experienced significant upheaval with the formation of a unitary Northern County in 2009.

Amid organisational restructuring, with budget and staff reductions, the 15 permanent employees that we interviewed found various ways to critique, or more exactly "distance" themselves, from the objectives of the local authority programme.

On the one hand, the restructuring process could be experienced as an administrative inquisition. Northern County, as one permanent project manager Philip argued, was seeking to determine "who he was" by having his whole career "boiled down" to "saying the right thing in an interview". The favoured project measures of work and performance at Northern County for Philip, in effect, undermined the meaningfulness of working relationships, ignoring an established professional self. Brad, on the other hand, a permanent project manager, described a mode of professional conduct that emphasised the importance of tacit organisational knowledge. Knowledge of a more localised and reflexive kind was being devalued through the requirement to produce accountable project management truths.

In a related way, others bemoaned the need for the evaluation of projects in meetings and through the continuous updating of documentation. As one project manager, Jennifer, put it: "I've got better things to do than come and sit in and discuss what is right and what is wrong with projects". Similarly, Simon, an administrator, stated: "There are less people to do the work and we've still got work outside of project work, a lot of work, you know?" At times, critiques developed by local government staff shaded into a broader anti-professional critique. "For me", as Jennifer put it during a discussion on PM methodology updates, "it is just a way for them [i.e. the project management professional associations] to make money. I understand it [PM methodology], but the thing is, I don't need a bit of paper to tell me". The recurring theme of professional self-interest was taken up by another manager, Eric. There was "an industry around it" he claimed. Here, a critique is advanced from the point of view of both the consequences of PM for work intensification and the superfluity of its expertise in fulfilling the real responsibilities of local government work. This mode of argument emphasises the self-serving activity of professional groupings through PM associations.

At other times, project managers and their lower level colleagues queried the programme less from the point of its questionable professional ambitions, and more in regard to the recruitment of highly paid freelance consultants. This concern related not only to the effects upon their own employment insecurity, but also a more general disquiet about the outsourcing of expert labour. At these moments, participants placed an emphasis on the worth, capabilities, and skills of local government workers, as those capable of carrying out the work involved in the investment programme themselves, and as those who should be provided with the capabilities to do so. According to Tina, a permanent project manager, a lack of "investment" in the workforce at the local authority meant that personal development had been neglected. She questioned the procurement of contracted expertise:

> We should have the skills in-house to do that work [the ICT investment programme], and if we haven't then why haven't we? … I mean, I do think they [freelance consultants] can bring a lot of experience, and they can bring knowledge of what has happened in outside areas, but in terms of council workers, it's like "my job is on the line and you are paying how much for a contractor? That is like three years of my salary!"

Statements of this kind appeared to be encouraged by the local government trade union. During our time at the authority the union was encouraging members to question the irrevocability of their situation and to act to avert the privatisation of labour and services. A key approach in this sense was its campaign to keep services in-house. Trade union documentation argued that staff were "the real experts" (Unison, 2012, p. 13) and should act to ensure their full involvement in programmes that might otherwise involve over-charging by consultants, resulting in substantial waste and the possibility of substandard service provision. Through this discourse the trade union posed an image of local government workers as "cost effective" experts in their own right.

On "the Tactics of the Weak"

Yet notwithstanding the various critiques and arguments discussed above, there were few indications of a desire for practical refusal. Jennifer, for example, deeply ambivalent, both attracted to the union discourse and sceptical of the claims of PM expertise, could nevertheless see benefit in PM as a way to realise autonomy in the labour market and end a working relationship that had become difficult and instrumental. This process in her case undermined a sense of collective identification with her colleagues but enabled her to foresee an alternative means of achieving a sense of "freedom" in her working life, of doing: "something independent, go off and do something different, or even take it [PM] somewhere else".

Others discussed the advantages of PM knowledge and practice less as a means of realising their "human capital", and more as a way of achieving safety and security at a time of crisis. In this respect, Harry, an ICT staff member with over twenty years of local government experience, described his hopes in using PM. In this case the benefits of expertise in an internal interdepartmental struggle were foregrounded; "Well, hopefully they'll [senior management, other departments in the council] see more of what we're doing". Making oneself and one's department visible and accountable through PM is addressed here as a way to demonstrate to others that both he and his department are performing ("they might see our worth a little bit more"). This argument is framed as a critique of having been left outside a formal network of accountability. Yet ultimately, there is an alignment between the judgements of a local actor and a broader governmental regime.

Another ICT staff member, Robert, with over twelve years of local government experience, explained his hopes in a similar way. As he put it: "I think it's easier to show the management what we actually do [by using PRINCE2^{TM}]". As the ICT unit's role in cost reduction across the authority took effect and became known, the defensive appeal of PM knowledge and practice was considerable for these subjects. Security became a matter of personal and departmental concern, so much so that these self-governing subjects appeared willing to abide by the "rules of the game". A related point was taken up by another of our subjects as he described a particular form of "empowerment". The "liberating" aspect of PM's governmental rationality would, Eric believed, provide a platform from which to state his case to his superiors. He would, as a manager, be better placed to proactively justify the economic rationale for the continuation of the IT department's work through the means of PM knowledge and practice, thus promoting the security of his own and his colleague's future employment.

Discussion and Conclusions

Munro (2012), adapting Dean (1999), characterises PM as a technology of agency and performance, one of an array of contemporary management techniques of government designed to guide apparently autonomous or free actors towards the achievement of specified ends. As such, the freelance purveyors of PM expertise under examination in our case can be conceived of as agents of governmentality. Contextualising their intervention in a field of power relations, the era of austerity and efforts by an array of authorities to normalise PM expertise in UK local government, our analysis of these essentially entrepreneurial consultants suggests they had found a means of self-expression in a working life akin to Handy's (1991) vision of the portfolio career. As PM, with its identity affirming images, interpellates or successfully hails these entrepreneurial subjects, a relay is established between the aspirations of governing authorities and a particular local field of power relations, echoing arguments elsewhere in this volume (see Büttner, Chapter 9, and also Shaw et al., Chapter 12, this volume). In this respect we would suggest a kind of pastoral logic (Foucault, 1978) in the way participants commonly described the deployment of project expertise as a matter of caring for others, implying a shepherding of the "flock" towards a new understanding with their best interests and wellbeing in view. This pastoral manner, which has been used by others to frame the practice of clinical leaders in the reform of the UK Health Service (Ferlie et al., 2013; Waring & Martin, 2016), would thus seem to have a wider applicability.

At the same time, for our freelance consultants projects also possessed an "expressive" character. These subjects framed their relationship to projects in terms of notions of "ownership", implying the achievement of personal goals and a kind of "between us" expertise only available to the experienced practitioner.

PM possessed a powerful, identity affirming character, an appropriate, and even ideal career outlet for the "freedom loving" consultant. Although working lives were conveyed as demanding, involving responses to crises (Eaton & Bailyn, 2000; Packendorff, 2002) and "bereavement" upon the completion of projects, projects were also judged a "solution" through which one could accumulate wealth and lead a more fulfilling life (Clegg & Courpasson, 2004; Muzio et al., 2011). The career was indeed, it seemed, a project of the self (Grey, 1994). Yet transcending Grey's concept of life subordinated to the career principle, for these subjects, notions and practices associated with PM expertise provided a framework through which other non-working aspects of life could be framed. "Private" norms of calculation and aspiration could be realised, where life itself, at least for some of our subjects, was amenable to project management. In such instances the potential application of PM's processes of rationalisation were indeed wide ranging, "enabling", and "productive".

Pursuing a critical Foucauldian analytic further (Barratt, 2008), how might we assess the costs of the case we have been considering? We would argue that "Total Place", which PM was designed to support in our study of a local authority, should not be viewed as merely another attempt to make political institutions function in a "quasi-business" manner (Diefenbach, 2009, p. 893). Alongside efficient and effective government, the supposed enhancement of "community", "partnership", "resilience" and, perhaps most of all, democracy, were also crucial objectives. Undoubtedly parochial in its sense of "place", indifferent to the global institutions and forces that seek to govern "places", and overly submissive to the economics of austerity (McKinnon, 2016), Total Place should not be diagnosed as simply another manifestation of a "neoliberal rationality" of government (Bevir, 2016).

PM, then, in this case is implicated in a hybrid scheme of government (Newman, 2005; Bejerot & Hasselbladh, 2011). For us, it is the tensions and contradictions of this specific hybrid scheme that are most striking. The stated ends of the expert freelancers suggest an orientation at odds with other objectives of "Total Place", notably the enhancement of supposedly democratic ends. To imagine oneself in a relation of "ownership" to one's work is to undermine the core principle of political accountability. Notions of "public service" and "public accountability" were noticeably absent in the discourse of our consultant subjects. Ultimately their practice evokes the "managerial stratum" characterised by Hirst (1996): members of a group, relatively homogeneous in attitudes, aspirations, and working methods, readily moving between public and private sectors. The manner in which such work devalues and undermines the ethics and practices of public institutions poses a profound threat to democratic ends.

The prospect of the extension and institutionalisation of PM expertise within the framework of Total Place and planned by the local authority, came with further contradictions and tensions. As such, the technology of PM is vulnerable to an array of criticisms of the deployment of management methods in the public sector (Du Gay, 2000). When the activities of local government are redefined in terms of the specification of "outputs" encapsulated in performance indicators, projects, and contracts (Power, 1994) there is not only a weakening of local political accountability but a delegitimisation of public provision (Newman, 2014). In project-based organising local government officers are assigned powers disproportionately in practices which "empower" them. As the work of government is redefined in managerial terms, bureaucratic ideals of impartiality and integrity associated with the defence of the public interest in a democratic polity are undermined (Du Gay, 2000). When the work of government is conceived in large part as an expert, technical, and managerial activity, the space for the practice of democratic citizenship and political engagement contracts (Brown, 2015).

As we have seen, however, efforts to enhance PM expertise among local government workers engaged in project-based work were not unproblematic. The early stages of the new initiative saw its targets identifying ways to rebuff and critique, or more exactly "distance" themselves from governmental discourses. For many there was another side to the new performance requirements, with permanent project managers and staff at the authority bemoaning the continuous inscribing of project activities. There were material concerns at stake, in a context of restructuring and the performance of additional project related work. Perhaps most common of all was the problem of the devaluation of local knowledge. Notions of tacit knowledge embedded in the working environment, evoking Michael Polanyi's (Polanyi, 1958; Nonaka & Takeuchi, 1995) concept of "personal knowledge", implied certain inherent limitations to the knowledge of external experts. In other instances, PM expertise was contested in the name of values and practices associated with the advancement of the public interest (Osborne, 1994; Du Gay, 2000; Barratt, 2009). This argument could be extended into a broader critique of the self-serving goals of PM as a profession, evoking neoliberal critiques of the pursuit of monopoly rents by professional bodies (Leicht & Lyman, 2006).

Nevertheless, for all the rebuffing, the logic of PM pervaded the discourse of local government workers. In this respect, our study suggests once again an array of perhaps more surprising "productive" effects. For some disenfranchised local government staff, PM expertise for all its weaknesses, was viewed as a standardised and reproducible form of "human capital" (Clegg & Courpasson, 2004; Weiskopf & Munro, 2012), offering a "way out" of the authority at a time of considerable turbulence and insecurity. Most common of all, however, was the tactical use for PM expertise. It was not PM's "liberating potential" or the more intimate rewards of project (or contract) "success" and "delivery" that was at stake. Rather PM became seductive and necessary as a "defensive" resource, for demonstrating personal and departmental achievements, thus protecting employment at a time of insecurity. We have illustrated a mode of "resistance", a tactical reversal (Foucault, 1978) or a turning around of instruments of power (de Certeau, 1984).

Critics argue (Rose, 1999) that subjects of government who are granted responsible autonomy, are increasingly required to act according to a "litigious mentality" in order to defend and justify their value and existence. Employees, while seeming to rebuff some of the effects of governmental discourses still, ultimately, reproduced them in a variety of ways. Fleming and Spicer (2003) have argued for the need to document the many different forms that "dis-identification" can take in contemporary organisations: the moments at which organisational actors abjure dominant discourses, only to reaffirm them in their actions. Dis-identifications in our case took diverse forms: in the expression of distrust for managers and their schemes, the professions, or indeed in a commitment to local knowledge and the customary values and practices of local government work.

Albeit in different ways, then, it is the expertise of PM that subjects look to for a way out of their predicament. Such "resistance" had little to do with efforts to overturn the influence of PM expertise, or even active support for the union, let alone the defence of local government as a "strategic" site for vital conditions that enable autonomy, solidarity, and citizenship (Newman, 2014). Indeed, in so far as they appear to set members of departments and individuals against one another in a competitive game, such resistance appears to us especially divisive. We should look elsewhere for the possibility of effective forms of resistance to the shattering of local government, perhaps to those movements of the Left debating the question of the organisation of the State (e.g. Shah & Goss, 2007) or the alliances of public sector trade unionists and activists that have emerged in response to austerity.

Finally, should we take the ubiquity of "projects" in our study as a sign of the "projectification" of society, a concept favoured by some critics to capture wide ranging changes in society informed by project-based concepts (Lundin & Soderholm, 1998)? After Foucault (Foucault, 1991; Dean, 1994), we remain suspicious of any global and epochal sociological diagnosis, with its implicit assumption of a unifying principle of social organisation and mode of argument that leaves little sense of a "way out". Ultimately our study of agents of projectification and the consequences of their intervention in a hybrid scheme of rule has sought to achieve a more modest ambition: to diagnose the effects of the deployment of a prevalent form of management expertise in a specific, endangered institutional setting.

References

Audit Commission (2009). *Final score: The impact of the comprehensive performance assessment.* London, England: Audit Commission.

Barratt, E. (2008). The later Foucault in organization and management studies. *Human Relations*, 61(4), pp. 515–537.

Barratt, E. (2009). Governing public servants. *Management and Organizational History*, 4(1), pp. 67–84.

Bejerot, E., & Hasselbladh, H. (2011). Professional autonomy and pastoral power: The transformation of quality registers in Swedish health care. *Public Administration*, 89(4), pp. 1604–1621.

Bevir, M. (2016). Introduction. In M. Bevir (Ed.), *Governmentality after neoliberalism*. London, England: Routledge.

Boltanski, L., & Chiapello, E. (2005). *The new spirit of capitalism*. London, England: Verso.

Bourn, J. (2004). *Improving IT procurement: The impact of the Office of Government Commerce's initiatives on departments and suppliers in the delivery of major IT-enabled projects*. London, England: National Audit Office. Retrieved from www.nao.org.uk/wp-content/uploads/2004/11/0304877.pdf

Brooke, R. (1991). The Enabling Authority. *Public Administration*, 69(4), pp. 525–532.

Brown, W. (2015). *Undoing the demos: Neoliberalism's stealth revolution*. New York, NY: Zone Books.

Byatt, S. I. (2001). *Delivering better services for citizens*. London, England: DTLR/LGA.

Cameron, D. (2011). Prime Minister's speech on modern public service. Prime Minister's Office, 10 Downing Street: UK Government. Retrieved from www.gov.uk/government/speeches/prime-ministers-speech-on-modern-public-service

CCTA (1997). *PRINCE2: An outline*. London, England: The Stationery Office.

Cicmil, S., & Hodgson, D. (2006). Making projects critical: An introduction. In D. Hodgson & S. Cicmil (Eds.), *Making projects critical*. New York, NY: Palgrave Macmillan, pp. 1–25.

Clegg, S., & Courpasson, D. (2004). Political hybrids: Tocquevillean views on project organizations. *Journal of Management Studies*, 41(4), pp. 525–547.

Cowell, R., & Martin, S. (2003). The joy of joining up: Modes of integrating the local government modernisation agenda. *Environment and Planning C-Government and Policy*, 21(2), pp. 159–179.

DCLG (2008). *National evaluation of the capacity building initiative: Final report*. London, England: Department of Communities and Local Government.

de Certeau, M. (1984). *The practice of everyday life*. Los Angeles, CA: University of California Press.

de Groot, J. (2006). Generating improvement from within. In S. Martin (Ed.), *Public service improvement: Policies, progress and prospects*. London, England: Routledge.

Dean, M. (1994). *Critical and effective histories*. London, England: Routledge.

Dean, M. (1999). *Governmentality: Power and rule in modern society*. London, England: Sage.

Diefenbach, T. (2009). New public management in public sector organizations: The dark sides of managerialistic "enlightenment". *Public Administration*, 87(4), pp. 892–909.

Downe, J., & Martin, S. (2006). Joined up policy in practice? The coherence and impacts of the local government modernisation agenda. *Local Government Studies*, 32(4), pp. 465–488.

Du Gay, P. (2000). *In praise of bureaucracy*. London, England: Sage.

Du Gay, P. (2008). "Without affection or enthusiasm": Problems of involvement and attachment in "responsive" public management. *Organization*, 15(3), pp. 335–353.

Eaton, S. C., & Bailyn, L. (2000). Career as a life path: Training, work and life strategies of biotech professionals. In M. Pieperl, M. Arthur, R. Goffee, & T. Morris (Eds.), *Career frontiers: New conceptions of working lives*. London, England: Routledge.

Ferlie, E., Fitzgerald, L., McGivern, G., Dopson, S. & Bennett, C. (2013). *Making wicked problems governable? The case of managed networks in health care*. Oxford: Oxford University Press.

Fleming, P., & Spicer, A. (2003). Working at a cynical distance: Implications of power, subjectivity and resistance. *Organization*, 10(1), pp. 157–179.

Forsyth, M. (1980). *Re-servicing Britain*. London, England: The Adam Smith Institute.

Foucault, M. (1978). "Governmentality" (lecture at the Collège de France, 1 February). In G. Burchell, C. Gordon, & P. Miller (Eds.), *The Foucault effect: Studies in governmentality*. Hemel Hempstead, England: Harvester Wheatsheaf, pp. 87–104.

Foucault, M. (1982). The subject and power. In H. L. Dreyfus & P. Rabinow (Eds.), *Michel Foucault: Beyond structuralism and hermeneutics*. Brighton, England: Harvester Wheatsheaf, pp. 208–226.

Foucault, M. (1991). What is enlightenment? In P. Rabinow (Ed.), *The Foucault Reader*. London, England: Penguin Books, pp. 32–50.

Grey, C. (1994). Career as a project of the self and labor process discipline. *Sociology: The Journal of the British Sociological Association*, 28(2), pp. 479–497.

Grint, K., & Holt, C. (2011). If total place, big society and local leadership are the answers: What's the question? *Leadership*, 7(1), pp. 85–98.

Handy, C. (1991). *The age of unreason*. London, England: Random House.

Hebson, G., Grimshaw, D., & Marchington, M. (2003). PPPs and the changing public sector ethos: Case-study evidence from the health and local authority sectors. *Work Employment and Society*, 17(3), pp. 481–501.

Hirst, P. (1996). Democracy and civil society. In P. Hirst & S. Khilnani (Eds.), *Reinventing democracy*. Oxford, England: Blackwell.

HM Treasury (2010a). Budget statement: Securing the recovery. Retrieved from https://assets.publishing.service.gov.uk/government/uploads/system/uploads/attachment_data/file/247878/0451.pdf

HM Treasury (2010b). June 2010 Budget. Retrieved from https://assets.publishing.service.gov.uk/government/uploads/system/uploads/attachment_data/file/248096/0061.pdf

HM Treasury/Communities and Local Government (2010). Total place: A whole approach to public services. Retrieved from http://webarchive.nationalarchives.gov.uk/20130129110402/http:/www.hm-treasury.gov.uk/d/total_place_report.pdf

Hodge, G., & Bowman, D. (2006). The "consultocracy": The business of reforming government. In G. Hodge (Ed.), *Privatization and market development: Global movements in public policy ideas*. Cheltenham, England: Edward Elgar.

Hodgson, D. (2007). The New Professionals: Professionalisation and the struggle for occupational control in the field of project management. In D. Muzio, S. Ackroyd, & J. Chanlat (Eds.), *Redirections in the study of expert labour: Medicine, law and management consultancy*. Basingstoke, England: Palgrave.

Kipping, M., Kirkpatrick, I., & Muzio, D. (2006). Overly controlled or out of control? Management consultants and the new corporate professionalism. In J. G. Craig (Ed.), *Production values: Futures for professionalism*. London, England: Demos.

Leicht, K., & Lyman, E. (2006). Markets, institutions and the crisis of professional practice. In R. Suddaby, & M. McDonough (Eds.), *Professional services firms*. Oxford, England: JAI Press.

Lundin, R. A., & Soderholm, A. (1998). Conceptualizing a projectified society. In R. A. Lundin & C. Midler (Eds.), *Projects as arenas for renewal and learning processes*. Boston, MA: Kluwer Academic.

Lyons, S. M. (2006). *The Lyons inquiry into local government: Prosperity, local choice and civic engagement*. London, England: The Stationery Office.

McKinlay, A., Carter, C., & Pezet, E. (2012). Governmentality, power and organization. *Management and Organizational History*, 7(3), pp. 3–15.

McKinnon, D. (2016). Governing urban and regional development. In M. Bevir (Ed.), *Governmentality after neoliberalism*. London, England: Routledge.

Miller, D. (2005). What is best "value"? Bureaucracy, virtualism and local governance. In P. du Gay (Ed.), *The values of bureaucracy*. Oxford, England: Oxford University Press.

Munro, I. (2012). The management of circulations: Biopolitical variations after Foucault. *International Journal of Management Reviews*, 14(3), pp. 345–362.

Muzio, D., Hodgson, D., Faulconbridge, J., Beaverstock, J., & Hall, S. (2011). Towards corporate professionalization: The case of project management, management consultancy and executive search. *Current Sociology*, 59(4), pp. 443–464.

Newman, I. (2014). *Reclaiming local democracy: A progressive future for local government*. Bristol, England: Policy Press.

Newman, J. (2005). Enter the transformational leader: Network governance and the micro-politics of modernization. *Sociology: The Journal of the British Sociological Association*, 39(4), pp. 717–734.

Nonaka, I., & Takeuchi, H. (1995). *The knowledge creating company: How Japanese companies create the dynamics of innovation*. Oxford, England: Oxford University Press.

Northern County (2009). Authority methodology document.

Northern County (2010a). Corporate plan: "Stronger together".

Northern County (2010b). ICT Investment Programme report.

Northern County (2010c). Transformation Service Programme.

OGC (2009). *Managing successful projects with PRINCE2*. Norwich, England: The Stationery Office.

Osborne, T. (1994). Bureaucracy as a vocation: Governmentality and administration in nineteenth-century Britain. *Journal of Historical Sociology*, 7(3), pp. 289–313.

Packendorff, J. (2002). The temporary society and its enemies: Projects from an individual perspective. In K. Andersson & A. Soderheim (Eds.), *Beyond project management: New perspectives on the permanent–temporary dilemma*. Malmo, Sweden: Libor.

Patterson, A., & Pinch, P. L. (1995). Hollowing out the local state: Compulsory competitive tendering and the restructuring of British public-sector services. *Environment and Planning A*, 27(9), pp. 1437–1461.

Polanyi, M. (1958). *Personal knowledge: Towards a post-critical philosophy*. Chicago, IL: University of Chicago.

Power, M. (1994). The audit explosion. Demos. Retrieved from www.demos.co.uk/files/theauditexplosion.pdf

Power, M. (2004). Counting, control and calculation: Reflections on measuring and management. *Human Relations*, 57(6), pp. 765–783.

Rose, N. (1999). *Powers of freedom*. Cambridge, England: Cambridge University Press.

Seldon, A., & Lodge, G. (2010) *Brown at 10*. London, England: Biteback.

Shah, H., & Goss, S. (2007). *Democracy and the public realm*. London, England: Lawrence & Wishart.

UK Cabinet Office (2016). Best management practice portfolio. Retrieved from www.gov.uk/government/publications/best-management-practice-portfolio

Unison (2012). Branch guide to securing in-house services. Retrieved from www.unison.org.uk/content/uploads/2013/06/On-line-Catalogue212783.pdf

Waring, J., & Martin, G. (2016). Network leadership as pastoral power. In M. Bevir (Ed.), *Governmentality after neoliberalism*. London, England: Routledge.

Weiskopf, R., & Munro, I. (2012). Management of human capital: Discipline, security and controlled circulation in HRM. *Organization*, 19(6), pp. 685–702.

Yeates, N., Haux, T., Jawad, R., & Kilkey, M. E. (2010). *In defence of welfare: The impacts of the spending review*. London, England: Social Policy Association.

CONTRIBUTORS

Barbara Allen is Senior Lecturer in Public Management and Policy at the School of Government, Victoria University Wellington, New Zealand. She is an expert in strategic public procurement and is interested in associated problems at the nexus of public, private, and the social sectors. Her research has involved in-depth evaluations of the Local Government Procurement Agenda in the UK, the Performance Improvement Framework in New Zealand, and Social Impact Bonds in the UK and New Zealand.

Simon Bailey is a researcher currently based at the University of Kent, UK. His interests are in the sociological study of medicine, organisation, learning, and policy. His research focuses on the emergence and formation of new practices, roles, and organisational forms in public service, with critical attention to changes in individual and organisational ethos amid contemporary moves toward a more entrepreneurial and financialised public sector.

Edward Barratt is a senior lecturer at Essex Business School, UK. His current research interests concern the histories of management and ethical codification in the British Civil Service and the history of knowledge management, especially in the early years of "New Labour" in Britain. He retains an abiding but critical interest in the potential for Foucauldian notions of governmentality to illuminate contemporary practices of organising.

Sebastian M. Büttner is Interim Professor of Comparative and Transnational Sociology at the Institute of Sociology, University of Duisburg-Essen, Germany. His major research foci are political sociology, sociology of Europe, and sociology of expertise. In the past few years, he has extensively studied the structures of expertise in EU governance and local effects of EU funding policy.

Josef Chaib is a researcher at Malmö University. He has a PhD in political science from Malmö University, Sweden. His research focuses on the organisation and government of welfare collaboration, political-administrative relations, and the role of knowledge in public administration and government.

Kath Checkland is Professor of Health Policy and Primary Care and Co-Director of the Institute for Health Policy and Organisation at the University of Manchester, UK, and a general practitioner working in a rural Derbyshire practice. Her work explores health policy, health systems, and organisations, with a particular focus on service commissioning and system change. She is a co-director of the Policy Research Unit in Commissioning and the Healthcare System (PRUComm).

Małgorzata Ćwikła is Assistant Professor in Management at the Institute of Culture, Jagiellonian University in Kraków, Poland. Her work is currently focused on the future of management, especially project management, and designing/projecting new organisational realities. She has background in management studies, cultural studies, and philology.

Stefanie Ettelt is Associate Professor in Health Policy in the Department of Health Services Research and Policy at the London School of Hygiene and Tropical Medicine, UK. She has a background in political science. Most of her work currently focuses on policy experimentation and evaluation, policy and institutional analyses, and the use of evidence in health policy making.

Mats Fred is a post-doctoral researcher at the Department of Global Political Studies at Malmö University, Sweden. He published his dissertation, "Projectification, the Trojan horse of local government" (Department of Political Science, Lund) early 2018. His interests include local government practices, organisational experiments, the practical outlet of EU policies, and the role of consultants in local and regional policy and politics.

Sebastian Godenhjelm is a political scientist and Senior Lecturer at the Swedish School of Social Science, University of Helsinki, Finland. His main research interests include public management, participation, actors, and processes in regional development in Finland and Europe. This research area is linked to the relationship between traditional forms of governing versus new forms of governance often characterised as temporary network-type project organisations.

Trish Greenhalgh is a general practitioner and Professor of Primary Care Health Sciences at the University of Oxford, UK. She leads a programme of research at the interface between the social sciences and medicine, working across primary and secondary care.

Patrik Hall is Professor of Political Science at the Department of Global Political Studies, Malmö University, Sweden. His current research interests lie in the broad field of reforms within public organisation, for instance the relation between bureaucracy and "new" public management and the growth of administrative work in the public sector. He is currently finalising a study regarding the growth and role of meetings in modern organisations.

Damian Hodgson is Professor of Organisational Analysis at Alliance Manchester Business School and Co-Director of the Institute for Health Policy and Organisation, University of Manchester, UK. His research centres on issues of power, knowledge, identity, and control in complex organisations, with particular interest in the organisation of health care and the formation and implementation of health policy. He is co-founder of the Making Projects Critical movement and has published widely on projectification and critical project studies.

Gemma Hughes is a health services researcher at the University of Oxford, UK. Gemma's research interests centre on critical analysis of the relationships between health and social care policy, practice, and lived experience. She has a professional background in the National Health Service (NHS) with extensive experience of service development and commissioning.

Beata Jałocha is Assistant Professor in Management at the Institute of Public Affairs, Jagiellonian University in Kraków, Poland. Her research focuses on projectification processes, mainly in public and non-governmental sectors. She also conducts projects, which are dedicated to the transformation of higher education institutions through action research.

Christian Jensen is Associate Professor at the School of Business, University of Gothenburg, Sweden. His primary research interests centre on different policy tools and implementation, and he has authored books, articles, and reports on various Swedish reforms. His current interests focus on managing big cities, innovation, and inter-organisational capacity building.

Staffan Johansson is Professor in Social Work at the Department of Social Work, University of Gothenburg, Sweden. His research is about human service organisations, including policy implementation, issues around collaboration and coordination the services for disadvantaged citizens, and also the roles of civil society organisation within the welfare state.

Tania Murray Li teaches in the Department of Anthropology at the University of Toronto, Canada, where she holds the Canada Research Chair in the Political Economy and Culture of Asia. Her latest book is *Land's End: Capitalist Relations on an Indigenous Frontier* (Duke University Press, 2014). Her interests include land, development, community, class, and indigeneity with a particular focus on Indonesia.

Karl Löfgren is Deputy Head of School and Associate Professor in the School of Government, Victoria University Wellington, New Zealand. Current research interests include digital governance and service delivery, public management, and policy implementation/organisational changes/reforms in public sector organisations. He is currently the book review editor for *Information Polity* (IOS Press), a member of the editorial boards for a number of academic journals, and is serving on the advisory board for the New Zealand practitioner magazine *Public Sector.*

Mikael Löfström is a senior lecturer at the Department of Business Administration at University of Borås, Sweden. His main research interests are in the area of governance, management of collaboration, inter-organisational relationships, public management reforms, and the projectification of the public sector.

Ewan Mackenzie is a research associate at Newcastle University Business School, Newcastle University, UK. His current research is in the sociology and politics of work in public and cultural sectors. In particular, he is interested in the intersection between neoliberalism, austerity politics, and everyday working life (both paid and non-paid).

Nicholas Mays has been Professor of Health Policy in the Department of Health Services Research and Policy at the London School of Hygiene and Tropical Medicine, UK, since 2003. He also directs the Department of Health and Social Care-funded Policy Innovation and Evaluation Research Unit. He has a background in social policy.

Dalia Mukhtar-Landgren is a senior lecturer at the Department of Political Science at Lund University, Sweden. Her interests include urban development planning and new forms of government in local politics. Her current research is on the development of new policy instruments through experimental governance, including social investments, social impact bonds, and the development of new planning instruments in relation to automatised vehicles in urban planning.

Sara Shaw is an associate professor at the University of Oxford, UK. She has a background in medical sociology and policy studies and she leads a programme of research focused on the organisation and development of healthcare policy and practice.

Stefan Sjöblom is a political scientist and Professor of Local Administration at the Swedish School of Social Science, University of Helsinki, and Associate Professor of Public Administration at the Åbo Akademi University, Finland. His main research interests include local and regional governance, participation, administrative reform policies, and evaluation studies. He has been a partner in several national and international research projects on governance, and local and regional development.

AUTHOR INDEX

SUBJECT INDEX